❖ Ukraine

Ukraine ❖ Birth of a Modern Nation

Serhy Yekelchyk

OXFORD
UNIVERSITY PRESS
OCM 71173938
2007

OXFORD
UNIVERSITY PRESS

Oxford University Press, Inc., publishes works that further
Oxford University's objective of excellence
in research, scholarship, and education.

Oxford   New York
Auckland   Cape Town   Dar es Salaam   Hong Kong   Karachi
Kuala Lumpur   Madrid   Melbourne   Mexico City   Nairobi
New Delhi   Shanghai   Taipei   Toronto

With offices in

Argentina   Austria   Brazil   Chile   Czech Republic   France   Greece
Guatemala   Hungary   Italy   Japan   Poland   Portugal   Singapore
South Korea   Switzerland   Thailand   Turkey   Ukraine   Vietnam

Published by Oxford University Press, Inc.
198 Madison Avenue, New York, New York 10016

www.oup.com

Oxford is a registered trademark of Oxford University Press

Yekelchyk, Serhy.
Ukraine : birth of a modern nation / Serhy Yekelchyk.
   p. cm.
Includes bibliographical references and index.
ISBN 978-0-19-530545-6; 978-0-19-530546-3 (pbk.)
1. Ukraine—History—19th century.   2. Ukraine—History—20th century.
3. Ukraine—Politics and government—19th century.
4. Ukraine—Politics and government—20th century.
5. Nationalism—Ukraine—History.   I. Title.
DK508.772.I45 2007
947.7′08–dc22   2006050900

9 8 7 6 5 4 3 2

Printed in the United States of America
on acid-free paper

❖

To the memory of my grandparents,

Leopold and Zynaida Yekelchyk

and Serhii and Kateryna Perelyhin

❁ Acknowledgments

The idea of this book dates back to 1998, when I was a graduate student at the University of Alberta in Edmonton. One day, Professor David R. Marples, for whom I was working as a research assistant, surprised me with a generous proposal to coauthor a history of twentieth-century Ukraine. We divided the chapters and began writing, but after a while both of us were sidetracked by other pressing obligations: my dissertation and David's many projects that have since then resulted in the publication of several books. After graduating in 2000, I moved to the University of Michigan at Ann Arbor for a postdoctoral year, taking with me the four chapters that I had written for the historical survey of Ukraine. A year later, the still unopened package moved with me to my new, permanent home base, the University of Victoria. At this point, David kindly suggested that I take over the project and write a short history of Ukraine on my own.

But as I studied my old chapters, I found them unsatisfactory. The years 2001 to 2003 saw a slow gathering of sources for a new draft. I began rewriting the text in January 2004, and the Orange Revolution in Ukraine later that year served as a powerful stimulus to stop procrastinating. Teaching courses on Ukrainian history also helped to spur me. The dozen students at the 2002 Harvard Summer School who took my Ukrainian history class and the forty-three University of Victoria students who in 2004 enrolled in my course on modern Ukraine prompted me to clarify many interpretations offered here.

Between 1998 and 2006, a number of colleagues volunteered to read chapters from this book, offering constructive comments and editorial suggestions. John-Paul Himka read every chapter, sometimes in more than one draft, and corrected my mistakes with his typical great erudition and goodwill. Besides David Marples, Mark Baker, Zenon Kohut, and Marko Pavlyshyn read the early drafts of some chapters that were written in Edmonton. As I was preparing a new draft in Victoria during 2004 to 2006, David Brandenberger and Heather Coleman came to my rescue as proverbial friends in need, reading several key chapters and suggesting numerous improvements. Alan Rutkowski and Benjamin Tromly also went through parts of my text or answered my queries. At the request of Oxford University Press, two anonymous referees, who were later revealed as Mark von Hagen and Hiroaki

Kuromiya, read my manuscript with a friendly yet critical eye. Both suggested a number of improvements that I endeavored to implement to the best of my abilities. Throughout the process of writing and revising the final draft, Marta D. Olynyk helped me enormously with the stylistic editing of all texts. A translator and editor based in Montreal, Marta has honored so many e-mail requests for urgent help with my work than I grew accustomed to sending her files before going to bed and getting them back in the morning, when it is already close to noon in Quebec.

During the academic year 2001–2002, the University of Victoria awarded me a work-study grant that enabled me to employ three student assistants: Lara Brown, Erin Scraba, and Trevor Rockwell. They proved to be enthusiastic helpers, checking sources and preparing the bibliography. Trevor went on to become my master's student while continuing as a research assistant on this project. He has helped to edit the manuscript and compiled the first draft of the Recommending Reading list. I also benefited from professional help from several people affiliated with the University of Victoria: cartographer Ole J. Heggen expertly prepared the maps for this book, and photographers Don Pierce and Chris Marshall helped to convert the color photographs I took in Ukraine into high-quality black-and-white prints. The Ukrainian artist Lena Kurovska (www.LenaKurovska.com) kindly granted permission to use her painting *The Orange Revolution* (2004) for the cover of the paperback edition.

I am grateful to Ron Suny for introducing me to Susan Ferber at Oxford University Press. An editor extraordinaire, Susan read my various drafts more closely than I ever did and suggested numerous excellent changes that had never occurred to me. In the process, she taught me to write for a wider audience than a small circle of academics. The most punctual of my correspondents, Susan also helped me complete this book by setting an example of true professionalism—in addition to her excellent editing, she always replied to e-mails on the same day and sometimes sent out FedEx packages on Christmas Eve. Thanks are also due to the people at OUP who skillfully shepherded my manuscript through the copyediting and production process, especially Christine K. Dahlin and Joy Matkowski.

Finally, I would like to express my great appreciation for the support and friendship of my colleagues at the University of Victoria, in both the Department of Germanic and Russian Studies and the Department of History. Although I did not ask any of them to read the manuscript of this book, they are responsible for the friendly and creative atmosphere for which UVic is famous, in addition to its fabulous location. Many thanks to my wife, Olga Pressitch, and our daughter, Yulia Ekeltchik, for tolerating my long hours of typing when the weather called for a picnic at the beach.

During the frantic, final push to finish the text in May 2006, Yulia also applied her advanced computer skills to the task of formatting reference material.

I dedicate this book to my grandparents, Leopold (1901–1979) and Zynaida (1908–2005) Yekelchyk, and Serhii (1908–1987) and Kateryna (1905–1975) Perelyhin. As alternately willing and reluctant participants in the great social upheavals and wars that shaped modern Ukraine, they lived through the tragedies and triumphs that my generation finds difficult even to describe.

✪ Contents

✥ Note on Transliteration

In this book, Ukrainian place and personal names are transliterated using the simplified Library of Congress system with soft signs, apostrophes, and diacritical marks omitted throughout. The masculine ending "-yi" is shortened to "-y," and initial iotated vowels are rendered with a "y" rather than "i." Most Ukrainian place names are transliterated from Ukrainian, including some that have established English forms derived from the Russian spelling; for example, Kyiv (Kiev), Dnipro (Dnieper), and Odesa (Odessa). Exceptions have been made for names of some historical regions, such as the Crimea and Galicia.

✣ Chronology

Ninth century	Formation of Kyivan Rus
980–1015	Reign of Prince Volodymyr
988	Adoption of Christianity
1019–1054	Reign of Yaroslav the Wise
1238–1264	Reign of Danylo of Halych
1240	Kyiv destroyed by the Mongols
1362	Kyiv annexed by Lithuania
1492	First documentary mention of the Cossacks
1569	Union of Lublin between Poland and Lithuania
1596	Creation of the Uniate Church
1648	Uprising against Polish rule
1648–1657	Bohdan Khmelnytsky rules as a Cossack hetman
1654	Treaty of Pereiaslav brings the Cossacks under Muscovite rule
1709	Tsar Peter I defeats separatist Hetman Ivan Mazepa
1772	Galicia becomes part of the Habsburg Empire
1840	Taras Shevchenko publishes his poetry collection *The Kobza Player*
1845–1847	Cyril and Methodius Brotherhood in Kyiv
1848	Supreme Ruthenian Council established in Lviv
1876	Literature in Ukrainian banned in the Russian Empire
1890	First Ukrainian political party created in Austria-Hungary
1898	Mykhailo Hrushevsky publishes the first volume of *History of Ukraine-Rus*
1900	First Ukrainian political party in the Russian Empire

1917	Revolution in the Russian Empire; the Central Rada convenes in Kyiv
1918	Establishment of the independent Ukrainian People's Republic
1918–1919	Reign of Hetman Pavlo Skoropadsky
1918–1919	Western Ukrainian People's Republic
1920	The Bolsheviks establish control over eastern Ukraine
1922	Ukrainian Socialist Soviet Republic joins the Soviet Union
1923	The Allies approve Poland's annexation of Galicia
1923–1933	Ukrainization campaign in Soviet Ukraine
1929	The Organization of Ukrainian Nationalists established
1932–1933	The Ukrainian Famine
1938–1949	Nikita Khrushchev's tenure as Communist Party leader in Ukraine
1939–1940	The Soviet Union annexes western Ukrainian lands from Poland and Romania
1941–1944	Nazi occupation of Ukraine
1954	The Crimea transferred from the Russian Federation to Ukraine
1963–1972	Petro Shelest's tenure as Communist Party leader in Ukraine
1965	Dissident Ivan Dziuba writes *Internationalism or Russification?*
1972–1989	Volodymyr Shcherbytsky's tenure as Communist Party leader in Ukraine
1989	First congress of Rukh, the Ukrainian popular front
1991	Declaration of independence
1991–1994	Presidency of Leonid Kravchuk
1994–2004	Presidency of Leonid Kuchma
2004	The Orange Revolution
2005	Viktor Yushchenko sworn in as president

✪ Ukraine

�֎ Ukraine

✜ Introduction

In late 2004, hundreds of thousands of orange-clad protesters occupied the Ukrainian capital's city center to protest electoral fraud and the poisoning of an opposition candidate. A very modern revolt, the Orange Revolution featured slogans text-messaged to cellular phones, protest songs set to rap, and big television screens on the streets showing larger-than-life opposition leaders. The events in Kyiv were one of the most televised revolutions in history. Although the Ukrainian media at first obeyed the outgoing regime in minimizing the protests, Western television crews worked freely, and viewers all around the world received daily updates from Ukraine. The images of Kyiv's Independence Square filled with demonstrators and the tents set up on Khreshchatyk Boulevard became familiar to a large international audience. Almost a "reality show" of a popular rebellion against corrupt authorities, the reports from Kyiv remained the top news until January 2005, when foreign viewers cheered the bad guys being voted off the new island of democracy. The winners of the Orange Revolution, meanwhile, faced the much less photogenic struggle to reform their country—an effort that would rarely be featured in international headlines.

The media coverage of the Orange Revolution did for Ukraine what the shrewdest politician could not: make millions of people around the globe care about the fate of democracy in Ukraine. Before this popular revolution, many of Ukraine's new sympathizers had known little about that land, which gained independence only in the late twentieth century with the collapse of the Soviet Union. Many journalists had to look at the map to find out where Ukraine was—in southeastern Europe, bordering on Russia in the east; on Russia and Belarus in the north; on Poland, Slovakia, Hungary, Romania, and Moldova in the west; and washed by the Black Sea in the south. Ukraine is a land of mighty rivers, most of them flowing southward and emptying into the Black Sea. The Dnipro (or Dnieper), in particular, has served for centuries as a chief trading route and is now a major source of hydroelectric power. Mountains are found only near Ukraine's borders: the Carpathians in the west and the Crimean Mountains in the south. Almost the entire country consists of vast plains that alternate with woodlands in central and northwestern Ukraine. The flat and treeless plains of southern and central Ukraine are now largely under cultivation, but for millennia the steppes (prairies) were wide-open avenues for invasion and migration. Ukraine is blessed with some of the best soil in the world, with the fertile *chernozem* ("black earth") found in most of the country's central belt. Ukraine's moderate continental climate, with its four distinct seasons, annual snowfall, and adequate precipitation in the summer, is conducive to agriculture, a traditional occupation of Ukrainians. A traveler arriving from western Europe, however, will find Ukrainian winters more severe. Kyiv's average temperature in January is only +21°F (-6°C), although the typical reading in July is, at +66°F (+19°C), the same as in Germany or Great Britain. Yet, a tourist can always escape southward to the Crimea, where the gentle Mediterranean climate, warm sea, and picturesque mountains provide an ideal vacation destination.

Ukraine is Europe's second-largest country after Russia, with an area of 233,100 square miles, or 603,700 square kilometers. Compared with other European countries, Ukraine is a bit larger than France and approximately the size of Germany and Great Britain combined. Yet each of these three western European countries has a larger population than Ukraine's 46.8 million people (a 2006 estimate). Economic development and the standard of life in today's Ukraine also cannot be compared with the leading Western economies, although in the late nineteenth and early twentieth centuries, the Ukrainian lands, rich in iron ore and coal deposits, showed considerable promise as one of the world's fastest growing industrial regions.

The name Ukraine comes from the word "borderland," and, indeed, for much of its long history this land has been a frontier. For thousands of years, it was a border between the open plain and the protective forest; for centuries, a three-way cultural borderland between Roman Catholicism, Eastern Orthodoxy, and Islam. In the last two hundred years, Ukraine has sat on a border between the oppressive Russian Empire and its more democratic European neighbors, between the Communist and capitalist social orders in Europe, between the Soviet Union and its European satellites, and, finally, between Russia and the European Union. The present-day boundaries of the Ukrainian state are very recent, dating to its independence after the Soviet collapse in 1991 and, before that, to the Soviet Union's territorial acquisitions and internal rearrangements during the twentieth century. Yet Ukraine's borders correspond very closely to the boundaries of Ukrainian ethnic settlement in Europe, in part because Stalin had taken upon himself the role of the gatherer of Ukrainian lands into a Ukrainian Soviet Socialist Republic, a constituent part of the Soviet Union. But while Stalin envisioned the Ukrainian republic primarily as a national homeland for ethnic Ukrainians, present-day Ukraine is, and always has been, a multinational land. Of the 48 million people counted in the last census in 2001, ethnic Ukrainians constituted 78 percent. Ethnic Russians represented the single largest national minority, at 17 percent of the population, but historically, the now smaller Polish and Jewish minorities have also been significant.

Puzzles related to Ukraine's historical identity continue to confuse foreign journalists and trouble local politicians. During the twentieth century, for example, the official spelling of the name of a major city in western Ukraine changed four times: from the German Lemberg under Austria-Hungary, to the Polish Lwów under Poland, to the Russian Lvov as a Soviet provincial center, to the Ukrainian Lviv. The Ukrainian capital of Kyiv is still given the Russian spelling of Kiev on most maps. Modern Ukrainian literature includes a number of great works, but the general reader will be more familiar with writers belonging to Ukraine only by birth, such as the Pole Joseph Conrad, the Jew Sholom Aleichem, or the Russian Mikhail Bulgakov. Even the literary giant Nikolai Gogol, who used his Ukrainian homeland as a setting for many of his works, wrote in Russian and is considered a Russian writer. Many historical events that took place in what is now Ukraine—the adoption of Christianity by Kyivan princes, the Cossack wars with Poland, the birth of Jewish Hasidism, the Crimean War, and the Chernobyl disaster, to name a few—are often seen as belonging to "Russian" or "Soviet" history.

❖

The question of how to construct Ukrainian history has long baffled historians and politicians. Ukraine is one of the world's youngest states, and a traditional political history of state building would not take its proponents too far. Contemporary Ukraine can be presented as a direct descendant of medieval Kyivan Rus, the seventeenth-century Cossack polity, and the 1918–1920 Ukrainian People's Republic, but these episodes of statehood do not link up into a coherent story. The discontinuities are just too great.

Another way to construct the history of Ukraine is to focus on the historical development of the Ukrainians, an Eastern Slavic nationality constituting the majority in the modern Ukrainian state. This, however, involves two dangers. First, by tracing the history of ethnic Ukrainians backward, one risks imposing the modern notion of national identity on a premodern population, which identified instead in religious, regional, or social terms. Second, more than 20 percent of Ukrainian citizens today are not ethnic Ukrainians but Russians, Jews, Poles, Belarusians, Crimean Tatars, and others who have lived for centuries in what is now Ukraine. They, too, should have a place in Ukrainian history. If one substitutes the history of the Ukrainians with the history of the lands included in the present-day Ukrainian state, even greater challenges emerge. The current borders of Ukraine are the product of Stalin's conquests in eastern Europe from 1939 to 1945 and Khrushchev's transfer of the Crimean peninsula from Russia in 1954. Dealing in turn with the very disparate historical experiences of various regions before they came to be a part of Ukraine would make for a catalogue of separate pasts, rather than a coherent analysis of historical processes. So, too, would a separate historical examination of each national minority.

This book does not follow in the footsteps of either the historians of the Ukrainian nationality (ethnic group) or those who trace the past of the lands that are now part of Ukraine. Instead, I argue that the present-day Ukrainian multinational state owes its existence to the Ukrainian national project—an endeavor to build a modern Ukrainian nation and provide it with a national homeland. The twentieth-century predecessors of today's Ukrainian state, the independent Ukrainian People's Republic (1918–1920) and the Ukrainian Soviet Socialist Republic (1918–1991), were both outcomes, if very different ones, of nationalist mobilization in the wake of imperial collapse. As the multinational empires were disintegrating in central and eastern Europe at the end of World War I, nation-states replaced them—if only briefly, as in the Ukrainian case—as an accepted form of political organization. The Bolsheviks soon took away Ukraine's real sovereignty, but they felt compelled to preserve a Ukrainian republic within the Soviet Union. Like the Ukrainian patriots before them, the Soviet bureaucrats created and maintained a national homeland for ethnic Ukrainians because they could not deny the right of self-rule to major, compactly settled nationalities. It is important, however, not to see these processes as a preexisting Ukrainian nationality acquiring the state structures to which it had long been entitled. Rather, a modern Ukrainian national identity itself was being shaped by the state structures, political events, and social processes unfolding in eastern Europe during the last three centuries. Ukraine as a modern nation-state did not come of age on its own but was made by politicians, writers, and civic activists—as well as by warlords and bureaucrats in faraway imperial capitals.

This book thus focuses on the emergence of a modern Ukrainian nationality in the age of popular mobilization and the shaping of a modern Ukrainian political nation from ethnic Ukrainians and Ukraine's national minorities. It views the gathering of Ukrainian ethnolinguistic territories into a single state structure as the result of twentieth-century geopolitics rather than a historical inevitability for the long-oppressed Ukrainian nation. This book also integrates the history of Ukraine's national minorities into its central narrative concerning the nineteenth- and twentieth-century project of creating a modern Ukraine through the making of modern Ukrainians. In other words, this book is about how the national mobilization of ethnic Ukrainians resulted in the emergence of a civic, multiethnic Ukrainian nation-state.

✪

The Ukrainian word for "nation," *natsiia*, has a different meaning from the English word "nation," usually understood as synonymous with "state." In Ukrainian, *natsiia* is an ethnic community of people who have a common origin, language, and culture—but do not necessarily possess a state of their own. The roots of this difference can be traced to the period before World War I, when nation-states predominated in western Europe and multinational empires ruled much of eastern and central Europe. In 1900, the lands populated by ethnic Ukrainians were split between the Russian and Austro-Hungarian empires, and the only viable vision of the Ukrainian nation at the time was that of a linguistic and cultural community of all Ukrainians. But even this vision in 1900 was not universally accepted.

The idea that humanity is naturally divided into ethnic communities is the cornerstone of modern nationalism, which developed in the late eighteenth and early nineteenth centuries. Thinkers of the time contended that nations were permanent and immemorial, defined by shared origins, religion, language, and customs. They also asserted that national self-realization in the form of a nation-state was a legitimate political goal worth going to war over. Nationalists today still subscribe to such views, but modern students of nationalism have little patience with the concept of nations as organic entities with unique, objective characteristics. Beginning in the 1950s, social scientists have connected the emergence of modern nations to industrialization and the development of print culture. Since the 1980s, the view of modern nations as "imagined communities" based on "invented traditions" has found considerable support among historians. Today, the majority of scholars think that a common territory, religion, language, and customs provide a basis for national identity. But it is nationalist mobilization—the political and cultural work of intellectuals—that transforms a population into a modern nation.[1]

In this book, I discuss the emergence of a modern Ukrainian nation during the last two centuries. The concept of "modern nation" as used here can be traced back to the French Revolution and German Romanticism. The understanding of nations as people, the idea of popular sovereignty, and the appreciation of ethnicity as a basis for self-rule all date back to the late eighteenth and early nineteenth centuries. This was also the time when modern nationalism began its slow spread into the lands of present-day Ukraine. This is not to say that the Ukrainians materialized out of thin air or were invented from scratch by nationalist politicians. Indeed, people who spoke closely related dialects, shared a religious tradition, and possessed similar customs lived in the region for centuries. Moreover, as will be shown in the following chapters, at several points before the advent of modern nationalism, local nobles, clergymen, and Cossacks (guards and settlers of the steppe frontier, who developed into a separate social group) understood themselves as a political "nation." Yet, it took the ideological innovation of modern nationalism to assimilate all social strata into the Ukrainian body politic and several generations of nationalist intellectuals to transform such a disunited population into a single nation.

In their discussions of this Ukrainian national movement, historians usually rely on the scheme proposed during the 1960s by Miroslav Hroch. This prominent Czech scholar studied the national movements of eastern European peoples who lacked a continuous tradition of statehood, native elites, and an indigenous literary tradition. Hroch argues that these nationalities usually undergo three consecutive stages in their national movement: initial academic interest in the nation's history and culture, elite creation and propagation of modern high culture, and this national elite's political mobilization of society on the mass level.[2] Ukrainian historians, including me, have tried to develop a periodization of the Ukrainian national movement that would correspond to Hroch's schema. In both the Russian and Austro-Hungarian empires, the academic stage took place during the late eighteenth and early nineteenth centuries. But difficulties begin with determining the exact dividing line between the cultural and political stages of the Ukrainian movement that historians place anywhere between the 1840s and the 1910s. Sometimes, political organizations emerged before a modern national culture could be fully developed; in other cases, oppressive policies forced retreats from political activity into "harmless" cultural work.[3] As the historian Roman Szporluk has pointed out, the policies of Ukraine's imperial masters or regional geopolitical factors—external to Hroch's sociological portrait of the national movement—frequently threaten to skew this simplistic model beyond recognition. In addition, in the age of nationalism, cultural and academic work has often been seen as constituting a political threat, making the separation of the two rather artificial and misleading.[4]

Perhaps the history of modern Ukraine is one that is meant to defy standard paradigms and explanations. After all, what theoretical model should be used in the case of the Soviet Union, which during the 1920s and early 1930s actively promoted the Ukrainian culture? One scholar proposes to see this period when a state uses its power to complete nation building as a fourth phase to be added to Hroch's three initial ones.[5] (After the long Soviet retreat into Russification, this stage could be said to have continued in post-Communist Ukraine.) Still, these steps explain only the development of the Ukrainian national movement, whereas the twentieth century saw the emergence of Ukrainian state formations that included significant national minorities. Although these polities were the result of the Ukrainian national project, all of them embraced, at least in theory, the concept of a civic or political nation, which included all citizens of Ukraine irrespective of their ethnicity. If anything, the history of Ukraine during the last century is the story of a conceptual change from an ethnic *natsiia* to a political nation situated against the backdrop of unusually turbulent and explosive times.

❖

At the time when modern historical scholarship was born in the eighteenth and nineteenth centuries, Ukrainians were a stateless ethnic group. Consequently, Imperial Russian historiography claimed Kyivan Rus, the Cossacks, and the colonization of the Black Sea's north coast as glorious pages in the history of Russian civilization. During the nineteenth century, Ukrainian romantic nationalists first proposed that some of these events actually belonged to Ukrainian history, understood as the past of the ethnic Ukrainians. Yet, most of them still saw the Ukrainians as a branch of the larger Russian nation. It was the great historian Mykhailo Hrushevsky, trained in Kyiv but working since 1894 in the Austro-Hungarian Empire, who finally separated Ukrainian history from Russian by claiming for it Kyivan Rus and presenting the history of the Ukrainian people and society as an uninterrupted process from ancient times to the present.[6]

In the Soviet Union, Ukrainian history was written first as a history of class struggle common to all nations. Later, regional history came to describe the emergence of the Russians' younger brother, who needed guidance in revolutionary struggles and socialist construction.[7] During the last decades of Soviet rule, multivolume collectively authored works became the preferred genre of history writing. In the Ukrainian republic, the state financed the writing and publication of an impressive eleven-volume *History of the Ukrainian SSR*, a compendium of official interpretations.[8] The collapse of Communism in 1991 heralded the return to freedom of thinking—and to the genre of single-author books. Aimed at replacing the *History of the Ukrainian SSR*, the book series Ukraine through the Centuries furnished many new details that inform this book.[9]

In an attempt to include wherever applicable recent archival revelations and new explanations of familiar events, I have taken advantage of a host of recent post-Soviet books and articles, the most important of which are found in the endnotes. One synthetic work deserves separate mention: Yaroslav Hrytsak's *Survey of the History of Ukraine: The Formation of a Modern Ukrainian Nation during the 19th and 20th Centuries* (1997)[10] does a superb job of introducing Western concepts and methodology into Ukrainian historical scholarship. Much of the subsequent work by younger Ukrainian scholars can be traced to their reading of this important work.

The endnotes to this book also document my intellectual debt to a number of Western historians of Ukraine, particularly those from North America and western Europe. Until the 1990s, Ukrainian history remained on the margins of Western academia, and almost all the scholars in this field were of Ukrainian descent. Some, like the late Ivan L. Rudnytsky (1919–1984) or Roman Szporluk (b. 1933), contributed greatly to the conceptualization of modern Ukrainian history, and today their works influence the development of post-Communist history writing in Ukraine.[11] Following the collapse of the Soviet Union, in 1995 the American historian Mark von Hagen called for a rediscovery of Ukrainian history as an ideal field of study for postmodern interest in the discontinuities and permeability of cultural borders.[12] Whether the profession listened or was just prompted by independent Ukraine's new strategic importance in Europe, Ukrainian history has become a growth industry since then, drawing to its ranks a new generation of scholars boasting no family ties to the region whatsoever.

Among students taking courses on Ukrainian history at an increasing number of Western universities, "heritage seekers" from among the Ukrainian diaspora or Jews and Mennonites whose ancestors had fled what is now Ukraine are also becoming a minority. Inquiring minds of the twenty-first century are attracted to Ukrainian history because it challenges the traditional story of the rise of nation-states and opens up new conceptual avenues. These students are joined by politicians and the general public, who in the wake of the 2004 Orange Revolution in Ukraine are watching this country as the principal arena of competition between Russia and the West. Although this book cannot provide these diverse audiences with exhaustive answers, I hope it will serve as a good starting point for an inquiry into modern Ukraine.

The book's structure reflects its focus on the age of social mobilization and mass politics. The first chapter surveys the history of what is now Ukraine from ancient times to the late eighteenth century. The second chapter discusses the development of the Ukrainian national movement during the nineteenth century. The narrative pace slows down, beginning with chapter 3, which deals with the period 1890–1917. Subsequent chapters provide a detailed analysis of the events of the Ukrainian Revolution, Soviet policies in Ukraine during the 1920s, Stalinism in Ukraine, the history of the Ukrainian lands outside the Soviet Union, the Ukrainian republic under Stalin's heirs, and Ukraine's role in the Soviet collapse. The final chapter discusses the developments in Ukraine beginning with the achievement of independence in 1991 and ending with the presidency of Viktor Yushchenko, the leader of the Orange Revolution.

What will be the next chapter of Ukrainian history? Many major trends discussed in this book—the construction of a nation-state, creation of a market economy, development of political democracy, and search for Ukraine's geopolitical place between the West and Russia—will continue to define Ukraine's future. But one of the principal themes in Ukrainian history during the last two centuries, the ethnic mobilization of Ukrainians and the emergence of independent Ukraine, may no longer be as central in the global world of the twenty-first century. Such issues as Ukraine's increasing inclusion into the international economy and the further spread of global mass culture, not to mention the diminishing role of the national government if Ukraine joins the European Union, will all challenge the idea of a nation-state as imagined by several generations of Ukrainian patriots. Yet, this will be a natural outcome. Modern Ukraine is the result of a nationalist project, but it was not built by nationalists and was always a multinational state. Now that it no longer needs to prove its right to exist, Ukraine of the twenty-first century will focus on building a functioning democracy and a better life for all its citizens.

The Historical Roots of Modern Ukraine

When Ukraine became independent in 1991, the new state began developing a historical pedigree that would anchor modern political realities in a venerable historical past. Carving a coherent national history from a bewildering kaleidoscope of past political, social, and cultural events was not a task unique to Ukrainian historians. The lack of a continuous state tradition might appear to be a major impediment, but Italian and German historians faced a similar problem. The temptation to write history backward, assuming that it would end with the creation of an independent Ukrainian state, was also typical of new national histories elsewhere.

In any case, Ukrainian scholars were not writing history from scratch. They could take on the interpretations developed by pre-Soviet patriotic historians of the so-called national school and kept alive among Ukrainian émigrés in the West. They were also influenced by the concepts and methods of the Soviet historical profession. For all their declared mutual enmity, both schools interpreted Ukrainian history primarily as the history of ethnic Ukrainians. In its Soviet version, Ukrainian history was inseparably connected to Russia's, whereas the national school narrated it as constant efforts to create a Ukrainian state. Yet in both cases, the history of ethnic Ukrainians was the cement holding together the story of state structures, social struggles, and cultural processes. Nationalists and Soviet ideologues both believed in ethnic groups that possess clearly defined features and share a common historical destiny. Grounding a nationality in an ancient past granted it legitimacy, and defining the exact moment of its emergence as a separate ethnic group justified present-day political boundaries. Hence, there was a perennial discussion of the Ukrainian "ethnogenesis" in both Soviet and émigré scholarship.

Present-day historians of Ukraine have inherited these concerns, although they write with a greater sensitivity to discontinuities, minority experiences, and other issues that are usually cut away during the carving of a traditional national history. To the credit of the Ukrainian historical profession, hardly any mainstream scholar has embraced eccentric theories claiming ancient archaeological cultures as proto-Ukrainian.[1] Rather, the new state and its historians honor the land's rich past, irrespective of its ethnic identification. The images of historical monuments selected for the first series of Ukraine's paper money, the *hryvnia*, range from the classical columns of a Greek Crimean colony (fifth century B.C.) to the churches of Kyivan Rus and Cossack Ukraine and that nineteenth-century masterpiece of French architecture in the Russian Empire, the Odesa Opera House.

✸✸ Whose Ancient Civilizations?

Like most of Europe, the territory of contemporary Ukraine was inhabited for tens of thousands of years before the first known civilizations appeared. The earliest traces of human existence unearthed thus far by archaeologists date from approximately 700,000 B.C. Still clearer evidence suggests that by the Upper Paleolithic Period (40,000–15,000 B.C.) clans of primitive hunters and gatherers populated most of the great Eurasian plain north of the Black Sea. The last glacier retreated by about 10,000 B.C., establishing practically the same climate and landscape that still exist in Ukraine. Agriculture developed at about 5,000 B.C. As humans learned to produce food by cultivating cereals and raising livestock, they switched from hunting and food gathering to a sedentary way of life.

Trypillian culture (4,000–2,500 B.C.; named by a nineteenth-century archaeologist after a village near his excavation site) is the best known early agricultural civilization on the territory of present-day Ukraine. The Trypillians lived in large settlements, used the wooden plow, and—from what we can gather from the ornamentation on their pottery—had a developed spiritual life. Artifacts of this advanced civilization in eastern Europe, which predated ancient Egypt, understandably occupy pride of place in Ukrainian museums, although few serious scholars see the Trypillians as progenitors of modern Ukrainians.[2]

Trypillian culture existed before written history, hence the need to invent a name for it. The first historically recorded people on the steppe north of the Black Sea were the Cimmerians (ca. 1,500–750 B.C.). Although Homer mentioned them in the *Odyssey*, the Greeks generally knew very little about the Cimmerians. Analysis of the archaeological evidence and the few available written sources has led scholars to believe that the Cimmerians were nomad horsemen from Central Asia. These invaders brought to the steppe the skill of horseback riding and the use of iron tools.

Around 750 B.C., the Cimmerians were displaced by the Scythians, a new wave of nomads from Central Asia. The classical world was by then coming to know its new neighbors better; the "father of history," Herodotus, left us an account of his trip to Scythia, which contains at times fantastic descriptions of the land and its inhabitants.[3] Like the Cimmerians, the nomadic Scythians were of Iranian stock, but they may have conquered and assimilated the local sedentary population.[4] In any case, the differentiation Herodotus makes is between the ruling stratum of "Royal Scythians" and the "Scythian plowers." In Soviet times, some patriotic scholars speculated that these Scythian plowers were, in fact, indigenous proto-Slavic agriculturalists. Although similar suggestions can still be found in both Ukrainian and Western textbooks, they remain unsubstantiated.[5] Whether proto-Slavs resided in the region or not, archaeological evidence suggests that from the earliest times, the ancient population of present-day Ukraine was multiethnic.

From the seventh century B.C. onward, several Greek colonies emerged on the Black Sea's northern coast. As trading outposts of the Aegean Greek city-states, the colonies engaged in active trade with the Scythians. The latter offered products probably extracted from the sedentary population: grain, fish, honey, furs, and slaves. In return, the Scythian elite acquired from the Greeks metal objects, wine, jewelry, and cloth. Ukrainian archaeologists have unearthed many examples of the beautiful artwork and jewelry made in characteristic "Scythian" style, which was distinguished by animal motifs. Whether produced by Scythian masters or the Greeks in response to the Scythians' requests, the findings attest to the well-developed cultural taste of the Scythian elite.[6]

Nevertheless, classical Mediterranean civilizations knew the Scythians primarily as fierce and skillful warriors. In 513 B.C., they withstood the invasion of King Darius I of Persia in what came to be the first documented war in the land that would one day be known as Ukraine. The Scythians successfully fought other nomads in the east and even expanded their territory westward until King Philip II of Macedon, the father of Alexander the Great, defeated them on the Danube in 339 B.C.

At about the same time, a new wave of nomadic tribes began arriving from the east. By about 250 B.C., the invaders, whom the Greeks knew as the Sarmatians, overwhelmed and probably assimilated the Scythians, taking over their hinterland empire. (The Scythians held out in the Crimea until 200 A.D.) Like the previous and future nomadic overlords of the Eurasian steppe, the Sarmatians were not culturally or ethnically homogeneous. In all probability, they were a loose confederation of tribes temporarily united under the most powerful one. The Sarmatians first fought the Greek colonies but then, imitating the Scythians, engaged in trade with them.

In the meantime, the Greek colonies on the northern coast of the Black Sea flourished. The prosperous cities of Tiras, Olbia, Chersonesus, Theodosia, Phanagoria, and Panticapaeum (Bospor) owed their wealth mainly to the grain trade with Scythians and Sarmatians, but also to fishing, wine making, and metalworking. In time, some colonies became independent of their Aegean Greek "mother cities." In the fifth century B.C., several colonies united into the powerful Bosporian Kingdom, which existed until 63 B.C., when the Romans defeated its last king, Mithradates VI.[7] From the second century B.C. onward, political instability and declining trade undermined the importance of the Greek colonies, now under the protectorate of the Roman Empire. In the following centuries, new streams of nomadic invaders almost swept away the once lively urban life along the coast.

The first nomadic incursion of the new millennium came not from the east but from the northwest. Late in the second century A.D., the Germanic tribes of the Goths conquered the Sarmatians. The new overlords also took over the coastal Greek cities. Gothic rule, however, did not last long in the steppe hinterland, where more nomadic invaders once again advanced from the east. This time, the new visitors passing through the Ukrainian steppe were not Indo-Europeans like the Scythians or Sarmatians, but Turkic peoples: the Huns in the late fourth century, the Bulgars and Avars in the sixth, and the Khazars in the seventh. In 1972, an eccentric Ukrainian author published a novel about Attila the Hun, who, he argued, was really a Kyivan prince with the recognizably Ukrainian name of Bohdan Hatylo,[8] but neither Attila nor other Turkic nomads were related to the Slavs. In fact, one can trace the movement of these itinerant tribes from Asia through the great Eurasian plain, which for millennia served as a kind of superhighway to Europe. Of these peoples, only the Khazars had a significant influence on the ancient Slavs.

The Khazars controlled the region north of the Black Sea and the Caucasus Mountains for more than two centuries, providing a stable environment for a new Eastern Slavic civilization emerging in their shadow. The Khazars conquered the steppe at the same time as the Byzantine Empire consolidated its rule in the Mediterranean, among other things reviving the Greek colonies on the Black Sea coast. With the old trade routes reopened, the Khazars now supplied grain, fish, honey, fur, and slaves to the coastal trading centers. Christianity, Islam, and Judaism were all practiced by the Khazarian elite until the turn of the ninth century, when the ruler, the *kagan*, and the nobility converted to Judaism. The political and commercial hub of the Khazar empire was located in the lower Don and lower Volga valleys, east of what is now Ukraine, yet its sphere of influence extended to the Dnipro Valley and the Crimea. The Khazars took control of the important trading routes linking Byzantium, northern Europe, and the Middle East; they also exerted dominance over the northeastern part of the Great Silk Road from China. Among the people living in the Khazar sphere of influence and paying them tribute, probably since the mid-eighth century, were the Eastern Slavs of the Dnipro Valley.[9]

The origins of the Slavs remain one of history's most controversial issues. There is no definitive evidence of their presence on the Eurasian plain until the sixth century, and the question of the Slavs' original homeland remains open. Most present-day scholars think that the Slavs were indigenous inhabitants of eastern Europe whose homeland was north of the Carpathian Mountains, in what is now east-central Poland and northwestern Ukraine.[10] Over the course of centuries, Slavic agriculturalists presumably spread out slowly in various directions. Some archaeologists interpret the so-called Zarubyntsi culture (ca. 200 B.C.–A.D. 200) and the Cherniakhiv culture (ca. A.D. 200–400), both located in the heart of present-day Ukraine, as evidence of Slavic settlement in the area. (Others identify these archaeological cultures with the Baltic tribes and the Goths, respectively.) It seems likely that the powerful tribal alliance of the Antes, which was described by Byzantine historians and existed from the fourth to the early seventh century, was at least partly Slavic. The oldest archaeological finds in Ukraine that can be connected to the ancient Slavs apparently date from the fifth century. Sixth-century Byzantine and Gothic historians made the first definitive identification of the Slavs' presence in the region.[11]

Judging by archaeological and written evidence, Slavic expansion into what is now central Ukraine intensified in the mid-seventh century. By that time, the warlike nomadic Avars, who had earlier crushed the Antes confederation, had moved westward. As the Khazars were consolidating their control over the Eurasian plain, several Eastern Slavic tribes firmly established themselves in the Dnipro Valley. These dozen "tribes," enumerated in the *Tale of Bygone Years*—a chronicle dating from the early twelfth century and still our main written source on the early history of the Eastern Slavs—were, in fact, large tribal confederations with their own leaders, cities, and numerous fortified settlements. The Polianians, with their capital in Kyiv, constituted the most powerful tribal alliance. The Eastern Slavs worked the land and raised cattle, both tasks apparently undertaken jointly by extended families or village communes. The tribes shared common pagan beliefs personifying the forces of nature, as well as a language that modern scholars think belonged to an eastern subgroup of the previously common Slavic tongue. (In modern linguistic classification, the Eastern Slavs are the Belarusians, Russians, and Ukrainians; Western Slavs include the Czechs, Poles, and Slovaks; and the Southern Slavs include the Bulgarians, Croats, Macedonians, Serbs, and Slovenes.)

During the eighth century, the Khazars took over at least some of the Eastern Slavic tribes. The Slavs were forced to pay tribute, but they also engaged in trade with their industrious eastern neighbors. In the mid-ninth century, when Khazar power weakened because of an internal political crisis and the onslaughts of the Pechenegs, new nomads from the east, the Slavic tribal leaders apparently decided to use the situation to their advantage. According to the *Tale of Bygone Years*, in 862 the Eastern Slavs invited the Varangians from Scandinavia "to come and rule over them." A certain Riurik first established Varangian rule in the northern Slavic settlement of Novgorod, thus founding a dynasty that would rule first in Kyiv and then in Moscow until the late sixteenth century. The ensuing unification of the Eastern Slavs under Varangian rule led to the creation of Kyivan Rus, a state from which present-day Ukraine, Belarus, and Russia all trace their history of statehood.

✪ Kyivan Rus and Its Inheritance

The Varangians' role in the creation of the first Eastern Slavic state has been the subject of fierce polemics for centuries. The "Normanist" theory holds that the Varangians (known in western Europe as the Vikings or Normans) were responsible for the founding of the Kyivan state; Russian and Ukrainian "anti-Normanist" historians have argued that the Varangians simply took over preexisting Slavic political structures. Although the controversy is by no means resolved, most present-day scholars see Kyivan Rus not as a Varangian state but as a product of interaction between the Varangian rulers and local Slavic society. The princes and their retinues preserved Scandinavian names for centuries, but the Varangians were small in number and quickly assimilated into the Eastern Slavic culture.[12]

The early political history of Rus is shrouded in mystery. According to the legend recorded in the *Tale of Bygone Years*, Kyiv was founded by three brothers, Kyi, Shchek, and Khoriv, and their sister Lybid. Because these names are Slavic, some scholars suggest that Kyi was a leader of the tribal confederation of Polianians. To assert the Slavic origins of the Ukrainian capital, the Soviet authorities erected a monument to the four founders on the banks of the Dnipro during the questionable celebration of Kyiv's alleged 1,500th anniversary in 1982. But regardless of who founded Kyiv and when, the city's advantageous location on the Dnipro, overlooking an important trade route, attracted the Varangians in the late ninth century. In 882, a Varangian chieftain by the name of Oleh (Helgi) sailed down the Dnipro from Novgorod and established himself in Kyiv. Oleh's relation to Riurik and his own successor, Prince Ihor, remains unclear.

The next hundred years saw the territorial expansion of the Kyivan state. Oleh repulsed the Khazars and in 907 concluded the first trade agreement with the Byzantine Empire. His successor, Ihor (Ingvar), and his widow, Olha (Helga), continued to unify the Eastern Slavic tribes by force; Olha also paid a state visit to the Byzantine capital, Constantinople. Her son, Sviatoslav the Conqueror (962–972), was the first Rus ruler with a Slavic name, but he went down in history as an archetypal Varangian warrior, spending most of his time in the field. He decisively defeated the Khazars in the east and destroyed their capital, subjugated the northern Slavic tribe of Viatychians, and marched his army as far as the Balkans. There, Sviatoslav conquered the Bulgarian Kingdom and went to war with the Byzantine Empire, apparently planning to establish a new capital on the Danube for his enlarged realm. Defeated by the Byzantines, however, Sviatoslav was ambushed and killed by the nomadic Pechenegs during his return to Rus. According to the chronicle, the Pechenegian khan had a wine chalice made out of Sviatoslav's skull.

The rule of Sviatoslav's son, Volodymyr I the Great (980–1015; also known as the Red Sun, the Baptizer, and St. Volodymyr), marked the beginnings of internal consolidation. The first Varangian rulers of Rus viewed their domain mainly as an object of exploitation, in the form of tribute collection and control over trade. Under Volodymyr, however, the Kyivan state began to emerge as an integrated polity and society. In 988, he accepted Christianity as the state religion, making a momentous cultural choice in favor of the Byzantine, later known as Orthodox, church. The chronicle contains an entertaining story about the emissaries that Volodymyr sent abroad to investigate his confessional options: Islam, Judaism, Catholicism, and Byzantine Orthodoxy. He reportedly rejected Islam with its precept of abstinence because "Drinking is the joy of Rus—we cannot live without it." Although the story sounds more like a legend than a description of actual events, scholars have found evidence supporting these diplomatic missions.[13] In any case, the tale highlights the early Kyivan state's position at the intersection of different cultures. The choice of Byzantine Christianity was determined not just by the beauty of its services, as the chronicle says, but also by the Kyivan state's close contacts with the Byzantine Empire.

The concept of religious unity and the hierarchical organization of the church served as models for state building. Volodymyr had the "idols" of pagan deities removed from public places and Christian churches built at the same time as he was removing the remaining local rulers from power and replacing them with his numerous sons or administrators. Volodymyr's military campaigns were chiefly in the west, and they resulted in new territorial acquisitions in what is now western Ukraine and Lithuania. At the same time, his marriage to a relative (a sister, the chronicle claims) of the Byzantine emperor greatly enhanced the prestige of the Kyivan princely house.

Volodymyr's son Yaroslav the Wise (1036–1054) reunited Rus following a prolonged internecine struggle after his father's death. He also crushed the nomad Pechenegs, who had been harassing the Kyivan state since the collapse of the Khazar empire in the east. Yet, Yaroslav is better remembered for his promotion of culture and education, as well as for having the customary laws updated and codified. The *Tale of Bygone Years* also records schools and a book-copying center created under Yaroslav, and the search for the hypothetical "Yaroslav's library," which may have survived in some ancient cave, is a perennial obsession of amateur Ukrainian archaeologists.[14] Following the example of the Byzantines, Yaroslav ordered the construction of the land's main church, the Cathedral of St. Sophia, named after the great cathedral in Constantinople, although not modeled on the original. The more austere original design of Kyiv's St. Sophia is now hidden under Baroque additions dating from the seventeenth and eighteenth centuries, but inside one can see the ancient frescoes and mosaics of Yaroslav's time.

During the reign of Yaroslav the Wise, Rus strengthened its ties with western Europe, particularly by the skillful use of marital diplomacy. Himself married to the daughter of the Swedish king, Yaroslav had the rulers of France, Norway, and Hungary as sons-in-law. Modern Ukrainians are particularly proud of Yaroslav's daughter Anna, who in 1049 married the French king Henri I and played a prominent role during the minority years of her son, King Philip I.[15]

Yaroslav failed, however, to secure the internal cohesion of his own realm, the largest in Europe. Like many other medieval states, Rus in his time remained a loosely knit group of principalities without a developed central administrative apparatus. To further complicate matters, the Riurikids did not follow the principle of primogeniture, under which power passed from a father to his eldest son. The intricate system they used—succession from elder brother to younger and from the youngest uncle to the eldest nephew in the family—fueled permanent fratricidal wars. In fact, both Volodymyr I and Yaroslav reached the Kyivan throne by force, in violation of any seniority system. In addition, the princes of Kyiv perceived Rus as the patrimony of the extended Riurikid family. In the manner of his predecessors, before his death Yaroslav divided the principalities among his sons and nephews, effectively dividing the strength of the state and leaving it without a single ruler.[16]

Combined with the internecine wars among the Riurikids, attacks by the Polovtsians or Cumans, new nomad newcomers from the east, soon undermined the unity of the Kyivan state. Aside from a brief respite during the reign of Volodymyr II Monomakh (1113–1125), when Kyiv restored its political authority and culture flourished again, the federation of principalities continued to disintegrate. Kyiv lost its primacy and during the twelfth century was plundered several times by the feuding princes. Some commentators have paid special attention to the events of 1169, when Prince Andrei Bogoliubskii of Vladimir and Suzdal (now in Russia) sacked, pillaged, and burned Kyiv in what they call the first act of Russian aggression against Ukraine.[17] But the twelfth-century princes did not think in modern ethnic categories, and

Andrei probably believed he was fighting other competitors for the patrimony of his grandfather, Volodymyr II Monomakh. More significant was his decision not to move his court to the conquered city, indicating Kyiv's decline as the country's political center. At its peak size in the thirteenth century, Kyivan Rus included much of today's Ukraine and Belarus, as well as a significant part of European Russia. But its principalities, now each with its own hereditary dynasty, effectively led separate political and economic existences.

From the emergence of Kyivan Rus to its decline, foreign trade played a paramount role in the state's economic life. The development of the Baltic–Dnipro–Black Sea trade route initially brought the enterprising Varangians to the banks of the Dnipro. Princes and merchants actively traded with Byzantium, offering slaves, honey, furs, wax, and grain. Merchants brought back wine, jewelry, fabrics, artwork, and metal weapons from the Byzantine Empire and the Middle East. By the twelfth century, however, the nomadic Polovtsians were seriously threatening the Dnipro trade route, the Arabs no longer controlled the Mediterranean trade, and Byzantium's economic importance was in decline. The Dnipro road "from the Varangians to the Greeks" lost its prominence, causing Rus to reorient its commerce westward, toward Poland and Germany. Yet, however important foreign trade may have been to the upper and middle classes, the overwhelming majority of the Rus population earned its living by cultivating the land.

Living in the midst of the Eastern Slavic population, the Varangians preserved their language and culture for only about a century, while new warriors continued to arrive from Scandinavia. The chronicles confirm the presence of other ethnic groups in Kyivan Rus, most notably Armenian, German, Greek, and Jewish merchants in major cities, as well as friendly Turkic settlers in the south of Rus, the so-called Black Caps (*chorni klobuky*).[18]

A cultural foster child of Byzantium, Kyivan Rus adopted its highly developed cultural tradition through the medium of the church. Unlike Rome, Constantinople allowed for the use of native languages in the liturgy, and in the late ninth century, two Byzantine missionaries from the Balkans, Cyril and Methodius, who at the time were proselytizing in the Czech lands, created a Slavic script for church purposes. Later developed by their Bulgarian disciples into the Cyrillic alphabet based on Greek letters, this script made possible the spread of a new literary language, so-called Church Slavonic, which came to serve as a vehicle of religious and secular literature in Kyivan Rus, as well as in other Slavic lands where Byzantine Christianity had taken hold, such as Bulgaria and Serbia.

Byzantine influences were especially noticeable in art and architecture. In fact, many of the early artists and architects of the Kyivan period were Greeks who had been invited to Rus by the princes. Among their lasting cultural contributions are icons (holy images on wood panels made with an egg-based paint) and the prohibition of statues and instrumental music in churches. In contrast, in literature the Byzantine influence usually reached Rus not directly but via Bulgaria. Religious forms and motifs dominated the literature of the Kyivan period; Christian treatises, sermons, hymns, and lives of saints were the subject matter of handwritten books. Occasionally, these genres allowed local authors to create fascinating pictures of everyday life (as did the monk compilers of the *Paterikon*, the lives of holy hermits in the Kyivan Cave Monastery) or to express the state ideology of the period (as did the eleventh-century head of the church in Rus, Metropolitan Ilarion, in his work "On Law and Grace"). Secular literature was represented mainly by chronicles, the most important of them being the *Tale of Bygone Years*, or the *Primary Chronicle*, dating from the early twelfth century. The only surviving work of Rus literary epic poetry is the magnificent *Lay of Ihor's Campaign*, portraying a minor prince's war against the nomads in 1185, although some scholars consider it a later forgery.[19]

Church Slavonic was the language of high culture that was used in all regions of Rus, but ordinary people apparently spoke a host of Eastern Slavic dialects from which the Ukrainian, Belarusian, and Russian languages would eventually develop. Scholars believe that modern Ukrainian is a lineal descendant of the colloquial language that was spoken in Kyiv a millennium ago. The question of when the specific traits of the Ukrainian language emerged is fraught with controversy, linked to Russian and Ukrainian claims to Kyivan Rus as the foundation of their history. Modern Ukrainian scholars are divided between those who stick to the traditional Soviet dating of the thirteenth to fourteenth centuries and those who trace the emergence of the Ukrainian language to the late eleventh or early twelfth centuries.[20] Irrespective of when the dialectal divergences began hardening, political divisions between what are now Ukraine and European Russia solidified following the Mongol conquest.

In 1237–1240, the Mongols, the last wave of nomadic invaders from the east, took Kyivan Rus into their immense empire, which had been founded by Genghis Khan. Led by Genghis's grandson, Batu Khan, their vast army was multiethnic and included many Turkic tribes. For this reason, Eastern Slavs called the invaders Tatars rather than Mongols. In a bloody war, the Mongol army devastated the Rus principalities one by one, taking advantage of their political fragmentation. Kyiv fell to the Mongols in December 1240, after a prolonged siege resulting in almost total destruction of the city. Following this devastating invasion, however, the Mongols did not interfere much in the internal life of Rus. Like other nomads before them, they collected tribute from the local princes and customs duties from major trading routes. The new steppe overlords even encouraged the revival of the trading centers on the Black Sea coast, this time by Italian merchants from Genoa, and engaged in trade with the Mediterranean civilizations in much the same way the Scythians had two millennia earlier.

Even before the Mongol attack, three new power centers emerged among the Rus principalities in place of declining Kyiv: Galicia-Volhynia in the southwest (present-day western Ukraine), Vladimir-Suzdal in the northeast (the present-day central part of European Russia, including the small town of Moscow, first mentioned in the chronicle for the year 1147), and Novgorod in the north (now also in Russia). The first two centers repeatedly attempted to unite around themselves the fragmented principalities, but for the time being the Mongols blocked such efforts. Still, both Galicia-Volhynia and Vladimir-Suzdal (and the latter's successor, Muscovy) claimed to be the political heirs of Kyivan Rus. Modern Ukrainian historians single out Galicia-Volhynia, which they prefer to call a "state" rather than just a "principality" of Kyivan Rus, as belonging to Ukrainian history.[21]

Located strategically on the major trade routes and possessing sub-stantial deposits of salt, a valuable commodity in those days, the lands of Galicia and Volhynia were united into a single and powerful principal-ity at the turn of the twelfth century. Under Prince Danylo of Halych (1238–1264), Galicia-Volhynia reached the apex of its political influence. Danylo subdued the powerful local aristocracy, checked the advance of the German knights in the west, and attempted to form a military coalition against the Mongols. To this end, he sought an alliance with his immediate western neighbors and in 1253 accepted a king's crown from the pope. After his efforts at organizing an anti-Mongol crusade failed, Danylo relied on his own forces to defeat the Mongols in 1255, before their overwhelming army forced him to submit in 1259. Under Danylo's successors, Galicia-Volhynia entered a period of stability that turned into a gradual decline. In the first half of the fourteenth century, his dynasty died out. Following a series of civil wars and foreign interventions in Galicia, neighboring Poland finally annexed it in 1378. Even before that, Volhynia had fallen under Lithuanian rule.

In the late fourteenth century, the Eastern Slavic lands that today con-stitute Ukraine were controlled by the Mongols in the east and a group of European neighbor states in the west: mainly Lithuania and Poland, but also Hungary (which took over Transcarpathia) and Moldavia (the northern part of Bukovyna). Among these western neighbors, the Grand Duchy of Lithu-ania was an especially impressive newcomer. Prince Mindaugas had united the warlike, pagan Lithuanian tribes only in the mid-thirteenth century, but his successors came to control large territories in eastern Europe between the Baltic Sea and the Dnipro Valley.[22] Having defeated the Mongols at Syni Vody (near the present-day Syniukha River in southern Ukraine) in 1362, the Grand Duchy absorbed most of the Eastern Slavic lands west and immediately east of the Dnipro, thus becoming the largest state in Europe. Simultaneously in the northeast, the princes of Moscow, with the Mongols' help, took the Vladimir-Suzdal Principality under their control. The stage was set for a contest between two ascendant powers for the territories of Kyivan Rus, as well as for the subsequent Ukrainian-Russian contest for its cultural legacy.[23]

The Eastern Slavic lands under Lithuanian rule preserved their political elite, social structure, laws, Orthodox religion, and language. The last, a nativized version of Church Slavonic, in fact became an official language of the state. In the late fourteenth century, former lands of Kyivan Rus constituted nine tenths of the Grand Duchy's territory. Ruthenian (an early-modern term for "Eastern Slavic," including future Ukrainians and Belarusians, but excluding the Russians) princes and nobles intermarried with the Lithuanian aristocracy and continued to exercise power as military commanders, administrators, and great landowners. In 1385, however, Lithuania entered a dynastic union with Poland, resulting in, among other things, an acceptance of Catholicism as the state religion. The Ruthenian elite had to fight for its political rights, which were restored to the Orthodox nobility only in 1434. Yet, the Ruthenian nobles also jealously observed the impressive political privileges their Polish counterparts had won from their kings. In 1569, when Poland and Lithuania entered into a closer constitutional union, the Ukrainian lands of Volhynia, Podolia, and Kyiv were incorporated into Poland proper with the assent of the local nobility.[24] It was also in the late sixteenth century that the Ruthenian lands in the Dnipro Valley came to be known by the name Ukraine, meaning "borderland." (The ethnic designation of Ukrainians, however, originated only in the nineteenth century.)

Even before the Ukrainian territories were united within the Polish part of the Polish-Lithuanian Commonwealth, a new and powerful enemy emerged in the south. The Tatars were originally the Turkic people who constituted the bulk of the multicultural Mongol army in the thirteenth century. In the late fifteenth century, the Tatars of the Crimea, who had settled on the peninsula after the conquest of Rus, seceded from the weakening Mongol Empire. The Crimean Tatar state, headed by its khan, became a vassal of Ottoman Turkey. Almost every year, beginning in the 1480s, the Tatars left their Crimean base to raid and ravage the Ukrainian lands. The nomads were especially interested in taking prisoners, who were then sold on the Crimean slave markets. It was the constant Tatar threat that brought about the emergence of the Cossacks, a social group that would greatly influence the course of Ukrainian history.

✸ The Cossack Period

Polish rule soon led to profound social and cultural changes in what would become the Ukrainian lands, now constituted as six palatinates (provinces) of the Polish-Lithuanian Commonwealth. Whereas in Kyivan Rus the boundaries among social groups were relatively fluid, the Poles introduced a European system of closed social "estates." The nobility was by far the most privileged of them. Ukrainian magnates continued to own vast landholdings and exercise considerable influence in the region, but the Polish kings made a point of awarding newly colonized territories on the steppe frontier to Polish nobles. Intermarriages, the social prestige of Catholicism, and the spread of the Polish educational system soon led to the assimilation of the Ruthenian nobility. In the early modern period, the loss of a native political elite, rather than foreign rule as such, meant the death of a nation, and the Ukrainian historical profession has spilled much ink condemning the nobility's "betrayal" of national interests. However, a revisionist Ukrainian scholar has argued recently that the Ruthenian princely and noble families continued functioning as a national elite until the early seventeenth century, thus ensuring the continuity of indigenous social and cultural structures between Kyivan times and the Cossack period.[25]

The social history of the era was complex. Cities and towns flourished under Polish rule, the largest of them enjoying self-government under the so-called Magdeburg law. The state and magnate town owners, however, encouraged German, Polish, and Jewish burghers to move in, while segregating or assimilating the Orthodox Ruthenians. In contrast, the situation of the peasantry worsened because sixteenth-century Poland was becoming the "breadbasket of Europe." To earn a handsome profit on the grain trade, the nobility introduced the manorial system of agriculture, resulting in the enserfment of peasants, who increasingly toiled in landowners' fields rather than paying them a modest rent as before. Conditions were different, however, in the sparsely populated Dnipro Valley, which was threatened by Tatar raids. To colonize these territories, Polish magnates granted peasants exemptions from taxes and labor obligations for up to thirty years.

Culturally, the inclusion of the Ukrainian lands into Poland exposed their residents to invigorating influences from the West. Unlike Muscovy, Poland fully experienced the European cultural revolution of the Renaissance with its humanist ideas and emphasis on learning, secular literature, and the arts. Through Polish mediation, another powerful intellectual watershed, the Reformation, also had some echoes in the Ukrainian lands.[26] Polish Catholicism launched a counteroffensive by the end of the sixteenth century, but the fertile intellectual climate of the time revitalized Ukrainian cultural life. Somewhat paradoxically, the resulting cultural upsurge took the form of an anti-Polish Orthodox revival. Seeing religion as the paramount identity marker, Orthodox magnates founded schools and established presses. In 1580, the town of Ostrih in Volhynia, the capital of the immensely rich "uncrowned king of Ukraine," Prince Kostiantyn Ostrozky, became home to the famous Ostrih Academy.[27] The following year, a press established in Ostrih published the first complete text of the Bible in Church Slavonic. Orthodox burghers also organized themselves into church brotherhoods to defend their religious, cultural, and corporate interests.

Religious polemical literature became especially widespread after the 1596 Brest Church Union. A crisis in the Orthodox Church and pressure from Polish Catholics prompted the majority of Ukrainian Orthodox bishops in the Polish-Lithuanian Commonwealth to sign an act of union with Rome, resulting in the creation of the Uniate (later known as the Greek Catholic or Ukrainian Catholic) Church, which preserved the Byzantine rite but recognized the pope as its head and supreme authority in matters of faith. The Polish government actively promoted the new church at the expense of the Orthodox. Initially, most bishops, but not the majority of the Orthodox Ukrainian population, accepted the Union. (In later centuries, the Uniate Church would establish itself in western Ukraine and serve as a focus of Ukrainian allegiances there.) In response, new Orthodox bishops were consecrated in Kyiv in 1620 to replace those who had crossed over to the Uniates. In 1632, the Orthodox Metropolitan Petro Mohyla established the first modern institution of higher learning among the Eastern Slavs, the Kyiv-Mohyla Academy.[28] Both the restoration of the Orthodox church hierarchy and the creation of this college would have been impossible without support from the Cossacks, who were emerging as the new defenders of Ukrainian social, political, and religious rights.[29]

The word "Cossack" comes from the Turkic word *kazak*, meaning "free man." Small groups of freebooters, hunters, and fishermen, most of whom were runaway peasants, began to settle on the southern steppe frontier in the fifteenth century. (There were few women among them, and women were later prohibited from living in the Cossack stronghold, the Zaporozhian Sich.) In the sixteenth century, when Polish governors and magnates began pushing for colonization of the Ukrainian steppe, they found it advantageous to recruit Cossacks as border patrolmen. The Cossacks were charged with defending the frontier from Tatar raids, but they also ventured far into the steppe in pursuit of the Tatars. Sometimes the Cossacks attacked Tatar settlements on the Black Sea, where they rescued captives and took booty. In the course of time, the Cossacks grew into a military force to be reckoned with. In 1552–1554, the legendary royal sheriff of Kaniv, an Orthodox soldier and hero of Ukrainian folksongs, Prince Dmytro Vyshnevetsky (Baida), founded a Cossack fortress on the lower Dnipro. He united several groups of Cossacks to man this new stronghold, which came to be known as the Zaporozhian Sich.[30]

As their numbers grew, by the late sixteenth century the Cossacks also developed into a distinct social group. The Polish kings granted them certain rights and freedoms and attempted at the same time to limit the number of Cossacks by establishing a "register" for them. However, the constant influx of fugitive peasants swelled the numbers and ignited antimagnate sentiments, resulting in several bloody Cossack uprisings against the Polish authorities at the turn of the seventeenth century. Under Hetman (elected Cossack leader) Petro Sahaidachny (1614–1622), the Cossacks participated in Poland's wars against Muscovy and Turkey. As head of a mighty army, Sahaidachny had enough authority to act as a protector of Orthodoxy in Ukraine. For example, he was instrumental in the restoration of the Orthodox Church hierarchy in 1620.[31] During the 1630s, the Poles suppressed several more Cossack uprisings. In 1638, they curtailed the rights of the Cossacks, reduced the register, and replaced the hetman with a royal commissioner.

Contemporary Polish writers referred to the decade of 1638–1648 in Ukraine as an era of "golden tranquility," but in fact social and religious tensions were increasing in the land. Settlers of the steppe borderland who had once been free found themselves turned into serfs and owing their landlords three to six days of labor per week. To make matters worse, the absentee Polish landowners leased their vast land estates to leaseholders, usually Jews, who then had to squeeze their investment and profit out of the peasants. Ukrainian burghers also felt disadvantaged in comparison with the Poles, Germans, and Jews. The Cossacks were unhappy with the limited register and aspired to recognition as a distinct social estate with guaranteed rights and freedoms. The Orthodox Church, which the Polish authorities had outlawed from 1595 to 1632, struggled against Catholic and Uniate inroads into its traditional territory and demanded full restoration of its legal rights and properties.

In this climate of growing discontent, a disaffected Cossack officer by the name of Bohdan Khmelnytsky (ca. 1595–1657) launched an uprising in 1648 that would redraw the map of eastern Europe. Initially motivated by a personal conflict with a local Polish official who had stolen his mistress and seized his estate, Khmelnytsky soon emerged as a national leader, great visionary, skillful general, and statesman among the Cossacks. The uprising quickly engulfed Dnipro (or central and eastern) Ukraine, in the process acquiring a new dimension. What had started as the Cossacks' rebellion against Polish rule also became a peasant war on the landowners and a religious war of the Orthodox against non-Orthodox (including Catholics, Uniates, and Jews). Led by Hetman Khmelnytsky, in May 1648 the united army of Cossacks, peasants, and their Tatar allies twice decisively defeated Polish troops at Zhovti Vody and Korsun. Khmelnytsky's army took control of Dnipro Ukraine and briefly occupied Galicia in the west. Those Poles, Uniate Ukrainians, and Jews who did not flee from the advancing rebel forces were massacred en masse. Jews in particular sustained terrible losses during the Khmelnytsky rebellion, with the number of estimated deaths ranging from more than 100,000 in contemporary Jewish chronicles to fewer than 16,000, according to present-day Ukrainian historians.[32] The Poles also resorted to mass killings of Ukrainian civilians. Ironically, it was an assimilated Ukrainian magnate, Prince Jeremi Wiśniowiecki (both a grandnephew of the legendary Cossack leader Dmytro Vyshnevetsky and father of the future Polish king), who came to be remembered by Ukrainians for his cruelty.

The armistice signed in the city of Zboriv in August 1649 created an autonomous Ukrainian Cossack state by putting three palatinates of the commonwealth under the authority of Hetman Khmelnytsky and banning Polish officials from governing there. The de facto independent polity soon developed its own military-administrative apparatus and foreign policy. Khmelnytsky, whom foreign observers sometimes compared with another rebel-turned-statesman, Oliver Cromwell, proved himself a skillful ruler. Present-day Ukrainian historians and politicians may be overstating his importance when they dub Khmelnytsky "Bohdan the Great" and "Father of the Fatherland" or present him as a modern nationalist fighting for his ethnic group's political independence.[33] However, the hetman did speak about the liberation of the "entire Ruthenian people," and recent research confirms that the concept of the Ruthenian "nation" (narod) as a religious and cultural community had been developing even before the Khmelnytsky revolution.[34] With the beginning of the revolt, the Cossacks assumed the role that had once belonged to the Ruthenian nobility—that of Ukraine's political class. Yet, their violent attacks on peasants and burghers of the same ethnicity and even the same religion during the Khmelnytsky wars serve as a reminder that a modern, egalitarian idea of nationality had not yet overwritten the boundaries between social estates.[35]

War with the Poles broke out again in 1651. Several times betrayed by the unreliable Tatars, Khmelnytsky sought anti-Polish alliances with other neighbors, notably the Ottoman Empire and Moldova. By 1653, when the war had reached a stalemate, the hetman drew closer to Orthodox Muscovy. In 1654, the Pereiaslav Treaty put the Cossacks under the protection of the tsar, although the exact meaning of this act remains controversial to this day. In contrast to the official Russian and Soviet position that Pereiaslav "reunited" Ukraine and Russia, Ukrainian historians have presented the treaty as merely a military alliance, dynastic union, or protectorate. Differences in interpretation surfaced almost immediately after the signing. Following their oath of allegiance, the Cossack leaders expected Muscovite envoys to also take an oath in the name of the tsar, which would oblige him to observe the Cossacks' traditional rights. The Muscovite boyars refused to do this, because they saw the tsar as an absolute monarch not accountable to his subjects.[36] Regardless of whether Khmelnytsky intended the Pereiaslav Treaty to be a temporary diplomatic maneuver or a unification of two states, according to its terms, the Cossack polity accepted the tsar's suzerainty while preserving its wide-ranging autonomy. In the long run, however, the Russian authorities gradually curtailed the Cossacks' self-rule while establishing their direct control of Ukraine.

After the prolonged Russo-Polish war (resulting from the Pereiaslav Treaty), Khmelnytsky's death, and internal feuding among the Cossack elite, Russia and Poland divided the Ukrainian lands in 1667. Poland retained the territories west of the Dnipro, and Muscovy controlled Kyiv and the lands east of the Dnipro. The Ottomans continued to rule in the south. In the second half of the seventeenth century, which came to be known as the period of the "Ruin" (*Ruina*), Ukraine was a battlefield for neighboring powers and feuding hetmans. During the Ruin, several hetmans attempted to break the union with Muscovy in favor of either Poland or Turkey. In 1708–1709, Hetman Ivan Mazepa made the last and most famous, albeit unsuccessful, effort by allying with the Swedish king Charles XII in his war with Russia.[37] On June 28, 1709, the Russian army under the command of Peter I and loyalist Cossacks decisively defeated the united Swedish-Ukrainian forces in the Battle of Poltava. As a result, Russia became a major European power, and Ukrainian autonomy began its final decline.

Even before Poltava, the tsars forbade Cossack hetmans to maintain foreign relations, stationed Russian garrisons in strategic locations in Ukraine, and entrusted Russian officials with collecting taxes there. After Mazepa's defeat, Russians, as well as German mercenaries, were increasingly appointed as senior officers in the Cossack army. In the 1720s, the real power in the Cossack polity, the Hetmanate, shifted to a body of Russian military administrators, the Little Russian Collegium.[38] ("Little Russia" was the official Muscovite name for Cossack Ukraine.) Proclaimed an empire in 1721, Russia during the eighteenth century gradually absorbed the Cossack autonomous state. The last hetman, a largely symbolic figure, was forced to resign in 1764 and never replaced. In 1775, the Russian army razed the Zaporozhian Sich, the troublesome Cossacks' stronghold, to the ground. Finally, in 1781, Empress Catherine II abolished the regimental administrative structure of the Hetmanate, creating instead three large provinces of the Russian Empire. The traditional territorial Cossack regiments were transformed into regular dragoon regiments in the imperial army.

The Cossack polity was not a full-fledged modern state, and it did not last long, but the Hetmanate furnished later generations with a precedent of Ukrainian statehood. The Khmelnytsky rebellion also led to profound social and cultural changes. With the Polish landowners expelled from the Cossack lands, the peasants regained their freedom. Entry into the new privileged social estate of the Cossacks was initially open to everybody; indeed, in 1654, half of the adult male population of the Hetmanate claimed to be Cossacks. However, the Cossack officer class soon evolved into a new, hereditary land-owning nobility that pushed for the renewed enserfment of the peasants. The Russian government skillfully played on the tensions between the Cossack elite and the lower classes, and soon Cossack officers, just like the Ruthenian nobles in Poland a century before, began assimilating with the empire's ruling class. The culmination of these processes came in the 1780s. In 1783, Catherine II deprived the Ukrainian peasants of the right to leave their landlords' land, thus turning them into serfs, and in 1785, she granted the Cossack officer class the rights and privileges of the Russian nobility.[39]

As early as 1686, the tsars subordinated the Orthodox Church in the Hetmanate to the patriarch of Moscow, which resulted in its transformation during the eighteenth century into an instrument of cultural assimilation. At the same time, however, clerics from Ukraine came to occupy high positions in the Russian Orthodox Church and helped to spread modern learning in Russia. Until the late eighteenth century, the arts and architecture of Cossack Ukraine displayed the influence of European Baroque, which is preserved today in the exquisite beauty of surviving churches and the unusual style of portraits of the Cossack elite.[40]

With the gradual assimilation of the officer class into Russian culture and the rank-and-file Cossacks' transformation into a stratum of free peasants, the social structures of the Hetmanate were disappearing at the turn of the nineteenth century. But the memory of the Hetmanate—enshrined in the so-called Cossack chronicles of the late seventeenth and eighteenth centuries—survived among the native nobility and would provide a living link between Cossack statehood and the Ukrainian national movement in the Russian Empire of the nineteenth century.

However, until the late eighteenth century, roughly half of Ukrainian ethnic territories were held by Poland. The lands immediately west of the Dnipro (the so-called Right-Bank Ukraine) were divided between Poland in the north and the Ottoman Empire to the south until the end of the seventeenth century. In 1699, Poland reacquired the Ottoman part of the region and again invited peasants to move into tax-free settlements on the steppe frontier. Yet, history was bound to repeat itself there. By the mid-eighteenth century, the magnates' attempts to enserf the settlers led to explosive social discontent, while the oppression of the Orthodox in Poland became an international issue. The Russian Empire claimed the right to protect its coreligionists, but it supported Poland in 1768 when a bloody rebellion of Cossacks and peasants engulfed all of Right-Bank Ukraine. Fearing that the revolt might spread to the Hetmanate, the Russian army helped crush the insurgents.[41]

Further west, the Ukrainian lands that formerly constituted the Galician-Volhynian Principality did not experience the Cossack movement. Khmelnytsky's army occupied them briefly in 1649, but Polish rule returned immediately afterward. By the early eighteenth century, the Ruthenian nobility and burghers had assimilated into Polish culture, all Orthodox parishes were converted to the Uniate Church, and the peasants were enserfed by the landlords. Just like in the former Hetmanate, only the villagers continued speaking an array of Ukrainian dialects and preserved traditional folk culture.

Two small westernmost enclaves of population descending from Kyivan Rus in the late eighteenth century had different masters. Northern Bukovyna, which until the Mongol conquest had been part of the Galician-Volhynian Principality, was subsequently annexed by Moldavia, which in turn became a dependency of the Ottoman Empire. Transcarpathia had lain under Hungarian and, later, Austrian rule since the eleventh century, but the region's highlander inhabitants managed throughout the ages to preserve their distinct Eastern Slavic identity.

Such was the setting of Ukrainian history until the last quarter of the eighteenth century, when the three major powers of the day would redraw the borders of eastern Europe, imposing their ideas of political legitimacy, population control, and modern culture on this confusing patchwork of regional identities and ethnic distinctions.

✣

To bring home the point that it has a venerable tradition of statehood, the present-day Ukrainian state uses the portraits of Kyivan Rus princes and Cossack hetmans on the front side of its paper money. Prince Volodymyr appears on the one-*hryvnia* bill, and Yaroslav the Wise on the two-*hryvnia* one. Bohdan Khmelnytsky, the founder of the Cossack state, graces the fiver, and Hetman Ivan Mazepa, who had attempted to break with Russia, is portrayed on the ten-*hryvnia* bill. (Larger denominations feature the portraits of later writers and politicians.) As material a symbol as they come of a nation's official historical pedigree, Ukrainian paper money shows the modern state's ability to "nationalize" the past by claiming the historical polities, rulers, and events preceding the emergence of the modern notion of "Ukraine." Just as France and Germany are entitled to claim Charlemagne's empire as "their" state, so is Ukraine descended from Kyivan Rus, which is also claimed by Russians and Belarusians. Modern Ukrainians are not challenged by other nations in celebrating the Cossacks as their national patrimony, but the 1654 union with Russia is now evaluated in a diametrically opposing fashion in the two countries—positively in Russia and negatively in Ukraine. All in all, although Ukraine is one of the world's youngest states, its past is as rich as any.

Imperial Bureaucrats and Nation Builders **2**

Between the late eighteenth century and the early twentieth, the present-day Ukrainian territories were divided between two empires. Ukrainians living west of the Russian-Austrian border pledged allegiance to the Habsburgs; their eastern conationals were subjects of the Romanovs. Both empires were large multinational entities united not by any modern ideology but by traditional allegiance to the ruling dynasty. But there was a crucial difference between the two: Throughout the nineteenth century, Russia remained an oppressive absolute monarchy, but the Habsburgs' subjects were able to participate politically and develop a civic society in the second half of the nineteenth century. Ukrainians in the two neighboring states, therefore, had markedly different political and cultural experiences, resulting by the turn of the twentieth century in their successful national mobilization in the west and a more ambiguous outcome in the east.

The nineteenth century has often been called the "age of nationalism." The American and French revolutions launched an era of political legitimacy that was no longer vested in the state, monarch, or nobility. Revolutionaries and German Romantic thinkers proclaimed new ideas: the people as a source of political authority, equality before the law, and the sovereignty of the nation. This ideology had unexpected implications in eastern Europe. While state borders divided the different nation-states in western Europe, eastern Europe was still dominated by multiethnic empires—Russian, Austrian, and Ottoman. There, the notion of popular sovereignty empowered the leaders of stateless nationalities. The modern concept of nationhood also originated during this period when, following German Romantic philosophers, intellectuals in eastern Europe embraced the new vision of nationality as a community based on shared language and culture. Scholars have helpfully divided the subsequent "national revivals" in eastern Europe into three general stages: "academic," when intellectuals pursued historical and folkloric research defining the national separateness of their people; "cultural," marked by the development of modern high culture and education in the national language; and "political," when mass mobilization for the nationalist cause took place.[1]

The history of the Ukrainian national movement confirms this general model, while also offering a healthy antidote to blind belief in teleological schemes. The scholarly, cultural, and political phases could overlap, have a reverse order, or be skipped, depending on powerful external factors, such as imperial repression and the international situation. European wars and imperial crises could shape the destinies of nationalities in defiance of any models. The success of the Ukrainian national revival was not preordained and instead depended on the combination of social factors and political circumstances that differed between the Romanov and Habsburg empires.

✜ Between Two Empires

In 1772, 1793, and 1795, Austria, Prussia, and Russia carried out the so-called three partitions of Poland. The three aggressive neighbors, all rising continental powers, eliminated from the map of Europe the internally unstable Polish state with its elected king, weak central government, and all-powerful gentry. Poland's Ukrainian lands were divided between Austria and Russia. During the first partition in 1772, Austria acquired Galicia, and in 1793–1795 the Russian Empire received the former Polish palatinates of Kyiv, Podolia, and Volhynia—the lands west of the Dnipro that remained under Polish control after the Khmelnytsky Rebellion and were known historically as the Right Bank. (The right and left banks of a river are determined in relation to an observer facing downstream. In the case of the Dnipro, the right bank is west of the river, and the left bank is east.)

At approximately the same time as the three powers were dividing the former Polish territories, the declining Ottoman Empire also had to relinquish many of its European possessions. In 1774, the Habsburgs annexed the mountainous region of Bukovyna, located south of Galicia, from the Principality of Moldavia, an Ottoman protectorate. Ukrainians predominated in the northern half of Bukovyna. That same year, the Russian army decisively defeated the Ottomans, wresting control of the Crimean Khanate, another valuable Ottoman protectorate in Europe, from the sultan. With the Crimean Tatars fleeing to Turkey en masse, in 1783 the Russian Empire formally annexed the Crimean Peninsula. Unlike the economically insignificant Austrian acquisitions, the Russian conquest of Crimea and the Black Sea's north coast opened up new trade opportunities on the Black Sea. With the Crimean Khanate extinguished, peasant settlers could now colonize the vast steppes of what is now southern Ukraine.

Imperial governments rearranged the administrative structure of Ukrainian lands, but for both contemporaries and later scholars it made more sense to speak of Ukraine's historical regions, each with its traditional name and unique cultural profile.[2] A traveler heading westward from Russia in the early nineteenth century would first pass through the Left Bank, the former territory of the Hetmanate and, since 1830, the imperial provinces of Chernihiv, Poltava, and Kharkiv. There, the social elite was a native nobility descended from the Cossack officer class, and the memory of the Cossack Ukraine was preserved well into the nineteenth century. After a century and a half of Russian rule, however, most local nobles assimilated into the Russian culture. A substantial number of ethnic Russians also settled on the Left Bank, especially in large cities.

After crossing the Dnipro, a traveler would enter the city of Kyiv on its high right bank. The golden domes of Kyivan churches could be seen from miles away. The city itself was under Russian control ever since Khmelnytsky's time, but other lands beyond the Dnipro, the so-called Right Bank (Kyiv, Podolia, and Volhynia provinces) had just been annexed from Poland. There, the Polish nobility remained the dominant social group, and Polish culture reigned supreme in cities. The Right Bank also had a sizable Jewish population, especially in cities and small Jewish towns, known as shtetls. During the eighteenth century, Hasidic Judaism, with its emphasis on spirituality, developed in the region. Russian imperial bureaucrats, who did not want their new Jewish subjects to move from the former Polish territory into Russia proper, restricted their residence to the so-called Pale of Settlement in the western provinces, including Jewish settlements in what are now Ukraine, Belarus, and Lithuania. The number of Jews in the Right Bank grew from some 110,000 at the end of the eighteenth century to over a million in 1880.[3]

A side trip to the Black Sea would take our traveler to the third Ukrainian historical region in the Russian Empire, the South (Katerynoslav, Kherson, and Taurida provinces). Until the late eighteenth century, it was a wild steppe, where the Cossacks clashed with the Tatars, but Catherine the Great and her successors lured to the region numerous colonists with offers of free land and tax exemptions. New settlers included Russian and Ukrainian peasants but also Greeks, Italians, Romanians, and Germans (among whom Mennonites were especially prominent). In the space of a few decades, the port city of Odesa on the Black Sea, founded in 1794 by a French governor in the service of the Russians with the help of Italian and Greek settlers, grew into a bustling metropolis, Ukraine's largest city and main trading center, where a dozen languages were spoken on the streets.[4]

Returning to the Right Bank and crossing the Zbruch River, a traveler would enter the Austrian Empire via the province of Galicia. Ethnic Ukrainians predominated in the province's eastern part, and Poles in the western. However, the numerical dominance of Ukrainian peasants (who still called themselves Ruthenians) meant little at a time when the nobility was the only political class. Most nobles in the region were Poles, many bureaucrats were Germans, and commerce was controlled by Jews. Ukrainians constituted a minority in the province's capital city, know in German as Lemberg, in Polish as Lwów, and in Ukrainian as Lviv.[5] Unlike the Russian Empire, however, where the overwhelming majority of ethnic Ukrainians belonged to the Orthodox Church—the Uniate Church in the Right Bank having been promptly dissolved by the imperial authorities—in eastern Galicia, the Uniate Church commanded the allegiances of local Ukrainians. Assimilation into the Polish culture was relatively easy for Ukrainians; religion was the major sticking point, because the Poles were Roman Catholics.

A short expedition south would take a traveler to Bukovyna, another new Austrian province with a considerable Ukrainian population. Previously part of Moldavia (one of the Romanian principalities), Bukovyna was more or less equally split into two halves, with ethnic Ukrainians forming a majority in the north and Romanians in the south. Because Orthodox Christianity had been a dominant religion in Moldavia, the Uniate Church could not make advances there, and Bukovynian Ukrainians remained Orthodox. Religion, thus, could not serve as a marker of national identity in Bukovyna, where both the Romanian upper classes and Ukrainians belonged to the same church. However, in this case, language served as an indicator of difference, because Romanian is not a Slavic language and is not comprehensible to ordinary Ukrainians, as Russian and Polish are.

In the early nineteenth century, visiting the last historical region of the Austrian Empire that is now part of Ukraine, Transcarpathia, would require traveling on horseback along narrow mountainous roads.[6] But a persevering traveler crossing the Carpathian Mountains from Galicia or Bukovyna would be rewarded by the colorful customs of the Eastern Slavic mountaineers, who had preserved their language under the rule of Hungarian kings since the eleventh century. Catholic Hungary, which in the late seventeenth century became part of the Habsburg Empire, helped establish the Uniate Church in Transcarpathia. Separated by mountain ranges from other Ukrainian lands and exploited by the Hungarian upper classes, the local Eastern Slavic population was the last group of the would-be Ukrainian nation to develop a modern national consciousness. The name we now use for the region, Transcarpathia, means the "land beyond the Carpathian Mountains" and is relatively recent. Indeed, this name is a product of the modern nationalist imagination, for Transcarpathia would appear to be located "beyond" the Carpathians only to an observer based in Kyiv or Lviv—the two centers of the Ukrainian national movement. Locals on their side of the mountains more often than not called their region Subcarpathian Rus, the land "under" or at the foothills of the Carpathians.[7]

In traversing all the diverse historical regions of what is now Ukraine, an early-nineteenth-century traveler—who would have probably communicated with Russian and Austrian imperial bureaucrats in French, the international language of the time—would notice important similarities between the two multinational empires. Both the Russian and Austrian empires were solidifying their control over newly acquired regions. In both polities, the Enlightenment ideas of rationality and good government led to administrative reforms, advances in education, and an increase in the number of civil servants. The growing imperial bureaucracies were adopting modern ways of counting, classifying, and ruling their new subjects. Yet some reforms of the "enlightened monarchs" also had positive consequences for their subjects.

In the Habsburg Empire, Maria Theresa (1745–1780) and Joseph II (1780–1790) limited the number of days a serf had to work for a landlord and gave serfs limited legal rights. Their educational reforms of 1775–1781 made elementary education compulsory and greatly increased the number of schools, including parochial schools with instruction in the region's native language. Finally, the two rulers professed religious tolerance and granted other churches in the new territories the same rights as the empire's dominant Roman Catholic Church. The Uniate Church (renamed the Greek Catholic Church in 1774, "Greek" here referring to its Byzantine rite) in particular benefited from imperial benevolence. For example, priests began receiving government stipends. In 1807, Vienna helped reestablish the office of metropolitan, or the church's supreme archbishop, with its seat in the Galician capital of Lviv. To raise the educational standards of the Greek Catholic clergy, the Austrian government opened a seminary in Vienna (1775), later replaced by a larger one in Lviv (1784). When Lviv University was established in 1784, a separate "Ruthenian" college was attached to it for the first twenty years, serving Ukrainian students who could not yet manage taking courses in Latin and German.[8]

The successors of Joseph II, Leopold II (1790–1792) and Franz I (1793–1835), revoked some of his reforms, but many changes proved irreversible. One notable alteration occurred in the nationalities policy, however. A patchwork conglomerate of a dozen major nationalities, the Habsburg Empire could not hope to assimilate them into the German culture of its Austrian ruling elite, for Austrians did not constitute a numerical majority. (In fact, in the age before modern nationalism and mass politics, imperial bureaucrats rarely considered assimilating minorities. Ensuring loyalty to the throne was their main concern.) But whereas Joseph II undermined the power of local elites in favor of a centralized state apparatus, his successors preferred cooperating with the existing ruling classes in various provinces. In the case of Galicia, this meant Vienna formed an understanding with the Polish gentry, much to the chagrin of Ukrainian peasants and the clergy.

The Russian empress Catherine II (1762–1796) had a different understanding of the Enlightenment program than her contemporary, Joseph II. Just as he was improving the situation of Austrian serfs, in 1783 she completed the establishment of serfdom on the Left Bank, the former territories of the Hetmanate. She, too, promoted education and bettered the position of priests, but these measures only furthered the absorption of the Ukrainian lands; education was uniformly in Russian, and the Orthodox clergy in Ukraine had long ago been made part of the Russian Orthodox Church. (The Uniate Church had existed in the territories annexed from Poland in the late eighteenth century, but Catherine began the process of converting Uniates into Orthodox believers.)

Higher education made important advances under another "enlightened monarch," Alexander I (1801–1825). On the initiative of the local nobility, in 1805 the first university in Russian-ruled Ukraine was established in Kharkiv. In 1834, Alexander's conservative successor, Nicholas I (1825–1855), established Kyiv University as a bulwark of Russian culture in the Right Bank, where high culture still remained largely Polish. Yet, the attitude of Russian imperial bureaucrats differed markedly from that of the Habsburg authorities, who recognized that Ruthenian peasants should hear royal decrees and church homilies in their own language, rather than the elites' own German. Russian ministers, many of them from assimilated Cossack families, considered Ukrainians the "Little Russian tribe of the Russian people" and thought their language a mere dialect of Russian. This being the case, education for Ukrainians equaled assimilation into Russian culture.

Such an attitude reflects the critical difference between the Austrian and Russian nationalities problems. The Austrian Germans were a small minority in their own empire, but ethnic Russians constituted roughly half of the Russian Empire's population. Until the late nineteenth century, the Russian government did not consider the option of assimilating minorities; the officials were satisfied with loyalty to the dynasty and, in the case of the Eastern Slavs, to the Orthodox Church. But this did not mean that imperial bureaucrats recognized Ukrainians and Belarusians as separate ethnic groups. Far from it, they were considered parts of the Russian people, thus bringing the "Russians" to a numerical majority in the Romanov empire.[9] The state's premodern blindness to ethnic distinctions during much of the nineteenth century had both good and bad consequences for Ukrainians. Individually, they could make careers anywhere in the Russian Empire as members of the dominant nationality.[10] As a group, however, they could not develop their culture, publish books in Ukrainian, or establish Ukrainian organizations.

✥ Little Russians into Ukrainians

The Ukrainian revival in the Russian Empire began in the Left Bank, but only partially because of the Cossack traditions preserved there. At the turn of the nineteenth century, most nobles descended from the Cossack officer class assimilated into Russian culture, just as the Ruthenian nobility in the Right Bank had become Polish two centuries earlier. Some still expressed nostalgia for the bygone rights and liberties of the Hetman state once ruled by their ancestors. Yet, their interest in the past, antiquarian in nature, developed into what can be called a "national revival" only with the infusion of new ideas about nationality. It was a new social group, the Ukrainian intelligentsia, that first based its claims not on the ancient Cossack freedoms but on the ethnic distinctiveness of the contemporary Ukrainian peasantry.[11]

The modern state's need for more bureaucrats and educators led to the growth of colleges and universities in the Russian Empire, beginning in the late eighteenth century. Their graduates, however, soon proved capable of generating unorthodox ideas. Among other things, the "intelligentsia" (the Russian word adopted into English and originally referring to intellectuals with a social conscience, usually critical of the authorities) first developed the modern idea of nationality as an egalitarian community of shared language and culture—in opposition to an elaborate social hierarchy of multinational empires held together by allegiance to the throne. The Ukrainian intelligentsia particularly appreciated the ideas of the German Romantic philosopher Johann Gottfried Herder, who in his *Letters for the Advancement of Humanity* (1785–1797) extolled the ethnic culture of the peasantry as the foundation of nationhood. Herder also had a high opinion of Ukraine, calling it the "new Greece" and predicting a bright future for it.

The intelligentsia's interest in the common folk, their speech, and customs marked the "scholarly," or heritage-gathering, stage of the Ukrainian revival. But few of its pioneers had a clear nation-building program in mind; more often than not, they wrote to defend their social group or to entertain friends. For example, the appearance (in Russian) of new works on Ukrainian history during the early nineteenth century was connected to the contemporary controversy over which former Cossack officers should be accepted into the Russian nobility. The author of the anonymous *History of the Rus People* (1800s), which circulated widely in written copies, glorified the Cossacks and called for self-government for their descendants. In contrast, the historian Dmytro Bantysh-Kamensky, in his four-volume *History of Little Russia* (1822), presented the "Little Russians," glorious as their history had been, as a branch of the Russian people and loyal servants of the crown. His argument tallied with the interests of the Cossack petitioners for nobility, but it also satisfied the imperial bureaucrats.[12]

Early literary works in the modern Ukrainian language failed to take nationality seriously. Those writing in the peasant vernacular at first sought to entertain their guests with the juxtaposition of "low-style" peasant speech and serious literary form. (Their listeners were accustomed to reading older books in a nativized Church Slavonic and modern serious literature in Russian.) This was the origin of the first book in modern Ukrainian, Ivan Kotliarevsky's *Eneida* (1798), a brilliant travesty of Virgil's classic *Aeneid*. The action was set in Ukraine, with Roman heroes who dressed and spoke like Ukrainian Cossacks. The situation changed only with the advent of Romanticism in literature. A reaction to the rationality of the Enlightenment, Romanticism emphasized irregularity, spontaneity, and emotion. In many countries, Romantic interest in nature developed into a fascination with peasant life and ethnic traits.[13] Romantic writers and folklorists in Ukraine grouped around Kharkiv University. There, a wager between two local litterateurs resulted in the appearance of the first "serious" prose works in modern Ukrainian. Hryhorii Kvitka-Osnovianenko wrote his *Little Russian Stories* (1833–1834) to prove that the peasant tongue could be used to convey sublime emotions.[14]

It was also in Kharkiv where the first grammar of the "Little Russian" peasant dialect, by Oleksii Pavlovsky, appeared in 1818 and where Prince Nikolai Tsertelev published his *Attempt at a Collection of Ancient Little Russian Songs* (1819). Philological and folklore studies became much more sophisticated in the 1820s and 1830s, owing to the efforts of Professor Mykhailo Maksymovych. He used his comparative analysis of Ukrainian and Russian folk songs to argue that the Ukrainians were a separate, if closely related, nationality. He was also one of the first to use the term "Ukrainians" instead of the official "Little Russian" designation that presumed membership in the larger Russian nation. Maksymovych's first collection of folk songs was called *Little Russian Songs* (1827), but the next two appeared under the titles *Ukrainian Folk Songs* (1834) and *A Collection of Ukrainian Folk Songs* (1849).[15]

Paradoxically, the imperial government supported the early stages of the Ukrainian revival. Concerned with the continuing domination of the separatist Polish gentry and Polish high culture in the Right Bank, St. Petersburg sought to prove the region's "Russian"—or, at least, Little Russian—heritage.

The Polish Uprising of 1830–1831, which began in Warsaw but spread to the Right Bank, only reinforced this concern. The Polish gentry rebels failed to attract the Ukrainian peasantry and were quickly defeated by the Russian army. Subsequent Russian measures included harsh repressions against the Polish nobility in the Right Bank, with 340,000 noblemen losing their noble status during the next twenty years.[16] But the government also took serious measures to replace Polish high culture in the Right Bank with Russian. In 1834, Kyiv University was established as a citadel of Russian schooling in a region where most educated people still spoke Polish. In their struggle against Polish influences in the Ukrainian lands, imperial bureaucrats enlisted some early Ukrainian patriots, such as Maksymovych, who served briefly as the first head of Kyiv University. In 1843, the Russian administrators also established a commission in Kyiv for the study of historical documents. Created to disprove Polish claims to the Right Bank, its voluminous publications eventually provided the foundation of Ukrainian historical scholarship.

In the 1840s, with the "academic" stage of the Ukrainian revival apparently complete, its center shifted to Kyiv. Instead of launching purely cultural work, however, Ukrainian patriots plunged into politics. In 1845, a group of young Ukrainian intellectuals in Kyiv established the Brotherhood of Saints Cyril and Methodius, a secret society whose members discussed the abolition of serfdom and creation of a free federation of Slavic peoples. Such a jump from culture to politics was logical in the oppressive Russian Empire, which in any case would not have allowed the free development of a separate Ukrainian culture. But the brotherhood's members did not go beyond heady political discussions and the preparation of programmatic documents. In 1847, the tsarist authorities exposed the group before it could start any serious propaganda work and punished its members with imprisonment and exile.

Mykola Kostomarov, a young Romantic author and historian with moderate political views who wrote the brotherhood's program, received only a light sentence and was able to resume his career. He eventually held the prestigious chair of Russian history at St. Petersburg University, even though he argued that historically Little Russians were a distinct nationality.[17] A much harsher sentence was levied on the poet Taras Shevchenko (1814–1861), a radical social thinker who believed that Ukrainians were a distinct nationality and should be a separate nation.

A serf orphan from the impoverished Ukrainian village of Moryntsi, Shevchenko was sent by his master to study drawing, which eventually led him to freedom and an education at the Imperial Academy of Fine Arts. Yet, it was the first collection of Shevchenko's poems, *The Kobza Player* (1840), that brought him fame. Using elements of folk songs, the peasant vernacular, and the bookish language of older writers, Shevchenko molded a new and vital

Ukrainian language, equally accessible to intellectuals and peasants. Unlike previous Ukrainian thinkers, who saw Little Russian identity as a regional version of Russianness, Shevchenko in his poetry portrays Ukraine as an independent nation, subjugated first by Polish and, later, Russian masters. For his antitsarist poetic manuscripts more than for his participation in the brotherhood, Tsar Nicholas I sentenced Shevchenko to ten years of army service as a private in Asia (then considered the equivalent of hard labor), with a prohibition against writing or drawing.

After being pardoned by the new tsar in 1857, Shevchenko was forbidden to live in Ukraine, but his poetry and status as a martyr for the national cause made him a hero to the younger generation. As a charismatic fighter against national oppression and social injustice, this literary genius of pure peasant stock became the symbol of new Ukraine. Many Ukrainian intellectuals considered Shevchenko the "father" of the Ukrainian people. He truly became a cult figure after his death in St. Petersburg in 1861 and subsequent reburial in Ukraine.[18]

The suppression of the Cyril and Methodius Brotherhood silenced the Ukrainian patriots. When Russia's defeat in the Crimean War (1853–1855) and the reformist program of the new tsar, Alexander II (1855–1881), led to a political liberalization, the Ukrainian movement resumed at its cultural stage. In theory, the abolition of serfdom in 1861 provided the Ukrainian intelligentsia with a broad peasant constituency to win to its case. In practice, however, the absence of a parliament and political freedoms, as well as the omnipresence of secret police and censors, limited their options to "harmless" cultural work.

Sometime in the late 1850s, in Kyiv a small group of young Polish nobles from the Right Bank, led by the student Volodymyr Antonovych, decided to "return" to the Ukrainian nationality of their ancestors. These young enthusiasts shocked polite society by wearing peasant dress and speaking Ukrainian, but their more important achievement was the creation in 1861 of the first *hromada* (community), a clandestine society devoted to the promotion of Ukrainian culture and enlightenment of the masses. Membership in the Kyiv Hromada soon grew to more than 200 young intellectuals and students, who concentrated on organizing Sunday schools for the peasantry, staging plays, and publishing books on Ukrainian subjects.[19] Ukrainian patriots in other major cities also established *hromadas* and began wearing embroidered peasant shirts to signal their allegiance to the Ukrainian nation—a custom that is still observed both in Ukraine and among diaspora Ukrainians. Ukrainian activists, including Shevchenko and Kostomarov, created a *hromada* in the imperial capital of St. Petersburg and started an influential monthly journal, *Osnova* (Foundation, 1861–1862), which published both literature and theoretical articles about Ukrainian identity. Shevchenko also wrote and published a Ukrainian primer for Sunday schools.

The imperial government observed with alarm the growing movement of "Ukrainophiles" (Ukraine lovers, a term the authorities invented and Ukrainian patriots accepted). Tsarist administrators worried about Ukrainian propaganda in Sunday schools, of which there were 67 in 1862, with an enrollment of thousands of students. They were also anxious because St. Petersburg saw the Ukrainophiles, wrongly, as allies or agents of Polish separatists on the Right Bank. In fact, *hromadas* had nothing to do with the Polish uprising of 1863, which, like the previous one, spread to the Right Bank but was suppressed by the Russian army, with the Ukrainian peasants watching on with indifference. Nevertheless, they were caught up in the whirlwind of subsequent repressions. In 1863, Minister of Internal Affairs Petr Valuev issued a secret circular letter to censors—known as the Valuev Edict—banning the publication of educational and religious books in the Ukrainian language. (Literature was still allowed.)[20] A number of Ukrainian activists were exiled to other parts of the empire, Sunday schools were closed, and the *hromadas* disbanded on their own. *Osnova* ceased publication one year earlier, not as a result of repressions but because of the Ukrainian movement's narrow social base; the number of subscribers, which stood at 1,400 in 1861, shrank to under 900.[21]

The recovery took almost ten years. The Kyiv Hromada renewed its activities in the 1870s, again under the leadership of Antonovych, who by then was a professor of Russian history at Kyiv University, and Mykhailo Drahomanov, a cosmopolitan intellectual and socialist who dreamed of Europe's transformation into a free federation.

Hromadas also reemerged in other cities. Their practical activities, however, were again limited to culture and scholarship.[22] The Ukrainophiles' major achievements included taking control of the Kyiv branch of the Imperial Russian Geographical Society (established in 1873), which provided cover for their folkloric and ethnographic research, and taking charge of the Russian-language newspaper *Kievskii Telegraf* (Kyivan Telegraph) in order to publish some pro-Ukrainian articles. In addition, *hromadas* in Ukrainian cities collected materials for a Ukrainian dictionary, staged amateur theatrical performances, and organized literary readings. Contacts and exchanges of publications with Ukrainians in the Austro-Hungarian Empire also developed at this time.

It was partly because of this connection that the imperial government launched a new crackdown on the Ukrainophiles in 1876. Persuaded by a renegade supporter of the Geographical Society that the entire Ukrainian movement was an Austrian plot against Russia, in 1876 Emperor Alexander

II issued the Ems Ukase (decree), so called because he signed it while vacationing at the German spa resort of Ems. This ruling banned the publication of all Ukrainian books and their importation from abroad, as well as the use of Ukrainian on stage. The imperial government also shut down the Kyiv branch of the Geographical Society and *Kievskii Telegraf*. Dozens of Ukrainian activists were fired from jobs in education and journalism, and many of them were exiled from Ukraine.[23]

The Ems Ukase rendered meaningless the Ukrainophile concept of apolitical cultural work. Those who remained in the Russian Empire had to lie low again. Antonovych was lucky to have kept his professorship—the imperial bureaucrats considered his historical works an important anti-Polish resource—and he continued quietly training the next generation of Ukrainian historians. Drahomanov, who lost his teaching position at Kyiv University, went to Switzerland, where he published the first Ukrainian political journal, *Hromada*, from 1876 to 1882. This periodical collapsed, however, when Drahomanov's increasingly radical socialist beliefs led Kyivan sympathizers to withdraw their financial support. Drahomanov thought that the Ukrainian problem was at once national and social, in that the Ukrainians, who suffered from national oppression, were overwhelmingly downtrodden peasants exploited by the Russian and Polish upper classes. Thus, he saw socialism, and even anarchism, as offering a solution to all of his people's ills. Instead of advocating Ukraine's separation from Russia, the committed federalist Drahomanov promoted the transformation of the Russian and Austro-Hungarian empires into a free federation of self-governing communes.[24] At the time, Drahomanov's theories had little influence on the Ukrainian movement in the domain of the Romanovs, but he became a mentor to young Ukrainian socialists in Austria-Hungary.

In the Russian Empire, meanwhile, cautious Ukrainophiles were losing the struggle for local youth to dynamic Russian revolutionaries. Since the early 1870s, the all-Russian movement of *narodniki*, or revolutionary populists, who believed in the peasantry's innate socialist instincts, earned many adherents among students in Ukraine. The populists used some of the same methods as the Ukrainophiles—studying peasant life, living in the villages, teaching in village schools—but their revolutionary agenda was much more radical. When their efforts to start a countrywide peasant uprising, including the 1877 attempt near Chyhyryn in Kyiv province, failed, the revolutionary populists turned to political terror. Ethnic Ukrainians were prominent among their leaders, including the group that succeeded in assassinating Alexander II in 1881, but the populists largely ignored the nationalities issue.[25] In any case, their influence declined after 1881.

The Ukrainophiles, in contrast, recovered somewhat during the 1880s. In 1881, Alexander III (1881–1894) modified the Ems Ukase to allow the publication of dictionaries and music lyrics in Ukrainian, as well as the staging of Ukrainian plays with permission from local authorities. This concession provided just enough breathing room for the Ukrainophiles to implement their modest plans. *Hromadas* cautiously sprang up again. Concerts also were held but had to feature an equal number of Ukrainian and Russian songs. As the only permitted medium of high culture, the Ukrainian theater flourished during the last two decades of the nineteenth century. Ukrainian realistic dramas and comedies from peasant life were hugely successful. The Tobilevych family was particularly influential during the early years of Ukrainian professional theater: Ivan (whose pen name was Ivan Karpenko-Kary) was a leading playwright, and his brothers Mykola (Mykola Sadovsky) and Panas (Panas Saksahansky) became the premier male actors. The graceful and talented Mariia Zankovetska, the leading Ukrainian actress, was as popular with the Russian public in St. Petersburg as with the Ukrainian intelligentsia. But if Ukrainian plays could be performed on their own—and with acclaim—in St. Petersburg, in Ukraine they had to be staged as double bills with Russian plays. For imperial bureaucrats in Ukraine, Ukrainian culture remained a political matter.[26]

✜ Ruthenians into Ukrainians

Ukrainians in the Habsburg Empire, who at the time called themselves Ruthenians (*rusyny*), experienced the early stages of national revival differently from their eastern brethren. Because a native nobility was absent and the secular intelligentsia minuscule, the clergy assumed leadership of the Ukrainian movement in Galicia. Unlike the Orthodox religion of Ukrainians in the Russian Empire, which united them with the dominant Russians, the Greek Catholic faith in Austria differentiated the Ukrainians from their Polish neighbors, thus underscoring their sense of separate identity. At the same time, the Greek Catholic Church retained, like the Orthodox, a married clergy, resulting in the reproduction of a Ukrainian clerical caste. After Maria Theresa and Joseph II improved the condition and education of Greek Catholic priests, the clergy emerged as true spiritual leaders of their nationality.

Students and graduates of church seminaries directed the academic stage of the national revival, which differed from the similar process taking place in Dnipro Ukraine. In Galicia, historical works, belles lettres, and folkloric research were secondary to animated discussions about the Ruthenian language, which were sparked in part by Vienna's decision to use it in elementary schools. A modified Church Slavonic with an admixture of Latin, German, and Polish words remained the language of church and publishing in Galicia, but it was so far removed from the peasant dialect as to be virtually unusable in elementary education. In discussing their options during the 1820s and 1830s, Ruthenian literati proposed a number of solutions: adopting standard Russian, switching to Polish, using the Polish alphabet to write in a Ukrainian peasant vernacular, and adopting a modern form of the Cyrillic alphabet for the peasant language. Each proposal had obvious implications for national identity, as they offered the Ruthenians the prospect of joining another nationality's high culture or, in the case of the last proposal, a chance to develop their own modern culture—a process central to nation building.[27] The political motives of Austrian imperial bureaucrats, who did not want the Ruthenians to ally with either the Poles or the Russians, and the example of the Czech and other Slavic national revivals, where peasant vernaculars were used as foundations for new literary languages, combined to ensure the eventual victory of the peasant speech written in modern Cyrillic.

The first book published according to these rules was prepared by a trio of Lviv seminary students during the 1830s: Markiian Shashkevych, Yakiv Holovatsky, and Ivan Vahylevych (known collectively as the Ruthenian Triad). Inspired by the example of Czech patriots and Kharkiv Romantic writers in the Russian Empire, they produced an almanac of poems, translations, folk songs, and historical articles—all written in the vernacular. *Rusalka Dnistrovaia* (Nymph of the Dniester), as it was called, did not pass muster with the church censors in Lviv, who were troubled both by the undignified language and potentially subversive folk songs. It was finally published in 1837 in Budapest, in the Hungarian part of the empire, but was banned in Galicia and read by only a narrow circle of the Ukrainian intelligentsia. Its publication, however, marked the first instance in the Austrian Empire of serious literature in modern Ukrainian.

The modest Ukrainian revival in the Habsburg Empire received an unexpected boost from the Revolution of 1848. Following the news about the revolution in France earlier that year, some Austro-Hungarian nationalities—in particular, Italians, Hungarians, and Poles—rebelled against imperial domination. Austrian Germans, too, demanded civil liberties and a parliamentary system. Although Galicia remained a political backwater far removed from the revolution's main battles, the Poles there quickly established a political organization, the Polish National Council, and pressed for autonomous status for this "Polish" province. The Austrian governor of Galicia, Count Franz Stadion, however, proved to be an adroit politician. Faced with the Polish threat, he decided to create a political counterweight in the Ukrainian movement.[28] With his encouragement, the Greek Catholic hierarchy established the rival Supreme Ruthenian Council, composed of conservative churchmen and lay intelligentsia and headed by Bishop Hryhorii Yakhymovych. The council promptly issued a momentous manifesto proclaiming the Ruthenians a people separate from the Poles or the Russians but of the same stock as their conationals in the Russian Empire. The Ruthenian leaders also petitioned the emperor to recognize them as a separate nationality and divide Galicia into a Polish western part and a Ruthenian eastern part; the first demand was implicitly accepted, but the second was often discussed but never implemented. The council also began publishing the first newspaper in Ukrainian, *Zoria Halytska* (The Galician Dawn), which ran from 1848 to 1857.[29]

Stadion's plan worked: The Ukrainian leaders did not support the Poles and remained loyal to the crown. Other concessions that helped extinguish the revolution included the abolition of serfdom in the spring of 1848 and the convocation of a parliament, the *Reichsrat*. Although they were politically inexperienced, the Ukrainians managed to elect twenty-five of the one hundred deputies from the province of Galicia (which until 1849 also included Bukovyna). Fifteen of the twenty-five were peasants, and, before the imperial authorities dissolved the unruly parliament, they made some bold political speeches in Ukrainian, protesting the compensation to landlords for the serfs' abolished labor obligations.

Led by the conservative senior clergy, the Galician Ukrainians as a whole sided with the Habsburgs in the Revolution of 1848 and were nicknamed the "Tyroleans of the East" for their loyalty to the Austrian crown. Early in 1849, the Supreme Ruthenian Council even organized a voluntary national guard, the Ruthenian Sharpshooters, to be used in the suppression of Hungarian rebels. The Austrian army, however, defeated the Hungarians with Russian help before the Ruthenians arrived. As a reward for their support and in continuation of Stadion's plan, in 1848 the imperial government established the Department of Ruthenian Language and Literature at Lviv University, and Yakiv Holovatsky became its first professor. The Austrian administrators also permitted the free development of Ukrainian culture. The Congress of Ruthenian Scholars was held in Lviv in 1848, and a permanent academic society, the Galician-Rus Matytsia, was established to promote Ukrainian education and publishing. The National Home, a cultural society with a wider range of activities, opened in 1849. After the Revolution of 1848, the Ukrainian movement in Galicia moved decisively into its cultural stage.

In Bukovyna, which had been part of Galicia and in 1849 became a separate province, there were few Ukrainian echoes of the revolution. In 1848, the local peasant outlaw Lukian Kobylytsia—who for his exploits earned a Robin Hood–like reputation in Ukrainian folklore—was briefly a member of parliament but was arrested before he could start a major peasant uprising against Romanian landlords, as he had done in 1843. In Hungarian-ruled Transcarpathia, the charismatic mining engineer Adolf Dobriansky emerged as a leader of the Ruthenian intelligentsia. Like the Greek Catholic clerics of Galicia, he professed loyalty to the Habsburgs and subsequently served in important administrative positions in the region. When the young emperor Franz Joseph I (1848–1916) asked Nicholas I for help against the Hungarian rebels, and the Russian army crossed Transcarpathia on its way to Hungary, Dobriansky acted as the official Austrian liaison to the Russians. Combined with the local intelligentsia's previous fascination with Russian culture, the passage of the mighty Russian army through tiny Transcarpathia solidified their belief that the Ruthenians living beyond the Carpathian Mountains were nothing but a branch of the larger Russian nation. Dobriansky became an informal leader of these "Russophiles."

The pro-Russian orientation soon became prominent in Galicia as well, paradoxical as it seemed after the Ukrainians' achievements in 1848. A new Austrian policy in the region was to blame for this change. Having suppressed the revolution, the Habsburgs dissolved the parliament and reestablished absolute monarchy, but simultaneously they sought a rapprochement with indigenous political elites in their borderlands. In Galicia, the Viennese government reached an accommodation with the Polish landed nobility, which no longer set its sights on an armed struggle for independent Poland. The symbol and chief promoter of this new policy was Count Agenor Gołuchowski, a Polish magnate from Galicia and a confidant of Emperor Franz Josef I. Having been appointed viceroy (governor) of Galicia in 1849, Gołuchowski served two more terms in the next twenty-five years and also held major ministerial positions in Vienna. Under his leadership, the Poles monopolized the province's administrative apparatus. Polish replaced German as the language of internal administration and the language of instruction at Lviv University and in high schools.[30]

Constitutional changes in the Habsburg Empire during the 1850s reinforced the government's power-sharing arrangement with the nobility of its principal nationalities. Military defeat at the hands of France and Piedmont-Sardinia in 1859 led to the creation of a central parliament and provincial diets (legislatures), although the electoral laws favored great landowners. Prussia's victory over Austria in 1866 resulted in the empire's transformation the following year into a dual monarchy, or the Austro-Hungarian Empire, with the Hungarian Kingdom receiving far-reaching autonomy. A revised constitution also granted Austrian citizens basic political freedoms, but the first taste of parliamentary politics was bitter for Ukrainians. Because very few of them were landlords, Galician Ukrainians, whose numbers roughly equaled the province's Poles, never managed to elect more than a third of the deputies to the provincial diet and usually held less than a fifth of the seats. After the constitutional deal with the Hungarians, the Polish elite in Galicia pressed Vienna for more concessions and more often than not received them.

The growth of Polish influence in the province disheartened the "Tyroleans of the East." Greek Catholic clerics and lay intellectuals, who acted as community leaders—the Supreme Ruthenian Council having dissolved on its own accord in 1851—increasingly turned their eyes to the east. Attracted by the might of the Russian Empire and the prestige of Russian culture, the Russophiles were also encouraged by the Russian government, which presented itself as a protector of foreign Slavs. The Galician Russophiles of the 1860s believed that the Ruthenians belonged to the same nationality as the Little Russians across the border, but that both constituted a subgroup of the greater Russian people.[31] The Ruthenian vernacular was, therefore, only a dialect of the Russian language. Until the end of the century, however, the Russophiles did not advocate a switch to writing in modern Russian and instead published their periodicals in a heavily modified Church Slavonic. This was in part because senior churchmen continued to play a prominent role among the Russophiles, but such linguistic conservatism disadvantaged them in the subsequent struggle for the peasantry's allegiance.

The younger generation of Galician Ukrainians also looked east, but they had Shevchenko and the Ukrainophiles as their models. Since the 1860s, the community activists in Galicia who saw their people as part of the same nationality as Ukrainians in Dnipro Ukraine, but distinct from the Russians, became known as the *narodovtsi* (national populists). Like the Ruthenian Triad, they wanted to develop the peasant vernacular into a modern literary language. The word "Ukrainian" did not become an ethnic denominator until the 1890s, but the dynamic Populists, who were mostly students, secular intelligentsia, and young priests, together with the Ukrainophiles in Russia, began developing a shared Ukrainian high culture. After several abortive attempts in the 1860s, the Populists founded journals in the vernacular, *Pradva* (Truth, 1867–1898) and, later, *Zoria* (Dawn, 1880–1897). The Populists also published a successful mass-circulation daily in the vernacular, *Dilo* (Deed, 1880–1939). Leading Ukrainian writers in the Russian Empire collaborated on these editions; wealthy Ukrainophile sympathizers from Dnipro Ukraine also contributed financially to these and other projects.[32]

Because the Russophiles dominated the older cultural organizations in Galicia, the Populists began establishing their own. The Prosvita Society (its name means "enlightenment"), created in 1868 in order to foster adult education, soon covered eastern Galicia with an impressive network of reading rooms. By 1903, Prosvita boasted 1,400 reading rooms and 66,000 members in its thirty-three branches.[33] The society also had an active publication program, with all titles appearing in vernacular Ukrainian. By the 1890s, the Populists branched out into economic organization, resulting in the creation of numerous Ukrainian cooperatives and credit unions. Emulating the Czech model of community mobilization, Ukrainian activists also established the gymnastics society Sokil and the firefighting association Sich.

Socially conservative and disadvantaged by their reliance on an antiquated bookish language, the Russophiles could not match the Populists' success in mobilizing the masses. They did create in 1874 an equivalent of Prosvita, the Kachkovsky Society, which published newspapers and later tried to gain a foothold in the cooperative movement, but membership and subscription numbers remained much smaller than those of their Populist rivals. As the Ukrainian movement in Galicia transitioned during the 1890s from a cultural stage to that of political mobilization, it did so under the slogan of a separate Ukrainian nationality entitled to the free development of its culture and some degree of self-rule.

During the last two decades of the nineteenth century, strategic considerations prompted Austrian imperial bureaucrats and the Vatican—both fearing Russian or Orthodox expansion into Austria's Slavic lands—to support the Ukrainian orientation in Galicia against the Russophiles. The government put prominent Russophiles on trial for high treason, while accepting (in 1893) the Ukrainian peasant vernacular as the official language of instruction in Ukrainian schools. The Vatican reformed the Greek Catholic Church, eliminating Russian sympathies among its hierarchy, which thereafter identified closely with the Ukrainian national cause.[34] Cultural development also assured the victory of the Ukrainian orientation. The Populists founded the first highly successful Ukrainian theater company in Galicia, and the greatest Galician literary talent of the time, Ivan Franko, wrote in the vernacular.

During the early 1890s, a compromise in parliament between the Populist politicians and the Poles resulted in the creation of a professorship in Ukrainian history at Lviv University (1894).[35] The appointee, Mykhailo Hrushevsky, was a Russian citizen and a former student of Antonovych in Kyiv, but he soon emerged as the leader of Ukrainian scholarly life in Galicia. Hrushevsky reorganized the Shevchenko Scientific Society, which had been established in 1873 with a grant from a wealthy benefactor in Dnipro Ukraine, into the Ukrainian equivalent of an academy of sciences. In addition, Hrushevsky began the publication of his monumental *History of Ukraine-Rus*, which built a solid historical foundation for the argument that Ukrainians constituted a separate nationality.[36]

It would be misleading, however, to see the Populists' victory as un-equivocal. In their sector of Galician society and culture, the Russophiles hung on well into the twentieth century. More important, acceptance of the Ukrainian orientation did not equal approval of the Populist social and political program, which was very moderate. Although a full spectrum of Ukrainian political parties did not develop until the last few years of the nineteenth century, radical socialists writing in the peasant vernacular made their first appearance as early as the late 1870s. The most talented among these young disciples of Drahomanov was the writer Ivan Franko (1856–1916).[37] The leftist critics of the Populists acquired a greater following during the 1880s, and in 1890 they became the first Galician political group to transform into a modern political party, the Radicals.

The competition between the Russophiles and Populists for popular al-legiance during the 1870s and 1880s was replayed in neighboring Bukovyna. There, the Ukrainians' situation was better because the Romanian upper classes lacked the influence in Vienna that the Poles had. Ukrainian schools, for example, outnumbered Romanian ones. A professorship in Ruthenian Language and Literature existed at the University of Chernivtsi (est. 1875) in the region's main city. By the late 1880s, the Populists dominated in Bu-kovyna as well, where they emulated Galicia's experience in educating and organizing the peasantry.

In contrast, Transcarpathia was now isolated from Galicia, not just by mountain ranges but also by the border between the Hungarian Kingdom and the rest of Austria. Direct Hungarian rule in the region after 1867 sup-pressed the previous Russophile tendency, leading instead to the assimilation of educated Ruthenians into Magyar (ethnic Hungarian) culture, a process encouraged by the local Greek Catholic Church. The Magyar language being very different from the Slavic languages, the assimilation of the peasantry did not advance too far, but Hungarian administrators did manage to completely destroy the Ruthenian school system in Transcarpathia. Unlike in Galicia and Bukovyna, where nationalist agitation had reached the masses, the local Eastern Slavic population at the century's end remained unaware of its exact place among modern nationalities.

❖

The writers, journalists, and historians of the nineteenth century first en-visioned Ukraine as a modern nation. They made a connection, at first an implicit one, between common language and culture—and the right to political sovereignty. In the long run, their literary works and political treatises proved weightier than the legacy of Kyivan princes and Cossack hetmans. Thus, it is no surprise that Ukraine's higher denomination bills feature intellectuals rather than warriors: Ivan Franko (20 *hryvnias*), Taras Shevchenko (50 *hryvnias*), and Mykhailo Hrushevsky (100 *hryvnias*). But the concept of "national revival" with which these names are usually associated in Ukrainian textbooks can be misleading. Many nineteenth-century patriots, in Ukraine and elsewhere, thought they were reviving their ancient nations, while in fact they were creating new, modern cultural and political communities. The competing nation-building projects in nineteenth-century Galicia, in particular, allow an exciting glimpse into the back rooms of modern European nationalism, where intellectuals "create" nations out of ethnographic masses.

At the dawn of the twentieth century, Ukraine was absent from the political map of Europe. The border between the Russian and Austro-Hungarian empires divided present-day Ukrainian territory into a larger eastern part and a smaller western one, whose historical trajectories were increasingly divergent. Eastern, or Dnipro, Ukraine had lost the last vestiges of political autonomy in the eighteenth century, and vague memories of Cossack glory and ancient freedoms were all that remained of the Ukrainian political tradition. Western Ukraine, the regions of eastern Galicia, Bukovyna, and Transcarpathia, was even further removed from its historical statehood during the princely era. To patriotic intellectuals at the time, defining "Ukraine" on the basis of its regions' distant claims to historical autonomy appeared difficult. Instead, nineteenth-century nationalism provided a new idea of what Ukraine was, namely, a territory populated by ethnic Ukrainians. By the late nineteenth century, an imaginary Ukraine stretching through the possessions of both the Romanovs and the Habsburgs already existed in the minds of nationalist activists.

More than 26 million strong in 1900 (22.4 million in the Russian Empire and 3.8 million in Austria-Hungary), Ukrainians were Europe's largest national minority and the second-largest Slavic people after the Russians. Their impressive numbers notwithstanding, both eastern and western Ukrainians fit the sociological criteria of so-called small peoples, or nondominant ethnic groups: the absence of a native ruling class, an incomplete social structure, an interrupted tradition of statehood, and discontinuities in the development of a literary language.[1] More important, before Ukrainian nationalists could begin to overcome these mighty social and political obstacles, they needed to define a modern Ukrainian identity. Nineteenth-century multinational dynastic empires, such as the Russian and Austro-Hungarian, allowed proliferation of multiple identities. For instance, a Ukrainian intellectual could be at the same time a loyal subject of the tsar, a member of the larger Russian cultural community, and a patriot of "Little Russia" (as Ukraine was officially designated). A nationalist mobilization of the people could succeed only after the notion of mutually exclusive national identities was established.[2]

In their ideological musings and efforts at popular mobilization, Ukrainian activists in Russia and Austria-Hungary operated under very different conditions. Many of twentieth-century developments in Ukraine were determined by dissimilarity between the Russian tradition of absolutism and social oppression and the Austrian tradition of parliamentarism and civil society.

✳✳ The Russian Empire: Industrialization and Social Change

At the turn of the century, Ukrainians remained essentially a "peasant people." In 1897, 95 percent of Ukrainian speakers in the Russian Empire lived in the countryside, and 87 percent were engaged in agriculture.[3] No wonder that during the revolutionary turmoil of 1905 and 1917, the land issue would become so closely intertwined with nationalist demands. The peasant emancipation of 1861 did not resolve Russia's longstanding "agrarian problem." Instead, it left peasants with huge redemption payments and no means to transform themselves into independent farmers. By 1900, the average size of a peasant landholding in Ukraine had decreased by half. As the traditionally high birthrate and improving health care made rural overpopulation unbearable, between 1896 and 1905 some 1.1 million Ukrainian peasants left, with the government's encouragement, to colonize the Russian Empire's territories in Asia, Siberia, and the Pacific coast.[4]

Most of those who stayed behind survived at a subsistence level, while jealously eyeing the approximately 5,000 huge noble estates in Ukraine that operated as large market producers. The majority of peasants had very little disposable grain for the market and toiled the noble lands as underpaid day laborers. During the 1902 disturbances in Poltava and Kharkiv provinces, the peasants' first action was to sack noble latifundia, a scenario that would be repeated during the revolutions of 1905 and 1917. Although Soviet scholars have emphasized the peasantry's increased social stratification, signified by the emergence of rich peasants (some 12 percent of households),[5] Ukrainian villagers in the early twentieth century did not yet perceive an internal social antagonism. Rather, they still saw all the peasants as "us" united against "them," the nobles and officials.

At the turn of the century, the peasants in Dnipro Ukraine were loyal to their family, village, region, church, and perhaps the tsar in faraway St. Petersburg. They knew they were not Muscovites, nor Poles nor Jews, but did not yet have a clear notion of allegiance to a broader Ukrainian nation. French peasants were in exactly the same situation until the advent of mass education and literacy.[6] Before nationalist propaganda reached them, and even afterward, Ukrainian villagers remained concerned primarily with the land issue.

The peasants' condition may have improved somewhat during the decade before World War I, but they still felt poor, exploited, and overtaxed. In 1905, the government canceled the remaining redemption payments for the land received during the emancipation, yet around the same time socialist and nationalist propaganda that was beginning to penetrate Ukrainian villages stirred rural discontent even further. Regardless of its agrarian strife, on the eve of World War I, Ukraine remained Europe's breadbasket, producing, primarily on large estates, 90 percent of the Russian Empire's (and 20 percent of the world's) wheat. Much of this grain was exported to finance the empire's economic modernization. Ukraine was also a world leader in the production of barley and sugar beets.

Industrialization began late in eastern Ukraine, and industrial development was only partly the product of local circumstances. Like elsewhere in Europe, railroad construction signaled the beginning of an industrial boom. The region's first railroad was built in 1865 to connect major grain-producing areas in Ukraine with the principal port of Odesa. For military reasons, during the following decade the government began investing heavily in railway construction in the strategically important borderland. The state-sponsored railroad expansion that began during the 1870s created a need for iron and coal, which were, conveniently enough, available in southeastern Ukraine. But it was foreign capital—French, Belgian, and English—that financed the industrial spurt in the Donets basin (Donbas) and Kryvyi Rih. The industrial boom reached its peak during the 1890s and 1900s, when foreign investors bankrolled construction in the region of dozens of large enterprises with modern Western machinery. While the Donbas developed into the empire's biggest coal producer, Kryvyi Rih and the lower Dnipro region became leaders in the metallurgical industry. Symbolic of foreign capital's dominance in Ukraine, the major industrial center of the Donbas, Yuzivka, was named after the Welshman John Hughes. (The city was later renamed Stalino and is currently known as Donetsk.) Ukrainian scholars estimate that Hughes transferred to the United Kingdom approximately 25 million gold rubles in profits from his Ukrainian enterprises.[7]

The expatriation of profits was only one of the problems that a late and foreign-led industrialization had created in the Ukrainian lands. Spectacular growth occurred in the extraction and elementary processing of coal and iron ore, rather than in the production of finished goods. This established Ukraine's profile as mostly a producer of raw materials for Russian industries and an importer of Russian finished products. Moreover, Ukraine's economic development was highly uneven, with an industrialized southeast and almost no industrial development on the Right Bank (that is, west of the Dnipro).

A small working class in the Ukrainian lands by and large did not identify with the Ukrainian nationality. Contemporaries explained the Ukrainian peasants' reluctance to move to the city and take up factory jobs by their spiritual connection to the land. One modern sociologist has offered a more prosaic explanation. In Russia proper, manorial agriculture had always been run at a loss, and the nobles often substituted the obligatory labor service with monetary rents, thus encouraging their serfs to hire themselves out to industry. This was not the case in Ukraine, where more fertile black soils and the proximity of markets made it profitable for landowners to exploit peasant labor in their fields. Consequently, when the industrial boom started in the Ukrainian southeast in the late nineteenth century, factory managers imported a skilled and mobile workforce from Russia. In 1892, 80 percent of workers in Yuzivka were newcomers from the Moscow region, and 42 percent of the 425,413 industrial workers in the Ukrainian provinces in 1897 had been born elsewhere. In the Oleksandrivsk metallurgical plant, Ukraine's largest factory, two thirds of the workers were ethnic Russians.[8]

In the decade before World War I, as well as during the war, the proportion of Ukrainians among new industrial workers rose, but it was too little and too late to change the balance. After the constitutional reforms of 1905, it was not Ukrainian nationalist organizations but Russian political parties and trade unions that would lead the way in organizing the working class in Ukraine. At a time of fluid and multiple national identities, a Ukrainian-speaking peasant moving to a factory fell under strong pressure to adopt the Russian language and Russian self-identification. Hryhorii Petrovsky, a prominent Ukrainian Bolshevik and deputy to the Russian parliament, was the most famous example of this trend. Although Ukrainian-born, as a worker in Katerynoslav he became completely assimilated and until the late 1920s listed his nationality as Russian.

In large part because of this assimilationist pressure, Ukrainian speakers were barely present in the cities and towns, compared with their predominance in the countryside. Although the regions' urban population more than doubled between the emancipation and the 1897 census, Ukrainians constituted only 30 percent of urbanites, compared with Russians (34 percent) and Jews (27 percent). In the largest cities, the percentage of Ukrainians was even lower.[9] Russians prevailed in the administrative and intellectual professions, and Jews were overrepresented in trade. Because of the long history of economic underdevelopment and unfavorable official policies, the native capitalist class in Ukraine remained small. Even the numbers of indigenous merchants and craftsmen, groups who had led national revivals in other eastern European countries, were insignificant. Of a total of 441,289 people in the Ukrainian provinces who in 1897 earned their income from investment, property, or trade, ethnic Ukrainians constituted only 17.5 percent.[10] Given the Ukrainians' similarly small representation among the intellectual professions (only 17 percent of lawyers and 10 percent of writers and artists in the Ukrainian provinces), this incompleteness of the people's social structure presented obvious challenges for nationalist mobilization. Of course, very few people at the time would have made such a reckoning of their nationality's "deficiencies"—only a few thousand Ukrainian activists could imagine their people one day exercising sovereignty in their land. The biggest challenge for Ukrainian patriots was not imagining their nation, however. Rather, it was surviving under the cumbersome bulk of the tsarist bureaucracy.

✖✖ The Russian Empire: Politics and Culture

Although Russia's last tsar, Nicholas II (1894–1917), had a weak and indecisive personality, he inherited an authority not constrained by a parliament or noble assembly. Until 1905, when the abortive revolution forced the tsar to establish a semiconstitutional regime, Russia remained an autocracy—a political system in which the monarch's will was limitless. The oppressive tsarist regime with its immense bureaucratic apparatus had prevented the development of autonomous organizations and public opinion, that is, civil society. In addition, it denied the empire's subjects any opportunity for political participation.

Although by the late nineteenth century the Russian government had accumulated an impressive list of repressions against the Ukrainian language and culture, it never had a coherent "Ukrainian" policy or, for that matter, a nationalities policy. The government did not pursue assimilation as the official course until the 1880s, and even then it inexplicably concentrated on the "indigestible" Poles and the Baltic peoples. Present-day scholars argue that the real flaw of the Russian imperial project was its failure to define a modern Russian identity.[11] Imperial bureaucrats never contemplated a mass Russification of Ukrainians because they were considered "Russian" already: the Little Russian branch of the Russian people. Rather than trying to assimilate the peasant masses, the authorities concerned themselves with preventing nationalists and radicals from reaching out to the villages. In 1917, this would present Ukrainian activists with an opportunity to mobilize the dormant peasant mass for the national cause.

During the last decades of the nineteenth century, however, the tsarist regime effectively suppressed any organizational efforts by the Ukrainian intelligentsia. Even the *hromadas*, which by then had been reduced to collecting materials for a Ukrainian dictionary and meeting privately in members' homes to listen to historical or ethnographic reports, were forced underground. At the same time, new ideological trends in Russia soon affected Ukrainian activists as well. The spread of Marxism and the beginning of the labor movement forced them to revisit the problem with which the previous generation of patriots had been struggling since the 1860s: Should the all-Russian issue of social liberation take precedence over the Ukrainian national cause?

The early 1890s in Ukraine saw the emergence of both the first Marxist circles and student nationalist groups, such as the Taras Brotherhood (1891–1893; named after Taras Shevchenko). By the end of the decade, underground political parties made their first appearance. The Russian Social Democratic Workers Party (1898), whose more radical wing was led by Lenin and known as the Bolsheviks, soon gained influence among the socialist intelligentsia and the Russian working class in Ukraine. For a long time, the Social Democrats refused to recognize the national question as a separate aspect of the struggle against tsarism. They also opposed the segregation of workers along ethnic lines into Polish, Jewish, and Ukrainian political organizations.

The first Ukrainian political party in the Russian Empire, the Revolutionary Ukrainian Party (RUP), was founded by a group of Kharkiv students in 1900. As new archival research by Ukrainian scholars confirms, RUP had managed to establish underground cells throughout Ukraine and during 1901 and 1902 helped stir peasant disturbances in Poltava and Kharkiv provinces.[12] The party's attempt to reconcile the aims of socialism and nationalism, however, eventually splintered the organization. The first to break away was the nationalist Ukrainian National Party, but more damaging was the departure of a larger socialist group that became known as Spilka (the Union) and cooperated with the Russian Social Democrats. The remaining RUPists, who included such future leaders of the Ukrainian Revolution as Volodymyr Vynnychenko and Symon Petliura, renamed their party the Ukrainian Social Democratic Workers' Party. They felt that only a national Ukrainian party could protect Ukrainian interests in a future socialist federation of Russia's peoples.

The moderates were also drawn into an organizational upsurge. First, they created the (apolitical) General Ukrainian Organization (1897) to coordinate the cultural activities of the remaining *hromadas*, but in 1904 they transformed this organization into the Ukrainian Radical Democratic Party (URDP). Like socialist Ukrainian activists, members of the URDP envisaged the empire's transformation into a democratic federation, but they had a more conservative take on social reform. The URDP soon established cordial relations with an all-Russian organization of moderate liberals, the Constitutional Democratic Party (popularly known as the Kadets).

New opportunities for the Ukrainian movement opened up during the "First Russian Revolution" of 1905, when massive strikes, army mutinies, and workers' insurrections led to the government's loss of control over some regions. In Ukraine, a number of peasant rebellions took place, with the rebels increasingly adding demands for a Ukrainian school to their traditional call for the seizure of noble estates. To quell discontent, the tsar established a limited constitutional regime. Freedom of speech and assembly enabled the Ukrainian parties to leave the underground and participate in the elections to the Duma, a parliament with little power in which the propertied classes were greatly overrepresented.

Because the socialists boycotted the elections to the First Duma (1906), the URDP gained strong representation there, although most of its candidates were elected on the Kadets' ticket. They created the Ukrainian parliamentary club, which formulated bold demands for autonomy and school instruction in Ukrainian. In the Second Duma (1907), Ukrainian socialists were better represented but, like the First Duma, the tsar soon dissolved it. Having suppressed the revolution, the government changed the electoral law to make sure that the conservative landowning nobility would be dominant in the subsequent Dumas. During the revolution, Spilka, which in April 1905 had joined the Russian Social Democrats as their regional organization, briefly became Ukraine's most influential party with some 7,000 members; it also managed to elect six deputies to the Second Duma.[13] But the advent of a conservative reaction in 1907 quickly demolished the radicals' grassroots organizations.

Concomitantly with the legalization of the *hromadas* as Ukrainian clubs in many cities, Ukrainian activists also followed the Galician example by setting up more than a hundred branches of the Prosvita Society and peasant cooperatives in the countryside. The revolution also allowed a brief proliferation of Ukrainian press and publishing. But even before it was cut short by renewed government repression after 1908, this revival was limited by the small number of literate Ukrainians who could afford subscriptions. Only one Ukrainian daily, the URDP's *Rada* (Council), existed continuously from 1905 until 1914, thanks to financial contributions from its publisher, Yevhen Chykalenko, and a few wealthy sympathizers. In its most successful years, *Rada* had about 4,000 subscribers.[14]

Following the defeat of the revolution, the tsarist regime began undoing the Ukrainian achievements. During 1907 and 1908, the police carried out arrests of radical activists, including a number of Ukrainian socialists. Under government pressure, Ukrainian clubs disbanded one by one, the URDP reverted to cultural work, and other parties disappeared or went underground. In 1910, the authorities closed down the Prosvita Societies and reinstalled the old ban on Ukrainian publications. These repressions were accompanied by hysteria in the Russian nationalist press, which branded all manifestations of Ukrainian culture as Austrian-sponsored political separatism or "Mazepism." The government crackdown effectively prevented the Ukrainian activists from beginning mass mobilization of the peasantry for the national cause. Moreover, in the realm of ideology, very few Ukrainian patriots even considered moving from the demand for autonomy toward the goal of national independence.

While the authorities again scaled down the Ukrainian movement to ethnographic research and amateur theater (and even that had to be conducted semilegally), a group of writers broke with an earlier populist tradition of descriptive realism. Mykhailo Kotsiubynsky's short stories and Lesia Ukrainka's poems marked the transition to modernism in Ukrainian literature. Volodymyr Vynnychenko, who early in his career had an option of building on the success of his Russian works, eventually chose the much less lucrative path of a Ukrainian litterateur. His psychological plays and novels portrayed new types of heroes in Ukrainian literature: professionals and urbanites. Although they were forced to publish in Ukrainian periodicals in Austria-Hungary, the Russian Empire's Ukrainian writers were beginning to engage modern issues.

For Ukraine's other peoples, the years from 1900 to 1914 were similarly a period of abortive national mobilization. The region's Russians did not think of themselves as a national minority and, regardless of whether they were radicals or moderates, remained generally concerned with all-Russian politics. A significant exception was Kyiv's notorious Club of Russian Nationalists (est. 1908), which devoted all its efforts to the denunciation of the Ukrainian movement.[15] The Jews, the second-largest minority, were profoundly traumatized by the pogroms of 1881–1883 and 1903–1905 that had often been instigated by right-wing Russian nationalists. Starting from the late 1890s, those Jews who had not emigrated became increasingly attracted to Russian social democracy, as well as to their national party of the same ideological inclination, the Bund, and to the nationalist Zionists. Both Jewish parties, together with the influential Polish Socialist Party, occasionally cooperated with Ukrainian activists in their common struggle for autonomy and cultural rights for the empire's nationalities.

The Bolsheviks, who would emerge as the winners of the all-Russian political struggles in 1917, were hostile toward Ukrainian national aspirations. In the years before the war, Lenin belatedly realized that one could not disregard nationalism as a transient phenomenon destined to die with capitalism. Consequently, the party and its authority on the nationalities, Joseph Stalin, proclaimed their adherence to the principle of national self-determination, as long as—and this was a crucial reservation—it was in the interests of the working class. Still, Lenin and Stalin did not foresee that the Ukrainian question would come to play such a major role in the revolution.

✸ Ukrainians in the Austro-Hungarian Empire

A parliamentary monarchy since the 1860s, the empire of the Habsburgs allowed Ukrainians a chance to participate in its political system and exercise their legal rights. No matter how frustrating the limitations of Austrian constitutionalism were, the possibility of public discussions of political issues, as well as the existence of autonomous social organizations, afforded Ukrainian activists a critical advantage over Ukrainians in the Russian Empire. Unlike the Romanovs, the Habsburgs recognized early on the importance of the nationalities issue. Because the Austrian Germans, the dominant nationality, were in the minority and had no chance of assimilating the empire's diverse ethnic groups, the Habsburg solution was to pit the nationalities against each other and make compromises with the stronger ones. The number of ethnic Ukrainians and Poles in Galicia was approximately equal, about 3.5 million each before World War I. Ukrainians clearly predominated in the eastern part of the province. Vienna, nevertheless, entrusted the government of the province to its leading stratum, the nobility, which was overwhelmingly Polish.

At the turn of the century, Galicia remained an agricultural society with a very small industrial sector. Some 95 percent of Ukrainians were peasants, who, much like their brethren in the Russian Empire, suffered from rural overpopulation and a shortage of land. One solution peculiar to Austria-Hungary was mass emigration overseas; between 1890 and 1914, 717,000 Ukrainians left for the United States, Canada, and Latin America.[16] Another result of the agrarian crisis was a gradual radicalization of the peasantry, which led to a series of impressive rural strikes in the early years of the twentieth century.

Only about 1 percent of the entire Ukrainian population was engaged in industry, primarily in food and lumber processing and also in oil production. The Viennese bureaucrats regarded Galicia as a supplier of raw materials and a market for manufactured goods from the more economically developed western parts of the empire. Beginning in the 1870s, however, foreign capital began aggressively exploiting the oil fields near Boryslav and Drohobych that on the eve of World War I were providing 4 percent of the world's oil. Ethnic Ukrainians constituted less than a fifth of the province's small working class, the majority of workers being Poles and Jews.

Galicia's few cities remained, above all, administrative centers in which the Polish language and culture predominated. Only the province's capital, Lviv, saw a significant population increase, although it was not comparable to the contemporary industry-driven urban growth in Dnipro Ukraine. With a population of 200,000 in the early twentieth century, Lviv was four times bigger than the province's next-largest city, yet by European standards, it was small and provincial. In the eastern part of Galicia, Ukrainians constituted less than a third of urbanites and in Lviv, about 20 percent. The Polish upper classes and Jewish merchants continued to outnumber them in cities and towns.

Although the absence of a native noble class and the near-absence of an indigenous bourgeoisie, a merchant class, and industrial workers allow scholars to speak of the Galician Ukrainians' "incomplete" social structure, by the late nineteenth century, they had developed a small secular intelligentsia that was dedicated to the national cause and comfortable with political participation. Another crucial dissimilarity to the Russian Empire was Ukrainians' religious difference from their closest neighbors. Unlike the Catholic Poles, nearly all the ethnic Ukrainians in Galicia belonged to the Greek Catholic (Uniate) Church, with its distinctive Byzantine rite.

The impressive national mobilization of Ukrainians in the two decades leading up to World War I began with an ideological conversion. During the 1890s, the populist intelligentsia in Galicia abandoned its previous ethnic self-designation as Rusyns, or Ruthenians, and began propagating a new name for its people, Ukrainians. The new term, of course, stressed that the Ukrainian-speaking population in both the Russian and Austro-Hungarian empires constituted a single nationality. The renaming also marked the victory of a modern Ukrainian identity over other national "projects" that had existed in eastern Galicia during the nineteenth century. During the 1890s as well, Ukrainian activists for the first time developed an idea of Ukrainian independence that would soon become universally accepted as the ultimate aim of the Ukrainian national movement.[17]

In 1893, the Austrian government implicitly acknowledged the Ukrainian populists' victory over the Russophiles by recognizing literary Ukrainian, in the form that had been standardized in the Russian Empire by Panteleimon Kulish, as an official language of instruction in Galician schools. By 1914, the eastern half of the province boasted 2,500 Ukrainian elementary schools and 16 state and private high schools. Ukrainian schools proved indispensable in preparing a cadre of national activists. Equally important, the new Greek Catholic metropolitan, Andrei Sheptytsky (enthroned in 1900), supported Ukrainian nation-building efforts, thus effectively restoring the church's position as a pillar of Ukrainian identity.

The national movement in Galicia would not have been the same without the inspiration of Dnipro Ukrainians, such as the ideologue of socialism and federalism Mykhailo Drahomanov and writers who could publish freely only in Galician periodicals. Drahomanov's influence was particularly visible in the views of the founders of the Radical Party (1890). By 1895–1896, however, these socialists, who had started as an opposition to the populists and Greek Catholic clergy, adopted the demand for Ukrainian autonomy and eventual independence. In 1899, the populists reconstituted themselves as the moderate National Democratic Party, which also proclaimed national independence as its final aim, while in the short run prioritizing the province's division into Ukrainian and Polish parts. The National Democrats soon became the most influential Ukrainian party in Galicia. The new Ukrainian Social Democratic Party (1900) occupied a position on the extreme left of the political spectrum. Quite apart from the Ukrainian parties were the Galician Russophiles, who, though largely defeated in the debate about the national identity of the local Eastern Slavic population, survived into the age of modern politics. In 1900, they organized the Russian National Party.

Relying on a vast network of Prosvita Societies, cooperatives, credit unions, and reading clubs, the Ukrainian parties were able to mobilize the peasantry for the national cause. After the introduction of universal manhood suffrage in 1907, they won twenty-two seats in the Vienna parliament (17 for the National Democrats, 3 for the Radicals, and 2 for the Social Democrats), in contrast to the Russophiles' two seats.[18] The inequality of electoral colleges, however, remained in the elections to the provincial diet, which allowed Poles to continue to dominate this legislative body. This only fueled Ukrainian-Polish antagonism in Galicia, which during the 1900s and 1910s, in addition to political debates, found its expression in student gang fights and political terrorism. In 1908, a Ukrainian student, Myroslav Sichynsky, assassinated the province's Polish viceroy, Count Andrżej Potocki.

Although in the early twentieth century the Ukrainian movement in eastern Galicia commanded great support among the masses, by 1914 it had not achieved any of its immediate goals: the division of the province, the establishment of a Ukrainian university, and the Ukrainian language's full equality with Polish in public life and education. Just before the war, however, Ukrainian politicians negotiated with Vienna an agreement calling for the establishment of a Ukrainian university, as well as separate Ukrainian and Polish chambers of the provincial diet and boards of education. The war put these plans on hold indefinitely.

Building on a firm foundation of the national church, schools, and village reading rooms, Ukrainian culture in Galicia blossomed in the early twentieth century. Readers could peruse some seventy Ukrainian periodicals, including

the influential Populist *Dilo*. In 1894, the Dnipro Ukrainian Mykhailo Hrushevsky was hired as the first professor of Ukrainian history at Lviv University.
His articles and the first volumes of his monumental *History of Ukraine-Rus*
soon provided the modern Ukrainian nation with a noble historical pedigree
going back to Kyivan Rus.[19] A present-day Ukrainian historian has unearthed
a telling detail of the spread of new historical memory among nationalist
activists: Beginning in the 1890s, an increasing number of babies born in
patriotic families received the names of ancient princes of Kyivan Rus, such
as Yaroslav.[20] Together with other scholars, Hrushevsky transformed the
Shevchenko Scientific Society into the Ukrainian equivalent of the Academy
of Sciences. By far the most prolific Ukrainian author of the time was Ivan
Franko, who wrote in practically all genres and was the first Ukrainian prose
writer to portray industrial relations. Vasyl Stefanyk and Olha Kobylianska
heralded the advent of modernism in literature; Kobylianska was also the
first Ukrainian author to engage feminist themes.

The political and cultural developments in Bukovyna generally followed,
if belatedly, the same pattern as in eastern Galicia. The Galician parties created
their branches there, and the only significant difference was the less important role of the church, which was Orthodox rather than Greek Catholic.
In Transcarpathia, however, the Hungarian ruling class did not allow any
Ukrainian political mobilization and even suppressed cultural life beyond
the level of elementary education and Greek Catholic church services.

✠ The Ukrainian Problem in World War I

The first total war requiring complete mobilization of economies and inflict-
ing horrendous civilian casualties, World War I was the outcome of Great
Power politics in Europe. Although not a major cause of the war, the Ukrainian issue had been a source of considerable tension between the empires
of the Romanovs and the Habsburgs. Russia claimed a special interest in
the fate of the Austro-Hungarian Slavs. In regard to Galicia, Bukovyna, and
Transcarpathia, tsarist statesmen secretly hoped to annex these "Russian"
lands, eliminating in the process these hotbeds of Ukrainian nationalism that
had been spilling over (or so they suspected) into Dnipro Ukraine.[21]

At the war's start in August 1914, the proverbial "Russian steamroller"
at first seemed to confirm its reputation. A large Russian army moved westward, capturing by early September all of eastern Galicia and Bukovyna.
Although the Russian army, which included conscripts from Ukraine, was
soon rebuffed by the Germans, Lviv remained in Russian hands until the
summer of 1915.

Ukrainian patriots in both empires welcomed the war. While eastern Ukrainians were probably playing it safe in the face of a popular patriotic mood in Russia, their western counterparts were hoping for the new political opportunities that Russia's collapse might bring. The leaders of the Ukrainian parties in Austria-Hungary immediately established the Supreme Ukrainian Council, headed by the prominent National Democrat Kost Levytsky; the council declared their people's loyalty to the crown and called for the formation of a Ukrainian military unit. Among the mass of volunteers, the army command eventually selected some 2,500 to serve in the Ukrainian Sich Riflemen. Meanwhile, hundreds of thousands of Ukrainians were conscripted to regular Austrian army units, as were millions of their brethren conscripted in the Russian Empire.

No declaration of loyalty could prevent the retreating Austrian troops from taking revenge on scores of "Rusyn" peasants and priests who were executed or sent to the infamous internment camp of Thalerhof on the false charge of spying for Russia. Then, the arriving Russian units began harassing local Ukrainian activists. The Russian authorities had no clear plan of how to incorporate Galicia into the empire, but the tsar's nationalistic governor, Count Georgii Bobrinsky, quickly shut down Ukrainian cultural organizations, periodicals, and cooperatives. With the assistance of local Russophiles, efforts were made to replace Ukrainian with Russian as the language of school instruction and to undermine the influence of the Greek Catholic Church. The imperial press hailed the "return" of Galicia and Bukovyna under the scepter of the Russian tsars, and in the spring of 1915, Nicholas II himself paid a visit to Lviv.[22]

Although the Austrian and German counteroffensive cut short this assimilatory experiment, it signified the growing role of ethnicity in the Russian imperial ideology, a process also underscored by the wartime persecution of ethnic Germans and Jews in Russia.[23] At the same time, Austria-Hungary sought to exploit the potential of Ukrainian nationalism against the Russian Empire when it allowed a group of socialist émigrés from Dnipro Ukraine, the Union for the Liberation of Ukraine, to propagate the idea of independent statehood among Russian POWs of Ukrainian nationality. With official support, the group set up a publishing venture in Vienna and dispatched its emissaries to a number of countries.[24] The Supreme Ukrainian Council, now renamed as the General Ukrainian Council, meanwhile, put forward a program of independence for Russian Ukraine and autonomy for eastern Galicia.

As the war progressed, the nationalities issue became increasingly prominent in both empires. The Russian retreat marked the end of organized Russophilism in Galicia because the movement's activists had either left for Russia with the retreating Russian troops or were later arrested by the

Austrian authorities. This left the Ukrainian national parties in a dominant and thus stronger position to push for their demands in Vienna, although the government never went further than promising to implement limited reforms after the war. Such pledges were aired again in late 1916, when the young Emperor Charles ascended to the throne following the death of the patriarch of European monarchs, Franz Joseph I. In the Russian Empire as well, Ukrainian cultural life began emerging from the underground, although political activities remained off-limits.

The war brought terrible destruction, human loss, and dislocation to Galicia and Bukovyna, where much of the fighting on the Eastern Front took place. On a more general scale, the colossal war effort caused extensive administrative and economic failures in the Russian and Austro-Hungarian empires. As the social and ethnic imperial order disintegrated, widespread resentment in both states grew against the central authority. With nationality emerging as the new focus of popular loyalties, the age of multinational dynastic empires was rapidly coming to a close.

❖

During the late nineteenth and early twentieth centuries, the industrial boom, urbanization, the advent of mass politics, and the first total war brought about a modern society in Ukraine. The notion of ethnicity was an important component of modern identity. By 1917, Ukrainian patriots in the Russian and Austro-Hungarian empires possessed a clear notion of belonging to a single Ukrainian nation that was entitled to some form of statehood and to the free development of its language and culture. However, national solidarity among the Ukrainian masses in Galicia presented a stark contrast to the confusion about national and social allegiances in Russian-ruled Ukraine. In neither empire did the Ukrainian movement have the strength or audacity to put forward a demand for political independence. The imperial collapse caused by World War I ultimately cleared the path for the Ukrainian Revolution.

The Ukrainian Revolution

Between 1917 and 1920, the collapse of the Russian and Austro-Hungarian empires allowed the creation of a Ukrainian state, for the first time uniting eastern and western Ukraine. The Ukrainian Revolution was at once the culmination of the Ukrainian national movement and an aspect of the larger political upheaval in eastern Europe after World War I—the turmoil best represented by the Russian Revolution. The revolution in Ukraine did not mean a clear-cut fight between socialists and nationalists—they were often the same people—but involved a confusing struggle between Ukrainian patriots of different stripes, as well as among the many varieties of local socialists and anarchists. Moreover, if the collapse of the Russian and Austro-Hungarian empires made the Ukrainian Revolution possible, the ensuing international struggle influenced its outcome. The military might of the German, Polish, Red, and White (anti-Bolshevik Russian) armies, together with the political decisions made by the victorious Allies after World War I, sealed the fate of the Ukrainian lands.[1]

The events of 1917 through 1920 established the contemporary notion of Ukraine as a geopolitical and cultural unit; the Great Powers of interwar Europe would have no choice but to regard Ukrainians as a separate nation. Yet, the course of the revolution disillusioned those Ukrainian intellectuals who had worked toward the "national awakening" of the peasantry. The chief interest of the peasants, who were far from being latent nationalists, was obtaining land. The government's failure to address this concern of its main constituency undermined popular support for the Ukrainian idea no less than the weakness of the native middle class, the Ukrainian national movement's late transition to a political stage, or the long history of tsarist repressions.

Not that there was a single Ukrainian idea, either. The fast-changing revolutionary governments envisioned very different Ukraines—autonomy within a democratic Russia, an independent socialist Ukraine, a conservative Ukrainian monarchy, a nationalist military dictatorship, to name a few—but none had much success in securing the victory of their particular version over others. Although "we now know" that Communism led Ukraine nowhere, the idea of a radical social transformation was also powerful in eastern Ukraine during the revolutionary period, even if it was as vague as that of Ukrainian self-rule.

The Ukrainians Organize

The Ukrainian Revolution as a political event began in the faraway northern capital of the Russian Empire, recently renamed from the German-sounding St. Petersburg to Petrograd. Beginning on March 8, 1917 (February 23 according to the Julian calendar or Old Style then in use in Russia, hence the February Revolution), street demonstrations to protest food shortages quickly escalated into a popular rebellion against the tsarist regime. The Volhynian regiment, composed mainly of Ukrainians, was the first to take sides with the crowds. Having lost control over the country, Nicholas II abdicated on March 15, and the same day the liberal members of the Duma formed the Provisional Government headed by Prince Georgii Lvov. Radical intellectuals and worker activists, meanwhile, established the Petrograd Soviet (Russian for "Council") of Workers and Soldiers Deputies, an institution soon replicated in other major cities. Adapting Lenin's term, most historians call the uneasy coexistence of the Provisional Government and the soviets the "dual power."

As in other non-Russian regions, the situation in the Ukrainian lands was even more complex, and it may be characterized as the "triple power," with nationalists being the third force. There, various political forces struggled not only to establish the scope of social revolution but also to define "Ukraine" as a political unit and determine its future relations with Russia. While the moderates sought to maintain civic peace, radical and nationalist intellectuals tried to channel the popular aspirations into their organizations. None of these forces had been strong enough to overthrow the tsar; it was the disintegration of the tsarist regime that allowed them to become major political players.

The old order in the Ukrainian provinces collapsed without bloodshed when, following several days of rumors, on March 13 a telegram from the Duma confirmed the victory of the revolution in Petrograd. Kyiv city officials, together with liberal politicians, took the lead by forming the Executive Committee of United Civic Organizations, which supported the Provisional Government. But in the next few days, socialists established soviets in major Ukrainian cities, starting with Kharkiv (March 15) and Kyiv (March 16). Finally, on March 17, Ukrainian activists set up a coordinating center of their own, the Central Rada (Ukrainian for "Council"). The influential historian Mykhailo Hrushevsky was chosen as its chairman, and practically all Ukrainian parties sent their representatives.

The Central Rada presided over the impressive revival of Ukrainian political and cultural life. Because the Provisional Government introduced freedom of speech and assembly, Ukrainian political parties could now emerge
from underground—and move considerably to the left in the process. The
moderate Society of Ukrainian Progressives became the Ukrainian Party of
Socialists-Federalists, which favored gradual reforms and opposed confiscation of large landholdings. Hrushevsky abandoned his former confederates
to join the revived Ukrainian Socialist Revolutionary Party, which voiced
radical proposals for land reform and quickly gained support among the
peasantry. Although the Socialist Revolutionaries were soon to become the
largest Ukrainian party and the voters' favorite, another revived socialist
party stayed at the helm for most of the Ukrainian Revolution. The Ukrainian
Social Democratic Workers' Party united the foremost young patriots of the
time, including Volodymyr Vynnychenko and Symon Petliura. As recent
publications of collected party programs confirm, the leading Ukrainian
forces of the time demanded merely territorial autonomy within a federal
Russian republic.[2]

With tsarist restrictions on national minorities lifted, Prosvita Societies,
Ukrainian cooperatives, and cultural clubs reemerged throughout the region.
The major Ukrainian daily of the prewar decade, *Rada*, resumed publication
as *Nova Rada*, and dozens of other periodicals in Ukrainian sprang up. The
Ukrainian national movement resumed its cultural work, which the tsarist
regime had cut short in the nineteenth century, but it was now operating
in a new political world. In the heady days of spring 1917, many Ukrainian
activists believed in their ability to "awaken" the masses. Indeed, for a while
the nationalist message seems to have found an enthusiastic response. On
April 1, an estimated 100,000 people marched in Kyiv under Ukrainian blue-
and-yellow flags in support of autonomy for Ukraine. In the summer, when
the Provisional Government allowed the creation of national military units,
some 300,000 soldiers of the disintegrating Russian army swore allegiance
to the Central Rada.[3] One should keep in mind, however, that the masses
may have been attracted by the Central Rada's combination of a nationalist
message with the slogans of land reform and universal peace.

To strengthen its legitimacy and build popular support, the Central Rada
organized a series of congresses in Kyiv, with delegates coming from all over
Ukraine. In April, the All-Ukrainian National Congress elected 150 representatives to the Rada. The Military Congress in May, the Peasant Congress
in June, and the Workers Congress in July delegated representatives to join
the Rada, which as a result grew to a body of 600 and had to create the Small
Rada to administer everyday business. Functioning now as a revolutionary
parliament of Ukraine, the Central Rada was de facto recognized as such

by most local soviets. Its main concern, however, was defining its relationship with the Provisional Government, which preferred dealing directly with its commissioners in the provinces. In retrospect, one can say that this distracted the Rada from such vital issues as land reform and the creation of a functioning administrative apparatus. But also understandable are the Ukrainian activists who focused on defining Ukraine's relations with its former imperial master.

Both the left wingers and the moderates in the Central Rada imagined autonomous Ukraine in a federation with Russia, but the Provisional Government at first refused any concessions to the nationalities until the planned convocation of the constituent assembly. With its proposals for autonomy rejected, on June 23 the Central Rada issued its First Universal (the historic name used by the Cossack hetmans for their decrees), proclaiming autonomy unilaterally.[4] The Rada also formed a Ukrainian cabinet of ministers, known as the "General Secretariat" and headed by Volodymyr Vynnychenko.

Deeply disturbed, the Provisional Government sent a delegation to Kyiv, led by the soon-to-be premier, Alexander Kerensky. As Germany and Austria-Hungary had just inflicted major defeats on the Russian armies, Petrograd became more susceptible to a compromise. Without acknowledging the Central Rada itself, it recognized the authority of the General Secretariat in five of the nine provinces where ethnic Ukrainians constituted the majority: Kyiv, Chernihiv, Poltava, Podolia, and Volhynia. At that point, the representatives of Ukraine's national minorities, who had been apprehensive observers of the struggle between Kyiv and Petrograd, finally agreed to join the Central Rada. The delegates of Russian, Polish, and Jewish political organizations took 202 of 822 seats in the Central Rada and 18 of 58 in the Small Rada.[5]

Yet, as the July elections to the city councils showed, the Ukrainian parties had a weak following in the politically crucial urban centers. In towns with a population under 50,000, they won 12.6 percent of the votes, and in cities with a population over 50,000, only 9.5 percent.[6] The elections to the All-Russian Constituent Assembly in November brought 67.8 percent of the vote to the Ukrainian parties, mainly to the Ukrainian Socialist Revolutionaries, while the Bolsheviks garnered a mere 10 percent. But in Kyiv, the Ukrainian parties received only 25 percent, and in Kharkiv, 13 percent.[7] The peasantry thus remained the Ukrainian movement's main support base, but the Central Rada did not satisfy the peasants' principal demand—the redistribution of land. To protest the postponing of land reform, in September the Ukrainian Socialist Revolutionaries refused to join the new General Secretariat. By the early fall of 1917, the peasants took matters into their own hands and began mass seizures of land belonging to the nobility or the crown.[8]

The Ukrainian government was losing both the trust of its constituency and control over the countryside. Like many socialists of the time, Vynnychenko and other Ukrainian leaders believed in the imminent "withering away" of the bourgeois state apparatus and standing armies. Blinded by this unrealistic dream, they neither created a strong national army out of the hundreds of thousands of soldiers who had declared loyalty to Ukraine nor organized a functioning bureaucracy out of thousands of patriotic teachers and petty officials. With civic order collapsing, local soviets in the cities and self-defense bodies in the countryside paid less and less attention to the proclamations issuing from Kyiv.

Meanwhile, the Ukrainian leaders were becoming increasingly frustrated with the Provisional Government. After the Bolsheviks in Petrograd overthrew Kerensky's government on November 7, 1917 (Old Style: October 25, hence the October Revolution), the Central Rada's troops supported the Kyivan Bolsheviks in their fight against the loyalist units of Kyiv Military District. Following the victory, however, the Rada claimed supreme authority over the nine Ukrainian provinces: Kyiv, Podolia, Volhynia, Chernihiv, Poltava, Kharkiv, Katerynoslav, Kherson, and Taurida (without the Crimea). The Rada's Third Universal (November 20) announced the creation of the Ukrainian People's Republic[9] as an autonomous unit in the future democratic federation of Russia's nationalities that was to emerge after the convocation of the Constituent Assembly.

Although their program proclaimed the nation's right of self-determination, the Bolsheviks had no intention of accepting the separation of Ukraine, which included major industrial and agricultural regions of the former Russian Empire. In December, they organized in Kyiv the All-Ukrainian Congress of Soviets that was to overthrow the Central Rada, but the Ukrainian parties managed to swamp the Bolsheviks with a mass of peasant delegates. The Bolshevik faction then moved to Kharkiv, where on December 25 another Congress of Soviets proclaimed the Soviet Ukrainian Republic. Bolshevik detachments arriving from Russia, together with local Red Guards, then began advancing on Kyiv.

The war against the Bolsheviks turned out to be a disaster for the Ukrainian republic. Most of the 300,000 soldiers at the Eastern Front who had previously pledged loyalty to the Central Rada had returned to their villages, and the standing Ukrainian army under Minister of War Symon Petliura consisted of 15,000 irregular "Free Cossacks" and volunteers. In what was in fact a civil war, morale mattered more than numbers, and the overall combat performance of the Ukrainian troops was disappointing. According to Ukrainian scholars, the Bolsheviks started their offensive with a force numbering no more than 8,000.[10] Yet, they were a better organized side with superior agitators, and they offered the frustrated masses the most radical social program. The campaign was won by persuasion rather than by force, as soldiers of the Ukrainian volunteer regiments defected to the Bolsheviks en masse.

The Central Rada also failed to build support among the workers. Of all the congresses convened by Ukrainian authorities in 1917, the Workers Congress was the most difficult to organize and, when it finally convened, the most critical of the government. Attempts by the authorities to control trade unions or establish separate Ukrainian ones failed.[11] In contrast, the Bolsheviks were becoming increasingly influential in Ukraine's cities. When the Red Army began advancing from the north, they staged successful uprisings in many cities. In Kyiv, troops loyal to the Central Rada managed to suppress a rebellion led by the workers of the Arsenal, later portrayed in Alexander Dovzhenko's famous movie *Arsenal*. One week later, the Ukrainian government was forced to abandon the city. In these final, tragic days of the capital's defense, on January 29, 1918, the Bolshevik forces at Kruty encircled and slaughtered a unit consisting of some 300 Ukrainian schoolboy volunteers—the victims becoming national martyrs for anti-Soviet Ukrainians.

Meanwhile, since December 1917, both Soviet Russia and the Ukrainian People's Republic were engaged in peace negotiations with the Central Powers. The Bolsheviks bitterly opposed Ukrainian participation, but Germany and Austria-Hungary favored the disintegration of the former tsarist empire and wanted to create several friendly states on its western fringes. By late January, it was clear to the Ukrainian leaders that their only salvation was in accepting the Central Powers' protection. As only a fully independent state could conclude an international treaty, on January 25, 1918, the Central Rada issued its Fourth Universal (backdated to January 22), proclaiming the independence of the Ukrainian People's Republic. Ukrainian sovereignty had been a reality since November, but the Ukrainian leaders remained reluctant to sever all ties with Russia. Contemporaries such as Hrushevsky and Vynnychenko were explicit about the external circumstances that forced this final step.[12]

On February 9, 1918, as the Bolshevik army was entering Kyiv, in Brest-Litovsk the Ukrainian representatives signed a separate peace treaty with the Central Powers, which recognized the Central Rada's authority over the nine provinces, plus Kholm province. Soviet Russia, which also signed a separate treaty, was forced to recognize the Ukrainian People's Republic. But more important were the secret clauses, which stipulated that Germany and Austria-Hungary would give Ukraine military help in exchange for deliveries of foodstuffs. Another secret agreement promised the unification of eastern Galicia and Bukovyna into a single "Ukrainian" crown land within the Habsburg monarchy.

Having taken Kyiv, the Bolshevik troops, led by the brutal Mikhail Muraviev, reportedly executed between 2,000 and 5,000 "class enemies" there,[13] but their control over the capital lasted only three weeks. A German and Austrian army of 450,000 bayonets forced them to flee, and by April, all nine Ukrainian provinces were cleared of Bolsheviks. Displaced to Russia, the Ukrainian Bolshevik leaders began preparing for a long struggle for Ukraine that they could not win without Russian backing. One of their first steps was to create the Communist Party (Bolshevik) of Ukraine or CP(B)U, which was, however, completely subordinate to its Russian big sister.

❖ The German Occupation and the Hetmanate

On its flight from Kyiv in early February, the Central Rada hastily enacted laws establishing an eight-hour workday and abolishing the right of private land ownership. Present-day historians argue that, in doing so, the Ukrainian socialists utterly misjudged the expectations of the peasantry, who wanted large estates to be distributed among individual peasant households instead of being "socialized."[14] These measures were even less popular with landowners and wealthier peasants, and after the Brest-Litovsk Treaty, the Rada's "socialist" legislation troubled the conservative German military administration in Ukraine.

The German high command in Ukraine soon became disappointed with its left-leaning protégé. The Ukrainian government had no functioning local administration, was unable to maintain order, and—most important to the Germans—was not of much assistance in collecting the grain that the Central Powers needed so badly. As early as in March and April 1918, the Germans took control of the railways, reversed the Rada's land legislation, and introduced martial law. They continued to tolerate the Central Rada only because it had to sign an economic agreement with Germany and Austria-Hungary promising the delivery by the end of July of 1 million tons of grain, 600 million eggs, and other foodstuffs and raw materials in large quantities. When such an agreement was signed on April 23, it sealed the fate of the Rada, which could not deliver on it.[15] Armed with this document, the German military took over the collection of foodstuffs.

In late April, the chief of staff of the German army group in Ukraine, General Wilhelm Groener, secretly met the Ukrainian conservative politician Pavlo Skoropadsky. A Russian-speaking collateral descendant of the eighteenth-century Cossack hetman, Skoropadsky was a former tsarist general who came to prominence in the summer of 1917 as the organizer of Ukrainian volunteer units. During their meetings, Groener told Skoropadsky about the German

plan to establish a Ukrainian monarchy and offered him the throne. Skoropadsky agreed, accepting at the same time the secret conditions limiting
the sovereignty of his future regime. On April 29, 1918, the congress of the
Ukrainian Union of Landowners proclaimed Pavlo Skoropadsky hetman of
Ukraine. That same day, the Central Rada, actually still in session in another
building in Kyiv, hurried through its last two legislative acts: the adoption of
the constitution and the election of Mykhailo Hrushevsky as the president
of the Ukrainian People's Republic. The historian's presidency lasted less
than a day.

The establishment of a new conservative regime occurred smoothly, almost without bloodshed. Skoropadsky, who is often dismissed by historians as
simply a German puppet, in fact represented the return to power of Ukraine's
prerevolutionary elites: tsarist bureaucrats, military officers, landowners, industrialists, and urban upper-middle classes. Restoration proved easier than
building a new state apparatus, because the old cadres of imperial bureaucracy
and officer corps gladly put themselves at the hetman's disposal. Ministries
were quickly reorganized and efficiently run, while local administration
was entrusted to provincial and district *starosty* (commissioners) appointed
from among gentry landowners or former tsarist officials. But most of the
hetman's administrators did not speak Ukrainian, and many secretly favored
the restoration of a Russian state that would include Ukraine. All the major
Ukrainian political parties refused to cooperate with Skoropadsky's regime,
resulting in repeated difficulties in forming a cabinet.

In retrospect, the Hetmanate's vision of Ukraine as a civic and territorial unit, rather than an ethnic and cultural unit, looks more attractive than
it did at the time. The Ukrainian historian Yaroslav Hrytsak notes insight-
fully that Skoropadsky "strove to introduce a new concept of the Ukrainian
nation that was founded not on knowledge of the Ukrainian language, but
on loyalty to the Ukrainian state."[16] But contemporary Ukrainian activists
did not appreciate this conceptual innovation and saw the hetman and his
officials at best as "Little Russians" from the imperial past and, at worst, as
closet Russian monarchists.

The hetman's government abolished all the laws, reforms, and institutions
of the Central Rada; it also banned strikes and resurrected censorship. Sensing
the alienation of the Ukrainian intelligentsia and the workers, Skoropadsky
tried to turn well-to-do peasants into the pillar of his regime by reestablishing
for them the privileged "Cossack" social estate of prosperous farmers. But
the Hetmanate's appeal to the peasantry was severely handicapped by the
government's association with wealthy landowners and German economic
exploitation. German punitive expeditions to quell peasant looters and the
forced collection of grain from the peasants soon provoked unprecedented

unrest in the countryside. In June, the left wing of the Ukrainian Socialist Revolutionaries organized a peasant rebellion of some 30,000 people in Kyiv region. Smaller revolts broke out elsewhere.

Paradoxically, of all the Ukrainian governments from 1917 to 1920, the Skoropadsky administration achieved the most spectacular successes in foreign politics, education, and culture. Under the leadership of Dmytro Doroshenko, the only known Ukrainian intellectual to become a minister, the hetman's foreign ministry succeeded in establishing diplomatic relations and exchanging ambassadors with the Central Powers, neighboring countries, and some neutral states, such as Switzerland and Sweden. A total of eleven foreign missions opened up in Kyiv.[17] The well-functioning hetman bureaucracy also managed to create 150 high schools with instruction in Ukrainian and two new universities. In the three existing universities, it opened departments of Ukrainian language, literature, and history. Skoropadsky established the Ukrainian Academy of Sciences, the National Library, the State Archive, the Ukrainian Academy of Fine Arts, the Ukrainian State Drama Company, and a number of other cultural institutions, many still in existence.[18]

Meanwhile, peasant discontent with German requisitions grew, and political opposition to the hetman became consolidated within the Ukrainian National Union, which in September made Vynnychenko its leader. At the same time as the State Ukrainian Theater Company of the Hetmanate was staging Vynnychenko's fashionable dramas, the author was busying himself with preparing a mass rebellion against Skoropadsky.

In the fall of 1918, with the defeat of the Central Powers imminent, the hetman made several desperate attempts to find another power base. At first, he negotiated with the Ukrainian National Union and seemingly secured a compromise, but the situation changed with the Central Powers' capitulation in November 1918 and commitment to withdrawing their troops from eastern Europe. Trying to please the Allies, who favored the restoration of a united Russia, Skoropadsky appointed an openly pro-Russian cabinet and issued a manifesto proclaiming Ukraine's federation with a "future non-Bolshevik Russia." But the hetman's final gamble only compromised him and caused the Ukrainian National Union to launch an armed uprising.

Vynnychenko and Petliura headed a five-person committee to coordinate the rebellion that was named the Directory, after the French revolutionary government of 1795 to 1799. Tens of thousands of peasants flocked to the Directory's headquarters in Bila Tserkva near Kyiv, and the best units of the hetman's army defected to their side. Among them were the elite Sich Riflemen, formed in Galicia during World War I and sent to Ukraine as part of an Austrian occupational force. On December 14, the Germans abandoned Kyiv. Leaving his abdication manifesto behind, Skoropadsky fled with them, disguised as a wounded German officer. The conservative experiment miscarried, leaving the eastern Ukrainian political scene to left-of-center contestants.

✿ Western Ukraine

As the Ukrainian political nation in the east was being born in the throes of agony, western Ukrainian leaders remained no more than sympathetic observers who could at most criticize Austrian policies in eastern Ukraine during their speeches at the Reichsrat. Badly shaken by military defeats, the Austro-Hungarian Empire still outlasted its Russian counterpart by almost twenty months. Moreover, in July 1918, the Habsburg officials announced that they had no intention of creating a Ukrainian crown land within the Dual Monarchy, as envisaged by the Brest-Litovsk agreements. Frustrated Ukrainian politicians anxiously awaited the changes that Austria's defeat in World War I was likely to bring about.

On October 16, 1918, in a desperate effort to save Austria-Hungary from dismemberment by the Allies, the young Emperor Charles (reigned 1916–1918) proclaimed his empire's transformation into a "free federation" of its peoples. On October 18, the Ukrainian deputies of the Reichsrat and provincial diets, together with representatives of major parties, established the Ukrainian National Council in Lviv. This body proclaimed the creation of a Ukrainian state within Austria-Hungary, including eastern Galicia, northern Bukovyna, and Transcarpathia. But while the council conducted talks with Vienna, on the night of October 31, a group of Ukrainian military in Lviv took power in the city. On the next day, November 1, the Ukrainian National Council declared the establishment of an independent Ukrainian state, soon officially named the Western Ukrainian People's Republic.

The young republic, however, was immediately opposed by a powerful enemy in its recently reconstituted neighbor state, Poland. Poles laid claim to all of Galicia, including its Ukrainian eastern part, where they predominated in the cities. Street fighting began in Lviv in early November; on November 22, a Polish uprising forced the Ukrainians out of their capital. The conflict developed into a full-fledged Ukrainian-Polish war, and it was against this background that western Ukrainians began their state building.

The Western Ukrainian People's Republic greatly benefited from the time-honored traditions of Ukrainian political and community life in Austria-Hungary. In contrast to eastern Ukraine, it had fewer problems in establishing an effective administrative apparatus and maintaining order. This was, in part, due to the preservation of the old system of county administration, with elected Ukrainian "commissars" replacing old "captains."[19] But perhaps more important was the fact that all western Ukrainian society united in the struggle with its traditional rival, the Poles, and social problems temporarily took a backseat.

In the Ukrainian National Council, which in late November was renewed by way of elections, the majority National Democrats collaborated peacefully with the opposition Radicals. The republic proclaimed basic political freedoms and minority rights, with 66 seats of 266 reserved for Poles, Jews, and Germans in the future parliament. Ukrainian-Jewish relations remained friendly in western Ukraine throughout the revolutionary era. The republic, however, never controlled all the territories it claimed. Romania quickly occupied the Ukrainian part of Bukovyna, and Transcarpathia remained under Hungarian control until its inclusion into the new state of Czechoslovakia. A functioning Ukrainian administration was set up only in eastern Galicia.

From the very first days of its existence, the Western Ukrainian People's Republic sought to unite with the Ukrainian state in eastern Ukraine, and indeed on January 22, 1919, the first unification of the two Ukraines was solemnly proclaimed in Kyiv. Although now only the "western province" of the Ukrainian People's Republic, the west, in fact, retained its autonomy, administrative structure, and laws. Moderate western Ukrainian politicians never quite found a common language with the socialist easterners, but political differences did not spell the doom for a united Ukraine. The war on two fronts did. The act of unification itself was proclaimed to the sound of Bolshevik guns in the east and Polish guns in the west, the two forces that would crush the Ukrainian state.

Because of their long tradition of national organization, Ukrainians in eastern Galicia were able to create something Kyiv never had—a reliable national army, the so-called Ukrainian Galician Army. If it were not for its grueling fighting against the much stronger Poles, the Galicians could have made a difference during the Civil War in eastern Ukraine. Short on senior officers, the army had many German and Austrian majors and colonels, and the two successive commanders-in-chief were former Russian generals, Mykhailo Omelianovych-Pavlenko and Oleksandr Hrekov. The army's greatest assets were its privates and junior officers—up to 60,000 conscientious and disciplined Ukrainian peasants and townspeople from eastern Galicia.[20]

The Ukrainian army began a counteroffensive in February 1919 and soon had Lviv encircled, but the arrival of major forces from Poland proper decided the outcome of the struggle in Galicia. The Allied negotiators at the

Paris Peace Conference allowed the Poles to persuade them that the specter of Communism might steal into Europe through the Ukrainian door. Eager to create out of an independent Poland a counterweight both to Germany and to Bolshevik Russia, the Allies abandoned the Wilsonian principle of self-determination in regard to eastern Galicia. To defeat the Ukrainians, the Poles used the 100,000-strong army of General Józef Haller that was trained and equipped in France. In theory, the Allies sent it to fight the Bolshevik plague, but in practice, it was employed against the Ukrainians. After a promising counteroffensive at Chortkiv in June, the Ukrainian Galician Army ran out of ammunition and retreated eastward.

In the spring of 1919, social problems also began troubling the western province. Peasants protested the authorities' failure to enact land reform, which envisaged the confiscation (with compensation) of large landholdings and their distribution among the peasantry. The Ukrainian National Council finally passed the land legislation in mid-April, but the actual redistribution was to start only after the war. The head of the Directory, Petliura, warned the leaders of the western province that their procrastination on the land issue could end in a social catastrophe.[21] Also in mid-April was a pro-Bolshevik workers' rebellion in western Ukraine's only industrial center, Drohobych.

But before internal problems had time to escalate, western Ukrainians lost the war to the Poles. On July 16, 1919, what remained of the Ukrainian Galician Army and the province's administration crossed the River Zbruch, which marked the old border between the Russian and Austro-Hungarian empires. Before that, in late June, the Allies agreed to the "temporary" Polish occupation of all Galicia, up to the Zbruch.

Having crossed into eastern Ukraine, the Galicians joined the struggling Directory on a tiny stretch of territory that it still controlled, with the center in Kamianets-Podilsky. It was there that eastern and western Ukrainians finally had an opportunity to unite their administrations and armies. But the National Democrat Yevhen Petrushevych, whom the Ukrainian National Council made a dictator of the western province in June, presided over a well-ordered bureaucracy of moderate nationalists. The Directory, on the other hand, had clear socialist leanings and no functioning administrative apparatus to speak of. Moreover, the two groups liked each other's enemies. The western Ukrainians could never reconcile with the Poles, but the easterners considered the Poles a natural ally against the Bolsheviks. In the same vein, the eastern Ukrainian patriots saw the Russian Whites as their mortal enemies, while the westerners did not mind collaborating with the Whites against the Bolsheviks. At the moment, both armies were preparing for a decisive fight against the Bolsheviks, but the lack of ideological unity in the middle of a brutal civil war would soon lead them into a tragic ambush.

✂ The Directory and the Civil War

When the Directory entered Kyiv following the fall of the Hetmanate in December 1918, it resurrected the Ukrainian People's Republic. However, no attempt to reconvene the Central Rada was made, nor was President Hrushevsky invited to play any political role. Instead, the five-member Directory assumed the highest executive and legislative authority. The Directory was dominated by two rival members of the Ukrainian Social Democratic Workers' Party, the ultra-socialist Vynnychenko and the more nationalistically inclined Petliura.

Vynnychenko, who initially served as the Directory's chairman, argued that the Ukrainian republic could survive only by "out-socializing" the Bolsheviks in competition for mass support. Accordingly, the Directory's first steps included declarations about confiscation of large estates without compensation, nationalization of industry, and workers' control of factories. Acting as though the Central Rada never existed, in late January 1919, the Directory convened a Labor Congress in Kyiv, which acted as an all-Ukrainian parliament and approved all of the government's measures.[22] But the Directory also engaged in nation building. It established Ukrainian as the republic's official language and proclaimed the autocephaly (independence) of the Orthodox Church in Ukraine, which was previously part of the Russian Orthodox Church. On January 22, 1919, the authorities organized a solemn ceremony in Kyiv to mark the unification of the eastern and western Ukrainian republics.

Before the Directory could implement any of its decisions, however, it had to evacuate Kyiv once again. The military situation in Ukraine worsened immediately after the Germans' departure in December 1918. Some 60,000 French troops landed in Odesa and other southern cities to support the Russian Whites, who promised the restoration of a united, anti-Bolshevik state. At the same time, the Bolsheviks began another invasion from the north. Vynnychenko desired a rapprochement with Soviet Russia; he even spoke about Ukraine's entry into a revolutionary war of Soviet republics (including Russia and Hungary, where a Communist rebellion was then underway) against the European reaction.[23] But his negotiations with the Bolsheviks were in vain, as their troops were fast advancing toward Kyiv. Peasants who had supported the Directory against Skoropadsky returned to their villages, and the Ukrainian government was again struggling to raise an army. Ukraine was about to become a battlefield in the Russian Civil War between the Reds and Whites. But these events may also be characterized as a Ukrainian civil war, for ethnic Ukrainians serving in the Directory's, Bolshevik, and White armies were killing each other for the victory of their respective vision of "Ukraine."

After the fall of Kyiv in February 1919, Vynnychenko resigned the chairmanship in the Directory. Petliura, whose orientation toward intensive state building and Allied aid seemed more appropriate, took over his duties. To facilitate the desired agreement with the Allies, who were suspicious of all socialists, Petliura created a nonsocialist cabinet, and he himself left the Social Democratic Workers' Party. (The disappointed Vynnychenko resigned from the Directory altogether.) But the nonsocialist cabinet existed only two months, exactly the time needed to reveal the futility of attempting to please the Allies, who were putting all their hopes in the Whites and the restoration of an "indivisible" Russia. By the time the socialists returned, it was too late to govern; the Ukrainian administration was constantly on the move westward, from Vinnytsia to Rivne to Kamianets-Podilsky.

The Bolsheviks' second tenure in Ukraine lasted about seven months. During this time, the Ukrainian Socialist Soviet Republic managed to alienate the Ukrainian leftist intelligentsia and the peasantry by using only the Russian language in administration, propaganda, and education. The government was headed at first by the Russian G. L. Piatakov, whose anti-Ukrainian views were well known, and then by a Russian of Bulgarian and Romanian background, Khristian Rakovsky, who had just recently served as the Soviet *Russian* envoy at the talks with the Directory and whose views differed very little from those of his predecessor. In cities and towns, the feared Cheka (security police) commenced its hunt for "counterrevolutionary" and "alien-class" elements. Finally, the Bolsheviks created hostility among the peasantry by sending out armed detachments of Russian workers to collect grain. Instead of distributing land to the peasants, the new authorities reorganized the confiscated large estates into state farms.

Such policies only fanned the flames of the peasant rebellion, which was often aimed at all outsiders. The whole countryside became a sea of anarchy divided up and controlled by local peasant chieftains, the so-called *otamany*. Some of them led peasant armies of many thousands and could influence national politics. Among the most famous were *otaman* Matvii Hryhoriiv, a former tsarist officer and left Socialist Revolutionary, who in the spring of 1919 drove the French forces out of Odesa but later turned against the Bolsheviks, and Nestor Makhno, a peasant anarchist, who concentrated his 40,000-strong army in the southern steppes, supporting in turn the Bolsheviks, the Directory, the Bolsheviks again, and finally, the idea of a peasant anarchist republic. Other colorful personalities whose memories survive in folklore include no fewer than three different female *otamanshas*, all named Marusia.[24]

The fact that one weak government was replacing another in Kyiv in 1919 had no impact on the countryside. World War I and the ensuing collapse of local institutions left the Ukrainian peasantry heavily armed, experienced in fighting, and more self-confident than ever. Although local peasant bands often switched their allegiance, sometimes fighting under the slogans of socialist revolution or independent Ukraine, their main interest was in survival, securing arable land, and looting. The revival of the term *otaman* suggested a spontaneous revival of Cossack traditions, but the rebels were not conscious Ukrainian nationalists. Rather, they were motivated by local concerns, prejudices, and naive anarchism.

The violent Jewish pogroms that claimed more than 30,000 lives were perhaps the most tragic consequence of the chaos in Ukraine in 1919. All sides in the Civil War perpetrated pogroms: the Whites, the Directory troops, the independent *otamans*, and the Red Army. With the exception of some White ideologically motivated pogroms, the anti-Jewish violence was usually carried out by drunken mobs of anti-Semitic freebooters against the authorities' orders. The troops subordinated to the Directory committed 40 percent of recorded pogroms—more than any other side,[25] resulting in their commander-in-chief, Symon Petliura, being branded in the West as a violent anti-Semite. Despite this localized violence against Jews, on a national level the Ukrainian People's Republic had a good record of treating its national minorities. It was the first modern state to establish a ministry of Jewish affairs and guarantee the rights of the Jewish culture. Yet, it lacked authority. The government issued well-intentioned orders condemning pogroms and attempted to investigate them.[26] In the meantime, marauding bands, often nominally considered to be part of the Ukrainian, Red, or White armies, simply moved on to the next village to perpetrate violence.

Like the Directory before them, the Bolsheviks in 1919 found governing Ukraine almost impossible. They barely had enough time to identify the problems before a well-organized White Army, equipped by the Allies, in June moved in from the Don region in the southeast. In July, Petliura's detachments, reinforced by the Ukrainian Galician Army, started advancing from the west. Beaten by both the Whites and the Directory, the Bolsheviks retired to Russia in late August, with the White general Anton Denikin in hot pursuit.

The units of the Ukrainian Galician Army and the (White) Volunteer Army entered Kyiv almost simultaneously, on August 30 and 31, 1919. For one day, the two armies occupied the city in friendly neutrality. The Ukrainian government hoped to obtain the Allies' support by acting in accord with the Whites. The Volunteer Army had no intention of recognizing Ukrainian statehood in any form, but it distinguished the "separatist" Petliura forces and the Galicians, who were seen as foreigners. After a day of uncertainty, when both the imperial Russian and the Ukrainian republican flags were flying at city hall, the Whites ordered the Galicians to withdraw from Kyiv. Reluctant to fight their potential allies, they obeyed. Soon it transpired that the Allies still did not want to deal with a Ukrainian government, even if it was friendly to the Whites. In the meantime, the Volunteer Army proceeded with its plan to reestablish the prerevolutionary social order: They restored land to large landowners, banned the use of the Ukrainian language, and arrested the Ukrainian intelligentsia. Amid the growing popular discontent against the Whites, the Directory finally declared war on them in late September.

Yet, military engagements with the mighty Volunteer Army brought the Ukrainian troops no success. In October, a typhus epidemic struck at a time when medical supplies were blocked by the Allies, killing about 70 percent of manpower (and up to 90 percent of the Ukrainian Galician Army). Defeated and decimated by the epidemic, the Ukrainians finally gave up. The Galicians entered into secret negotiations with the Whites that ended in the Ukrainian Galician Army's subordination to Denikin on November 6.[27] At the same time, Petliura reached an agreement with the Galicians' sworn enemy, Poland. The rupture between the two Ukrainian governments was now complete, and the military catastrophe assured.

The Poles moved into the provinces of Volhynia and Podolia, where Petliura and his government were traveling in several railroad cars. What remained of the Directory was attacked by local peasant bands; the state treasury was stolen, and the staff of the war ministry was left behind.[28] On November 15, Petliura was officially proclaimed a dictator and fled to Warsaw soon afterward. Another dictator, Petrushevych, the leader of the western province, was on his way to Vienna. Some Ukrainian units stayed behind to pursue what would later be called the "Winter March" across the Right Bank, but this was essentially a guerilla action marginal to the fate of the Russian Civil War.

As these events were unfolding near the Polish border, in Ukraine's central provinces the Reds were beating back the Whites. In December 1919, the Bolsheviks took Kyiv for the third time, and on this occasion they seriously reevaluated their Ukrainian policy. Their debacle in Ukraine earlier that year was caused primarily by peasant resistance, but Lenin rather dogmatically translated it into a national framework, concluding that more attention to national rights was needed. The Kremlin allowed the formal independence of Soviet Ukraine (in federation with Soviet Russia), official recognition of the Ukrainian language, and a more careful agrarian policy. On Lenin's insistence, Ukrainian Bolsheviks formed an alliance with the influential leftist splinter group of the Ukrainian Socialist Revolutionary Party, the so-called Borotbists ("Fighters"), who provided the Soviet authorities with Ukrainian-speaking cadres.

To placate the countryside, the Bolsheviks terminated the creation of state farms and communes and opted instead for a massive distribution of confiscated land to the peasantry. In the spring of 1920, the authorities distributed 15.5 million *desiatynas* (14.2 million hectares) of land,[29] effectively presenting themselves as a government that was finally satisfying the peasantry's age-old dreams. Forced requisitioning of grain from the peasants to feed cities and the Red Army soon destroyed this effect and led to new revolts and punitive expeditions beginning in the summer of 1920.[30] But by then, the Bolsheviks had already secured victory in the Civil War. (The Whites held out in the Crimean peninsula until November 1920, but they no longer presented a major military threat.)

Petliura, in the interim, negotiated with the Poles for a joint anti-Soviet expedition. Poland was indeed interested in war with the Bolsheviks, not so much to defeat them as to create a buffer Ukrainian state between Soviet Russia and itself. The Polish leader Józef Piłsudski was also confident in the French and British support of his cause. After Petliura agreed to recognize the Polish claim to eastern Galicia and the western part of Volhynia, a joint offensive of Polish and Ukrainian troops against the Bolsheviks began in April 1920. Initially, it was a success. Kyiv was taken in May, and the last cabinet of the Ukrainian People's Republic was installed there. In June, however, the Red Army responded with a powerful counteroffensive, which by August brought it to the outskirts of Warsaw. The Poles managed to push it back but in October made a truce with the Soviets. The remnants of Petliura's army were interned in Poland. In March 1921, the Treaty of Riga among Poland and the Soviet republics of Russia and Ukraine sealed the status quo. Poland recognized Soviet Ukraine but kept eastern Galicia and western Volhynia. The Bolsheviks required considerable time and effort to suppress peasant insurgents of various political stripes, but their victory was no longer in question. The Ukrainian Revolution was over.

❖❖

Because the independent Ukrainian state created during the revolution did not survive beyond 1920, history textbooks in present-day Ukraine often feature sections on the reasons for the Ukrainian Revolution's "defeat." The catalogue usually includes the overwhelming might of Soviet Russia and Poland, a weak sense of national solidarity among ethnic Ukrainians in the Russian Empire, and the siren call of Bolshevism. All these factors indeed were at work from 1917 to 1920. Yet, it is misleading to evaluate the success or failure of the Ukrainian Revolution in relation to the aim its leaders did not formulate until later in the process—independence. The Ukrainian Revolution began as a general movement for national rights, a more democratic society, and a better economic order. Various political groups and regional factions emphasized different aspects of this general agenda, but no one group ever managed to unite the majority of the population under its banner. The revolution began not because the Ukrainian movement had enough popular support to rise in revolt but because the empires had collapsed, leaving a power vacuum for new politicians to fill. Under the circumstances, the revolution accomplished much, in that it established the modern idea of Ukraine and forced the Bolsheviks to create a Ukrainian republic within the Soviet Union.

Soviet Ukraine in the 1920s:
The Ukrainization Drive

5

The Ukrainian lands that became part of the Soviet state were constituted as the Ukrainian Socialist Soviet Republic. Although in 1936 for some reason the Kremlin reversed the word order, making Ukraine and other republics "Soviet Socialist," the nature of the republic's sovereignty changed little in the next seventy years. Moscow made all major decisions concerning Ukraine, and every political turn of the center was immediately imitated in the Soviet Ukrainian capital of Kharkiv. Nevertheless, Ukrainian statehood mattered. For the first time in modern history, eastern Ukrainians had a territorial entity with borders closely corresponding to the ethnic boundaries of Ukrainian settlement. A part of the Soviet Union, the Ukrainian republic nonetheless provided a symbolic national homeland for generations of Soviet Ukrainians.[1]

The Ukrainian people obtained a territorial and administrative framework on which to build their modern, if Soviet, identity. Soviet Ukrainian statehood furnished them with political institutions, leaders, state symbols, and state support for the national language and culture. This Bolshevik concession was in response to the challenge of the Ukrainian Revolution. The events of 1917 through 1920 established a precedent for a national polity and stimulated the growth of national consciousness among all the ethnic groups residing in Ukraine. The national mobilization of Ukrainians and other peoples began before the establishment of Soviet power, but the Bolsheviks attempted to disarm the forces of nationalism by placing themselves at the head of this mobilization drive. This was the main theoretical rationale for their policy of Ukrainization and for the similar promotion of minority languages and cadres—Polish, Jewish, Greek, German, and so forth—in regions where they were compactly settled within Ukraine.[2]

The Bolsheviks also faced a number of formidable practical tasks in Ukraine, most notably the pacification of the rebellious peasantry and the inclusion of locals into the new administration. Yet, Lenin saw these pragmatic objectives as mere components of the Soviet power's most daunting mission in the non-Russian regions, the integration of the nationalities into the socialist order. The road to Soviet modernity led through the industrial and cultural development of the borderlands, which would bring all Soviet peoples into socialism. Before the Bolsheviks could embark on this grandiose project, however, the embattled economy backfired on them.

✪ Economy: Destroyed and Revived

Three years of civil war ruined the Ukrainian economy, which had already been heavily damaged by the war effort in 1914 through 1917. Industrial production fell almost to zero, transport and commerce were disorganized, and food and fuel shortages haunted the cities. Faced with economic collapse in all territories under their control, the Bolsheviks adopted the policy of "War Communism"—an emergency program of industry nationalization, grain requisitioning, and universal labor conscription. Initially, the new masters of the country did not worry too much about the collapse of the "capitalist economy," for they saw it as an opportunity for an instant leap into Communism. To some Bolshevik dreamers, War Communism opened a door into an egalitarian society of the future, where there would be no private property or free market, and where products would be distributed according to need.

In reality, however, life on the other side of the door was gloomy. In the villages, compulsory grain deliveries amounted to virtual confiscation carried out by armed detachments. To manage the nationalized factories and distribute food rations, the authorities created a vast bureaucratic machine that was notoriously inefficient. The end of economic ruin was nowhere in sight. Ironically, as desperate city dwellers tried to exchange any goods they possessed for food, some Bolshevik theorists actually celebrated the skyrocketing inflation as a sign of the "withering away of money."

In Ukraine, the Civil War delayed the implementation of the Soviet economic policy. Most of the elements of War Communism were first introduced in the republic during the spring and summer of 1919 and then reestablished after the defeat of the Whites early in 1920. These economic policies immediately led to widespread peasant resistance, so in the spring of 1920, the Bolsheviks placated them with a large-scale land distribution program. At the same time, faced with the need to fulfill the requisitioning quotas, the authorities established the Committees of Poor Peasants (Russian: *kombedy*, Ukrainian: *komnezamy*), hoping for their assistance against the rich, who were thought to be hoarding grain. But a new wave of peasant rebellions soon thwarted the requisitioning efforts. In October 1920, Lenin complained, "We take bread from Siberia, take it from the Kuban, but we cannot get it from Ukraine, because war is in full swing there and the Red Army has to fight against the bandits proliferating there."[3]

All in all, War Communism failed as an economic model. It could provide subsistence levels of production and distribution but was unable to stimulate economic recovery. In 1921, industrial production in the Ukrainian lands was only one tenth of the prewar figure, and trains ran just once a week between the major cities. The daily bread ration in the cities was reduced to a mere 100 grams. As soon as the Civil War ended, the population openly rebelled against War Communism policies. Early in 1921, peasant resistance to grain requisitioning became overwhelming, and workers in many Ukrainian cities went on strike, forcing the authorities to use military force against workers in what was officially a "workers' state."[4] As the Bolshevik leadership was discussing the possibility of undoing War Communism in March 1921, an anti-Bolshevik mutiny broke out on the Baltic naval base of Kronstadt—famous for its role in the October Revolution—stressing the urgency of reform. (Incidentally, the mutiny began shortly after a large contingent of disaffected peasant recruits from Ukraine arrived at Kronstadt.)

At the same time as the Red Army was suppressing the Kronstadt rebellion, Lenin announced at the Tenth Party Congress (March 1921) a temporary return to market economy, in the form of the New Economic Policy (NEP). Overcoming objections from less pragmatic Bolshevik firebrands, Lenin persuaded the congress that a tactical retreat toward capitalism was necessary to prepare a later strategic advance toward socialism. The Soviet leader variously estimated the length of this retreat at either ten or twenty years. Ukrainian historians have revealed only recently that the CP(B)U Central Committee initially passed a contradictory resolution declaring that the NEP was unnecessary in general and unacceptable in Ukraine in particular, but if Soviet Russia launched it first, it would have to be introduced in the republic.[5] Yet Lenin's authority, together with the mass peasant uprisings, soon reined in the hard-liners in the Ukrainian leadership.

Under the NEP, instead of arbitrarily confiscating all uncovered food "surpluses," the state required peasants to pay a fixed tax in produce and, later, in cash. The products remaining after payment of the tax could be sold on the open market. However, in Ukraine the introduction of the NEP came too late to prevent the unfolding famine. In addition to the general disorganization of agricultural production and the harsh requisitioning quotas of 1920 and 1921, a drought struck in Ukraine and the (Russian) Volga region in 1921, resulting in mass famine. The contemporary official estimate of deaths in the republic was 235,000, but present-day Ukrainian historians believe that the total number of the dead and their (estimated number of) unborn children might have been more than a million.[6] In the summer of 1921, the Soviet government appealed to the West for help, opening the door to a massive American relief effort.

In the long run, the return to market relations in agriculture produced encouraging results, especially after 1923, when a tax in cash replaced the one in produce, and industrial goods became available for peasants to purchase. The "tactical retreat" also worked for the economy in general. Later in 1921, the government began denationalizing small industries; private enterprises developed, particularly in consumer industries and service. In a short period of time, Ukrainian authorities leased to private owners as many as 5,200 enterprises—roughly half of the republic's total number of enterprises. In 1923, the state earned an impressive 850 million gold rubles in lease payments in Ukraine.[7] Although large industries remained state-owned, the centralized allocation of resources was partially replaced by contracts between firms. Slowly, the revival of big industries began. But the NEP went furthest in the revival of private shops and the service industry, with the number of private trade establishments in the republic ballooning to 106,824 in 1926.[8] Owing especially to the growth of privatized agriculture, trade, and consumer industries, by 1927 Soviet Ukraine's GNP attained pre–World War I levels.

For all the successes of the NEP, the Bolsheviks remained uneasy about this policy. Indeed, although agriculture recovered rapidly, the decision about how much grain to sell resided with "petit bourgeois" peasant owners rather than state planning organs. The peasants tended to sell less than before the revolution, for the simple reason that not enough reasonably priced, good-quality consumer goods were available for them to buy. In 1927 and 1928, the government initiated a fierce ideological campaign against the main producer of grain, the well-to-do farmer. The press presented the latter as a kulak (or *kurkul* in Ukrainian), a monstrous exploiter of poor peasants and someone who refused out of "class hatred" to sell grain to the Soviet state. At about the same time, the authorities began cracking down on private traders and entrepreneurs.

These developments were taking place against the backdrop of a theoretical debate in the Kremlin about how to industrialize the country. Led since 1925 by Stalin's men, the Ukrainian leadership unreservedly sided with their patron, who first defeated Trotsky with the help of the moderates and then adopted Trotsky's radical idea of rapid state-sponsored industrialization at the expense of the peasantry. The days of the NEP were numbered.

Defining the State and the Party

The victorious Bolsheviks proclaimed the Ukrainian Socialist Soviet Republic an independent state of workers, peasants, and soldiers. Even though the 1919 constitution of Soviet Ukraine did not mention any federative links with

Soviet Russia, in fact both were ruled by their respective Bolshevik parties, and the CP(B)U was merely a constituent part of the Russian Communist Party (Bolshevik). This, together with the presence of the Red Army on its territory, put Ukraine firmly within the Soviet Russian "political space." All the republic's institutions copied their Russian counterparts, and Soviet Russian laws automatically applied on Ukrainian territory.

Until 1934, Soviet Ukraine's capital was in Kharkiv, an eastern industrial city located close to the Russian border, which, unlike Kyiv, had not been associated with the Ukrainian national governments of 1917 through 1920. Following the Russian example, the Soviet Ukrainian political system was based on soviets (councils) of worker, peasant, and soldier deputies that existed in every village, city, district, and province. The All-Ukrainian Congress of Soviets (renamed the Supreme Soviet in 1927) served as a republican parliament, but it was in session only twice a year for several days. In any case, the electoral system favored workers and soldiers. Peasant votes counted for less, and former tsarist and nationalist officials, priests, and members of "exploiting classes" were disenfranchised until 1936. The government of Soviet Ukraine was called the Council of People's Commissars (the word "minister" was considered bourgeois), and it included only Bolsheviks.

Before the creation of the Soviet Union, Soviet Ukraine was linked to the Russian Socialist Federated Soviet Republic through a December 1920 treaty of economic and military assistance, which merged the republics' key ministries. But Ukraine, like Belarus and the Transcaucasian Soviet Republic, was supposed to conduct foreign affairs independently of Russia. Both Soviet Russia and Ukraine, for example, signed the 1921 Treaty of Riga, which formally ended the Polish-Soviet war. By 1922, the Bolshevik Party decided to clarify the lines of authority between the center and the republics and, in the process, establish a clear framework for Soviet nationality policy. Stalin stood for the inclusion of other republics into Soviet Russia as its autonomous units, whereas the Ukrainian leaders of the time (in particular, Khristian Rakovsky, Mykola Skrypnyk, and Volodymyr Zatonsky) defended their republic's sovereignty.[9] At the last moment, Lenin interfered to engineer the creation in December 1922 of the Union of Soviet Socialist Republics (USSR) as a federation of four, theoretically equal, national republics: the Russian Federation, Ukraine, Belarus, and the Transcaucasian Federation. (In 1929, the Kremlin carved out more national polities from the Russian and Transcaucasian federations, bringing the number of Soviet republics to nine. In 1936, their number increased to eleven.)

According to the union treaty and the 1924 constitution, all matters of military, foreign relations, foreign trade, transportation, and communications became exclusive prerogatives of the center. Republics preserved their own people's commissariats, which were empowered to deal with economic, social, and cultural affairs, although the central government gradually established all-Union structures on top of most republican ministries. The constitution proclaimed the right of every republic to secede freely from the USSR. However, the universal domination of the Bolshevik Party and Red Army effectively made secession unthinkable for the next sixty-five years. Significantly, the Russian Republic, unlike all the others, did not have a separate Communist Party organization—the All-Union Communist Party (Bolshevik) represented "Russian" interests well enough.

From its very inception, the Ukrainian Bolshevik organization's biggest problem was building an indigenous power base. The CP(B)U has been widely perceived as foreign to Ukraine. Founded as a separate party relatively late, in April 1918, by July of the same year it had a minuscule membership of 4,364 people. It grew impressively to 38,000 in 1920 and 56,000 in 1922, but these numbers are deceptive because approximately half of the membership in 1920 was Communists from Red Army units recently stationed in Ukraine. Just as before the revolution, the Bolsheviks in Ukraine tended to be ethnic Russian or Jewish urban dwellers unable to reach out to the Ukrainian peasantry. The 1922 party census recorded the growing ethnic gap between the rulers and the ruled in the republic of some 26 million people. That year, 48 percent of the republic's 56,000 Bolsheviks were serving in the Red Army, and only 14 percent of the Communists in the military were ethnic Ukrainians. Among the CP(B)U members, 23 percent recorded their ethnicity as Ukrainian, although only 11 percent knew the Ukrainian language.[10]

At the end of the Civil War, the Ukrainian political scene was slightly more heterogeneous than the Russian one, featuring some twenty political parties and organizations, including at least three different Communist parties. In addition to the CP(B)U, the latter included the Ukrainian Communist Party (Borotbists) and the Ukrainian Communist Party—both leftist splinter groups of earlier Ukrainian parties and featuring larger percentages of ethnic Ukrainians than the CP(B)U.

The two leading parties of the Ukrainian Revolution, the Ukrainian Party of Socialist Revolutionaries and the Ukrainian Social Democratic Workers' Party, both had left factions that during the Civil War allied themselves with the Bolsheviks. The numerically strong pro-Communist Socialist Revolutionaries were associated with the newspaper *Borotba* (The Struggle) and became known as the Borotbists. During the Civil War, this peasant-based party collaborated with the Bolsheviks but insisted on the wide-ranging autonomy of future Communist Ukraine. In 1919, the Borotbists constituted themselves as the Ukrainian Communist Party (Borotbists), which, with 15,000 members, was nearly as large as the CP(B)U itself. In March 1920, the Borotbists agreed to dissolve their party and join the CP(B)U on the understanding that this was the only way to preserve a separate Ukrainian republic. Of the 4,000 Borotbists who joined the Bolsheviks, all but 118 were excluded from the CP(B)U during the party purge of August 1921,[11] but many Ukrainian-speaking Marxist intellectuals from among the remaining handful would become prominent in the republic's political and cultural life during the 1920s and early 1930s.

The much smaller group that split from the Ukrainian Social Democrats early in 1919 also favored the independence of Soviet Ukraine. In January 1920, this group constituted itself as yet another Ukrainian Communist Party, called the Ukapists (from the Ukrainian abbreviation of the party's name, UKP). Never numerically strong, the party had only 200 or 300 members in the early 1920s. Its importance lay, rather, in the fact that it served as a magnet for those Communists who opposed the Bolshevik's centralist and assimilationist tendencies. Tolerated as an impotent rival, the Ukapists survived until January 1925, when most of their remaining members were admitted to the CP(B)U. This was the last legal political party in the republic other than the Bolsheviks. All other socialist parties still in existence after the Civil War were disbanded by the Bolsheviks between 1921 and 1924; in many cases, their leaders were put on trial.

Yet the autonomist trend in Ukrainian Communism did not die with the dissolution of the Borotbists and Ukapists. It soon emerged that an autonomist undercurrent was present even within the Bolshevik leadership in Ukraine. Some, like Lenin's protégé Mykola Skrypnyk, had long believed that each nation would advance to socialism through the development of its own proletarian institutions and culture. Others, like Trotsky's client Khristian Rakovsky, made a spectacular turnaround from a denial of the Ukrainian nation's very existence to a defense of the republic's interests. As the head of Soviet Ukraine's government from 1919 to 1923, Rakovsky's power and prestige were rooted in Ukrainian state institutions, economic strength, and distinct national identity. Not surprisingly, he soon turned into a protector of local interests. In particular, he actively promoted Soviet Ukraine's separate foreign relations, which resulted in the republic becoming a signatory to forty-eight international treaties and winning full diplomatic recognition from such countries as Germany, Italy, Poland, and Turkey. Both Skrypnyk and Rakovsky were among the most outspoken opponents of Stalin's plan to absorb other Soviet republics into the Russian Federation. At the Twelfth Party Congress in April 1923, Rakovsky openly clashed with Stalin over the republic's rights in the future union. Ukrainian historians have uncovered archival evidence that Rakovsky attempted to resign as Ukrainian premier after his vision of confederation was rejected.[12]

The "autonomists," however, never had a secure majority within the CP(B)U. Ever since its inception, the party had been deeply split into two or three rival regional factions. Whereas the Kharkiv-Kyiv group supported Skrypnyk, the Katerynoslav-Yuzivka[13] wing challenged the necessity of an indigenous power base in principle. The Russifiers were led by one of the secretaries of the CP(B)U Central Committee, Dmytro Lebid—a protégé of yet another powerful man in Moscow, Grigorii Zinoviev. Lebid elaborated the theory of the struggle of two cultures, arguing that the "higher" Russian culture of the urban proletariat should supplant the "backward" Ukrainian culture of villagers. The party was supposed to promote this "progressive" assimilation.[14] The factional and ideological split among Ukrainian Bolsheviks enabled the Moscow leadership to impose its agenda on the local ruling elite. This process culminated in the 1925 appointment of Stalin's trusted lieutenant, Lazar Kaganovich, as Ukraine's new party boss.

Fortunately for Ukraine, though, in 1923 the Kremlin began to promote a new agenda that encouraged national diversity. Aimed at disarming nationalism, the new policy also sought to grant legitimacy to the new Soviet republics, to build support for the Bolshevik cause among non-Russians, to educate and mobilize minorities in their own languages, and to show the world an example of a Marxist solution to the nationality problem. The result was what a present-day scholar has aptly called the "affirmative action empire."[15]

✥ Ukrainization and National Communism

In 1923, the Twelfth Party Congress in Moscow adopted the policy of indigenization, or *korenizatsiia* ("putting down roots"). Like the NEP, this policy had to be pushed through by the top leadership despite widespread opposition, especially among Russian-speaking party functionaries in the national republics. Both CP(B)U First Secretary Emmanuil Kviring and Second Secretary Dmytro Lebid sided with Russian-speaking bureaucrats. Yet, the center successfully imposed its will in Ukraine and elsewhere. Moreover, because Ukraine was the most populous non-Russian republic of the USSR, the indigenization policy—known in its application to Ukrainians as "Ukrainization"—advanced further there than in other regions.

The practical dimensions of Ukrainization included actively recruiting Ukrainians to the party and state apparatus, fostering the development of Ukrainian culture, and expanding education and publishing in Ukrainian. The Ukrainization drive began in the summer of 1923 with a series of rather unrealistic decrees, one ordering the Ukrainization of the school system within the next two years and another obliging all state employees to learn Ukrainian within one year or lose their jobs. Although such tasks could not be accomplished so quickly, the authorities did organize language courses for state employees, while simultaneously trying to increase the proportion of ethnic Ukrainians in their ranks. But the indigenization policies did not spread to book publishing and the press until the mid-1920s.

Both Kviring and Lebid, who revealed themselves as less-than-ardent Ukrainizers, were recalled to Moscow in 1925. Stalin's trusted assistant, Lazar Kaganovich, became the new chief of the CP(B)U and was given the title "General Secretary," which would be used by Ukrainian party leaders until 1934. As Kaganovich recalls in his memoirs, Stalin briefed him on the situation in Ukrainian party leadership in the following way. There are, Stalin said, seven members in the Ukrainian Politburo, but they have fourteen different opinions on every question, because each of them contradicts himself as well as the others.[16] Kaganovich handled well the challenges of his new job. A Ukrainian Jew, he spoke some Ukrainian and, more important, pursued Ukrainization vigorously as long as it was the party line. Many former Borotbists whom Lebid had purged from the CP(B)U were brought back and entrusted with responsible positions. The most prominent ex-Borotbist, Oleksandr Shumsky, became the people's commissar of education.

The energetic Kaganovich then pushed for the speedy Ukrainization of the party, state bureaucracy, education, and the press. The new, again unrealistic, deadline for the complete Ukrainization of the state apparatus was set for January 1, 1926. By 1927, however, 70 percent of the state's business was being carried out in Ukrainian—in contrast to only 20 percent in 1925. In 1927, ethnic Ukrainians for the first time constituted more than 50 percent of both party members and government officials.[17] Yet, Ukrainian historians who have examined these data in more detail argue that these numbers were achieved mainly by bringing the "native cadres" into the lower ranks of the apparatus. Of the 1,898 top-ranking Bolshevik bureaucrats in Ukraine, only 345 knew the Ukrainian language in 1926. Also, the authorities finessed these figures by defining several levels of language proficiency. In 1927, 39.8 percent of all state employees knew Ukrainian "well" and 31.7 percent "satisfactorily," which inflated the proficiency rate to the total of 71.5 percent. In practice, "satisfactory" command of the language was often a euphemism for knowing a couple of Ukrainian words.[18]

After a slow start in the early 1920s, the Ukrainization of education and the press progressed quickly in the second half of the decade, especially during Mykola Skrypnyk's tenure as the people's commissar of education from 1927 to 1933. By 1929, 83 percent of all elementary schools in the republic and 66 percent of secondary schools offered instruction in Ukrainian. An impressive 97 percent of ethnic Ukrainian students were enrolled in Ukrainian schools—a colossal achievement when compared with the tsarist ban on schooling in Ukrainian. Ukrainization proceeded at a slower pace at the college and university level, but the gains were impressive nonetheless because this process had to begin literally from scratch. The breakthrough in publishing was no less remarkable. In 1922, only 29 percent of all books printed in the republic were in Ukrainian, and the thirty newspapers in Ukrainian (most of them small-circulation local papers) were dwarfed by 102 Russian newspapers (including almost all the large-circulation press). By 1931 and 1932, 88 percent of all periodicals in the republic, including most major papers, were in Ukrainian, and 77 percent of books were published in that language.[19] Of course, this did not mean that Ukrainian books dominated the republic's book market, as three quarters of the books sold in the republic were published in Russia. Urban readers also eagerly consumed the Russian-language newspapers published in Moscow.

Overall, new research both in Ukraine and abroad questions the traditional picture of Ukrainization as a successful policy that produced cities, factories, and offices dominated by Ukrainian-speakers. Ukrainian historians now warn against "exaggerating the real results" of the policy. Their overseas colleagues argue that Ukraine's cities became bilingual rather than Ukrainian-speaking, and Russian culture continued to predominate among the working class and bureaucracy, although these now included more ethnic Ukrainians. This meant, of course, that linguistic Ukrainization was not comprehensive.[20]

But Ukrainian cultural gains should not be underestimated. Whatever their real intentions and subsequent reservations, Soviet authorities effectively sponsored the completion of the nation-building process in Ukraine by creating full-fledged national high culture, education, and administrative apparatus.

The indigenization program was intended to disarm nationalism by granting non-Russians the forms of national life but not real sovereignty. Yet, because most Soviet nationalities were also territorial entities akin to western European nations—complete with formal borders and distinct economic interests—the emergence of local elites and the use of ethnicity as an instrument of mass politics led to so-called nationalist deviations in many republics during the 1920s. People who are retrospectively labeled as "national Communists" (the term itself originated after World War II) believed that each nationality should combine the construction of socialism with nation building. Even within a single republic, national Communists never represented a united political front. Rather, national Communism existed as an underlying ideological resistance to centralization and assimilation in several high-profile incidents discussed here.

During Stalin's meeting with a delegation of Ukrainian Communists from Poland in the fall of 1925, Ukraine's Commissar of Education, Oleksandr Shumsky, suggested that the CP(B)U should be led by an ethnic Ukrainian. According to him, replacing Kaganovich with Premier Vlas Chubar would greatly enhance the party's image. In addition to questioning the political limits of Ukrainization, Shumsky criticized its slow pace, especially in industry and trade union work. Stalin reportedly answered that putting an ethnic Ukrainian at the helm of the republic was not yet expedient.[21] The party boss followed up, however, with a longer letter to the Ukrainian leadership in April 1926. He claimed to sympathize with Shumsky's concerns but rejected the Ukrainian minister's proposals. The forcible Ukrainization of the Russian or assimilated proletariat in Ukraine was unacceptable, for it could provoke the workers' alienation from the party and the growth of ethnic hostility. It was also unnecessary, because in the long run, the influx of Ukrainian peasants into the expanding industrial sector would surely change the national composition of the Ukrainian working class. Stalin also warned that, without party supervision, all-out Ukrainization might evolve into a struggle against the Russian culture and "its highest achievement, Leninism."[22]

Taking their cue from Moscow, Stalin loyalists in Ukraine organized the campaign against Shumsky. During 1926 and 1927, he was publicly criticized as a "deviationist" and removed from all positions of responsibility. While Shumsky found little open support within the CP(B)U, the Ukrainian Communists in Polish-held eastern Galicia did not fear expressing solidarity with his views. The Communist Party of Western Ukraine even raised the matter, unsuccessfully, before the Communist International.

As the Bolsheviks were busily denouncing "Shumskyism" at home and abroad, a new "nationalist deviation" emerged in Soviet Ukraine. In 1928, a young economist by the name of Mykhailo Volobuiev published two controversial articles in the official journal of the CP(B)U, *Bilshovyk Ukrainy* (The Bolshevik of Ukraine). He argued that first the tsars and now the Soviet central planners in Moscow subjected Ukraine to colonial exploitation. According to him, in the mid-1920s, the Soviet government was collecting about 20 percent more in taxes than it spent in the republic, while the investment funds raised in Ukraine were used to construct new factories far away in the Urals. Volobuiev asserted that the Ukrainian economy was a distinct entity, which the republic's leadership should completely control, because only economic independence could overcome the legacy of colonialism. Party ideologues forced Volobuiev to repudiate his views, but the fact that he was allowed to contribute such a discussion piece to the party's official journal was in itself significant.[23]

Manifestations of national Communism abounded in particular in culture and scholarship. In 1925, the leading prose writer of the decade, Mykola Khvylovy, called upon the Ukrainian creative intelligentsia to adopt a European artistic orientation. Condemning provincialism and the imitation of Russian cultural models, he coined the scandalously famous slogan, "Away from Moscow!"[24] Stalin himself took the time to dismiss Khvylovy's views in his 1926 letter to the CP(B)U Central Committee and to condemn the writer for his demand that the Ukrainian intelligentsia turn westward. After this letter, Khvylovy was subjected to relentless criticism and forced to denounce his views.

In 1928, the authorities denounced as "deviationist" another leading party intellectual, the head of the Ukrainian Institute of Marxism-Leninism, Matvii Yavorsky. He considered the revolution in Ukraine not only a part of the Russian Revolution but also a product of the Ukrainian people's struggle for their liberation. The party leadership accused Yavorsky of inventing a distinct Ukrainian revolutionary movement, expelled him from the party, and initiated a general investigation of other possible nationalist deviations in Ukrainian historical scholarship.[25]

Finally, the case of Mykola Skrypnyk demonstrates the complexity of ideological struggles during the 1920s. As a prominent Ukrainian statesman in the 1920s, he was both an active promoter of Ukrainization and the first critic of the "national deviationists" Shumsky and Khvylovy. Present-day scholars rightly see Skrypnyk as the leading Ukrainian national Communist but have trouble reconciling these two sides of his work.[26] Although retrospectively Skrypnyk is placed among national Communists, it is helpful to emphasize that during the 1920s he did not see himself as an ally of Shumsky, Khvylovy, Volobuiev, and others—nor was he seen as such by the party leadership. Only after the political fault lines changed in the early 1930s did he become stigmatized as a nationalist deviationist.

Although the heights of Ukrainization were still to come, attacks on national Communists during the late 1920s indicated the party's more stringent line on Ukrainian nation building. Scholars have long explained this change as Ukrainization advancing too far for the Kremlin's liking, but new research connects it to the political (rather than social) consequences of Ukrainization—above all, to the development of national Communism.[27] Whatever the cause, the authorities reacted harshly. During the party purge in 1929, special commissions expelled 24,204 party members, or 9.8 percent of the CP(B)U's total membership, including a great number of national Communists.[28]

Parallel to the Ukrainization drive for ethnic Ukrainians, the program of indigenization also benefited Ukraine's numerous national minorities. By

1931, twenty-five nationality districts and more than a thousand nationality village councils were established in places compactly settled by Russians, Jews, Germans, Poles, Bulgarians, Greeks, Czechs, Albanians, Moldovans, Belarusians, and Swedes.[29] Within these enclaves, the minorities had the right to use their own language in courts and the administration. Education and the press in minority languages flourished in both nationality areas and larger multicultural cities. Many Russians, as the former dominant nationality of the empire, were vexed by both Ukrainization and the creation of administrative units for other nationalities, yet for the minorities the policy of indigenization opened up exciting avenues of unhindered cultural development. By the late 1920s, especially notable were the revival of the Yiddish-language culture of Ukraine's 1.6 million Jews and the Tatar renaissance in Crimea. (The Crimean peninsula, although adjacent to Ukraine, was administratively attached to the Russian republic until 1954.)

❖ Society and Culture in the 1920s

Although the Ukrainization of cities remained incomplete, it was accompanied by important social changes. The number of urban dwellers increased steadily from 4.2 million in 1920 to the prewar total of 5.6 million in 1928, and the growth was mainly due to migration from the countryside. As a result, the share of ethnic Ukrainians among the urban population grew from 33 percent in 1920 to 47 percent in 1926. For Ukrainian peasants arriving in big cities during the 1920s, the move no longer meant assimilation into Russian culture. The de facto bilingualism in Ukraine's cities meant that they were no longer outposts of Russian language and culture stranded in a Ukrainian peasant sea. A villager moving there during the late 1920s would have found Ukrainian street signs, posters, theaters, schools, and even Ukrainian-speaking bureaucrats and police to deal with. According to one memoirist, even prostitutes in big cities began speaking Ukrainian![30]

The number of industrial workers grew from 260,000 after the Civil War to 675,000 in 1927, and the majority of new recruits were ethnic Ukrainian peasants taking up jobs in industry. Although published data vary, sometime in the late 1920s, ethnic Ukrainians came to constitute the majority of the republic's working class—a momentous change for the traditionally "peasant nation."[31] On one of the landmark Soviet projects of the time, a gigantic hydroelectric dam on the Dnipro called Dniprohes, two thirds of the workforce was Ukrainian. Ukrainization programs slowed down the assimilation of workers into Russian culture, for the first time producing a Ukrainian working class with some degree of national consciousness. It did not, however, become a support base for nationalists or even national Communists, for by then the Bolsheviks completely dominated the ideological sphere.

The standard of living improved very slowly during the 1920s. Party and state bureaucracy enjoyed privileges owing to their status, as did the numerous petty entrepreneurs of the NEP era, the so-called nepmen, owing to their business success. The proletariat, in whose name the battles of the Civil War were fought, seems to have gained little in the promised brave new world. Most workers toiled ten-hour shifts for inadequate wages. Urban dwellings remained overcrowded, as almost everyone lived in "communal apartments" where each room was occupied by a separate family. Before the industrialization drive begun in the late 1920s, unemployment had been a major problem in Ukraine's cities, which were also plagued by crime and a growing number of beggars. Partly to alleviate the population's misery, in 1924 the authorities lifted the ten-year prohibition on hard liquor, which the tsarist government had introduced at the beginning of World War I. Instead of moonshine, the thirsty populace consumed the traditional vodka, while the treasury greatly benefited from the state monopoly on the production of this alcoholic beverage. Although the authorities encouraged workers to attend the theater, it was cinema that really became the mass entertainment of the time, with the public preferring Western movies to early Soviet films. Spectator sports, especially the future national sport of soccer, did not develop in earnest until the mid-1930s.

Rural life changed even less. The peasants owned more land than ever, but they were overtaxed and did not have urban consumers' access to goods and services. Mass culture arrived in the countryside about 1925 in the form of radio loudspeakers, which became the principal medium of conveying political information. Early Soviet legislation guaranteed women full civic equality, but most of those who took advantage of the new educational and career prospects were young urban women. During the 1920s, the state did not make much progress with political mobilization of Ukrainian peasant women, most of whom regarded the progressive laws that legalized abortion and made divorce easy as threats to traditional family life.

Although much weakened under Bolshevik pressure, Orthodox Christianity and other religions still held sway over the majority of Ukraine's population during the 1920s. Seeking to undermine the dominant Russian Orthodox Church, the state was more tolerant toward its splinter groups, in particular the "Living Church" and the Ukrainian Autocephalous (i.e., independent) Orthodox Church (UAOC). A belated result of the Directory's 1919 decree, the UAOC was officially established in May 1920. Lacking support from properly consecrated bishops, the new church had to bend canon law in ordaining its original hierarchy and priests, who were later considered "illegitimate" by other Orthodox churches. With the silent support of the authorities, however, the UAOC took over numerous church buildings, including the majestic St. Sophia Cathedral in Kyiv, and introduced the Ukrainian language in church services where Church Slavonic had reigned before. But as much as they wanted to undermine the Russian Orthodox Church in Ukraine, the Bolsheviks had no intention of creating another strong religious organization in its place. As the UAOC gained popular following, in the late 1920s, the government imposed heavy taxes on its parishes and ousted the head of the church, Metropolitan Vasyl Lypkivsky, from office.

A combination of the Soviet emphasis on mass education and the Ukrainization policies fueled an impressive cultural flowering during the mid- to late 1920s. The Bolsheviks' plan to eliminate illiteracy by 1927 proved too ambitious, but in that year more than 70 percent of urban dwellers and more than 50 percent of villagers could read and write—compared with the aggregate literacy rate of 28 percent in 1897. As in other parts of the Soviet Union, the 1920s witnessed radical experiments with school curriculum and forms of instruction, as well as the replacement of "bourgeois" universities with so-called Institutes of People's Education. Unlike in other republics, though, Ukrainian authorities made considerable progress in the Ukrainization of higher learning. In 1927, knowledge of Ukrainian became mandatory for both college-level admission and graduation; in 1928, 42 percent of students received instruction in Ukrainian. Impressed with the advances of Ukrainization, many distinguished scholars returned from abroad. In 1924, Mykhailo Hrushevsky came back to Kyiv to head the Historical and Philological Section at the Academy of Sciences.

During the NEP years, the Soviet authorities generally tolerated freedom of artistic expression as long as it did not openly contradict the regime's ideology. The official "soft line on culture," combined with state-sponsored Ukrainization, resulted in one of the most creative and experimental periods in the history of Ukrainian culture.[32] A cohort of brilliant young poets, including Pavlo Tychyna, Maksym Rylsky, and Volodymyr Sosiura, won the hearts of the growing Ukrainian reading public. The painters Mykhailo Boichuk and Anatol Petrytsky developed the native modernist artistic style. The composers Borys Liatoshynsky and Lev Revutsky shaped a symphonic genre previously absent in Ukrainian music. The experimental theater of the young director Les Kurbas was acclaimed by the public, while the genius of the film director Alexander Dovzhenko won international recognition. Because of cinema's influence on the masses, the Bolsheviks tried to manipulate this art to serve ideological indoctrination. Dovzhenko's silent movies, however, succeeded as art despite their massive and largely inefficient—because the audiences were confused by the director's metaphoric images—propaganda content. His trademark poetic and symbolist style is evident even in *Earth* (1930), a film commissioned to promote collective agriculture but ranked by an international jury at a Brussels world fair in 1958 as one of the ten best movies of all time.[33]

The artistic level of the Ukrainian revival was uneven, though. Dozens of newly minted "proletarian writers" produced ideologically correct trash; others freely borrowed yesterday's topics from Russian literature. The sophisticated literary products of the Ukrainian symbolists, futurists, and neoclassicists were often published next to third-rate propaganda scribblings. The pro-Bolshevik mass literary organization Pluh (The Plow) made a point of promoting proletarian literature through a network of writing workshops for peasants. Other literary groups looked for ways to develop a new, socialist culture without compromising artistic standards. In 1925, Mykola Khvylovy united a group of Marxist writers and "fellow travelers" into VAPLITE (the Ukrainian acronym for the Free Academy of Proletarian Literature). The members of this literary organization insisted on maintaining high artistic standards; in search of cultural models, they turned to western Europe rather than Russia, inspired by Khvylovy's controversial motto, "Away from Moscow." But no less intense was the internal discussion among writers about ways of developing new Ukrainian culture.[34]

Having condemned Khvylovy, the party leadership found it desirable to strengthen the loyalist Ukrainian branch of the All-Union Association of Proletarian Writers. The authorities turned this organization into their literary mouthpiece, while undermining all others, and slowly increased their ideological control over culture. For the time being, the Bolsheviks were unaware of the dangers inherent in the full-fledged Ukrainian high culture that developed on their watch and with their active help.

❖

An innovative and contradictory period marked by ambiguous state policies, the 1920s in Soviet Ukraine was ultimately a time of unfulfilled promises. The economic freedom and social diversity associated with the NEP turned out to be the Bolsheviks' concessions to the market and society that they could not yet subdue. The policy of Ukrainization, which the national Communists saw as transforming their republic into a socialist polity for ethnic Ukrainians, demonstrated the party's more pragmatic effort at disarming nationalism and reaching out to the population in its native tongue. State-sponsored

Ukrainization completed the process of national mobilization, which had begun in the Russian Empire, but it mobilized the Ukrainian masses for the task of socialist construction. Concerned about Ukrainization's political consequences, such as "national Communism," by the end of the decade Stalinist bureaucrats were reconsidering their affirmative action policies. Ukrainian culture, meanwhile, flourished in an atmosphere of relative freedom and state support, a climate that would not last long.

Stalinism: Famine and Terror

Since the mid-1920s, the Bolshevik leadership, frustrated by the economic and social ambiguities of the NEP, had been discussing ways to resume the country's advance toward socialism. In the debates about how to transform Soviet society, Joseph Stalin first sided with the moderates Nikolai Bukharin and Aleksei Rykov to defeat his opponents on the left but then adopted a leftist call for rapid industrialization at the expense of the peasantry. In the process, he denounced his erstwhile allies as ringleaders of the "right opposition." The party leadership in the Ukrainian republic sided with Stalin no matter what his position. When in mid-1928 Kaganovich returned to Moscow, he was replaced as the Ukrainian party boss by Stanislav Kosior, an ethnic Pole and an experienced party bureaucrat who had worked both in Ukraine and in Moscow. A Stalin loyalist, Kosior faithfully supported his patron during the ideological struggles of the late 1920s. Like other regional branches of the Bolshevik Party, in 1929 the Ukrainian party organization underwent a purge of "rightists," resulting in the expulsion of 24,000 (almost 10 percent) of Ukrainian Communists.[1]

As a result, by his fiftieth birthday, which was celebrated with great fanfare in 1929, Stalin emerged as the unchallenged leader of the USSR.[2] Prompted by a series of real and perceived crises—the imaginary threat of foreign invasion, the slackening of industrial growth because of the lack of large investments, and difficulties with the collection of grain—he launched a program of radical social transformation that the Soviets called the "great breakthrough" and later scholars dubbed "Stalin's revolution from above."

A combination of large-scale industrialization, forced collectivization of agriculture, and the suppression of "bourgeois" culture changed the face of the Soviet Union in general and Soviet Ukraine in particular. In pushing their country into the industrial age, the Bolsheviks relied on state coercion and control that also helped establish a Stalinist political system. Intensive industrialization and urban growth transformed Ukraine's social fabric by making Ukrainians more modern, but modern in the Soviet sense. Collectivization and the Famine of 1932 and 1933 destroyed the Ukrainian peasantry as a social force capable of resisting the authorities. The Terror eliminated the indigenous political class. The repeated cleansing of the

Ukrainian intelligentsia, which began in 1930, undermined the national culture and instilled Stalinist cultural values that included the preeminent role of Russian culture in the USSR. By the end of the decade, the state had abandoned the policy of Ukrainization and destroyed the cultural life of Ukraine's national minorities. The Stalin regime, however, preserved the Ukrainian republic's political and cultural institutions, now totally devoid of sovereignty and initiative.

✸✸ The First Five-Year Plan

At the heart of the Stalinist economic transformation was the substitution of state planning for market relations. With the dismantling of NEP, the state took over the economy and converted itself into a gigantic and highly centralized corporation managing both production and distribution of goods. In the Soviet "command economy," central planning was supposed to demonstrate its advantages over the chaos of capitalist economies. In reality, Moscow could effectively control only the output figures. The system of a state-owned economy required a huge bureaucracy, but it did not promote quality or innovation.

In addition, planning itself was more of a slogan than reality. In 1928, Gosplan (state planning commission) drafted a five-year plan for accelerated economic growth, but policy makers revised its targets upward so many times that its original purpose was lost. Retroactively approved by a party conference in the spring of 1929, the first five-year plan (1928–1932) was revised repeatedly, evolving from an ambitious program to a set of entirely fantastic goals. For instance, the party leadership kept raising the targets of annual industrial growth from 16 percent (1928) to 22 percent (early 1929) to 32 percent (late 1929) to 45 percent (1931). These were symbolic goals meant for public consumption, and the official propaganda was used to motivate the population. In reality, the proper computation of official figures would yield an average annual industrial growth of less than 16 percent and today's scholars consider even this number inflated. In Ukraine, the targets for coal extraction in the Donbas were raised from 27 to 53 to 80 million tons per year, but the actual figure reported in 1933 was 45 million tons. The production of cast iron in the republic was to increase from 2.4 million tons to 6.6 million but actually went up to 4.3 million tons.[3] These corrections notwithstanding, Ukraine's industrial growth was impressive.

The first five-year plan emphasized the development of heavy industry, and the Ukrainian republic became its showcase. After intense lobbying, the Ukrainian leadership managed to secure for the republic the status of a primary industrialization region, which brought with it major financial allocations. Measured in 1928 rubles, total state investments in Ukrainian industry grew from 438 million in 1929 to 1,229 million in 1932.[4] Of some 1,500 new Soviet industrial plants constructed during the first five-year plan, 400 were begun in the Ukrainian SSR. Built between 1927 and 1932, the mammoth Dniprohes hydroelectric dam on the Dnipro—Europe's largest—became the poster image for Soviet industrialization. The press devoted an equal amount of attention to celebrating the new smokestack industry in Ukraine, in particular the giant Kharkiv tractor factory and Zaporizhzhia steel mill. Costing 933 million rubles, the latter was the most expensive construction project in interwar Ukraine.[5]

There was little industrial construction on the Right Bank, which the authorities viewed as a potential theater of war in the event of a conflict with Poland or Germany. Generally, most capital investments were channeled into the traditional industrial areas in the Donbas and the lower Dnipro region, with such cities as Dnipropetrovsk, Kryvyi Rih, and Zaporizhzhia reaping the greatest benefits. In addition to regional economic imbalances, some contemporary Ukrainian specialists were concerned about the republic's general economic profile. In 1932, a conference of Ukrainian economists passed a resolution criticizing the continuing practice of exporting raw materials to the Russian republic and importing finished goods from there. Apparently, the central planners envisioned Ukraine as the Soviet hub of coal extraction and ferrous metallurgy. In 1932, Ukraine supplied about 70 percent of the USSR's coal, iron ore, and pig iron—but only 23 percent of the country's finished metal products.[6] There was even less local production of consumer goods. In general, Stalinist centralization soon led to the Ukrainian economy's direct subordination to Moscow. In 1927, the republic controlled 81 percent of the industry in Ukraine, but by 1932, this figure dropped to 38 percent.[7]

The breakneck tempo of industrialization, combined with the suspension of market mechanisms and fixation on gross output figures, led to inefficiency and poor quality. The press blamed chronic faulty construction, breakage, and bottlenecks on resistance from "old specialists" educated under the tsarist regime. Beginning with the 1928 show trial of fifty-three engineers accused of "wrecking" (sabotage) in the mining town of Shakhty in the Donbas (on the Russian side of the Ukrainian-Russian border), the authorities silenced engineers and planners who were arguing for a more reasonable rate of industrial development. When in early 1933 Stalin announced that the first five-year plan had been fulfilled at the end of 1932, no one dared to dispute his figures. Even if the official numbers were greatly inflated, however, Western scholars' estimates of 50 percent industrial growth from 1928 to 1932 put the speed of

Stalin's industrialization on par with the post–World War II economic boom in Japan and West Germany. As a result of the first five-year plan, Soviet Ukraine turned into a major industrial power.

In the second (1933–1937) and third (1938–1941; unfinished because of World War II) five-year plans, the Ukrainian republic's share of investments dropped once the Kremlin began spending heavily on industrial construction in Siberia. In Ukraine, the emphasis was shifted to the development of transportation, machine building, and the chemical industry. According to official Soviet data, after 1932, Ukraine lagged behind the Russian republic in industrial growth. By 1940, industrial production in Soviet Ukraine had increased 7.3 times in comparison with the 1913 figure, although in the USSR as a whole, it increased 7.6 times and in the Russian Federation, 8.9 times.[8] Even so, on the eve of World War II, Ukraine became one of Europe's leading industrial regions. In terms of the volume, if not the quality, of the metal and machines produced, it was ahead of France and Italy and almost achieved parity with the United Kingdom.

The capital needed for industrialization had been squeezed out of the peasantry, and the Ukrainian countryside felt the full impact of low grain prices and the compulsory deliveries that allowed the state to sell grain abroad and feed the cities cheaply. But urban dwellers were no better off than peasants, because the government needed to keep down consumption in order to invest a larger share of the national product in heavy industry. In 1928, the Soviet leadership restored food rationing in the cities, which lasted until the mid-1930s. Nor was the housing situation a priority for a state that prioritized machinery above social conditions. Beginning especially in 1930, the in-migration of new workers from the countryside exacerbated existing social tensions in the cities already crammed with workers and urbanites living in communal apartments, crowded dormitories, and makeshift shacks.

The rapid growth of cities and industrial towns was of particular significance in Ukraine, where the majority of workers and city dwellers had historically been ethnic Russians and Jews. Rapid industrialization created a labor shortage, prompting peasants to seek a better life in industrial centers and on construction sites. During the 1930s, the percentage of ethnic Ukrainians among the republic's industrial workers increased from 52 to 66 percent. The legacy of tsarist times, when the division of labor coincided with ethnic boundaries, was finally overcome. Even more impressive were the advances ethnic Ukrainians made in the cities. Between 1926 and 1939, the republic's urban population ballooned from 5.4 to 11.2 million, and by 1939, ethnic Ukrainians, at 58 percent, were a clear majority in cities and towns.[9]

Western scholars have previously interpreted these statistics as an indication of ethnic Ukrainians' impressive "social mobilization" during the late 1920s and early 1930s. But there is no evidence that these figures translated into increased self-assertiveness on the part of the Ukrainian working class. Party functionaries certainly did not encounter any nationalist resistance on the factory floor. If anything, the authorities were frustrated by their inability to control the massive influx of people to the cities or to curb huge rates of labor turnover.[10] In December 1932, the government introduced internal passports and a system of residence permits in the cities. To combat worker migration and absenteeism, it passed tough new laws on "labor discipline." The authorities also found the low productivity of labor frustrating. Their first response was to institute "socialist competition" between enterprises and among brigades within each factory, with the winners receiving red banners and some material rewards. Two mines in the Donbas had the distinction of being the first enterprises in the Soviet Union to challenge each other to a "socialist competition." Searching for better material stimuli for workers, in 1931 the Soviet leadership abandoned the Communist principle of wage equality. Henceforth, skilled workers and "shock workers" who regularly overfulfilled their norms received better salaries, rations, and bonuses, which reduced labor turnover during the second five-year plan.

✸ War on the Peasants

A self-proclaimed party of industrial workers, the Bolsheviks always distrusted peasants as independent small producers with "petit-bourgeois instincts." The revolutionaries dreamed of one day eliminating that major obstacle to socialism, private landholding, which had a much stronger tradition in Ukraine than in Russian provinces, where a peasant commune had long held sway over village life. The NEP forced the Bolsheviks to put on hold their experiments with state farms and agricultural communes, but they never abandoned their plans for a future socialist transformation of agriculture. Collective and state farms, which had been created on a voluntary basis during the early 1920s, attracted only the very poorest, some 3 percent of rural households. In 1927 and 1928, the government stepped up the campaign for voluntary collectivization, but in Ukraine fewer than 6 percent of peasant households joined collective farms, and they brought with them less than 4 percent of arable land. It is little wonder that in the original draft of the first five-year plan, Soviet economic planners envisaged the collectivization of only 12 percent of the land under cultivation in the Ukrainian SSR.

Stalin and his associates abandoned this cautious approach to collectivization after a crisis of their own creation. The government financed industrialization by keeping grain prices low in order to maximize gains from grain exports and minimize rationing expenditures within the country. But the laws of the market turned against the Bolsheviks. Beginning in 1927, the peasants started switching to the cultivation of other crops; they also hoarded grain, although not nearly on the scale the Kremlin imagined. Unwilling to give up his grand vision of industrialization, Stalin initiated a campaign of coercion, which slightly improved grain deliveries. As the crisis dragged on, forced closures of markets and the requisitioning of grain once again became the norm, just as they had been during the Civil War. By February 1929, having defeated Bukharin and other economic moderates, Stalin was about to begin a socialist offensive against the countryside. As the Soviet Union's traditional breadbasket, Ukraine would suffer disproportionately.

After increased coercion yielded even better grain deliveries in 1929, in the fall of that year, Stalin called for the all-out collectivization of agriculture. The Kremlin revised the timetable for Ukraine twice, first estimating the collectivization of 30 percent of households by 1932, but soon escalating its demands to 100 percent by the end of 1930. During the winter of 1929–1930, the government dispatched to the countryside tens of thousands of workers, soldiers, and party activists who declared one village after another "collectivized." Most peasants were bullied into submission under the threat of repressions and prospects of higher taxes and grain procurements if they did not join.

In the language typical of the time, the Stalinists presented the campaign for the all-out socialization of the countryside as a class war, a crusade against the rich peasants or kulaks. Because the term "kulak" (*kurkul* in Ukrainian) had never been clearly defined, anyone resisting collectivization could be branded one. The press proclaimed that kulaks were wealthy peasants who exploited hired labor, but in reality, many of those who were hiring help were disabled war veterans, widows, and families with a number of small children. A peasant whom Soviet statisticians classified as "wealthy" had an income less than half of an average worker's salary. But the authorities needed to punish one group of "enemies" to subdue the rest of the peasant mass. In 1929, an official survey using economic criteria classified only 73,000 peasant households in the republic as kulak, but the state ended up confiscating property from more than twice this number. In 1934, the Ukrainian authorities announced the "dekulakization" of 200,000 households, roughly a million peasants.[11] The government divided kulaks into three categories: anti-Soviet activists, who were to be shot, imprisoned, or exiled; rich exploiters, who were to lose all their property and be exiled; and politically harmless kulaks, who as politically unreliable were forbidden to join collective farms and had to accept inferior land in the vicinity. Those who were subject to deportation were rounded up and jammed into railroad cars heading for Siberia, Central Asia, and the Soviet Pacific region. The mortality rate was staggering, especially among peasants who were dumped in frozen Siberia and the Soviet Arctic and abandoned to fend for themselves. Present-day scholars estimate that in 1930 the Soviet authorities deported some 75,000 "kulak" families from Ukraine. The available number for the first half of 1931 stands at 23,500 families.[12]

The campaign against the kulaks did not remove the source of peasant resistance to forced collectivization. Local revolts in Ukraine included one in Chernihiv province, where the soldiers of the Twenty-First Red Army Regiment joined the peasants. Between February 20 and April 2, 1930, alone, the authorities registered 1,716 anti-Soviet incidents in the Ukrainian countryside. During the first three months of that year, peasant resistance resulted in 46 Soviet officials being killed, 84 wounded, and 763 physically assaulted. Women's riots were widespread because peasant women felt that the authorities would not politicize their actions to the same degree as men's resistance.[13] But most peasants opted for passive forms of defiance, such as fleeing to the cities or slaughtering their farm animals rather than surrendering them to collective farms. During the first five-year plan, the republic lost half of its livestock; the number of pigs declined from 7 to 2 million.

As in other parts of the USSR, minor officials in Ukraine often opposed the violent methods of collectivization. During 1930, the authorities dismissed about a fifth of lower-rank administrators in the republic on charges of "right deviationism." Even Oleksandr Shlikhter, the people's commissar of agriculture in Ukraine and a respected old Bolshevik who had joined the revolutionary movement in 1891, spoke against the administrative excesses during a Ukrainian Central Committee meeting in November 1929. The republic's leadership quietly retired the old Bolshevik to an academic position.

In early March 1930, just as chaos and violence in the countryside reached a high point, Stalin unexpectedly called a halt to the forced collectivization. He published a hypocritical article in the party's main newspaper, *Pravda* (Truth), in which he shifted the responsibility for coercion onto overzealous local functionaries and announced that the socialization of the land should be strictly voluntary. During the spring and summer of 1930, half of the peasants who had been herded into collective farms spontaneously decollectivized. Between March and October, the share of collectively tilled land in Ukraine fell from 71 percent to 34 percent of the total.

The Kremlin, however, renewed its offensive in the fall of 1930. By manipulating taxes and delivery obligations, it soon made private farming practically impossible. In 1932, taxes on individual farms in Ukraine outpaced their average profit, which resulted in the share of collectivized households jumping to 70 percent and arable land belonging to collective farms, to 80 percent.[14] By the mid-1930s, practically all land under cultivation in the republic was collectivized or owned by the state.

For ideological reasons, the Bolsheviks favored large state farms (*radhospy*; Russian: *sovkhozy*), which were essentially agricultural factories with staff classified as workers rather than peasants. But in the early 1930s, the state did not have the resources to create them everywhere. The overwhelming majority of Ukrainian peasants, therefore, joined collective farms (*kolhospy*; Russian: *kolkhozy*). Twenty-three thousand strong by the end of 1932, collective farms were ostensibly voluntary cooperatives that delivered set quotas of produce to the state and distributed the remainder among their members in accordance with the number of worked "labor days."

The official propaganda exalted collective farming for its alleged high level of mechanization and resultant productivity gains. In fact, before World War II, there was hardly any increase in the production of food grains, and Soviet tractors looked like reliable machines only in propaganda films. (And even there, as in Alexander Dovzhenko's celebrated film *Earth*, village activists are seen urinating in the tractor's cooling system to get it working.) During the 1932 harvest, Ukraine had on average one tractor per collective farm; by August, 70 percent of tractors in Dnipropetrovsk province were inoperative. Rather than distributing tractors to collective farms, the authorities preferred concentrating them and other machinery at machine and tractor stations (MTSs). With their trained repair teams and complement of propagandists, the MTSs, numbering 594 by the end of 1932, projected into the Ukrainian countryside an image of Soviet modernity as industrial and intensely ideological.

Forced collectivization, which was carried out in the Ukrainian SSR more rapidly and violently than in other Soviet regions that were viewed as less important granaries, created chaos in agriculture. Because of unusually favorable weather conditions in 1930, a good harvest of 23.1 million tons of grain (or 27 percent of the Soviet Union's total harvest) concealed the transformation's early debilitating effects. But the all-Union government squeezed Ukraine disproportionately by taking from the republic 7.7 million tons or 38 percent of the grain consigned in the USSR. Although the 1931 harvest was smaller, at 18.3 million tons, the Kremlin set the republic's grain quota at the same figure of 7.7 million and used the army and the police to ensure grain collection. The government managed to collect some 7 million tons in Ukraine, but it left the peasants with hardly enough grain to survive the winter and only half the seed grain needed for the following year. Ukrainian officials pleaded with Moscow to lower the quota for 1932, and it was indeed revised downward to 6.2 million tons.[15]

The 1932 harvest, however, was considerably lower than the two previous harvests—only 14.6 million tons. Scholars have cited various reasons for such a decline: the drought in 1931, the disruption of agriculture because of collectivization, the peasants' lack of enthusiasm in the collective farm fields, and even infestations from crop diseases that contemporaries had not recognized. Although all of these factors probably contributed to the Famine of 1932 and 1933, most Western and Ukrainian historians now agree that the Famine was caused primarily by the Kremlin's ruthless policy of grain procurement. In addition to meeting the regime's economic aims—the Soviet planners apparently overestimated the harvest, resulting in pressure on local authorities to deliver more than was possible—this strategy reflected the government's desire to suppress peasant resistance to its policies.

The Ukrainian peasants were already starving in the fall of 1932, when troops and party activists descended on the countryside to ensure the fulfillment of the republic's grain quota. Recent archival research and oral history projects provide terrifying glimpses of the last kernels of grain (and last morsels of food) being taken from villages during violent house-to-house searches, swollen children dying from malnutrition, and even cases of cannibalism.[16] The authorities preferred to believe that the peasants were hoarding grain on a large scale and continued the searches even as whole villages were dying out. After August 1932, even the smallest theft of property from collective farms carried the death penalty. The introduction of the passport system in the same year prevented starving peasants from escaping to the cities, and the Russian-Ukrainian border was sealed off, lest the Famine victims flee to the Russian republic. Starving peasants tried to escape into nearby cities, and their corpses lined Ukraine's roads.

The Famine was at its height in early 1933, when the Kremlin castigated the republic's leadership for its "lack of vigilance." New research shows that Stalin linked the grain-requisitioning crisis to alleged Ukrainian nationalist infiltration of the party that was made possible by Ukrainization.[17] This conclusion had dire consequences for the Ukrainization policies, but it also explains the government's murderous ruthlessness in carrying out grain procurements in the starving republic. For the Stalinists, peasant resistance in Ukraine, whether real or imagined, was associated with Ukrainian nationalism.

During 1932 and 1933, the USSR continued to export Ukrainian grain abroad and refused relief offers from foreign "capitalists." The Soviet government denied all reports about the Famine, and such prominent Western journalists as Walter Duranty, then a Moscow-based reporter for the *New York Times*, willingly assisted in the cover-up while asserting privately that Famine victims numbered in the millions.[18] According to Stanislav Kulchytsky, the leading economic historian of twentieth-century Ukraine, between 3 and 3.5 million people in the republic died of starvation and malnutrition-related diseases, and the total demographic losses, including a Famine-related reduction in the number of children born, can be estimated at between 4.5 and 4.8 million people.[19] In present-day Ukraine, the Famine of 1932 and 1933 (usually referred to in Ukrainian as *Holodomor*, or terror-famine) is mourned officially as the greatest national tragedy, an act of ideologically motivated mass murder similar to the Holocaust and the Armenian Genocide.[20]

✸ The Great Terror

Stalinist social transformations of the late 1920s and early 1930s included the so-called Cultural Revolution, which manifested itself in the suppression of "bourgeois" culture and the purge of old specialists. Paralleling developments in the Russian republic, the attacks in Ukraine began with a denunciation of engineers, which soon developed into a purge of writers and a reform of the Academy of Sciences. Unlike in Russia, however, in Ukraine the Cultural Revolution evolved into a crusade against "nationalist deviations," which lasted throughout most of the 1930s. Owing to the combination of all-Union campaigns with local purges, the republic experienced more waves of mass arrests than Russia. The year 1937 symbolized the Stalinist terror for all Soviet citizens, but in Ukraine there were two such years, 1933 and 1937.

The beginnings of the Terror date back to the spring of 1930, when the republic's authorities staged a show trial of the fictitious Union for the Liberation of Ukraine. (An organization with a similar name did exist during World War I, but it was long since defunct.) Held in the Kharkiv opera theater and broadcast over the radio, the trial was used to compromise the old Ukrainian intelligentsia. The prosecution accused its representatives of plotting to separate Ukraine from the Soviet Union, organizing resistance to collectivization, and even conspiring to kill Stalin. The forty-five leading scholars and writers who were put on trial included the alleged head of the organization, Serhii Yefremov, vice president of the Academy of Sciences and a prominent literary scholar. All but nine of the accused were indicted and imprisoned. Most of them were never heard from again.

The majority of the defendants belonged to the generation that had developed modern Ukrainian culture during the revolution and the 1920s. Many were associated with the Ukrainian Autocephalous Orthodox Church. A simultaneous attack on the UAOC began just before the trial. The church was forced to dissolve itself, and all but two of its thirty-four bishops were arrested between 1930 and 1934.

The show trial also discredited the Ukrainian Academy of Sciences, which the authorities purged, in the process abolishing many of its research institutes, among them Hrushevsky's history section. The security police accused both Hrushevsky and his main Marxist critic, Matvii Yavorsky, of participation in a nebulous Ukrainian National Center, which it "uncovered" in 1931. Former members of the Ukrainian Party of Socialist Revolutionaries, students of Hrushevsky, and Galician émigrés were the majority of those who were indicted in this case. Hrushevsky was also arrested and, under pressure from the investigators, even admitted to being a member of the fictitious organization. But the higher authorities eventually decided not to include him in this case—possibly saving him for future trial. The aging historian was released and transferred to Moscow, where he continued his scholarly work under close police supervision. Hrushevsky died in Russia in 1934. From the labor camps, his nemesis Yavorsky wrote courageous letters denouncing Stalinism and was executed in 1937.[21]

Late in 1932, when Stalin became convinced that the difficulties with grain procurement were the work of Ukrainian nationalists, the Kremlin issued a decree warning against the nationalists' use of Ukrainization as a cover-up. The same resolution abolished Ukrainization in the areas of compact Ukrainian settlement in the Russian republic.[22] The policy of Ukrainization within Ukraine was never officially abolished, but an unspoken retreat from it began in 1933. In January 1933, Stalin dispatched to the republic his envoy Pavel Postyshev, who became the second secretary of the Ukrainian Central Committee and was charged with ensuring grain collection and stamping out "nationalist counterrevolution." At the height of the Famine, Postyshev could not do much about the former, but he did order the removal of 237 district party secretaries (out of 525) and had most of them arrested.[23] His major success, however, was bringing down the most prominent advocate of Ukrainization, Mykola Skrypnyk, who was people's commissar of education until February 1933. After official criticism of his policies developed into an open campaign of denunciation, Skrypnyk shot himself in July 1933.[24] He followed the example of the leading prose writer and national Communist, Mykola Khvylovy, who had killed himself two months earlier.

A purge of Ukrainian intellectuals and party activists ensued. Late in 1933, the Kremlin officially reversed the long-standing Bolshevik axiom that Russian Great Power chauvinism was a greater danger to the Soviet state than non-Russian nationalism. Party resolutions and newspaper articles concentrated on uncovering "nationalistic deviations" in the republic. Postyshev announced that the enemies had used the policy of Ukrainization to isolate Ukrainian workers from the beneficent influence of Russian culture. Accordingly, the secret police went after thousands of people who had been involved in Ukrainization: teachers, scholars, writers, and bureaucrats in charge of culture. During 1933, nearly 100,000 Communists were expelled from the Communist Party of Ukraine, and many of them were arrested. Dozens of writers and the former commissar of education, Oleksandr Shumsky, were imprisoned as members of the fictitious Ukrainian Military Organization.

The change in the Soviet nationalities policy had similar consequences for Ukraine's ethnic minorities: Jews, Poles, Germans, Greeks, and others. What made their situation even worse was the regime's suspicion of diasporic peoples, whose allegiances might remain with their homelands abroad. During the early 1930s, the government restricted indigenization programs among the minorities and purged their leading intellectuals. The Jewish Section of the CP(B)U was dissolved in 1930, German farmers suffered heavily during the collectivization and the Famine, and Poles, together with Germans, were from 1934 to 1936 deported from Ukraine's border regions to Soviet Asia.[25] Finally, in 1938 and 1939, the government abolished all national districts and village councils that still existed in the republic and closed down minority schools with languages of instruction other than Ukrainian or Russian.[26] Only ethnic Russians, the 10 percent of the population representing Ukraine's largest minority, escaped this attack on the nationalities. If anything, the retreat from the indigenization policies strengthened the role of Russian culture in Ukraine.

Nevertheless, Russians suffered along with Ukrainians and other nationalities during the indiscriminate terror that was waged from 1934 to 1938. Beginning on an all-Union scale as a response to the December 1934 assassination of Sergei Kirov, the Bolshevik leader of Leningrad, mass terror claimed hundreds of thousands of lives and sent millions to the infamous Gulag (the Russian acronym for the main administration of labor camps). The irrationality of the party's self-immolation during the Great Terror prompted a number of explanations. Scholars have variously interpreted the purges as a natural renewal mechanism in the Stalinist system that did not know free elections, as a result of the Kremlin's struggle against local party tsars, or as Stalin's way of replacing the old Bolsheviks and bourgeois intellectuals with his cadres. Most agree that the Terror started from a settling of scores with former political opponents but snowballed into the unmasking of enemies everywhere. The public atmosphere of a besieged fortress and the quotas established for the large security police force swept thousands of party functionaries, intellectuals, and ordinary citizens into the Terror machine.

Like elsewhere in the Soviet Union, in Ukraine the worst years of the Great Terror were 1937 and 1938, when the number of people arrested in the republic totaled 267,579; of these, 122,237 were executed.[27] The lists of executed "enemies of the people" included former Ukrainian party leaders Kosior and Postyshev, as well as hundreds of the Ukrainian republic's highest officials. Of the sixty-two members of the CP(B)U Central Committee who had been elected in 1937, fifty-five lost their lives during the purges. Only one of the eleven members of the Ukrainian Politburo, the Central Committee's decision-making core, survived the Great Terror.[28]

A new study of the Terror in the Donbas shows that certain segments of Ukrainian society were hit harder than others. They included party and state officials, people with past non-Bolshevik political affiliations, industrial managers and engineers, intellectuals, clergy, and national minorities. But it would be wrong to assume that most of the victims were party members and intellectuals; nonparty workers and peasants still constituted a majority of the repressed. Women were far less likely to be arrested than men, perhaps because of their less prominent social roles in Stalinist society.[29] Another recent study demonstrates that citizens of Polish or German extraction suffered disproportionately as potential "enemy spies," constituting 18.9 percent and 10.2 percent, respectively, of those arrested during 1937, while their shares in Ukraine's general population were only 1.5 percent and 1.4 percent, respectively.[30]

Relying on blackmail and torture, the People's Commissariat of Internal Affairs (NKVD) multiplied the number of confessions daily, until the Stalinist leadership stopped the bacchanalia of terror in 1938. Arrests and executions continued on a smaller scale, including a final purge of the top police brass in Moscow and Kyiv. At last, Stalin appeared satisfied that the country had been cleansed of hidden enemies. In Ukraine, the Great Terror effectively exterminated the political generation that had taken part in the revolution—either on the side of the national, non-Communist governments or on the Bolshevik side. The purges eliminated even the theoretical possibility of organized resistance to the regime and created a new Soviet elite, the "class of '38"—an insecure and cynical generation of chameleonic bureaucrats who owed their allegiance neither to the revolution nor to the nation but to their supreme master in the Kremlin. One person who started his career in 1938 as a party functionary in Dnipropetrovsk province in Ukraine was the future Soviet leader Leonid Brezhnev.

✥ Mature Stalinism

The 1934 decision to move the Ukrainian capital from Kharkiv back to Kyiv was made in the Kremlin and came as a surprise to the members of the CP(B)U Central Committee.[31] Having curbed Ukrainization, the Soviet leadership was ready to reclaim Kyiv, the traditional center of Ukrainian culture and politics. The city in which they had felt insecure ever since the revolution was to be remade into a model proletarian urban center projecting Soviet Ukrainian identity westward, to the Right Bank and to Ukrainian lands abroad.

Although no official announcement ever abolished the policy of Ukrainization, Postyshev repeatedly criticized what he called "forced Ukrainization" and the hidden nationalist enemies who had promoted it.[32] Bringing the Ukrainian language closer to Russian, the authorities abolished Skrypnyk's alphabet and language reforms of the late 1920s. The 1930s saw a marked decline in Ukrainian-language publishing in the republic. During this decade, the share of Ukrainian book titles fell from 79 percent to 42 percent, and newspapers from 89 percent to 69 percent. The number of students attending Ukrainian schools declined less conspicuously, from a high of 88 percent in 1932 to 82 percent in 1939.[33] But the introduction of Russian in 1938 as a compulsory subject in all schools, beginning in second grade, indicated that the Soviet authorities were no longer averse to assimilation. (Russian was taught in most Ukrainian schools before that, but only from third grade and with fewer hours per week.[34]) Beginning in the mid-1930s, the press hailed Russian as the Soviet lingua franca and the language of the Communist future.

The regime's increased Russocentrism was but one aspect of the so-called Great Retreat from proletarian internationalism. Under Stalin, the idea of world revolution lost its primacy to the notion of building socialism in one country, and the state gradually incorporated Russian nationalism into its ideological arsenal. Ukrainians and other nationalities were welcome to celebrate their great ancestors and national traditions, so long as these did not undermine the cult of the Russian "elder brother." At the same time, mature Stalinism openly abandoned the revolution's egalitarian ideals by cementing the privileges of the new class of bosses. During the late 1930s, the state confirmed its new respect for traditional family values by banning abortion and making divorces difficult to obtain. A general shift from revolutionary experimentation to conservatism also took place in education and culture.[35]

The turn to social conservatism and the Great Terror marked the emergence of mature Stalinism under which the party, together with the NKVD and other ministries, was just one of the supreme leader's instruments. The Stalin cult, or obligatory adulation of the leader, emerged as the central ideological feature of mature Stalinism, surpassing and absorbing both Marxism and the myth of the revolution. The press also promoted local cults of republican party leaders, presenting them as Stalin's disciples and faithful assistants.

Early in 1938, the Ukrainian SSR acquired a new "leader of the Ukrainian people" and Stalin's pupil in the person of Nikita Khrushchev, an ethnic Russian from Ukraine, who had started his party career in the republic but grew to prominence in the Moscow city party organization. Khrushchev had to bring his team over from Moscow because the bulk of the Ukrainian leadership had been arrested, as a result of which the state apparatus had all but stopped functioning. Like his predecessors, Khrushchev had no qualms about completing the elimination of "enemies." Before the Terror subsided in the republic at the end of 1938, he had authorized arrest lists with tens of thousands of names.[36] But for those in Ukraine who had survived the Famine and the Great Purge, Khrushchev's reign symbolized a return to "normality."

Having secured their hold over political life, the Stalinists could afford to adopt a new constitution in December 1936, which proclaimed the republics' right to secede from the USSR and contained every sort of democratic freedom imaginable—each one of them fictional. In January 1937, Ukraine produced its carbon copy of the all-Union constitution. During the 1937 elections to the Soviet parliament, the Supreme Council, 99 percent of Ukrainian voters supported the official list, the only one available. According to the new system introduced that year, loyal citizens did not have to mark anything on the ballot and could walk with it directly to the ballot box. Those who entered the voting booth immediately raised suspicions that they were crossing out the official candidate's name. In June 1938, Ukraine's voters "elected" in a similar fashion the republic's own Supreme Council of 304 deputies. The handpicked legislators included 186 ethnic Ukrainians and 111 Russians,[37] a clear imbalance, given that the Russians' share in the general population was around 10 percent.

During the mid-1930s, the government gradually eliminated food rationing in the cities and somewhat improved the living standard, although it still remained abysmally low. The second and third five-year plans paid more attention to consumer goods, though some social groups had greater means to acquire them. The new class of bosses reaped most of the benefits, and the peasants, the least. The impact of the new policies on the working class was mixed. Since 1934, workers were paid according to a piecework system based on volume of production and qualifications, although the most productive of them, the "shock workers," received additional honors and bonuses. A larger income gap opened up with the emergence of the Stakhanovite movement. Alexei Stakhanov was a miner in the Donbas who in 1935 overfulfilled his work quota fourteen times by mining 102 tons of coal in less than six hours. Of course, the mine's management orchestrated this feat by providing Stakhanov with several helpers who handled secondary tasks. Yet, the press made this simple miner into the poster boy of a nationwide campaign to increase productivity and master new production techniques. His emulators, who enjoyed extraordinary material rewards, soon appeared in various industries, although the authorities were careful not to sponsor too many of them—a Stakhanovite mass movement would make planning impossible.

Finally, mature Stalinism incorporated literature and the arts into its massive political education network. The government had dissolved all competing literary groups and in 1932 enrolled loyal writers into the Union of Soviet Writers, a cross between a ministry of literature and a writers' guild. Similar organizations were later established for artists, composers, and cinema workers, and all of them had branches in Ukraine. The First Congress of Writers in 1934 defined a new official style in culture, Socialist Realism, which was aimed at connecting "what is to what ought to be." Like their Russian colleagues, Ukrainian cultural figures had no choice but to produce works portraying Soviet people acquiring Communist consciousness through participation in revolution or selfless labor. This master plot is evident in the quintessential socialist realist novel, Nikolai Ostrovsky's *How the Steel Was Tempered* (1932–1934), a heroic tale of the revolution and Civil War in Ukraine written in Russian by a Ukrainian Komsomol activist. In Ukrainian literature, Andrii Holovko, the author of novels about the class struggle and party work in the village, emerged as the early star of Socialist Realism. Subtler and more politically ambiguous was the prose of Yurii Yanovsky, especially his popular novel *Horseriders* (1935), which portrayed the Civil War in Ukraine as a fratricidal but righteous struggle. The Terror was especially harsh on Ukrainian poets. Those who survived it—the three biggest names being Maksym Rylsky, Pavlo Tychyna, and Volodymyr Sosiura—switched to hailing Stalinism in simple poetical language. A large new cohort of readers discovered Socialist Realist literature through these works, because by 1939 the drive to eliminate illiteracy had resulted in 90 percent of Ukrainian citizens under the age of fifty being able to read and write.[38]

The establishment critics taught Ukrainian artists that Socialist Realism meant naturalistic and didactic painting. After producing his great silent movie *Earth* (1930), with its complex symbolism and lyrical images of nature, Dovzhenko released his first sound film, *Ivan* (1932), which celebrated industrialization in less ambiguous terms. In 1939, the director followed Stalin's advice to make *Shchors*, an even more Socialist Realist tale focusing on the life of a Soviet hero of the Civil War in Ukraine.[39] As Russian writers were reclaiming their nation's heroic past, the playwright Oleksandr Korniichuk started the same process in Ukraine with his play *Bohdan Khmelnytsky* (1938), which the director Ihor Savchenko turned into an acclaimed movie in 1941.

Traditional and conservative as it was, the official culture of mature Stalinism promoted optimism and celebration. "Life has become better, life has become more joyous, comrades," Stalin proclaimed in 1935, and the tone of all cultural production reflected this. Postyshev's proposal that year to revive the tradition of Christmas trees received Stalin's approval and gave birth to the new Soviet custom of "New Year's trees." Like the rest of Soviet citizens during the 1930s, Ukrainians applauded the exploits of Arctic pilots and explorers, participated in physical culture parades, and sang songs from new sound films. Significantly, they chanted the immensely popular songs in Russian from the Moscow-made blockbusters *Happy-Go-Lucky Guys* (1934), *Circus* (1936), and *Volga, Volga* (1938)—all of which were shown in Ukraine without dubbing or subtitles. The epitome of Stalinist mass culture, the Russian musical film combining lighthearted comedy and a correct ideological message, had no equivalent in Ukrainian cinema. As the Stalin regime increasingly identified with the Russian language and tradition, Ukrainian culture became relegated to the background.

During the 1930s, Soviet newspapers boasted that industrialization, collectivization, and mass literacy had propelled Ukraine from backwardness into the bright age of socialism. Such propaganda stories overlooked the dark side of Stalinism—an inefficient command economy dominated by smokestack industries, depressing agricultural production carried out by recalcitrant collective farmers, and a political culture of subservience enforced by the threat of terror. There could be no open discussion of the Famine. While transforming Ukraine into a modern industrial society, Stalin's revolution from above crushed the two social strata that had traditionally been the backbone of the national movement—the peasantry and the intelligentsia. Collectivization and the Famine devastated the former, while the Terror decimated the latter. Other nationalities residing in Ukraine experienced a similar decline. At the same time as Moscow's centralization drive took away much of the republic's economic sovereignty, the Russian culture began regaining its privileged position. The Soviet state no longer emphasized Ukrainian nation building, and its actions smacked of imperial absorption.

Western Ukrainian Lands between the Wars: The Birth of Radical Nationalism

Following the end of World War I, the victorious Allies organized a series of conferences in Paris to redraw the map of Europe. Although they outwardly embraced the idea of national self-determination that had been promoted by U.S. president Woodrow Wilson, not all the peoples of Europe were awarded their own nation-states. As they dismantled the Austro-Hungarian Empire, the Allies divided the empire's ethnic Ukrainian lands among two new states (Poland and Czechoslovakia) and an expanded Romania. Poland and Romania also managed to acquire some Ukrainian territories that had belonged to another defunct empire, tsarist Russia. As a result, western Ukraine, which is best defined in the interwar period as the Ukrainian-inhabited territories outside the Soviet Union,[1] was now larger than it had been under the Habsburgs. More than 7 million strong by the early 1930s, western Ukrainians constituted one of the largest stateless minorities in interwar Europe.

The Paris Peace Conference made provisions for the protection of minority rights. New states pledged to ensure equal treatment for all their citizens, protect minority languages and schools, and even grant autonomy to larger ethnic groups—but most of them soon reneged on their promises. In particular, interwar Poland and Romania became what one modern sociologist has called "nationalizing states," openly using state power to promote the status of their titular nationalities and assimilate or marginalize their national minorities.[2] Such policies, however, had the unintended effect of strengthening the notion of a separate Ukrainian national identity or—in the areas where nation-building processes had been obstructed during the nineteenth century—of ensuring the domination of self-described "Ukrainians" over conationals who still identified themselves as Rusyns or members of the larger Russian nation. As the language of politics became increasingly restricted to an ethnic idiom, socialism began losing ground in western Ukraine. The disgruntled population was abandoning the "organic work" of civic nationalism in favor of radical nationalist ideas. By the late 1930s, the underground nationalist movement, which embraced terrorist methods, captured the majority of politically active youth in western Ukraine. But their separatist struggle would not achieve its main goal, the collapse of the oppressive Polish state. This did not come about until renewed war in

Europe in 1939. Regardless of the strength of Ukrainian nationalism in the region, the fortunes of western Ukraine would once again be decided by the great geopolitical powers of the day.

✨ Ukrainians in Poland

The reestablished Polish state included two regions where ethnic Ukrainians constituted a majority: eastern Galicia and western Volhynia. Although Poland had controlled all of Galicia since the summer of 1919, the Allies kept postponing the decision on the province's status until 1923, when they finally awarded all of it to Poland. This act antagonized the Ukrainian majority in eastern Galicia who had placed high hopes on the Allies' goodwill and protested Polish control by boycotting the elections of 1922. Still traumatized by the defeat of the Western Ukrainian People's Republic, Galician Ukrainians demonstrated a highly developed national consciousness. The Greek Catholic Church and numerous Ukrainian civic organizations served as the mainstays of national life, making the imposition of Polish control difficult. In contrast, western Volhynia, which Poland acquired after the Polish-Soviet war of 1920, was an undeveloped agrarian region with a predominantly Orthodox population. Illiterate and almost untouched by nationalist propaganda, the peasants of Volhynia had little notion of their ethnic identity. As a present-day Polish historian has shown, during the 1931 census, around 700,000 of the region's residents could not decide on their native language and nationality, choosing to simply identify themselves as "locals."[3]

While Soviet Ukraine was undergoing rapid industrialization and urbanization, Ukrainian lands in Poland retained their traditional character as an agrarian backwater. The production of oil in Galicia declined, a result of the depletion of deposits, a lack of investment, and the high cost of extraction. The small Ukrainian working class in Galicia and its minuscule counterpart in Volhynia found employment primarily in forest industries and food processing. The situation became even worse during the Great Depression. With the collapse of agricultural prices and a lack of industry to relieve rural overpopulation, villagers saw immigration as the only way to radically improve their lives. But during the interwar period, the United States and Canada restricted their admission of immigrants from eastern and southern Europe, as well as Asia. Still, some 150,000 western Ukrainians managed to emigrate between the wars, mostly to Argentina, France, and Canada. Those remaining faced a daily struggle for survival on tiny plots of land.

More than half of all Galician peasants possessed landholdings of less than two hectares or five acres. Agrarian reform was slow to arrive, and when the Polish government finally began the voluntary partitioning of large estates, it awarded most of the land in Ukrainian territories to Polish colonists.[4] The Ukrainian peasants' hunger for land remained unsatisfied, and during the 1930s, nationalists used rural discontent to strengthen their support in the countryside. This constituency was essential to their power base because a majority of urban residents were either Poles or Jews and upward of 90 percent of the region's Ukrainian population lived in the villages of eastern Galicia and western Volhynia.

The only economic success story in the region was that of the rural Ukrainian cooperative movement, which, beginning in the late nineteenth century, grew rapidly as a counterweight to Polish-controlled state and economic agencies. By the late 1930s, eastern Galicia boasted some 4,000 Ukrainian cooperatives with a total membership of more than 700,000.[5] The most important of them was Maslosoiuz (Dairy Union), which helped 200,000 farmers market their products in Poland and abroad. Large cooperative organizations stabilized prices and provided peasants with agricultural education. In addition, they supported Ukrainian cultural life and provided managerial or clerical jobs for the national intelligentsia.

Ukrainians' economic disadvantages were combined with the discriminatory policies of the Polish government. In accordance with the Allies' wishes, the Polish constitution of 1921 guaranteed the rights of minorities, but few of these provisions were ever enforced. The government abolished the former province of Galicia as an administrative unit and divided its eastern part into three smaller palatinates (*województwa*) with their borders drawn in such a way that Ukrainians could not achieve large voting majorities. To bring attention to the fact that eastern Galicia was to be considered Polish territory, authorities in Warsaw began referring to the region as "Eastern Little Poland."

Next, Ukrainian cultural institutions came under attack. The Polish administration closed down two thirds of the Prosvita Society's reading rooms and abolished Ukrainian Studies departments at Lviv University. The authorities reneged on their promise to establish a separate Ukrainian university while complicating the Ukrainian students' matriculation at existing institutions of higher learning. In 1921, Ukrainians responded by establishing an illegal Ukrainian Underground University, which lasted almost four years and enrolled up to 1,500 students. In 1924, the state banned the use of Ukrainian in government agencies and began transforming the old Austrian system of Ukrainian elementary schools into a bilingual one in which Polish was dominant.

Polish discrimination against organized Ukrainian life peaked in the fall of 1930. In response to nationalist-incited peasant attacks on Polish estates, government troops occupied the region, dismantled Ukrainian cultural institutions, indiscriminately brutalized the population, and made thousands of arrests. Having suppressed peasant discontent, the authorities tried 909 Ukrainian activists, including five deputies to the Sejm (House of Deputies). The "Pacification" of 1930 further alienated Ukrainians from the Polish state and caused an international outcry over Warsaw's treatment of its national minorities.

Although local governors acted more or less in accord with the general assimilationist views of the Polish establishment, new research indicates that Poland lacked a truly coherent nationalities policy during the late 1920s. The early 1930s saw the creation of a special National Committee attached to the Polish Council of Ministers that issued recommendations for the "state assimilation of national minorities," complemented several years later by an official program for "strengthening Polishness" in the eastern borderlands. Neither program was systematically implemented, however, imbuing Polish nationality policy with a distinctly ad hoc and inconsistent character.[6] From the very beginning, the Polish authorities made a point of referring to Ukrainians by their premodern name, Rusyns. In the 1930s, the government went a step further when it began encouraging Ukrainian ethnographic subgroups (Boikos, Lemkos, and Hutsuls) to view themselves as distinct nationalities. To further undermine the Ukrainians' national solidarity, the government also supported the remaining Russophile activists. Yet these attempts to "tribalize" Ukrainians were never as high on the government's agenda as efforts to insulate western Volhynia from nationalist ferment in neighboring Galicia.

In Volhynia, Polish authorities attempted a compromise with the Ukrainian population. The palatinate's governor from 1928 to 1938, Henryk Józewski, offered concessions to Ukrainian politicians and ensured that Ukrainian peasants in Volhynia would benefit from the parceling of large estates. Yet, his positive program was undermined by other measures instituted by the central government, such as Polonization of elementary education, a ban on Ukrainian umbrella cooperatives structures in Volhynia, and, especially, persecution of the Orthodox Church.[7]

While Poland's concordat with the Vatican protected the rights of the Greek Catholic Church, Orthodox Ukrainian congregations were left at the mercy of the Polish administration. At first, the government tolerated the Orthodox faith in Volhynia because there it feared the spread of Greek Catholicism, which had become conflated with Ukrainian nationalism. In the 1930s, though, as Galician political influence in Volhynia became a fact of life, the official policy evolved from forcing Orthodox church services to be conducted in Polish to outright seizure of parish property. During the "re-vindication" campaign, hundreds of churches that had been converted under Russian imperial rule from the Greek Catholic rite to Russian Orthodoxy were converted again—this time to mainstream Polish Roman Catholicism. Hundreds of other parish churches were simply destroyed.

Together with economic hardships in Galicia and Volhynia, the Polish government's infringements on local linguistic, educational, and confessional traditions added to the growing dissatisfaction among all strata of Ukrainian society. A few Ukrainian political parties and social organizations offered the only safety valve against an explosion, but this function depended on how effectively they could defend their constituency.

✥ Ukrainian Political Parties and the Rise of the OUN

By the mid-1920s, mainstream Ukrainian political forces grudgingly acknowledged eastern Galicia's inclusion into the Polish state and began participating in Poland's political life. In 1925, a merger of several smaller parties led to the creation of the Ukrainian National Democratic Alliance (in Ukrainian: UNDO), a reincarnation of prewar National Democrats that now returned to its traditional role as the leading Ukrainian party.[8] The UNDO was a moderate liberal party that enjoyed the support of the Ukrainian establishment. Without abandoning the ideal of national independence, it focused on the further development of Ukrainian civil society. The Prosvita Societies, cooperatives, and the main Ukrainian newspaper *Dilo* all backed the UNDO, as did the influential head of the Greek Catholic Church, Metropolitan Andrei Sheptytsky, and the head of the Union of Ukrainian Women, Milena Rudnytska. Founded in 1921 to improve the position of women in society and mobilize them for the national cause, this latter organization had 45,000 members by the mid-1930s. Other early successes of moderate nationalists included the foundation of Plast (the Ukrainian scouting movement, which the government banned in 1930) and the establishment of private secondary schools. As the Polish authorities forced Ukrainian public schools to offer bilingual education, the Native School Society began an impressive fund-raising campaign, resulting in more than half of all Ukrainian-language secondary schools being privately operated (and thus exempt from the bilingualism requirement) by the decade's end.

Given its vast network of affiliates and supporters, the UNDO had no trouble capturing 50 percent of the Ukrainian vote in the 1928 elections and dominating the Ukrainian representation in the Polish Sejm and Senate. (That year, a total of forty-six Ukrainian deputies were elected to the Sejm, and eleven became senators.[9]) But the years of the Great Depression brought an increase in both nationalist and leftist violence. The ensuing government crackdown on Ukrainian organizations underscored the moderates' failure to protect Ukrainian interests by legal means. In 1935, the UNDO made its last attempt to reach a compromise with the Polish authorities. As a result of the "Normalization" agreement, the government guaranteed Ukrainians a fixed number of seats in parliament, together with an amnesty for political prisoners and credits for Ukrainian cooperatives and banks. Vasyl Mudry, the new leader of the UNDO, became deputy speaker of the Sejm. However, following the death in the same year of its authoritative leader, Marshal Józef Piłsudski, Poland moved rapidly to the right. Lacking the political will to accommodate the country's minorities, successive governments instead revived earlier proposals for the assimilation and colonization of the borderlands. In the late 1930s, the Ukrainian public, especially the new generation of disaffected young men and women, grew increasingly frustrated with the UNDO's fruitless "collaborationism." Conflicts divided the party, leaving Ukrainian politics without a strong center.

The pro-Soviet left offered an alternate solution to western Ukraine's problems—unification with Soviet Ukraine. During the 1920s, pro-Soviet sentiment was widespread among Ukrainians in Poland, who envied the success of Ukrainization in the Communist-dominated lands to the east. For a time, even Yevhen Petrushevych, the former head of the Western Ukrainian People's Republic, joined this pro-Soviet camp. The opening of the Communist Party archives in the 1990s revealed that a number of Ukrainian organizations in Poland, including the Prosvita Society, private schools, publishing houses, the Ethnographic Museum, and even the Shevchenko Scientific Society had all benefited from covert Soviet financial aid.[10] Although none of these bodies were pro-Communist, the Soviets clearly hoped to develop a Ukrainian fifth column in Poland that one day might lead to the expansion of the Soviet Ukrainian republic.

There were overtly pro-Soviet organizations as well. In 1923, local Communist groups united to form the Communist Party of Western Ukraine (KPZU), which became an autonomous branch of the Polish Communist Party. Although banned by the Polish government in 1924, the KPZU operated legally through its front organization, the Workers' and Peasants' Socialist Union. During the 1928 elections, the Communists won 48 percent of the vote in western Volhynia, where their ideas appealed to poor peasants. Even in eastern Galicia, they polled a respectable 13 percent. The KPZU, however, identified with the "national Communists" in Soviet Ukraine, and its protests against Stalin's nationalities policy soon led to a falling-out with the Soviet authorities that was compounded by the end of Ukrainization and the Famine of 1932 and 1933. By the mid-1930s, pro-Soviet sentiments in western Ukraine had all but disappeared, but it was Stalin who wrote the last chapter in the history of the KPZU in 1938 when he ordered it dissolved, along with the entire Communist Party of Poland, on the grounds that it was a "band of spies and provocateurs."[11]

The moderates' fruitless "collaborationism" and the destruction of the radical left cleared the way for the ultranationalists. The Ukrainian radical right made its first appearance in the early 1920s, when young veterans of the Ukrainian-Polish War, led by Colonel Yevhen Konovalets, set up the Ukrainian Military Organization. From its very inception, the movement embraced terror as a way of destabilizing Polish control over the Ukrainian population. In 1921, the nationalists tried to and nearly killed Piłsudski during his first state visit to Lviv; the following year, they assassinated Sydir Tverdokhlib, the leader of the Ukrainian Agrarian Party, which had refused to participate in an election boycott. Nationalist violence and terrorism continued throughout the interwar period.

At a conference in Vienna in 1929, the Ukrainian Military Organization united with other student and émigré nationalist groups into the Organization of Ukrainian Nationalists (OUN). Although Konovalets became the recognized leader of the organization, its main ideologue was Dmytro Dontsov, a charismatic émigré from eastern Ukraine, who was not even formally a member of the OUN. A former socialist, Dontsov preached integral nationalism, a doctrine exalting the ethnic nation as a supreme form of human organization entitled to its own state. He saw the democratic and socialist beliefs of Ukrainian nationalists as the main reason for the Ukrainian Revolution's failure and as a more effective alternative offered the slogan "The Nation above All." Influenced by Nietzsche, Schopenhauer, and Italian fascism, Dontsov fantasized about the will of a strong minority, which alone could ensure his people's survival in a world where nations struggled with each other. His "nationalism of the deed" envisaged the future Ukrainian state as ethnically homogeneous and run by a nationalist organization with a supreme leader as its head.[12] The OUN translated these heady ideas into a rallying call for Ukrainian independence and revolutionary terror.

The radical right soon grew into a mass movement. War veterans, impoverished peasants, and educated Ukrainian youth excluded from the Polish workforce all flocked to integral nationalism. University and high school students, who did not share the previous generation's belief in parliamentary democracy, became the vanguard of the OUN underground. In response to the Polish government's oppressive measures, the organization waged a campaign of terror and sabotage against the Polish state; nationalist ideologues spoke of this campaign as growing into a popular rebellion against Polish rule.[13]

But the OUN did not spare the lives of those compatriots who opposed its program. In 1934, the OUN carried out sensational political assassinations of Minister of Interior Bronisław Pieracki and Ivan Babii, a respected Ukrainian high school principal who forbade his students to join the OUN. Both the UNDO and the Greek Catholic Church condemned the nationalist terror, and the Polish authorities imprisoned hundreds of nationalist activists in the infamous Bereza Kartuzka concentration camp.

The OUN had inherited from the Ukrainian Military Organization its contacts with German military intelligence. Ukrainian nationalists were naturally attracted to revanchist circles in Germany seeking to overturn a postwar settlement that they, too, found unjust. Captivated by the Nazis' anti-Polish and anti-Communist stance in the late 1920s, the Ukrainian radical right generally welcomed Hitler's rise to power. But differences soon emerged between the moderate OUN leadership abroad that was working to secure German support for the Ukrainian cause and radicals on the ground in Poland who developed a cult of violence and self-reliance. After a Soviet agent killed Konovalets in Rotterdam in 1938, the OUN split into a more moderate OUN-M, headed by Konovalets's lieutenant Andrii Melnyk abroad, and the more radical OUN-B, led by the head of its Galician branch, Stepan Bandera. Internal struggles from 1938 to 1941 left the OUN in disarray. As a result, the most dynamic force in western Ukrainian society, with a membership in the tens of thousands, was ill prepared to protect its people when foreign armies began marching in.

✣ Ukrainians in Romania and Czechoslovakia

At the end of World War I, the Kingdom of Romania acquired two regions inhabited by approximately a million ethnic Ukrainians. It absorbed the agrarian, poverty-stricken former Russian province of Bessarabia, with a significant Ukrainian population in its southern part,[14] and the former Austrian province of Bukovyna, which boasted a vibrant Ukrainian political and cultural life. Like Poland, interwar Romania pursued a policy of assimilation, although it was formulated more clearly and enforced more strictly. Although the Ukrainian and Romanian languages had little in common, the official ideology of the ruling National Liberal Party classified local Ukrainians as Romanians who had forgotten their ancestral tongue. For the first decade of Romanian rule (1918–1928), Bukovyna was ruled by martial law, allowing authorities to dissolve Ukrainian cultural groups, ban newspapers, and eliminate the Ukrainian public school system. The government also abolished the chairs of Ukrainian Studies at the University of Chernivtsi. The Orthodox

Church, to which most Ukrainians in the region belonged, was subordinated to the Romanian Orthodox Church and ordered to begin the introduction of the Romanian language into its services. Paralleling events in Poland, the land reform that took place in the 1920s benefited Romanian colonists rather than the Ukrainian peasantry.

Ukrainian political and cultural life experienced a brief revival between 1928 and 1933, when the National Peasant Party held power in Romania. Ukrainian political organizations, such as the Ukrainian National Democratic Party, had been allowed to operate since 1922, although they were not allowed to put forward their slates of candidates during elections.[15] Renamed the Ukrainian National Party in 1927, the organization now focused on uniting Bukovynians in defense of the national cause, sharing with the only Ukrainian weekly in Bukovyna the ideological platform of the Galician UNDO. This brief revival was cut short when the Romanian National Liberal Party returned to power in 1933. As political frustration grew among Bukovynian Ukrainians during the mid-1930s, increasing numbers of them joined underground groups of radical nationalists; this process accelerated in 1938, when Romania became a military dictatorship under King Carol II and dissolved all political parties and remaining Ukrainian social organizations.

While Ukrainian civic life in Bukovyna declined under Romanian rule, the position of Ukrainians in Transcarpathia improved greatly. The Czechoslovak Republic was the only new state in eastern Europe that remained a liberal democracy during the entire interwar period. It was also the only polity outside the USSR where the state supported education, culture, and the use of the Ukrainian language in local administration. Such benevolence was the result of the Czechoslovak state's general pro-Slavic policies and its specific interest in the elimination of Hungarian influences in Transcarpathia. The local "Rusyns," who numbered about half a million, had no ill feelings toward Prague. In fact, during a referendum in 1919, Rusyn émigrés in the United States approved the inclusion of their former lands within the new state of Czechoslovakia.

Although Czechoslovak promises of regional autonomy were never enacted, Transcarpathia—its official name was Subcarpathian Rus—remained a distinct province in which locals held many administrative positions and elected offices. The government invested in the economic modernization of this mountainous region, primarily focusing on the construction of a hydroelectric system and bridges. Overall, however, Transcarpathia continued to be an agrarian backwater. During the 1920s, Rusyn peasants benefited from land reform, which broke up some large estates, yet poverty persisted in the countryside. The most notable positive change was in education. During the first decade of their rule, the Czech authorities increased the number of regional schools with instruction in Ukrainian, Rusyn, or Russian from 34 to 425. The government recognized and partially subsidized two Ukrainian institutions of higher learning: the Ukrainian Free University in Prague and the Ukrainian Husbandry Academy in Poděbrady. In addition, Prague extended financial support to Transcarpathian cultural organizations and established the Subcarpathian Rusyn National Theater.

The cultural renaissance of the 1920s provoked a debate about national identity in Transcarpathia. In essence, it was a belated replay of nineteenth-century ideological struggles in Galicia, with three groups competing for the loyalties of the local Eastern Slavic population. Russophiles and Ukrainophiles saw the Transcarpathian peasants as belonging to the larger Russian or Ukrainian nations, respectively. Rusynophiles argued that the local Rusyns constituted a separate Eastern Slavic nationality. As a result, many cultural organizations in the region competed against each other; this was the case especially with the networks of the Ukrainophile Prosvita Society and the Russophile Dukhnovych Society. The leadership of the Greek Catholic Church in Transcarpathia retained pro-Hungarian sympathies and eventually came to embrace the Rusyn option. As in Galicia, however, the Ukrainophile current soon emerged as the most dynamic political force.[16] At the forefront of the Ukrainophiles' activities were the Prosvita Society, the Plast scouting organization, and the Christian National Party. Led by the Greek Catholic priest Avhustyn Voloshyn and later renamed the Ukrainian National Union, the party had an UNDO-like agenda.

Disturbed by the growth of a potentially separatist Ukrainian national movement, in the mid-1930s, the Czechoslovak government offered official support to the Rusynophile current, which consequently survived until World War II. Radical Ukrainian nationalism made few significant inroads in the region, largely because of the availability of other political options. Transcarpathia was a model of regional cosmopolitanism during the interwar years, hosting all possible political and national configurations from Communists to the OUN underground, as well as Russians, Ukrainians, and Rusyns.

✸✸ The Rising Threat of War

Because of its strategic location in eastern Europe, in the spring of 1939, tiny Transcarpathia became the site of the first armed conflict in Europe since the end of World War I. The region also produced the first attempt to proclaim Ukrainian independence since the revolutionary struggles of 1917 through 1920. The events began to unfold in September 1938, when Britain and France sacrificed the territorial integrity of Czechoslovakia to the dubious cause of "appeasement" at Munich. As Nazi Germany absorbed the western part of the Czechoslovak Republic, the leaders of Slovakia and Transcarpathia demanded their long-promised autonomy. In October, the Prague government appointed Josef Tiso as premier of an autonomous Slovakia and the Russophile Andrei Brodii as premier of newly autonomous Subcarpathian Rus. Within two weeks, however, Czech authorities became nervous about Brodii's apparent pro-Hungarian orientation and arrested him. A new regional administration composed mostly of Ukrainophiles was established under Avhustyn Voloshyn.

Meanwhile, Hitler proceeded to dismember Czechoslovakia. In November, he awarded his Hungarian allies the southwestern part of Transcarpathia, including its capital, Uzhhorod. Voloshyn's government moved to the city of Khust. From there, it commenced the Ukrainization of the administration and educational system in the region, which it renamed Carpatho-Ukraine. In addition, the cabinet established the Carpathian Sich, a military force of approximately 5,000 soldiers, who were mostly enthusiastic Ukrainian youth from Galicia—many of them members of the OUN.[17] In February 1939, the elections to the local parliament brought Voloshyn's Ukrainian National Union a resounding victory, with 86 percent of the vote.

Legally, the region remained part of Czechoslovakia, but the Transcarpathian leaders pinned their hopes on Nazi Germany, which briefly considered playing the "Ukrainian card" against Czechoslovakia and perhaps even the Soviet Union. After the November 1938 meeting between Voloshyn and Hitler's foreign minister, Joachim von Ribbentrop, Germany opened a consulate in Khust and concluded two economic agreements with the autonomous region.[18] Foreign diplomats and Ukrainian nationalists alike speculated that Hitler was plotting to use Transcarpathia as a stepping-stone for an attack on the USSR. At the Eighteenth Party Congress held in Moscow in early March 1938, Stalin publicly ridiculed the talk about the "incorporation" of the 30-million-strong Ukrainian SSR into Transcarpathia, with its population of 700,000.[19]

Only days later, on March 14, Hitler's real strategy became apparent when he ordered the invasion of Czech lands, forced Tiso to proclaim Slovak independence, but authorized Hungary to take over the second autonomous region, Transcarpathia. As the Carpathian Sich fought valiantly to delay the Hungarian advance, on March 15, 1939, the Transcarpathian parliament proclaimed the Republic of Carpatho-Ukraine politically independent. Voloshyn, who had been elected president, had to flee Khust in the face of the Hungarian advance on the same day; it took the Hungarian army only a couple of days longer to establish its control over the region. Hungary would rule Transcarpathia until 1944.

The next military act to be played out on Ukrainian soil would occur only after the official start of World War II. On August 23, 1939, Nazi Germany and the USSR stunned the world and their own citizens by concluding a nonaggression treaty, accompanied by trade agreements. The Molotov-Ribbentrop Pact, named after the two countries' foreign ministers, put an end to the long-running propaganda war between Germany and the Soviet Union. More important, it contained a secret protocol dividing eastern Europe into spheres of influence. Poland was to be partitioned, with its eastern regions falling under Soviet control. On September 1, 1939, having secured Stalin's cooperation, Hitler ordered an attack on Poland that launched World War II.

On September 17, after the German army had broken Polish resistance, Soviet troops invaded from the east, ostensibly to protect Poland's Ukrainian and Belarusian minorities.[20] The Polish army did not put up serious resistance, and the Soviets lost fewer than 500 soldiers in the entire campaign. Local Ukrainians welcomed the end of Polish rule but were unsure what to expect from their new masters. General (later Marshal) Semen Tymoshenko, the commander of the Soviet army group in Poland and himself a Ukrainian, issued leaflets presenting the invasion as the "historic reunification of the great Ukrainian people."[21] The Kremlin, indeed, had decided to attach western Ukraine to the Ukrainian SSR. In October 1939, the Soviet authorities organized elections in eastern Galicia and pressured voters to support one official slate of candidates. The resulting National Assembly petitioned the USSR for the region's incorporation into Soviet Ukraine, and permission was duly granted on November 1, 1939. (Western Belarus was included in the Belarusian SSR.) The Red Army seized further territories allotted to Stalin according to his secret agreement with Hitler in June 1940, coercing Estonia, Latvia, and Lithuania to "voluntarily" join the Soviet Union. At the same time, having threatened Romania with war, the USSR annexed northern Bukovyna and Bessarabia. Bukovyna and the Ukrainian-populated southern region of Bessarabia were directly incorporated into the Ukrainian SSR, while the remaining part of Bessarabia and the former Moldovan autonomy within Soviet Ukraine were constituted as a new union republic, the Moldovan SSR.

In line with the official rhetoric about "reunification," the Soviet authorities initiated an impressive campaign to Ukrainize education and culture in western Ukraine. In eastern Galicia, by far the best example of Soviet policies in the newly conquered territories, existing bilingual schools were Ukrainianized, alongside thousands of new Ukrainian language schools—a total of 5,798 in the fall of 1940.[22] Lviv University, too, was Ukrainianized and named after the prominent writer and civic figure Ivan Franko. New Ukrainian theaters and a branch of the Ukrainian Academy of Sciences were established in the region. Many leading western Ukrainian intellectuals found employment in these new institutions, while others, disturbed by the closing of such indigenous Ukrainian establishments as Prosvita and the Shevchenko Scientific Society, fled to German-occupied Poland. The process of Ukrainization was accompanied by intensive political reeducation of western Ukrainians. In 1939 alone, the Ukrainian Politburo allotted to the "western provinces" 500,000 copies of the Ukrainian edition of the *Short Course in the History of the All-Union Communist Party (Bolsheviks)*, the famous compendium of Stalinist ideological axioms.[23]

To the majority of local Ukrainians, Soviet economic policies initially appeared inoffensive enough. Most Ukrainian peasants felt little apprehension about the nationalization of industry and trade that had been controlled by foreign corporations, as well as by resident Poles and Jews. Villagers greeted the confiscation of large Polish estates even more enthusiastically, as the government redistributed about half of the land among the poor peasantry. However, the Stalinist regime soon began threatening the traditional structures of western Ukrainian society. The remaining half of the newly seized land was awarded to state-organized state and collective farms, which the peasants were increasingly pressured to join. Existing cooperatives were reorganized or dissolved. The Greek Catholic Church was expropriated of its extensive landholdings, and religious instruction in schools was abolished. Stalinist bureaucrats also disbanded all Ukrainian political parties and closed down "bourgeois" Ukrainian newspapers.

The frightening face of the new regime was truly revealed in 1940, when mass arrests and deportations began. The majority of Ukrainian political activists had fled to the German occupation zone in September 1939, but the Soviets arrested as many of the remaining prominent nationalists, industrialists, and civil servants as they could, focusing not only on Ukrainians but also on Poles and Jews. In 1940, the new authorities began mass deportations of Polish colonists, former government employees, and propertied classes to labor camps and police-supervised settlements deep inside the USSR. The majority of the deportees were Poles, but the long arm of the Stalinist security apparatus also swept up a large number of ethnic Ukrainians, who were deemed unreliable because of their social background, political past, or suspected anti-Soviet sentiments. Sorting through the NKVD's Byzantine record-keeping system is difficult, but present-day Ukrainian scholars have determined that during 1939 and 1940, some 312,000 families or between 1,170,000 and 1,250,000 people were deported from western Ukraine to Siberia, the Arctic Circle, and Soviet Central Asia. Ethnic Ukrainians constituted about 20 percent of the deportees.[24]

Most Ukrainians fleeing from Soviet-occupied lands resettled elsewhere in Poland, especially in the Lemko and Kholm (Chełm) regions, which had substantial Ukrainian populations. Like the rest of former Poland, these districts were now part of the General Government, a German colony that was first in line for incorporation into the Third Reich. There, the Nazis tolerated some degree of Ukrainian social and cultural life as a counterweight to the Polish majority, which they distrusted. To coordinate these activities and to protect the interests of their conationals, Ukrainian activists managed to establish in Cracow the Ukrainian Central Committee (UCC), headed by the geographer Volodymyr Kubijovyč. In a short time, the UCC created a network of Ukrainian schools, cooperatives, and youth organizations for the local population.[25] The Ukrainian Autocephalous Orthodox Church, which reestablished itself in the Kholm region, provided religious life. The OUN, which had largely missed the fateful events of 1939, also built up its presence in the General Government. With almost all Ukrainian territories under Soviet control, the nationalists hoped that the Nazi-Soviet Pact would prove to be temporary, as a war between Germany and the USSR was their only chance to undo Stalin's domination of their country.

❖

As the brutal Stalinist regime was shaping Soviet Ukraine into a modern industrial society, the Ukrainian lands in Poland, Romania, and Czechoslovakia remained agrarian backwaters. Popular frustration over national discrimination and assimilation attempts by Polish and Romanian authorities resulted in the rise there of a Ukrainian radical right, which professed the aim of independent statehood. The Organization of Ukrainian Nationalists, which embraced terror as a political weapon, developed into the most dynamic force in western Ukrainian society, attracting masses of disgruntled young men and women. Tiny Transcarpathia stood apart from this trend because of the Czechoslovak government's liberal policies, yet this westernmost region was the first to be drawn into the whirlwind of the international conflicts leading to World War II. No matter how strong the radical nationalists had been in Galicia and Bukovyna, they, too, proved powerless when the Soviet Army marched in. With OUN members watching in disgust, Stalin stole their thunder by uniting all ethnic Ukrainians in a single polity, the Ukrainian Soviet Socialist Republic.

Figure 1. The Zbruch Idol

With no explanatory plates anywhere in sight, few people passing by on an average day through this small park in central Kyiv would know that the stone column with primitive bas-relief is a copy of the Zbruch Idol, a tenth-century sculpture thought to represent a pagan Eastern Slavic deity. Discovered in 1848 on a hill overlooking the River Zbruch in western Ukraine, the nine-foot original remains in a Polish museum. Archaeologists continue debating the complex symbolic meaning of the carvings, thought to reflect the ancient Slavs' vision of the world. The column's upper part portrays a four-faced deity, which, based on the monument's phallic form, scholars guess must have been the god of fertility. Some skeptics dismiss the Zbruch Idol as a nineteenth-century forgery; others question its attribution to ancient Slavs, as the chronicles mention only wooden idols and no similar stone deities have been found in the Eastern Slavic lands. In a sense, the Zbruch Idol remains as enigmatic to scholars as its replica is to passersby in this Kyivan park.

Figure 2. King Danylo
In his search for allies against the Tatars, Prince Danylo of Halych looked
westward. In 1253, his talks with the pope about an anti-Tatar crusade led to
the dispatch of a papal delegation to Galicia-Volhynia to crown Danylo
as king and thus the equal of other European monarchs. Nothing came of
Danylo's plans for a crusade and his collaboration with the pope, but he and
his two immediate successors retained the august title. Later Ukrainian historians who wanted to stress Galicia-Volhynia's difference from northeastern
principalities (and thus, Ukraine's historical closeness to Europe rather than
Russia) called Danylo "king"; Russian and Soviet scholars who insisted on
the unity of the Rus principalities styled him "prince." After the collapse of the
Soviet Union, the former interpretation triumphed. This equestrian statue with
the inscription "King Danylo" was erected in Lviv in 2001 to mark 800 years
since Danylo's birth. The ruler's hand points westward to Europe.

Figure 3. Bohdan Khmelnytsky

Not many nineteenth-century statues remain in Ukraine, where radical political changes during the twentieth century were often accompanied by the destruction of the previous regime's monuments. The equestrian statue of Bohdan Khmelnytsky (1888) has survived, but the meaning of this monument has changed many times. When it was constructed on the square where Hetman Khmelnytsky staged his triumphant entrance into Kyiv in 1648 as the liberator of Cossack Ukraine from Polish rule, the tsarist authorities saw this sculpture as commemorating Ukraine's "return" to Russia. Early Soviet ideologues despised Khmelnytsky as a feudal lord and exploiter of the peasantry and boarded up his monument with wooden panels during parades. Since Stalin's time, Khmelnytsky again came to be revered as the forerunner of the Russian-led "friendship of peoples," with novels and operas celebrating his statesmanship. Finally, since the late nineteenth century, Ukrainian patriots have considered this statue a monument to the founder of the first Ukrainian state—an interpretation that predominates in independent Ukraine.

Figure 4. Taras Shevchenko

Ukraine's national bard Taras Shevchenko (1814–1861) never visited Lviv, and his historical poems speak with disdain about the Uniate (Greek Catholic) Church, which is considered the national church in Galicia. But in the late nineteenth century, ethnic Ukrainians living in various historical regions and attending different churches accepted him as the common symbol of the new Ukraine and spiritual "father" of all Ukrainians. The Soviet authorities presented Shevchenko as an intuitive socialist and friend of Russian revolutionaries. They built several monuments to the poet in Dnieper Ukraine, but from the 1960s on, these became meeting spots of nationalist dissidents. Perhaps because of this, the Soviets did not allow the statue of the national poet to be erected in troublesome Lviv. The striking monument in the photo was built in the center of Lviv between 1992 and 1996 with funds collected by the Ukrainian diaspora. The stela on the left, the "Wave of National Revival," features images from his poetry.

Figure 5. The Arsenal

Founded in 1764 as a cannon factory, the Arsenal is one of Ukraine's oldest industrial enterprises. It grew into a large plant during the late nineteenth century. (The building in the photo dates from the 1850s and originally doubled as a citadel; the two upper floors are later additions.) The Arsenal's history illustrates well the overwhelming influence that Russian political parties had on the working-class movement in Ukraine. Russian-speaking socialist intellectuals organized illegal reading circles in the factory as early as the 1880s, and they successfully mobilized the factory's workers during the massive strikes of 1903 and 1905. Ukrainian parties never had any significant following in the Arsenal or among the Ukrainian working class in general. A stronghold of the Bolsheviks, during the revolution the Arsenal served as a base for two Bolshevik-led rebellions, the first in 1917 against the tsarist garrison and the second in 1918 against the Ukrainian People's Republic. Marks left by the Ukrainian troops' machine guns are still visible on the building's walls. The Soviet-era black memorial plaque with bas-relief commemorates the bloody and unsuccessful 1918 rebellion.

Figure 6. Mykhailo Hrushevsky

This impressive monument to Mykhailo Hrushevsky was unveiled in
1998 in the center of Kyiv, next to the building (in the background)
where the Central Rada held its sessions in 1917 and 1918. After the
Soviet Union's collapse, the Kyiv municipal authorities, in honor of Hrushevsky, renamed the main avenue on which both the Parliament and
the Cabinet of Ministers buildings are located. This lionization of Hrushevsky, who played a largely symbolic role in the revolution, is highly
significant. The real rulers of revolutionary Ukraine, Vynnychenko and
Petliura, do not fit the post-Communist pantheon of great Ukrainians as
well as this widely respected historian and cultural figure. Vynnychenko
was too far to the left, and Petliura's name has been associated with the
violent civil war and the surrender of Galicia to the Poles.

Figure 7. Les Kurbas

One of the names that best symbolizes the flourishing of Ukrainian culture in the 1920s is Les Kurbas (1887–1937), a modernist theater director who almost single-handedly reformed the Ukrainian theater. He replaced nineteenth-century realistic plays of morals with modern Ukrainian dramas and Western classics, introducing to the Ukrainian scene the avant-garde techniques of expressionist theater. In Kyiv in 1922, Kurbas established an experimental studio named "Berezil" (March) that soon became one of the country's premier theater companies. Many leading Ukrainian actors of the twentieth century trained there. During the early 1930s, the director increasingly came under fire for staging modern Ukrainian plays that the party condemned as "nationalistic." In 1933, the secret police arrested him during a crackdown on Ukrainian intelligentsia and imprisoned him in the infamous prison camp on the Solovki Islands in Russia's far north. He was executed there in 1937. This small, intimate statue of Kurbas was erected in Kyiv in 2002.

Figure 8. Bykivnia

Most victims of the Great Terror were shot at night, one by one, in special rooms inside major prisons. In the early hours of the morning, unmarked trucks drove their bodies to secret burial sites. Those executed in Kyiv between 1937 and 1941 were buried in the forest near the village of Bykivnia on the city's eastern environs. When the Nazis captured Kyiv during World War II, they organized excavations there and published reports about Bolshevik crimes. Later, Soviet authorities tried to save face by claiming that these were the graves of Soviet POWs executed by the Germans. The truth was acknowledged only in 1989, and the monument in this photo was unveiled in 1995. It marks the turnoff from a highway into Bykivnia Forest. Estimates of the number of people buried there range from 6,329 (reflecting the actual body count during selective excavations) to figures above 120,000.

Figure 9. Lviv University

This splendid palace was built in Lviv in 1877 through 1881 in Viennese neo-Renaissance style to house the Galician diet (provincial legislature). In 1923, the government of the newly restored Polish state transferred the building to Lviv University. Only those identifying themselves as Polish citizens were accepted as students, and until 1925, young Ukrainians who did not recognize Polish control over eastern Galicia were not admitted, attending instead the Ukrainian Underground University. After Ukrainians began enrolling in Lviv University during the late 1920s, the Polish authorities restricted their maximum number to 15 percent of the student body. There were no professors of Ukrainian nationality until 1933. Such discriminatory educational policies only aggravated discontent among young Ukrainians, who joined the nationalist underground in large numbers. After the Soviets "liberated" Lviv in 1939, they transformed this Polish institution of higher learning into a Ukrainian university named after the writer Ivan Franko.

Figure 10. Babi Yar

This is a Soviet-era (1976) monument to the victims of Babi Yar. The official line held that in this ravine the Nazis killed "Soviet civilians and POWs," and the authorities harassed Jews who marked the anniversaries of September 29, 1941, as their national tragedy. For this reason, the sculptors did not place Jewish civilians in the forefront and opted instead for young men presumably representing Soviet POWs or underground fighters. Since the Soviet Union's collapse, several small memorials have been erected nearby, each claiming the memory of Babi Yar for a smaller, more exclusive, group of victims. They include monuments to Jews who died there, POWs of the nearby Syrets concentration camp, and executed Ukrainian nationalists. Perhaps the most touching is a small nonpartisan memorial to the children who perished in Babi Yar—a bronze group of abandoned, broken toys.

Figure 11. The Friendship Arch

During the postwar period, the "friendship of peoples" emerged as the Soviet ideological line on the nationalities issue, according to which the Soviet Union was the voluntary creation of member nations, each of them flourishing in the socialist family under the guidance of elder brother Russia. The Friendship of Peoples Arch in Kyiv celebrates the historical "fraternal relations" between Russians and Ukrainians. The Soviet authorities originally planned to open this monument in time for the Pereiaslav Treaty's 325th anniversary in 1979, but the stumbling command economy could not deliver the materials on time. A thirty-meter-long "rainbow" of stainless steel was finally unveiled in 1982. Beneath it stand larger-than-life figures of fraternal Russian and Ukrainian workers, as well as a seventeenth-century Muscovite boyar and a Cossack dignitary. These days, young Ukrainians on skateboards and mountain bikes enjoy the steps leading to the monument.

Figure 12. The Supreme Rada

Built on the edge of a beautiful park in central Kyiv for the specific purpose of housing the Soviet Ukrainian parliament, this example of Stalinist neo-classicism, with its six Corinthian columns and statues of workers and peasants guarding the main entrance, in 1940 earned architect V. Zabolotny a coveted award for artistic or scholarly achievement, the Stalin Prize. Yet, the Supreme Rada itself played the largely symbolic function in the Soviet system of rubber-stamping decisions made in the headquarters of the Communist Party of Ukraine on nearby Ordzhonikidze (now Bankova) Street. That all changed with the first free elections in the republic in 1990, which shifted the center of political life to the parliament. The building's octagonal great hall became the scene of acrimonious debates among the deputies, while protesters of all stripes often marched to the Supreme Rada and camped in the park across from the main entrance. It was in this building that the deputies passed the Declaration of Independence during an emergency session on August 24, 1991.

Figure 13. Independence Square (Maidan)

Until the early nineteenth century, what is now Kyiv's central plaza was a wasteland known as Goat Swamp. After newly paved streets united the historical parts of the city, however, Khreshchatyk Square became the city's natural center. Renamed and reconstructed many times since, the location acquired a new name for the sixtieth anniversary of the Bolshevik Revolution in 1977—October Revolution Square—as well as a massive monument to Lenin. With the fall of Communism in 1991, the new Ukrainian authorities removed the statue (while leaving a smaller one at the other end of Khreshchatyk Boulevard) and renamed the plaza Independence Square. However, no appropriate new monument was constructed until 1999 through 2001, when the municipal government had the square rebuilt in a tacky style without any prior public discussion, much to the chagrin of Kyivan intellectuals. A huge Independence Column in the center is topped by an angel-like figure of a woman in a gold-embroidered Ukrainian costume. The new look of Independence Square became familiar to TV viewers worldwide during the 2004 Orange Revolution as the backdrop of the huge protest rallies. Enterprising street vendors now offer tourists cans with liberating "Maidan air" for five dollars and up. (Although "maidan" is Ukrainian for "square," after the Orange Revolution, Maidan with a capital "M" came to refer exclusively to Kyiv's Independence Square.)

Ukrainian Lands in the Mid-Nineteenth Century

Boundary of Ukraine, 2006
International boundaries
Provincial boundaries

AUSTRIAN EMPIRE

HUNGARIAN KINGDOM

GALICIA

TRANSCARPATHIA

BUKOVYNA

Chernivtsi

MOLDAVIA

BESSARABIA

PODOLIA

VOLHYNIA

RIGHT

BANK

KYIV

RUSSIAN EMPIRE

CHERNIHIV

LEFT
BANK

POLTAVA

KHERSON

SOUTH

TAURIDIA

KHARKIV

KATERYNOSLAV

CRIMEA

BLACK SEA

SEA OF
AZOV

Lublin
Pinsk
Chernihiv
Kursk
Voronezh
Zhytomyr
Kyiv
Lviv
Uzhhorod
Kamianets-Podilsky
Kharkiv
Poltava
Katerynoslav
Novocherkassk
Chisinau
Odesa
Kherson
Symferopol

Buh
Vistula
San
Pripet
Dnipro
Desna
Seim
Vorskla
Donets
Don
Ros
Dnipro
Southern
Buh
Dniester
Prut
Danube

N

0   100 kms
0   50 miles

Map: Ukrainian Lands in Interwar Europe

Boundary of Ukraine, 2006
— International boundaries
- - - Republic boundaries
········ Provincial boundaries

POLAND
BELORUSSIAN SSR
RUSSIAN SFSR
UKRAINIAN SSR
CZECHOSLOVAKIA
TRANSCARPATHIA
HUNGARY
GALICIA
VOLHYNIA
BUKOVYNA
BESSARABIA
MOLDOVIAN ASSR
ROMANIA
CRIMEAN ASSR
KUBAN
RUSSIAN SFSR

Warsaw
Brest-Litovsk
Pinsk
Lublin
Chelm
Lutsk
Lviv
Ternopil
Homel
Chernihiv
Kyiv
Zhytomyr
Kursk
Voronezh
Kharkiv
Poltava
Luhansk
Iuzivka
Novocherkassk
Rostov
Kamianets-Podilsky
Vinnytsia
Ielyzavethrad
Katerynoslav
Kryvyi Rih
Zaporizhzhia
Chernivtsi
Chisinau
Odesa
Mykolaiv
Kherson
Symferopol

Vistula
Buh
Pripet
Dnipro
Desna
Seim
San
Ros
Dnipro
Vorskla
Don
Donets
Don
Dniester
Prut
Southern Buh
Danube

SEA OF AZOV
BLACK SEA

0   100 kms
0   50 miles

N

Nazi Occupation and the Soviet Victory

Following the Soviet annexation of Galicia, Volhynia, and Bukovyna in 1939 and 1940, Stalinist ideologues had to redefine their notion of "Ukraine." Much of their prior propaganda had belabored the alleged opposition between the happy life of Soviet Ukrainians under socialism and the suffering of their brethren in Poland and Romania under the power of landowners and capitalists. With most of the Ukrainian ethnic lands now united in the Ukrainian SSR, an important change had to take place in the republic's ideology. Official pronouncements began celebrating the reunification as the completion of Ukrainian nation building. In its address to Stalin in November 1939, the republic's Supreme Soviet stated, "Having been divided, having been separated for centuries by artificial borders, the great Ukrainian people today reunite forever in a single Ukrainian republic."[1]

Such unusual pronouncements signaled the reshaping of Soviet Ukrainian identity, as did feverish efforts at Sovietizing lands that were now to be known as the western provinces. Faced with the need to absorb millions of nationally conscious western Ukrainians, Stalinist ideologues attempted to define a national identity for Soviet Ukraine that would be sufficiently national to unite east and west and socialist enough to facilitate the unified nation's membership in the Soviet Union. The titanic clash between Nazi Germany and the USSR that began in 1941 did not actually interrupt this ideological project. For most of the war, the celebration of the "great Ukrainian people" served as a major mobilization tool, albeit one increasingly supplemented by singing the praises of Russian guidance. Only during the postwar ideological freeze did the authorities make serious efforts to reinstall Soviet values as the dominant component of the Ukrainian national identity.[2]

One of the major reasons for this retreat was the spread during the war of an alternative, nationalist understanding of nationhood. Although the Nazis did not encourage Ukrainian nationalism, toward the end of the war, the Ukrainian nationalists in western Ukraine emerged as an independent military and propaganda force to be reckoned with. Beginning in late 1943, the Soviet authorities' struggle to reestablish control over the area and absorb it ideologically would provide a backdrop for much of postwar Ukrainian history.

✣ Ukraine as a Battlefield

Nazi Germany's all-out assault on Soviet territory on June 22, 1941, took the Soviet leadership by surprise. The Kremlin disregarded numerous warnings from abroad, including reports from Mykola Hlushchenko, a prominent Ukrainian Postimpressionist artist and Soviet spy in Germany and France.[3] Afraid of provoking war with overt military preparations, Stalin did not authorize a command for combat readiness until two hours before the German attack, and thus Soviet troops were completely unprepared. The Nazi Blitzkrieg ("lightning war"), involving fast-moving mechanized formations supported by air attacks, initially worked against the Red Army as well as it had in Europe during the previous two years. Its officer ranks decimated during the Great Terror, the large Red Army had poorly trained conscripts, and most of its weapons were obsolete. During the first months of what would become known as the Soviet people's "Great Patriotic War," high rates of desertion and voluntary surrender indicated the soldiers' low morale.

With the beginning of the war, the Soviet high command transformed the Kyiv and Odesa military districts into Southwestern and Southern Fronts, respectively. But these fronts could not withstand the German army group "South." Three regular German armies and a Panzer army advancing into Ukrainian territory were assisted by two Romanian armies, as well as by Slovak and Hungarian divisions. Lviv fell on June 30, followed by Zhytomyr on July 9. Kyiv was already within easy reach, but the Germans paused to regroup and resupply, giving the Red Army an opportunity to reinforce the city's defenses. In August, the Germans annihilated the Soviet Southern Front, capturing most of the Ukrainian southeast (Kirovohrad, Kryvyi Rih, and Dnipropetrovsk). In September, the Panzer army of Heinz Guderian helped to encircle five Soviet armies around Kyiv. Against his generals' advice, Stalin refused to order withdrawal and, on September 19, Kyiv became the biggest and most important Soviet city ever to fall into German hands. The Soviet losses during Kyiv's defense in July through September of 1941 were staggering: 616,304 dead and around 665,000 taken prisoner.[4] The commander of the Southwestern Front, Colonel General M. P. Kyrponos, and most of his staff died in action.

With the fall of Odesa to Romanian forces on October 16 and that of Kharkiv to the Germans on October 25, the battle for Ukraine was over. The Red Army held on to a small area in the northeast and to the Crimean peninsula in the south, which was at the time technically a part of the Russian republic. After the Soviet forces finally stopped the German advance in the Battle of Moscow, they made an unsuccessful attempt in the spring of 1942 to liberate the Donbas region and Kharkiv. This counteroffensive brought nothing but heavy losses, and in the summer of 1942, the Nazi armies resumed their advance. In July, they drove the Red Army from the Crimea. On July 22, 1942, Soviet troops abandoned the last Ukrainian town they held, Sverdlovsk in Voroshylovhrad (Luhansk) province, and retreated to Russia.

From the very first days of the war, heavy fighting and German bombing raids inflicted upon Ukraine terrible loss of life and destruction. More than 3 million of the republic's residents joined the Red Army; 200,000 of them volunteered in the first days of the war.[5] But the majority of these soldiers were either killed or taken prisoner within a couple of months. By the end of 1941, the Germans held 3.6 million Soviet POWs—an estimated 1.3 million of them Ukrainians—who had less than a 50 percent chance of surviving harsh treatment and disease in labor camps. Before the Soviet troops retreated, in many cities the secret police executed nearly 9,000 political prisoners, inmates with sentences longer than three years, and even some "unreliable" civilians who had been hurriedly arrested after the onset of war.[6]

The Soviet authorities relocated 3.5 million Ukrainian bureaucrats, intellectuals, workers, and their families to Russia and Soviet Asia. They encouraged the rest of the population to leave as well, but many people hoped that life under the Nazi occupation would prove tolerable. Ukrainian Jews, many of whom remembered the German occupation in 1918 as a time of relative social order before the pogroms of 1919, were largely unaware of Nazi racial policies. The Soviet authorities, who did not want to be seen as protecting Jews and leaving other nationalities to their fate, did not take measures to evacuate them en masse. Instead, the government concentrated all its efforts at dismantling and removing more than 800 major Ukrainian industrial plants and factories, some 170 from Kyiv alone, along with a third to half of their workers. These enterprises eventually resumed work in Siberia and Soviet Asia, contributing greatly to the ultimate Soviet victory in the war.

Whatever could not be evacuated was destroyed according to a "scorched earth" policy that Stalin had proclaimed in his first wartime radio address on July 3. In most cases, this policy meant simply disabling remaining industrial equipment and power stations, driving cattle eastward, and destroying liquor and food stashes. Yet there were also spectacular acts of demolition. The large blast furnaces in Kryvyi Rih were blown up, and the Donbas mines flooded. When, in a panic, Soviet military engineers prematurely dynamited the Dniprohes dam, a torrent of water caused death and damage in the city of Zaporizhzhia. Before abandoning Kyiv, the Red Army blew up all four bridges across the Dnipro. The city itself had suffered almost no destruction during its defense, but Soviet agents exploded mines under many landmark buildings after Kyiv's occupation by the German army, hoping to kill enemy generals and other dignitaries. The resulting fire devastated much of the city center.[7]

Beginning in the fall of 1941, Nazi reports from the Eastern Front stressed the hardening resistance of the Red Army. As the Soviet command began enforcing harsh measures against desertion, voluntary surrender, and unauthorized retreat, it also stepped up patriotic propaganda, which in Ukraine portrayed Soviet soldiers as descendants of the heroic Cossacks. (The patriotic film *Bohdan Khmelnytsky* was often shown to the troops before their departure for the front.) However, by the time the Red Army could match the Germans in morale, all Ukrainian territory had already been lost to the enemy.

❖ Nazi Rule

Although Ukrainian nationalists had long hoped that the German victory over the Soviet Union would lead to the creation of a Ukrainian state, the Nazis had no such plans. Having conquered Ukraine, they divided it into several administrative units. Galicia became a district of the General Government of Poland, and most of Dnipro Ukraine was included in the Reichskommissariat Ukraine, essentially a colony of the Third Reich. Because of their proximity to the front, Ukraine's easternmost regions, including the city of Kharkiv, remained under German military administration. Finally, Romania reclaimed Bukovyna and acquired considerable territory in the southwest, including the major port of Odesa. These lands became the Romanian province of Transnistria (that is, the region located "beyond the Dniester River").

In western Ukraine, where the Soviet conquest in 1939 and two years of heavy-handed Stalinist rule had alienated much of the population, the Germans were initially greeted as liberators. This was not the case in the east, where the people generally adopted a wait-and-see attitude. While small groups of activists either welcomed the arriving Nazi troops or organized resistance against them, masses of city dwellers were busy looting state stores and warehouses and making provisions for the uncertain future. It initially appeared that the German military authorities were prepared to tolerate local initiative in social and cultural matters. Indeed, during the month or two before the more severe Nazi civil administration became entrenched, many workers showed up at their factories, teachers reopened their schools, and peasants began dividing the collectivized land and cattle among themselves. Ukrainian cultural organizations and the Prosvita Societies emerged in cities and in the countryside. Hundreds of Orthodox priests came out of hiding to lead a modest religious revival. Assisted by thousands of nationalist volunteers from western Ukraine, Ukrainian activists in the Reichskommissariat began establishing local administrations, newspapers, and police.

At that point, the Nazis could have won considerable support by announcing some form of Ukrainian self-rule and the privatization of land, yet the German administration remained conspicuously silent regarding its future plans for Ukraine. This lack of clarity was intentional. Nazi racial theories pictured Slavs in general and Ukrainians in particular as *Untermenschen*, a "subhuman" species at best worthy of being enslaved to the German master race. Hitler envisaged the future German agrarian colonization of Ukraine requiring, in the short run, the decimation and enslavement of the local population, as well as the destruction of all major cities.[8] There was, however, some disagreement among Nazi bureaucrats as to how to treat the conquered territories until the war was over and they could proceed with implementing these plans. Minister for Occupied Eastern Territories Alfred Rosenberg thought that allowing non-Russians self-government would mobilize them against Bolshevism. In contrast, Erich Koch, the brutal Reichskommissar of Ukraine, was not prepared to make any concessions to the locals. All doubts about Nazi policy in the region were removed in September 1941, when Hitler utterly dismissed the idea of allowing self-government in the occupied territories: "In 1918 we created the Baltic states and the Ukraine. But now we have no interest in the continued existence of the Eastern Baltic states and a free Ukraine."[9]

Consequently, the German occupation policy in Ukraine was one of plunder, enslavement, and extermination. To kill all the Communists, Jews, and Roma (Gypsies) they could identify, Nazis set up special execution units, the Einsatzgruppen, that were staffed by the SS and Gestapo personnel. On September 29 and 30, 1941, in Kyiv, German machine gunners from Einzatzgruppe C shot 33,771 Jews, whom the local auxiliary police herded into the infamous ravine of Babi Yar (Babyn Yar). In other Ukrainian cities, the Nazis moved Jews into ghettos, which were gradually emptied by waves of executions. The total number of Ukrainian Jews who perished in the Holocaust is estimated at 1.4 to 1.5 million.[10] As in other occupied countries that experienced the Holocaust, the local population produced some willing and unwilling accomplices, a mass of passive bystanders, and a minority who had courage to hide Jews. Unlike in western Europe, in Ukraine sheltering Jews meant certain death in case of discovery. Still, as of 2004, 1,984 Ukrainian citizens have been honored by Israel as "Righteous Gentiles" for saving Jews during World War II.[11] Although Metropolitan Sheptytsky did not receive this accolade, he may well be the most famous example of assisting Jews in wartime Ukraine. On the metropolitan's orders, some 150 Jews were hidden in Greek Catholic monasteries in Galicia.[12]

Although not singled out for immediate extermination, Ukrainians were subjected to racial segregation and genocidal policies. As German-only shops, restaurants, and trams appeared in Ukrainian cities, the Nazi administration curtailed medical services for the locals, closed down all universities, and abolished education beyond the fourth grade. Seeing no point in the existence of large Slavic urban centers in the future German agricultural colony, the Nazis forbade independent food deliveries to Kyiv and other cities, causing mass starvation and a population exodus to the countryside. Hitler visited his armies in Ukraine several times and during 1942 and 1943 spent considerable time in his Eastern Front headquarters near Vinnytsia, but he did not bother to visit a major Ukrainian city. (Neither did Benito Mussolini, who briefly stopped in Ukraine in August 1941.)[13] Tellingly, the capital of the Reichskommissariat was not Kyiv but the small provincial town of Rivne. Similarly, because Ukraine was to become an agricultural colony, the Nazis did not attempt any serious reconstruction of industry in Ukraine beyond the establishment of repair facilities and the extraction of some rare minerals.

The German regime quickly antagonized the Ukrainian population. Hostage taking and mass executions in response to any act of resistance shocked urbanites, who would long remember gallows on their streets as the most visible symbol of the Nazi rule. In Kyiv, the Germans turned Babi Yar into a killing field where, in addition to 33,771 Jews, they executed more than 100,000 POWs, suspected Communists, Ukrainian nationalists, and even some players of Dynamo Kyiv soccer club, which had the audacity to beat the German Air Force's amateur team. Entire villages and their inhabitants were obliterated in response to local partisan attacks. Among the repulsive everyday practices of Nazi rule was the institutionalization of corporal punishment in the workplace, including the public flogging of peasants for minor offences—a practice reminiscent of tsarist times.[14]

German economic policies were not attractive either. In an effort to extract maximum produce for the needs of the Reich and the army, the Nazi administration decided to preserve the hated Soviet institution of collective and state farms. This policy allowed the Germans to collect some 5 million tons of grain in Ukraine during the war but dashed the peasants' hopes of getting back their land. To provide the Reich with cheap labor, the Nazis also conscripted healthy young workers in Ukraine. Thinking they would get to see Europe and earn a living there, some youths initially volunteered for the program, but word soon spread about the slave labor and inhuman treatment that the *Ostarbeiter* ("Workers from the East") were forced to endure in Germany. Then, the Nazis resorted to force by rounding up young people in public places, sending 2.3 million Ukrainian citizens to Germany as part of this forced labor program.[15]

The Nazi policies were somewhat milder in the General Government (in Galicia), where the administration allowed Ukrainians into the lower ranks of civil apparatus as a counterweight to the Poles, whom the Germans did not trust. There, Ukrainian co-ops and schools reopened, and cultural life flourished. Yet, the Nazis relied on political terror and economic exploitation in Galicia as well. Romanian rule in the south was generally more lenient than the German regime, although the Romanian administration banned Ukrainian newspapers and aggressively promoted Romanian culture in the region.[16]

♻ Ukrainian Nationalism and the Challenge of the Total War

Ukrainian nationalists had long hoped for a replay of World War I, when the empires that had dominated eastern Europe fought each other to exhaustion and collapsed, making possible the brief existence of a Ukrainian state. Because the Soviet Union now controlled almost all Ukrainian ethnic territories, the OUN placed its hopes on its natural rival, Nazi Germany. At a minimum, the nationalists wanted to use their collaboration with the Germans to establish their own military formations and gain a foothold in eastern Ukraine. Their boldest dreams involved independent statehood. Both branches of the OUN felt that, irrespective of the war's outcome, their promotion of Ukrainian self-government and culture in the occupied territories could benefit the national cause in the long run.

Mindful of the lessons of World War I, when the Ukrainian legion of the Austro-Hungarian army became the nucleus of the Ukrainian armed forces during the revolution, the nationalists sought to establish Ukrainian military formations that would fight on the German side and yet preserve their national character and connection to the nationalist leadership. In April 1941, the German military established two such units that were officially known as the battalions Nachtigall and Roland and unofficially as the Legions of Ukrainian Nationalists. Staffed with activists of the OUN-B, the two battalions participated in the Nazi attack on the USSR. Nachtigall was part of the German forces that took Lviv.

As soon as Lviv was captured on June 30, 1941, OUN-B activists in the city proclaimed the creation of an independent Ukrainian state. Bandera himself did not attend a hastily convened "National Assembly," which bestowed the title of "Head of the National Congress" or premier on his lieutenant, Yaroslav Stetsko. Although the OUN-B managed to secure statements of support from Metropolitan Sheptytsky and some Galician civic leaders, the Germans were taken aback by the Ukrainians' initiative. The Gestapo arrested Stetsko and

Bandera and demanded that they withdraw the declaration of independence. The two refused and, together with some other senior Banderites, spent most of the war in detention.[17]

The OUN-M had intended to issue a similar proclamation in Kyiv, but the Germans' major falling-out with the Ukrainian nationalists occurred before the capital was even taken. Just prior to the war, both branches of the OUN began organizing in the General Government so-called expeditionary groups, which were to follow the German armies into eastern Ukraine. Thousands of young activists joined the groups with the aim of conducting nationalist propaganda and organizing political life in the occupied territories. But as the nationalist emissaries moved into Soviet Ukraine, a bitter feud developed between the two factions, involving assassinations and mutual denunciations to the Nazis. Already upset with the declaration of independence, the Germans decided to crack down on the Ukrainian nationalists. They executed a number of Banderites, broke their networks in Galicia, and disbanded most of their expeditionary troops. In August 1941, the military command withdrew Nachtigall and Roland from the front. Following reorganization into a single regular guards battalion, the Ukrainian legionnaires served in Belarus until the end of 1942, when the unit was dissolved and most of its Ukrainian officers arrested.

Quite apart from German repressions, expeditionary groups found it difficult reaching out to eastern Ukrainians, who highlighted social welfare and civil rights as the issues of greatest importance. Historians have shown that the locals were often taken aback by the integral nationalists' message of ethnic exclusivity, as well as by their virulent anti-Russian and anti-Jewish attitudes.[18] This wartime encounter between Ukrainian patriots from western and eastern Ukraine proved a sobering experience for the integral nationalists, whose ideology would evolve later in the war to incorporate the concerns of eastern Ukrainian audience and de-emphasize racial theories.

Their problems notwithstanding, the Melnykites sought in late 1941 to establish themselves as the leading political force in eastern Ukraine, where the Banderites could no longer operate legally. In October, the OUN-M created in Kyiv the Ukrainian National Council as a potential nucleus of a Ukrainian government. In November, the Melnykites organized a patriotic rally in Bazar near Kyiv. Their aim was to demonstrate to the Germans the popular support for the Ukrainian cause, but the event instead alarmed the occupation administration. In response, the Nazis unleashed the Gestapo and the Einsatzgruppen on the Ukrainian nationalists. Hundreds of nationalist activists were arrested and shot in various cities, including Kyiv, where the poet Olena Teliha and other leading Melnykites perished in Babi Yar. The Germans cracked down on Ukrainian patriots throughout the Reichskommissariat, regardless of whether they belonged to OUN-B or OUN-M or had no affiliation to either organization. The local administrations, newspapers, schools, and police were thoroughly purged of patriotic Ukrainians, who were replaced in many cases with local Russians. The authorities also shut down and arrested the leaders of most of the Ukrainian cultural and civic organizations. By early 1942, the nationalist gamble on using the German invasion to promote Ukrainian national assertion ended in a fiasco.

In the General Government, the Nazi authorities remained more tolerant toward Ukrainian cultural and civic life but dashed the hopes of establishing a political representation. The Ukrainian National Council that the moderate Ukrainian leaders such as Kost Levytsky and Metropolitan Sheptytsky had created in July 1941 was disbanded in March 1942. Afterward, the only Ukrainian representative body that the Germans still recognized was the Ukrainian Central Committee that had existed in Cracow since 1939 under Volodymyr Kubijovyč, and they insisted on treating this association as a welfare organization with no political standing. The UCC was successful in organizing relief for children, famine victims, and the Ukrainian POWs who had been captured in 1939 during the German-Polish war. In addition, it supported Ukrainian education and publishing. But Kubijovyč also did not shy away from acting as a de facto spokesman for Ukrainians in the General Government. He established contacts with local German administrators and was probably the only Ukrainian ever to be received by the chief of the Gestapo, Heinrich Müller.[19] Using his German connections, Kubijovyč tried to protect the Ukrainian interests in the General Government. In 1943, he successfully intervened with Governor General Hans Frank to stop the killing of Ukrainian peasants in the Zamoś region for their alleged resistance.[20]

When the tide of war turned against the Germans in 1943, it was the UCC whom they approached with the proposal to form a Ukrainian volunteer division in the German army. In organizing recruitment, Kubijovyč encountered opposition from the Banderites, who were at that time building up their guerrilla army, but found support from the Melnykites and the Greek Catholic Church. In April, Otto Wächter, the governor of the District of Galicia, proclaimed the formation of the SS Volunteer Galicia Division. Some 82,000 youth volunteered to fight against Ukraine's "most terrible enemy—Bolshevism,"[21] but only 13,000 were selected and eventually became soldiers. Following the period of training, the Galicia Division finally saw action in July 1944 near Brody in western Ukraine, where the Soviet Army crushed the Thirteenth German Army Corps to which the division was attached. Most of the Ukrainian volunteers were either killed or taken prisoner, but the German command subsequently raised more recruits and in 1944 and 1945 used the division against Slovak and Yugoslav partisans.[22]

By the time the UCC had helped to form the Galicia Division, however, the nationalist guerrilla resistance to the Nazis was also in full swing. The Ukrainian Insurgent Army (UPA, the *Ukrainska povstanska armiia*) grew out of a small anti-Soviet partisan force in the forests of Volhynia and Polissia that emerged in 1941 and was led by an independent activist, Taras Bulba-Borovets. The group changed its name to the UPA in the spring of 1942, when it began attacking the Germans. As the local population was antagonized by the Nazi policies, both OUN-B and OUN-M established guerrilla units as well, which fought the Germans in the Ukrainian northwest. In 1943, the Banderites forcibly united the nationalist partisans under their command. Roman Shukhevych, a former officer of Nachtigall, became the UPA's commander in chief. An estimated 40,000 UPA fighters waged war against the Germans, Soviet partisans, Polish guerrillas, and regular Soviet troops. In addition, in the summer of 1943, UPA forces in Volhynia began attacking local Poles. During 1943 and 1944, an estimated 35,000 Polish civilians and an unknown number of Ukrainian civilians in the Volhynia and Chełm regions fell victim to mutual ethnic cleansings perpetrated by the UPA and the Polish insurgents.[23]

In 1943, the OUN-B announced that it was fighting against both Nazi and Bolshevik imperialism and for democratic freedoms. When the Soviet Army entered eastern Galicia in July 1944, the UPA and some other political groups formed a clandestine Ukrainian Supreme Liberation Council, which proclaimed a pluralist platform calling for a democratization of Ukraine's socioeconomic and political life. The suppression of xenophobic elements in nationalist ideology reflected a more diverse support base of a Ukrainian movement that was both anti-Nazi and anti-Soviet. At the same time, the ideological change was part of the nationalist leadership's attempt to position itself as a democratic movement of national liberation that would be more acceptable to the Western Allies. Yet, with the West not interested in dealing with the enemies of their valued Soviet partner, Ukrainian nationalists remained caught between the Soviet rock and the German hard place.

⁑ The Return of Soviet Power

Having survived a series of crushing military defeats in 1941 and 1942, the Stalinist state mobilized the entire society for its war effort. The Soviet military command raised and trained a huge fighting force, which was motivated by both Stalinist patriotic propaganda and the news about the Nazi atrocities in the occupied territories. Heavy industry, which had been moved beyond the Ural Mountains, was soon outproducing Germany in every category of armaments. In addition, military and food supplies began arriving from Great Britain and the United States through the Lend-Lease program. Bolstered with this material support, in January 1943, the Soviet Army solidly defeated the Germans in the Battle of Stalingrad, which marked a turning point in the war. The Germans nevertheless fought fiercely and in February managed to push back the Soviets, who had briefly retaken Kharkiv. Yet, following the Battle of Kursk in July and August 1943, history's largest battle in terms of the number of troops and armaments involved, the Soviet army resumed its advance into Ukraine.

Soviet partisans in Ukraine greatly assisted the army's offensive. Beginning in late 1942, the German military command saw partisans as a major threat to its supply and communication lines west of the Dnipro. In addition to harassing the Germans, some 2,000 partisan units projected a Soviet presence into the occupied territories. The most conservative Western estimates put the number of pro-Soviet guerrillas in Ukraine at 40,000, but the leading Ukrainian authority on World War II, the late Mykhailo Koval, considered the 1946 official estimate of 200,000 not far off the mark. Although the statistics on the partisans' ethnicity are incomplete, the existing data indicate that some 55 percent were Ukrainians.[24] (A large percentage of Soviet guerrillas were professional military, a multinational group in which Russians were over-represented.) Perhaps the most famous partisan commander in the republic was the colorful Sydir Kovpak, whose 1,600-strong detachment accomplished an impressive raid behind German lines from Polissia through Galicia and to the Carpathian Mountains in the summer of 1943.

Assisted by the partisans who were blowing up the railways in the German rear, the Soviet troops pushed steadily westward, taking one Ukrainian city after another. By the end of August 1943, the Soviets had liberated Kharkiv and reached the Dnipro. After long and fierce fighting, they crossed the river and took Kyiv on November 6. Following a major battle at Korsun during January and February 1944, the Soviet Army recovered most of the pre-1939 territory of the Ukrainian republic. In July, it took eastern Galicia, with Lviv falling on July 27. In October 1944, when the Red Army entered Transcarpathia, the Soviet press pompously celebrated the liberation of all the Ukrainian lands.[25] The festivities signaled to the international community Stalin's decision to annex this former Czechoslovak region and include it in the Ukrainian republic.

In an attempt to mobilize Ukrainian patriotism for the war effort, the Soviet leadership renamed the army groups that took part in the liberation of the republic the First, Second, Third, and Forth Ukrainian Fronts. Soviet Ukrainian intellectuals, who produced most of the official propaganda in Ukrainian during the war, seized on this opportunity to elevate the national history and culture. On the recommendation of the film director Dovzhenko, the military Medal of Bohdan Khmelnytsky was created in 1943. Ukrainian writers and scholars promoted the cult of the Cossacks and the celebration of Shevchenko as their nation's founding father. In late 1943, however, the Kremlin indicated its displeasure with the growth of Ukrainian patriotic propaganda by condemning as nationalistic Dovzhenko's film script *Ukraine in Flames*. In 1944, Ukrainian intellectuals were emboldened again by the creation of separate Ukrainian ministries of defense and foreign affairs and by the appointment of some leading writers to important government positions.[26] But it soon became clear that this was no more than Stalin's ploy to get an extra seat in the United Nations. Together with the USSR and Belarus, Ukraine did become one of the UN's founding members, yet the party eventually abandoned or rendered hollow all of the wartime Ukrainian state-building projects.

Instead, during the last years of the war, Soviet propaganda stressed the historical unity of the Ukrainian and Russian peoples, with the latter characterized as the historic dominant player in their relationship. The Stalinist regime made only one notable concession to popular identities that surfaced during the war—it accepted a larger role for religion in a socialist society. In Ukraine, it meant state support for the Russian Orthodox Church, which in 1943 had reached an understanding with the Kremlin. The state suppressed the Ukrainian Autocephalous Orthodox Church, which had reestablished itself in Ukraine during the war.[27] As soon as the Red Army took Galicia, the Soviet administration there also began repressions against the Greek Catholic Church.

This change in Soviet policies was more than abandonment of wartime reliance on non-Russian patriotism as a mobilization tool. It also reflected the Kremlin's growing concern with the strength of Ukrainian nationalism, especially in the western regions. Newly released documents show that Soviet partisans there clashed with the nationalist guerrillas as early as 1942, and during the spring and summer of 1944, the UPA became a major obstacle to the establishment of Soviet control over the area.[28] The rebels not only slowed the advancing Red Army with their attacks but also fatally wounded General Nikolai Vatutin, the commander of the First Ukrainian Front. They attacked Soviet bureaucrats and security officials in the towns and villages of western Ukraine, as well as local activists who collaborated with the Stalinist authorities. During the winter of 1944–1945, massive Soviet military and security forces descended on the western Ukrainian countryside in a brutal campaign of repression. Declassified documents reveal that during 1944 and the first six months of 1945, the Soviets reported killing 91,615 nationalist guerrillas and detaining 96,446.[29] Even if these numbers were exaggerated, a slaughter of this magnitude effectively eliminated large-scale armed re-sistance. Smaller nationalist detachments continued their war of terror for years after the war's end, however.

As the Red Army advanced into Galicia, a large part of the local intel-ligentsia fled with the retreating German forces. This group joined numerous refugees from eastern Ukraine who had been prominent in public life dur-ing German rule and feared retaliation or simply wanted to escape further Stalinist repressions and deprivations. (Only a minority among the refugees had collaborated with the Nazis.) Although the overwhelming majority of them eventually returned to the USSR, a significant percentage of Ukrainian Ostarbeiter and POWs chose to stay in the West because of memories of poverty at home and because they feared repression on their return to the USSR. In 1946, there were some 160,000 to 200,000 Ukrainian "displaced persons" (DPs) in the Western allies' occupation zones in Germany and Austria, as well as smaller numbers in Italy, France, and other European countries.[30] Following a prolonged struggle against forced repatriation to the Soviet Union, the majority of the DPs resettled in North America, Australia, and Britain.

✢✢ The Sovietization of Western Ukraine and High Stalinism

With his mighty armies having been key to the Allies' success in Europe, Stalin persuaded the United States and Great Britain to recognize the Soviet territo-rial acquisitions of 1939 and 1940. Stalin, President Franklin D. Roosevelt, and Prime Minister Winston Churchill reached a preliminary agreement on this issue during their first conference in Tehran (November 1943). At the second conference in Yalta (February 1945), the Big Three finalized the most difficult question of Poland's borders by moving the Polish state west by about 200 miles. The Allies assigned eastern Galicia, western Volhynia, and Polissia to the USSR, and they compensated the Poles with former Ger-man territories in the west. In addition, the Soviet Union reacquired from Romania the Ukrainian-populated northern part of Bukovyna and pressured Czechoslovakia to officially surrender Transcarpathia (in 1945). For the first time in modern history, all the Ukrainian ethnic lands were united in a single state structure, that of the Ukrainian Soviet Socialist Republic. Unwittingly, the Stalinist conquests made possible the emergence of the present-day united and independent Ukraine.

The Soviet plan to absorb western Ukraine included several population exchanges with Poland resulting in the departure of 810,415 Poles and the arrival of 482,880 Ukrainians.[31] This spelled the end of the centuries-long

Polish presence in Ukraine, as well as a closure to the bitter Polish-Ukrainian conflict in Galicia. But the authorities were less concerned with ethnic purity in western Ukraine than they were with its political loyalty. Between 1944 and 1950, they exiled to Siberia 203,662 western Ukrainians, mostly family members of nationalist guerrillas.[32]

No reliable statistical information is available on the number of victims in the bloody war between Soviet security detachments and the UPA that enveloped the western Ukrainian countryside during the immediate postwar years. According to new research, the United States and Britain began supporting the Ukrainian insurgents as early as 1946, and the Soviet discovery of this backing fueled the emerging Cold War.[33] Meanwhile, the main forces of Ukrainian partisans withdrew to the forest area along the Polish-Ukrainian border, as well as to eastern Poland, to escape systematic security sweeps through the villages of eastern Galicia and Volhynia during 1945 and 1946. After the partisans ambushed the Polish deputy minister of defense, General Karol Świerczewski, the Polish government organized Operation Wisła, a punitive military action against the UPA. During the spring and summer of 1947, Polish, Soviet, and Czechoslovak troops suppressed the guerrilla resistance in Poland's eastern regions and forcibly resettled some 150,000 of the remaining local Ukrainian population in the country's northwest.[34] By 1948, organized resistance on the Soviet side of the border had ended as well. Isolated groups of nationalists continued their propaganda and sabotage efforts until the early 1950s, but they no longer imperiled Soviet control of western Ukraine.

Although the Stalinist authorities held off any major socioeconomic transformations in the region until they defeated the UPA, they made no postponement on the ideological front. After the death of Metropolitan Sheptytsky in November 1944, the official press immediately began attacking the national church of Galician Ukrainians. In 1946, with the church's bishops in prison, the Soviet functionaries staged a sobor (ecclesiastical council) of the Greek Catholic Church that "reunited" it with the Russian Orthodox Church and turned its church buildings and other resources over to the Moscow Patriarchate.[35] At the same time, the new administration organized an intensive political propaganda campaign in the western provinces. Local schools, newspapers, and district party committees were staffed with tens of thousands of Russians and reliable eastern Ukrainians.

By 1948, the Soviet authorities felt secure enough to begin the forced collectivization of the region's agriculture, which was largely completed by 1951.[36] Because the official concept of socialist transformation also included industrialization, Moscow made a point of developing industry and mineral extraction in western Ukraine as well. During the first postwar decade, the region's industrial output increased fourfold, and Lviv-made buses and radios became a familiar sight throughout the Soviet Union. No longer a peasant society, western Ukraine acquired a sizable indigenous working class and a professional stratum. Notwithstanding the influx of Russian workers and the spread of the Russian language in higher education, postwar western Ukraine remained, in the historian Roman Szporluk's words, one of "the least Soviet," as well as "the least Russian and the least Russified," areas in the USSR.[37] To prevent a resurgence of nationalism, Soviet bureaucrats neither pushed for linguistic assimilation in the west nor encouraged significant Russian in-migration. With their long tradition of communal organization for the national cause, western Ukrainians staunchly adhered to their language and produced one of the lowest levels of party membership per thousand of population. Khrushchev must have been referring to western Ukrainians when, in his 1956 Secret Speech, he mentioned Stalin's wish to deport the Ukrainians in the same way that the Chechens, the Crimean Tatars, and other unreliable ethnic groups had been. The deportation of the Ukrainians was never attempted because "there were too many of them and there was no place to which to deport them."[38]

As Stalinist bureaucrats in western Ukraine busied themselves with Sovietizing the reconquered lands, their colleagues in the east focused on rebuilding the ruined economy. The extent of wartime destruction was such that most industries had to be rebuilt from scratch. Nevertheless, the fourth five-year plan (1946–1950) proved a success because in a command economy, the government could concentrate investments and workers' labor on a single task, rebuilding heavy industry. By 1950, the republic's industrial output already exceeded the prewar levels; by the end of the fifth five-year plan (1950–1955), it was more than twice the prewar figure. In the absence of foreign investments, the authorities achieved such a feat by demanding sacrifices from a population that was forced to underconsume.

In contrast with industry, Ukrainian agriculture during the postwar decade did not benefit from heavy state investment. Khrushchev's bold projects to consolidate collective farms into large "agro-cities" could not overcome wartime devastation and the lack of workers (especially men who had perished in the war). Although the authorities eventually abandoned their restructuring plans, the republic's grain harvests in 1950 and even in 1955 could not match the prewar levels. Combined with agriculture's other woes, the drought of 1946 led to a famine in the countryside. As in 1932 and 1933, ruthless grain collection policies and official denial of the problem cost the Ukrainian peasants dearly. The only official data showing the famine's scale are the number of people diagnosed in 1947 with dystrophy (serious weight loss and weakness associated with impaired nourishment): 1,154,198. Present-day scholars estimate the number of starvation-related deaths at anywhere from 100,000 to a million.[39]

Khrushchev, who incurred Stalin's wrath by asking for famine relief, in 1947 briefly lost his party leadership in the republic to the Kremlin's trusted troubleshooter, Lazar Kaganovich. While he could not organize a breakthrough in agriculture, Kaganovich sought to uncover national- ist deviations in Ukrainian culture and scholarship. His efforts were part of a general postwar ideological freeze, known as the Zhdanovshchina, after Andrei Zhdanov, Stalin's lieutenant who in 1946 had started the cam- paign for a return to a strict party line on cultural issues. But if the Russian Zhdanovshchina was an attack on liberalism and Western influences in the arts, its Ukrainian variety focused on combating the alleged manifestations of Ukrainian nationalism.[40] Beginning under Khrushchev and gaining mo- mentum under Kaganovich, the ideological purification campaign resulted in numerous denunciatory meetings and firings, as well as several decrees on "political mistakes" committed by Ukrainian writers, historians, literary scholars, and theater directors.

The authorities' prolonged struggle with the UPA in western Ukraine may have been one of the reasons for this ideological purge, which came to an end in late 1947 after Khrushchev regained Stalin's favor—and the posi- tion of first secretary. Under Khrushchev and his colorless successor, Leonid Melnikov (first secretary in 1949–1953), the Ukrainian bureaucracy under- went an impressive consolidation. Ideologically, the apparatchiks explained the victory as proof of the Soviet power's vitality and used their war record as a justification for career advancement.[41] Owing to an extensive recruit- ment campaign, by 1949 the CP(B)U had recovered its prewar strength of 680,000 members. Ethnic Ukrainians made further strides in securing their majority in the party, occupying more than 70 percent of the ranking posi- tions in the party apparatus.[42] In the party's Central Committee, a group of younger Ukrainian functionaries, who had risen to prominence during the war and were Khrushchev's appointees, became increasingly influential. Yet, the all-important post of the first secretary remained in the hands of ethnic Russians such as Khrushchev and Melnikov.

In 1951, the Kremlin checked the growing self-confidence of the Ukrai- nian establishment with a surprise denunciation of Volodymyr Sosiura's popular patriotic poem "Love Ukraine" (1944) as crypto-nationalistic. This was followed by a comprehensive campaign against "nationalist deviations" in all other genres of Ukrainian culture. Beginning in the late 1940s, the Stalin- ist authorities also harassed Ukrainian Jews, whose employment prospects worsened considerably after the bizarre anti-Semitic campaigns against "root- less cosmopolitans" in 1949 and "killer doctors" in 1953. Until Stalin's death in March 1953, the republic's population remained in a state of uncertainty, with rumors circulating about a forthcoming major purge in Ukraine.

❖

World War II, which led to the deaths of more than 8 million Ukrainian citizens,[43] left the republic in ruins. As a result of Stalin's imperial conquests in eastern Europe, however, Soviet Ukraine's territory increased by a quarter and its population by some 11 million, for the first time uniting almost all ethnic Ukrainians in one state. The Stalinist unification unwittingly fulfilled the old nationalist dream of the state unity of Ukrainian lands, a project that only a Great Power could accomplish after the Ukrainians failed to defend their unity during the revolutionary period. More than any other event in the twentieth century, the war defined contemporary Ukraine as a political and geographical notion. Yet, the postwar Ukrainian Soviet Socialist Republic was anything but a nationalist dream. With a regimented socialist economy, public life strictly controlled by the party, and Ukrainian culture increasingly under attack, the republic's national identity seemed a meaningless form filled with Stalinist content.

Ukraine under Stalin's Heirs

Stalin died in March 1953, leaving his successors a multinational world power, a socialist state covering a sixth of the globe's dry land and controlling additional satellites in Europe and Asia. Having won the bloodiest war in human history, the Soviet Union quickly managed to restore its industrial base. The Kremlin had eliminated all enemies real and imagined, including the almost complete suppression of Ukrainian nationalist insurgents in the newly incorporated territories. Stalinist bureaucrats did not fully control the fabric of everyday life, but they boasted the creation of a new Soviet person. Indeed, throughout the country, an increasing number of citizens had internalized Communist ideology and Soviet patriotism. Yet, Stalin's heirs realized that they could no longer ask for sacrifices from the people without providing them with a better life. They repudiated terror and eliminated the worst irrational features of Stalinist governance, while preserving their commitment to the socialist project. For more than thirty years, the successors of Stalin tried to construct Soviet "normalcy"—a socialist society not burdened by wars, reconstructions, and the purging of enemies.

For the Ukrainian Soviet Socialist Republic, this postwar normalcy meant impressive industrial development, urbanization, and the development of a fully modern society—but also tight political control from Moscow and gradual marginalization of Ukrainian culture. World War II, the Holocaust, and forced population exchanges with Poland had made the republic more ethnically homogeneous than ever. But this trend was soon counterbalanced by the influx of ethnic Russians and assimilationist pressures prompting Ukrainians to switch to the Russian language. Having lost much of its rich multiethnic past, the republic became more "Ukrainian" but also more culturally "Russian."

While experiencing postwar deprivation and striving to improve everyday conditions, many Ukrainians saw tensions related to the republic's rights and national identity as marginal, of interest only to the narrow stratum of the intelligentsia. After all, life was indeed becoming better and distinctively modern. Ukrainian citizens, with urbanites among them now outnumbering villagers, were moving into new apartments, enjoying free medical services, and buying their first refrigerators and television sets. The Ukrainian republic led the way in the development of Soviet computers, airplanes, and intercontinental ballistic missiles. Big cities had their homegrown hippies and Beatles fans. Yet, the foundation of the republic's political identity, the Ukrainian national project, was bound to reemerge in a moment of crisis—as the only platform that could unite the republic's elites and ordinary citizens against the Soviet center.

✜ De-Stalinization and Khrushchev's Reforms

Succession struggles in the Kremlin unexpectedly confirmed Ukraine's political importance. In his abortive bid for power, Lavrentii Beria, Stalin's long-serving chief of the secret police, attempted to court the non-Russian nationalities, Ukrainians in particular. In June 1953, he engineered the removal of Khrushchev's successor in Ukraine, First Secretary Leonid Melnikov, on charges of being insensitive to the nationalities issue in western Ukraine. Melnikov, an ethnic Russian, was allegedly responsible for introducing Russian-language instruction at local universities and promoting newcomers from the east over native cadres. (Such policies were, indeed, pursued in the region as part of a general Sovietization drive, but Melnikov did not invent them.) Melnikov's replacement was Oleksii Kyrychenko, a long-time protégé of Khrushchev and the first ethnic Ukrainian to lead the Communist Party of Ukraine or CPU—as the CP(B)U was renamed in 1952—since the early 1920s.[1] Ethnic Ukrainian bureaucrats were promoted to other important positions in the republic, and even after Beria lost his bid for power, the victors did not reverse the personnel changes in Ukraine.

The Ukrainization of the apparatus continued in large part because of Khrushchev's rise to prominence in the Kremlin. Having served for a decade as the Ukrainian party chief, Khrushchev considered the republic his power base and was not averse to wooing its population with such political gestures. He went even further in 1954, when the whole Soviet Union lavishly celebrated the 300th anniversary of the Pereiaslav Treaty. The attendant statement from the Communist Party of the Soviet Union (CPSU) Central Committee, the so-called Theses on the tercentenary, affirmed the official interpretation of Pereiaslav as beneficial for the Ukrainians and the alleged desire to "reunite" with Russia as Ukrainian history's main theme.[2] Between the actual anniversary in midwinter and its official celebration in May, the Kremlin announced an unprecedented "gift" from one Soviet republic to another. As a token of everlasting friendship, the Russian Federation ceded the Crimean peninsula to Ukraine.

The historic homeland of the Crimean Tatars, the peninsula was constituted politically as the Crimean Tatar Autonomous Soviet Socialist Republic within the Russian Federation between 1921 and 1945, even though from tsarist times, Russian and Ukrainian settlers made up the majority of its population. In the spring of 1944, however, Stalin had all the Tatars deported en masse to Soviet Asia for their alleged collaboration with the Nazis. The next year the Kremlin formally abolished the Crimea's autonomous status and turned it into a regular Russian province. A new wave of predominantly Russian settlers replaced the deportees, and by the time of Stalin's death, the Crimean economy had largely recovered from wartime ruination. Its famous resorts on the Black Sea again became the favorite destination for Soviet vacationers, and the Crimean wine industry flourished once more. The Soviet military rebuilt Sevastopol as a base of the Black Sea Fleet. Connected by land only to Ukraine, the Crimea has always had closer economic ties with this republic than with Russia. Its integration into the Ukrainian economy intensified after 1954, and more ethnic Ukrainians moved into the region, but no cultural Ukrainization occurred. For the sake of appearances, the republic's authorities transferred to the Crimea one Ukrainian theater company,[3] but ethnic Russians retained their numerical majority, and Russian culture continued to predominate on the peninsula.

The jubilee rhetoric and the transfer of the Crimea in effect elevated the Ukrainians to the role of the Russians' junior partners in running the Soviet state. Ukrainian-born functionaries could and did make their careers in Moscow and elsewhere in the USSR. Especially after Khrushchev established his unchallenged authority in the Kremlin during the late 1950s, dozens if not hundreds of his protégés from Ukraine moved to high positions in Moscow. Political support from the Ukrainian leadership helped Khrushchev in crucial moments, especially during the succession struggles of 1954 and during his attempted ouster by party hardliners in 1957. As a reward, in 1957 the Soviet leader promoted Kyrychenko to Moscow to become one of the secretaries of the CPSU Central Committee. Kyrychenko's successor in Kyiv, Mykola Pidhorny, also an ethnic Ukrainian, earned a similar promotion in 1963 and went on to play a major role in Soviet politics during the late 1960s and 1970s (when Soviet and Western media used the Russian spelling of his name, Nikolai Podgorny).[4]

Meanwhile, a tradition emerged in Ukraine, in contrast with Stalin's time, to staff the upper levels of the party bureaucracy with functionaries of indigenous nationality. At its height, after the Eighteenth Congress of the CPU in 1954, all secretaries of the CPU Central Committee and all eight full members of its Politburo were ethnic Ukrainians. Although personnel changes later reduced the Ukrainian bureaucrats' complete domination, this general trend continued into the 1960s. Three quarters of ranking party and state posts in the republic during the late 1950s and 1960s were held by ethnic Ukrainians. Scholars have interpreted this as an emergence of a new Ukrainian political elite in the post-Stalin period,[5] but in view of the bureaucrats' eagerness for promotion elsewhere in the USSR, not too much Ukrainian patriotism can be attributed to them.

Even if they were not patriots of their republic, the Ukrainian functionaries of Khrushchev's time operated in a radically different political and cultural atmosphere than under Stalin. Khrushchev's famous Secret Speech at the party's Twentieth Congress in 1956 condemned Stalin's cult and state terror as aberrant deviations from genuine Marxism. The Twentieth Congress accelerated the rehabilitation of political prisoners that had been going on quietly since Stalin's death, although this process remained slow. According to data from KGB archives, of the 961,645 Ukrainian citizens who had been repressed on political charges between 1929 and 1953, the authorities rehabilitated only 290,967 between 1953 and 1961.[6] Khrushchev's rehabilitation was a limited process; nationalist insurgents, Nazi collaborators, and those convicted of various conspiracies before the Great Terror rarely received a hearing. Beginning in 1956, however, some former UPA fighters and their family members were allowed to return to Ukraine after their terms of exile expired. During the first year, some 60,000 came back to western Ukraine, making the republic's authorities worried about the spread of nationalist sentiments. In the future, returnees were forbidden from settling in the western regions, and those already there were pressured to leave.[7]

Restoring the reputation of the statesman Mykola Skrypnyk, the symbol of Ukrainization, who took his own life after being denounced as a nationalist in 1933, was no less significant than clearing the names of those "convicted" by Stalinist special tribunals. From 1956 to 1958, the Writers' Union spearheaded a campaign to rehabilitate dozens of writers who were victims of the Great Terror. Official party decrees annulled previous condemnations of specific Ukrainian literary and musical works.

As in other parts of the Soviet Union, the rehabilitation of repressed cultural figures constituted part of the "Thaw," the general process of cultural liberalization after Stalin. In Ukraine, Alexander Dovzhenko's 1955 newspaper article calling for a "broader understanding of Socialist realism" was received as a call for creative freedom. Dovzhenko, who died in 1956, was lionized posthumously as one of Ukraine's greatest cultural figures, and dozens of writers and poets began pushing the limits of acceptability in literature. After a prolonged silence during Stalinism, writers' calls to protect the Ukrainian language sounded openly during the Thaw.

Although most noticeable in politics and culture, de-Stalinization spread to the economy as well. The priorities of postwar reconstruction reflected the core values of the Stalinist state. Heavy industry had to be rebuilt first, because state prestige and military might depended on it. In contrast, food shortages and the lack of consumer goods did not constitute a major concern. Soviet agriculture stagnated during Stalin's last years, as it received almost no investments during postwar reconstruction. Yet, Khrushchev saw the declared aim of the Soviet project, Communism, as a social order under which ordinary people would live better than under capitalism. His unrealistic call in 1957 to catch up with and overcome the United States in the production of meat, milk, and butter may sound naive today, but for contemporaries it was a refreshing change after decades of deprivation and famine.

As a major agricultural region, during the late 1950s, Ukraine benefited from impressive increases in state purchasing prices on grain (sevenfold), potatoes (eightfold), and cattle (fivefold). This, together with debt forgiveness, rejuvenated collective and state farms, which could now afford modest improvements. On one of his visits to Ukraine, Khrushchev decided to abolish the Machine and Tractor Stations, once established by Stalin as machinery depots and political supervision centers for nearby farms, and in 1958, the state sold the stations' equipment to the collective farms. During the late 1950s, agricultural production in Ukraine on average grew by 8 percent per year.[8] Food supply to the cities and farmers' standard of life both began improving during this time. Thousands of Ukrainian agricultural specialists, however, left for Kazakhstan and eastern Siberia, where they were recruited to work on Khrushchev's "virgin lands" scheme to cultivate unused land there.

Although the general idea of these reforms was sound, specific agricultural experiments under Khrushchev could be as destructive as some of Stalin's measures. In 1955, the state decreased by half the allowable size of individual plots, the parcels of land near their houses that collective farmers were permitted to keep. While ideologically suspect, these private plots contributed greatly to the economy. They not only fed peasant families but also allowed them to sell the surplus at city markets, thus alleviating food shortages there. The cut in their size, thus, hurt both peasants and urban consumers. Another damaging experiment was connected to Khrushchev's infamous infatuation with corn. During the late 1950s, the Soviet leader issued the directive to devote 20 percent of arable land in Ukraine to this crop, at the expense of the traditional wheat. By the decade's end, the growth in agricultural production had slowed down. Two years of bad harvests, 1960 and 1963, delivered the final blow to Khrushchev's dream of beating the United States in food production. For the first time in its history, in 1963 the Soviet Union was forced to purchase grain from abroad. In 1962, citizens' discontent over rising prices on food in state grocery shops and farmers' markets led to isolated clashes with police and vandalism of shops in Ukraine.[9]

In industry, Khrushchev rightly saw bureaucratic centralization as the main source of problems, but his solution was decentralization, rather than market competition. A reduction in the number of federal ministries in Moscow began soon after Stalin's death. Between 1953 and 1956, some 10,000 major enterprises and organizations were transferred to the command of Ukrainian ministries, thus increasing Kyiv's share of the republic's industry from 36 to 76 percent. During the same period, more than 60,000 bureaucrats in the republic lost their jobs as part of an administrative efficiency campaign.[10]

These early measures may have been helpful in prolonging the Soviet industrial boom. Massive postwar reconstruction launched a period of impressive industrial growth during the 1950s that began slowing down only early in the following decade. Building on this momentum, in 1957 Khrushchev abolished more central ministries and introduced regional economic councils (*sovnarkhozy* in Russian; *radnarhospy* in Ukrainian) that had comprehensive authority over economic development in their areas. Originally, there were eleven such councils in Ukraine, although in 1960 their number grew to fourteen, and a republican coordinating body, the Ukrainian Economic Council, was established. As a result of this reform, Ukrainian authorities gained operational control over 97 percent of the republic's industry.

Khrushchev aimed to prevent situations in which Ukrainian factories in close proximity could not work together because the central planners had linked them with partners in other regions. After Stalin's death, dozens of such cases were discussed at various conferences. For example, the Kyiv power station repair facility received electric cable from the city of Kuibyshev in central Russia, even though a large factory was producing just such a cable in Kyiv. Timber for scaffolding arrived from Arkhangelsk in the Russian north, although it did not differ from that produced locally.[11] But the Kremlin soon discovered that investing local authorities with economic power bred regionalism. Managers and party bosses eagerly guarded their regions' interests, while overall industrial growth continued slowing down. In the early 1960s, Moscow gradually reversed its course, first consolidating Ukraine's fourteen regional economic councils into seven and later into three.[12] After Khrushchev's fall in 1964, the Kremlin restored power to the central ministries.

An attempt to decentralize the party command structure became the last hurrah of de-Stalinization. In 1962, Khrushchev pushed through the decision to divide all provincial and lower-level party committees into "industrial" and "agricultural" streams. In Ukraine, this reform was implemented, amid the growing displeasure of party functionaries, in all but nine primarily agricultural western oblasts. Khrushchev caused further discontent among party bureaucrats with his project to limit tenure in party offices to three terms. In 1964, Khrushchev's Ukrainian clients and the people he had promoted to Moscow were among the most active plotters against him. In the summer of 1964, the majority among the party leadership forced Khrushchev into retirement.

‡‡ Two Models of Soviet Ukrainian Identity

Just as the personality and views of the party leader in Moscow shaped Soviet policies in general, those of the party boss in Ukraine influenced the party line in the republic. In the absence of true democratic mechanisms and with the godlike Stalin no longer in the Kremlin, now occupied by a fellow bureaucrat, local leaders increased their authority even further. In the case of Ukraine, the policies of two post-Stalin first secretaries of the CPU, Petro Shelest (1963–1972) and Volodymyr Shcherbytsky (1972–1989), reflected not just two different styles of leadership but two models of a Soviet Ukrainian identity—one defending the republic's economic interests and culture and the other encouraging centralization and assimilation. The replacement of Shelest by Shcherbytsky in 1972 signaled the restoration of the Kremlin's firm grip on Ukraine.

Shelest was one of those dignitaries whose support for the coup against Khrushchev proved crucial in 1964. A colorful figure known for speaking his mind, Shelest made a career in industrial management before switching to party work during the 1950s. There has been much retrospective mythologizing since Shelest's fall in 1972, especially because official charges against him included being soft on nationalism and promoting economic regionalism. Rumors circulated in Ukraine about his secret support of dissidents, and Shelest himself—when he reappeared in public during the late 1980s—claimed to have been a forerunner of Gorbachev's glasnost.[13] Since the 1970s, Western analysts have debated whether Shelest could be categorized as a "national Communist" or representative of "Ukrainian autonomism."[14]

Now that declassified archives and memoirs have shed new light on the Shelest period, the first secretary emerges as a staunch Communist who, nevertheless, understood the protection of Ukraine's economy and culture to be his duty as the republic's party boss.[15] Official ideology saw socialist construction and the development of Soviet nations as two complementary processes. For Shelest, a Soviet Ukraine meant a strong Ukraine with a fully developed economy and national culture. Thus, when he had to clash with Moscow bureaucrats over his republic's interests, he saw himself as defending Leninist nationality policy, not undermining the Union.

This is not to deny that Shelest's position also reflected the interests of the postwar Ukrainian elites. Immediately before his accession to power in 1963, he headed the CPU's Bureau for Industry and Construction, which oversaw the work of regional economic councils. Both his own background as an industrial manager and his work at the bureau to develop the republic's economic self-management influenced Shelest's later policies as a Ukrainian party leader. He expressed dissatisfaction with the central planners' neglect of Ukraine's needs and insisted that investments in the republic should match its contribution to the all-Union budget. Understandably, Shelest opposed the Kremlin's decision to divert investment from Ukrainian coal and metallurgy to Siberian oil and gas.

Shelest's position also reflected his role as leader of the large and growing Communist Party of Ukraine, now more "Ukrainian" than ever. Party membership in Ukraine between 1958 and 1972 increased from 1.1 to 2.5 million, with the share of ethnic Ukrainians reaching a new high of 65 percent. Ukrainian functionaries continued to dominate the CPU Politburo: In 1971, nine of ten full members and all five candidates belonged to the indigenous nationality.[16] (Note that the Kremlin approved all these high appointments. The Ukrainization of the republic's highest leadership was not seen as rebellious or contradicting the Soviet nationalities policy.) As the head of the CPU, Shelest was justifiably proud of his party's role as "political vanguard" of the Ukrainian people. Those working in the CPU Central Committee apparatus under Shelest remember the first secretary's intense dislike of the term "the republic's party organization," which stressed the political reality of the CPU as being de facto a territorial unit of the all-Union Communist Party. Instead, Shelest preferred the official (and more independent-sounding) name, the Communist Party of Ukraine.[17]

A native speaker of Ukrainian, Shelest always used this language during public appearances in Ukraine. The first secretary often praised the Ukrainian language and heritage in his speeches, in contrast to his predecessors and successors. Most of the records of the CPU Central Committee dating from his time in office were kept in Ukrainian. Apparently with Shelest's approval, in 1965 the Ukrainian minister of higher education, Yurii Dadenkov, issued a circular letter about the Ukrainization of college instruction, although it was soon withdrawn. Yet, it is a mistake to assume that Shelest bonded with the Ukrainian intelligentsia or secretly encouraged dissidents. Contemporary observers in the West speculated that Shelest or some of his associates had encouraged the dissident Ivan Dziuba to write the programmatic book of Ukrainian dissent, *Internationalism or Russification?* but Dziuba himself denied this.[18] In a recent newspaper interview, the poet Dmytro Pavlychko shed light on what Shelest's relations with outspoken intellectuals were really like:

"He summoned me and said, 'Shorten your tongue!' And to do him justice, he protected me from arrest and gave me an apartment in Kyiv."[19] Obviously, Ukraine's party boss did not want mass arrests or other serious trouble on the "ideological front," but he was no ally of the Ukrainian intelligentsia.

Shelest's own book, *Our Soviet Ukraine* (1970), was used as a public excuse for his demotion, and for that reason it received some rather unwarranted attention in the West.[20] Although this work has a patriotic tenor, glorifying the Cossacks and the achievements of Soviet Ukraine, it, like most books published by high officials at the time, was ghostwritten and carefully edited in the CPU Central Committee. Shelest's personal contribution was minimal; his diary contains at best mentions of "going through the material for the book." Thus, if this work documents any deviations from Soviet ideology, they are not Shelest's personal transgressions but rather tropes that had been commonplace in the 1960s but sounded ambiguous in the new political climate of the mid-1970s.

No closet nationalist, Shelest's commitment to democratic reform is also doubtful. During the 1968 Prague Spring, he was the most hawkish of Soviet leaders and pressed for military intervention, lest the disease of liberalism spread to neighboring Ukraine. In economic policy, he continued to emphasize heavy industry at the expense of the production of consumer goods. His rise and fall had more to do with changing alliances and the buildup of power among the highest Soviet leadership than they did with his Soviet-style Ukrainian patriotism.

The story of Shelest's fall begins with the ouster of Khrushchev eight years earlier. The 1964 coup was carried out under the slogan of a return to "collective leadership" and indeed, during the first years of the new regime, decisions were made by the ruling triumvirate of Leonid Brezhnev, Aleksei Kosygin, and Mykola Pidhorny. By the late 1960s, however, Brezhnev, who was first secretary of the CPSU Central Committee, emerged as the country's unquestioned leader. (In 1966, the party congress restored the historical name of his post, "General Secretary.") Unlike Stalin, and Khrushchev during his last years, the new party chief ruled by consensus, balancing the positions of the powerful interest groups. In the process, Brezhnev was building one of the most extensive patronage networks in the Soviet Union, which after his death would be referred to as the "Dnipropetrovsk mafia."

Like Khrushchev, Leonid Brezhnev was an ethnic Russian who was born and began his party career in Ukraine. Trained as an engineer, he joined the party bureaucracy in his native Dnipropetrovsk province in 1938, taking advantage of the vacancies created by the Great Terror. Interestingly, at the time he listed his nationality as "Ukrainian," apparently trying to present himself as an indigenous functionary. (He changed his nationality to

"Russian" when he was promoted to a high position in Moscow during the 1950s.)[21] Having caught Khrushchev's eye during the war, Brezhnev rose through the ranks in Ukraine, Moldova, and Kazakhstan before his move to Moscow. For Shelest, another unfaithful client of Khrushchev's, Brezhnev was his equal and former coconspirator but not a patron. If anything, Shelest was closer to another triumvir, Pidhorny. As soon as Brezhnev accumulated more power in the Kremlin, his relations with powerful republican chiefs, such as Shelest, became tense.

In Ukraine, Brezhnev found an alternative to Shelest in Volodymyr Shcherbytsky, an old friend from Dnipropetrovsk province.[22] In the early 1960s, Shcherbytsky served briefly as the republic's premier before being sent back to Dnipropetrovsk to serve as provincial first secretary. In 1965, Brezhnev helped him regain the premier's position, a managerial rather than political job at the time, but Shelest lasted for seven more years, as Brezhnev needed to accumulate considerable authority before removing him. Preparations began in earnest in 1970, when the Ukrainian KGB chief loyal to Shelest was replaced, along with all provincial KGB heads. A crackdown on dissidents followed, complete with a press campaign against Ukrainian nationalism that made Shelest appear lax. Finally, in May 1972, Brezhnev suddenly transferred the Ukrainian party leader to a managerial job in Moscow as deputy premier of the USSR and then sent him into retirement. Only a year later, the Ukrainian public learned about Shelest's "mistakes" from an editorial in a party journal. He was declared guilty of idealizing the Ukrainian past, promoting economic self-sufficiency, and abetting "nationalist deviations."

The new first secretary, Shcherbytsky, owed his political career to his association with the Dnipropetrovsk clan and his personal friendship with Brezhnev. In contrast to Shelest, historians usually present him as Moscow's obedient puppet and even as a "Little Russian," as opposed to a nationally conscious Ukrainian. But such a characterization only obscures the complex processes within the Ukrainian elite. Those who knew Shcherbytsky before the early 1960s, for example, remember him as a Ukrainian-speaking patriot much like Shelest.[23] Only later, when he began positioning himself vis-à-vis Shelest as a political rival and a better agent of the center, did Shcherbytsky's persona begin evolving into that of a Russian-speaking administrator tough on Ukrainian nationalism.

True to his promise, Shcherbytsky began his rule with repressions against dissidents and the wider circle of the Ukrainian intelligentsia from 1972 to 1974. During the 1973 exchange of party cards campaign, some 37,000 members were purged from the CPU, many of them for "ideological mistakes." Dozens of nonconformist academics lost their jobs, and some historical journals and musical ensembles were terminated. In this purge, Shcherbytsky was ably assisted by the CPU's new ideological secretary, Vasyl Malanchuk, whose father had been killed by nationalist guerrillas in western Ukraine and who thereafter launched a personal ideological crusade against Ukrainian nationalism. The appointment of an ethnic Russian, Ivan Sokolov, as the CPU's second secretary reduced the postwar domination of Ukrainians in the republic's highest leadership.

Shcherbytsky did not oppose the central planners as fervently as Shelest, but it would be misleading to see him as Moscow's representative in the republic. Like many Soviet provincial party secretaries or republican party leaders, he "worked the phones" to secure investments and consumer goods for Ukraine while disdainfully referring to central bureaucrats as "Muscovite boyars."[24] But Shcherbytsky's commitment to his republic had clearly defined limits. Together with millions of Ukrainian soccer fans, he took part in the general rejoicing when the Dynamo Kyiv soccer team beat Moscow clubs, but he almost always spoke Russian in public, and his seventeen-year rule saw a steep decline in Ukrainian-language publishing and education.

✸✸ The Sixties Generation and Dissent

The creeping assimilationist pressure encountered resistance from the Ukrainian intelligentsia. The cultural Thaw during the 1950s brought to prominence a new generation of writers and artists. Coming of age during the time of rehabilitation, the first cultural exchanges with the West, and somewhat relaxed ideological control, this brilliant cohort of creative Ukrainian youth adopted the name *shistdesiatnyky* (the "sixties," or the generation of the sixties). They rebelled against party control over artistic expression and condemned the conformism of their older colleagues. Prominent sixties included poets Ivan Drach, Lina Kostenko, Dmytro Pavlychko, Vasyl Symonenko, and Mykola Vinhranovsky; prose writers Volodymyr Drozd, Valerii Shevchuk, and Hryhir Tiutiunnyk; literary critic Ivan Dziuba; film director Serhii Paradzhanov; theater director Les Taniuk; and artists Alla Horska and Panas Zalyvakha. This generation was not united by a single creative style or by any coherent ideology. More traditional in form, the civic poetry of Vasyl Symonenko seemingly has little in common with Ivan Drach's contemporary bold experiments with words. The sixties also had different relations with the government; some reached accommodation with the authorities, others suffered repression, and yet others retreated into isolation. Yet, their search for new creative forms helped shape present-day Ukrainian culture, and their democratic impulses eventually translated into political dissent.

For all the youthful vigor of the sixties, a senior establishment writer produced the most controversial novel of the decade. In 1968, Oles Honchar, the chairman of the Ukrainian Writers' Union, who protected and encouraged the sixtiers, published the novel *The Cathedral*. Depicting a town in eastern Ukraine whose residents are trying to save an old Cossack church from being dismantled, the message of the novel, rather than its more traditional style, caused a sensation. *The Cathedral* was read as a passionate plea to preserve historical monuments that anchor modern Ukrainian identity in the Cossack past. The authorities soon banned the book—after the first secretary of Dnipropetrovsk oblast, Oleksii Vatchenko, thought he recognized himself in one of the main characters, a heartless and assimilated bureaucrat.[25] Yet, the official ban on *The Cathedral* merely made it more popular among the Ukrainian intelligentsia. Of course, only a tiny minority of its readers belonged to an organized political opposition.

During the Brezhnev era, Ukrainians earned a reputation of being overrepresented in the dissident movement and among the ranks of Gulag prisoners. Yet, Ukrainian dissent was never a united movement. Rather, this label encompassed very different traditions, organizations, and ideological orientations among various nonconformist groups. Most Ukrainian oppositionists shared a concern about civil rights best expressed by the famous Russian dissident Andrei Sakharov, but local issues of national rights and religious freedoms were equally important to them. Contrary to what might be expected, the origins of Ukrainian dissent are not found in wartime Ukrainian nationalism. The last groups of nationalist insurgents hid in the forests of western Ukraine until the early 1950s, and the first dissident organizations emerged by the decade's end, but these dissidents did not have a nationalist pedigree. In sharp contrast to the peasant membership, conspiratorial methods, and populist anti-Marxist ideology of wartime nationalism, the dissent of the 1960s was a product of the Soviet system itself. The first archetypal dissidents came out of the sixties movement, and these well-educated young intellectuals called for a return to the "Leninist" nationality policy and other reforms within the existing system.

At first, the dissidents limited their discussions to small informal circles, and their topics to the preservation of the Ukrainian language and culture. The Club of Creative Youth in Kyiv provided these outspoken intellectuals with a semiofficial outlet until its dispersal in 1963. At Kyiv University in 1963, a scholarly conference on the Ukrainian language turned into a demonstration against assimilationist policies. A monument to Taras Shevchenko, located in a park across the street from the university, became a traditional gathering place for nonconformist youth, and KGB agents frequently photographed the participants. Official criticism of the Ukrainian sixtiers in 1963 scared some of them away and hardened the resolve of others.

One result was the politicization of *samvydav* (self-publishing, *samizdat* in Russian), unofficial literature copied on typewriters or by hand and distributed secretly. At first mostly forbidden literary works, by the mid-1960s Ukrainian *samvydav* developed into bold political journalism.[26] During the 1965 crackdown on dissidents, the Ukrainian KGB arrested some sixty intellectuals involved in *samvydav*. But these harsh measures backfired. A young official journalist assigned to cover the trials, Viacheslav Chornovil, ended up writing a *samvydav* book about the accused and served a prison sentence for it. Another manifestation of protest occurred at the 1965 Kyiv premiere of Serhii Paradzhanov's internationally acclaimed movie, *Shadows of Forgotten Ancestors*. Before the film's screening in the capital's largest movie theater, the literary critic Ivan Dziuba addressed the audience and powerfully denounced the arrests. Later that year, Dziuba sent Shelest a letter protesting the repressions and assimilationist tendencies in culture. He enclosed a copy of his manuscript, *Internationalism or Russification?* which became the most celebrated manifesto of Ukrainian dissent.[27]

Quoting Lenin extensively, Dziuba argued that the Soviet authorities abandoned "Leninist" nationalities policy in favor of assimilation. A close reading of his text reveals that Dziuba constructed his ideal "Leninist policy" from a very selective reading of party documents dating from the period of Ukrainization. The real value of his book lies in the contrast between the promotion of the Ukrainian language and culture during the period of Ukrainization and the state's quiet retreat to encouraging assimilation during the later period. Perhaps most damagingly, Dziuba compares cultural assimilation in Soviet Ukraine to tsarist colonial policies. Yet he, like the majority of the sixties, did not question the legitimacy of the Soviet state or hint at the possibility of Ukraine's separation. In contrast, the Ukrainian Workers and Peasants Union (1959–1961), a small western Ukrainian organization led by Levko Lukianenko, thought Ukraine should separate from the USSR and build Communism on its own. (Its proletarian name notwithstanding, the union consisted entirely of low-level Soviet functionaries.)[28]

Despite the predominance of a "reformist" trend, the Ukrainian dissident movement produced several more radical nationalist thinkers. The colorful historian Valentyn Moroz, whose writings echoed those of Dmytro Dontsov, cherished the cult of the heroic individual. He rejected the Soviet system in principle in his book, *Report from the Beria Reserve* (1970), which was written in the Gulag. Another radical was Stepan Khmara, who took over the editorship of the *samvydav* journal *Ukrainian Herald* in 1972. Under its first editor, Viacheslav Chornovil, the journal mostly reported violations of civil rights and the principle of national equality. After Chornovil's second arrest, Khmara adopted an openly nationalistic discourse, speaking of the "ethnocide" of Ukrainians in the Soviet Union. The (partial) opening of the Ukrainian KGB archives has allowed Ukrainian scholars a detailed look at such small radical groups as the Ukrainian National Front, established in the city of Ivano-Frankivsk in western Ukraine during the early 1960s. In contrast to the intellectual Marxist sixtiers, this organization, which was made up of veterans of the Ukrainian Insurgent Army and young Galician villagers, advocated independence and circulated old nationalist propaganda literature.[29]

The mainstream of Ukrainian dissent, however, insisted on working in the open and holding the Soviet authorities to their promises. Writing letters of protest to party and state bodies became the favorite legal weapon of nonconformist intellectuals. In 1965, a number of writers and scholars signed a petition in defense of arrested dissidents; three years later, 139 intellectuals signed a letter to Brezhnev, protesting the arrests and rampant assimilation. That same year, more than 300 people in Brezhnev's home base of Dnipropetrovsk signed the "Letter from Creative Youth" to decry the disappearance of the Ukrainian language in that city. By the late 1960s, annual meetings in May near Shevchenko's statue in Kyiv to mark the anniversary of the poet's funeral became forums full of dissident youth. In 1967, the KGB violently dispersed the gathering, leading to an unprecedented manifestation of protest before the CPU Central Committee building. The Ukrainian minister of interior arrived there late at night to appease the crowd of protesters. After another mass gathering at the Shevchenko monument in 1972, the authorities cancelled the festival of arts, Kyivan Spring '73, fearing that it would provide a venue for more protests.[30]

In 1972, the authorities commenced a new crackdown against dissent by arresting hundreds of people in different parts of Ukraine and imposing much harsher sentences than in 1965 and 1966. Some leading figures, most notably Dziuba, renounced their views in exchange for freedom. Rather than eradicating Ukrainian dissent, however, the state offensive radicalized it by crushing the protesters' hopes of working within the system and gradually transforming it. Those who ended up in remote prison camps in Russia began issuing radical appeals, denouncing their Soviet citizenship, and demanding recognition as political prisoners.[31]

Meanwhile, international developments gave dissidents an unexpected boost. In 1975, the Soviet Union signed the Final Act of the thirty-five-nation European Conference on Security and Cooperation at a meeting in Helsinki. Signatories formally recognized the postwar political borders in Europe—an important gain for Soviet diplomacy—but also agreed to observe basic human rights and allow the monitoring of their compliance. After Soviet newspapers published the Charter of Human Rights, dissidents immediately sensed an opportunity to make the state honor its promise. In May 1976, the first Helsinki Committee was established in Moscow as an open public association monitoring the state's human rights record. Similar groups emerged in other Soviet republics, the largest one in Ukraine.

The Ukrainian Group for the Promotion of the Implementation of the Helsinki Accords, popularly known as the Ukrainian Helsinki Group (UHG), was created in November 1976 and united representatives of different trends in dissent. Mykola Rudenko—a Soviet war hero, a longtime establishment writer, and recent convert to the opposition who wrote a lengthy critique of Marxist economic theory—became the leader of the group. Its members included political prisoners of Stalin's time, dissidents of the 1960s, adherents of banned Ukrainian churches, and oppositionists from ethnic or religious minorities (such as the prominent Jewish activist Iosif Zisels and the son of the jailed Baptist leader, Petr Vins). United by their concern about civil and national rights, rather than narrow ethnic nationalism, the UHG members coordinated their work with similar groups in Russia, Lithuania, Georgia, and Armenia. But they did not exclude the possibility of Ukraine's future secession from the USSR if it was decided by free and fair elections.

In the spirit of its legalistic philosophy, the UHG insisted on its right to work openly. By 1980, the group had issued about sixty declarations, appeals, and bulletins registering violations of human and national rights in Ukraine. Twenty-four of the group's thirty-nine members were imprisoned, eventually serving a combined 170 years.[32] Six (including Rudenko) were forced to immigrate; four eventually died in the Gulag. By the early 1980s, the Ukrainian Helsinki Group was disabled by repressions, but its members in both the Gulag and foreign exile remained committed to the cause. Unlike its sister group in Moscow, the UHG never officially dissolved. (Surviving members would reestablish the group during Gorbachev's reforms.)

The struggle for freedom of religion represented a notable trend in Ukrainian dissent. Of the two banned churches, the Greek Catholic Church continued to operate as a "catacomb church." By the late 1970s, it had several bishops and hundreds of priests, most of them formally employed as clerks or laborers but covertly serving the faithful in western Ukraine. The KGB constantly harassed the church and imprisoned numerous priests. In 1963, however, following Pope John XXIII's personal intervention with the Soviet authorities, they released the head of the church, Metropolitan Iosyf Slipy, who went to Rome. In 1982, the lay activist Iosyf Terelia organized a committee for the defense of the Greek Catholic Church, a dissident group campaigning to legalize the church. The Ukrainian Autocephalous Orthodox Church was not functioning in Ukraine, although some activists kept sending appeals to the authorities on its behalf. One of these petitioners, the

Reverend Volodymyr Romaniuk (in the 1990s, Patriarch Volodymyr), was sentenced to ten years in 1972. Khrushchev's antireligious campaign in the late 1950s and early 1960s also inflicted heavy losses on the Russian Orthodox Church in Ukraine, which the authorities otherwise tolerated and had previously used as an instrument of assimilation. The campaign resulted in the forced deregistration of nearly 4,000 parishes, with new registration not allowed until the late 1980s.[33] The Soviet authorities likewise harassed the Baptists, Pentecostals, Adventists, and Jehovah's Witnesses in Ukraine. These religious groups often sought permission to emigrate from the Soviet Union, as did many Ukrainian Jews, whose religious and cultural rights were severely limited and who were subjected to anti-Semitic harassment. In addition, the state restricted the Jews' social and educational opportunities. The Crimean Tatars, in contrast, demanded permission to return to Crimea from their exile in Soviet Asia.

Other expressions of dissent in Soviet Ukraine included occasional workers' protests and strikes. Dissident groups had hardly any contact with the workers; the UHG, in fact, ignored socioeconomic questions. When isolated strikes took place, usually to protest food shortages and rising prices, they were concentrated in the Donbas region, where the dissident movement was barely represented. In 1978, a group of Donbas workers led by Vladimir Klebanov established an independent trade union, the Free Trade Union Association of the Soviet Working Class. The organizers emphasized that they had nothing in common with oppositionist intellectuals or Ukrainian "nationalists," but the authorities arrested them anyway.[34] Worker unrest would not emerge as a serious political factor until well into the Gorbachev period.

Overall, the dissidents did not attract mass support in Ukraine or elsewhere in the Soviet Union. More or less reliable data for the period 1960 to 1972 puts the total number of Ukrainian citizens engaged in dissident activities, including simply signing petitions, at 942 individuals—this in a republic with a population of 45 million.[35] But given the omnipotence of the KGB and the party's strict control over public expression, the dissidents' achievements were remarkable. Most adults were aware of the dissidents and their demands, irrespective of whether this information originated from Western radio broadcasts or denunciations in Soviet newspapers.

Because Ukraine shared a long border with Poland, Czechoslovakia, Hungary, and Romania, any discontent in these Soviet satellites also put the Ukrainian leadership on high alert. Events in Hungary in 1956, Czechoslovakia in 1968, and Poland in 1980 and 1981 were widely discussed in Ukraine, although there was no serious spillover of organized protest. The Prague Spring, in particular, reverberated in Ukraine because it changed the situation of the Ukrainian minority in Czechoslovakia. The legalization in Czechoslovakia of the (Ukrainian) Greek Catholic Church and the publication there of works by Ukrainian dissidents explain why Shelest insisted on Soviet armed intervention there.[36]

✣ Soviet Modernity in Ukraine

Although neither the dissident movement nor social unrest seriously troubled the Soviet system in postwar Ukraine, the causes of its crisis—which by the early 1980s had become obvious to all, including the highest leadership—had their origin in the system itself.

Ukraine's economic performance continued to deteriorate during Brezhnev's tenure in the Kremlin. Following the reversal of Khrushchev's decentralizing reforms in 1965, all-Union ministries again assumed supreme control over the republic's economy. That year, the Kremlin commenced another economic experiment, a reform that was informally named after the Soviet premier Aleksei Kosygin but was actually based on the suggestions of the Kharkiv economist, Professor Yevsei Liberman. The reform was aimed at eliminating the gross value of output as the key index of plan fulfillment, which led to the production of mountains of low-quality goods. Instead, more emphasis was placed on sales and profit—although both remained problematic concepts in an economy where the State Committee on Prices determined all prices and various planning agencies regulated production. Introduced only in industry, the reform brought some short-term gains but in the long run was undermined by the continued existence of central planning.[37] In the absence of market mechanisms, which would ensure quality, competitive cost, and prompt response to consumer demand, economic imbalances were exacerbated.

Like elsewhere in the USSR, the impressive growth rate of the postwar reconstruction years began slowing down in Ukraine in the late 1960s. According to (inflated) official data, growth rates in Ukrainian industry between the five-year plans of 1966–1970 and 1981–1985 decreased from 8.4 to 3.5 percent, and in agriculture, from 3.2 to 0.5 percent.[38] An inefficient heavy industry required massive investment of capital while showing a diminishing rate of return. The decline also reflected the attrition of physical plants and the use of outdated technologies, especially in the aging mining and metallurgical enterprises in the Donbas and the lower Dnipro region. Machine building in Ukraine continued receiving heavy investment, but much of it went into the production of military equipment. For the first time in Soviet history, the ninth five-year plan (1971–1975) envisaged a faster growth rate for consumer goods industries than for capital goods industries. In Ukraine, light industries grew in the western provinces, significantly changing the economic profile of that region.

With the Donbas coalfields showing the first signs of exhaustion, local natural gas deposits and hydroelectric dams along the Dnipro began playing a bigger role as energy sources during the 1960s. Construction of nuclear power stations in the republic commenced during the 1970s, the first two (Chernobyl and Rivne) becoming operational in 1979. By then, the intensive exploitation of natural gas deposits in Ukraine made further large-scale production economically unfeasible until the advent of new technologies. As a result, Ukraine became heavily dependent on Siberian oil and gas for its energy needs—a factor of little significance at the time but a serious economic and political problem for present-day Ukraine.

Ukrainian agriculture recovered somewhat after the reversal of late Khrushchevian innovations (such as the obsession with corn) and the allocation of even bigger investments, but the USSR was no longer able to satisfy its grain needs. The importation of grain, primarily from the United States and Canada, continued uninterrupted from 1963 until the Soviet collapse. In Ukraine, collectivized agriculture was as inefficient as elsewhere. Large investments allowed for a modest quantitative increase, but mechanization, labor productivity, and yield per acre remained abysmally low. By the early 1980s, one agricultural worker in the republic tilled an average of only 5.8 hectares or 14.3 acres, compared with 105 hectares or 259.5 acres for the average American farmer. Undeveloped infrastructure and the low motivation of collective farmers resulted in up to 40 percent of grain being lost during harvesting and transit.[39] At the same time, the villagers enthusiastically tilled their one-acre private plots, which provided a third of the total agricultural production on just 3 percent of the land under cultivation.[40]

The 1960s and 1970s saw significant social changes in Ukraine. The low tempo of population growth, rapid industrialization, and mass migration to cities signaled the advent of modern urbanized society. In 1966, the republic's city dwellers outnumbered villagers. By 1979, 53 percent of the once overwhelmingly agrarian ethnic Ukrainians lived in urban areas. Soviet living standards rose considerably during the post-Stalin era, especially between the late 1950s and early 1970s. Khrushchev was the first to seriously address the housing crisis with a massive residential construction program, even if at the cost of lowering standards; from 1956 to 1964, more apartments (measured in total square meters of new living space) were built in Ukraine than during the entire period from 1918 to 1955.[41] His successors continued residential construction, albeit still at a rate that did not match demand. (Most Soviet citizens, especially in the cities, were theoretically entitled to free accommodations from the state with only minimal maintenance payments.) In 1974, 1.3 million families in Ukrainian cities were on the housing wait-list, and the average urban resident had just 12.6 square meters of living space. More and more families owned household appliances, but Soviet Ukraine lagged behind the West in terms of both their quality and quantity—60 television sets, 49 refrigerators, and 16 vacuum cleaners per 100 families in 1974.[42]

Soviet Ukraine during the Brezhnev period remained a society of concealed privilege and inequality, with bureaucrats and managers at the top of the social hierarchy. The elite had access to quality housing, country villas, exclusive resorts, limos, and subsidized shops carrying the best food and cheap imported goods. With wage differentials reduced substantially during the late 1950s, the rest of society felt deprived of access to these commodities rather than unable to afford them. For social and ideological reasons, the state kept prices relatively low but could not satisfy demand. For instance, subsidies reduced the prices on meat sold at state shops, but high-quality meat could be bought only after hours of queuing—that is, if it was delivered at all—or, at much higher prices, at farmers' markets in cities. Newspapers celebrated salary increases, and Soviet Ukrainians' savings kept growing, but they were engaged in a permanent hunt for food, clothing, and furniture. Queuing for long hours—for years, in the case of cars, and for decades, in the case of apartments—became a way of life.

What the ideologues called a "developed socialist society" was not without gender inequality either. Since the war, Soviet Ukrainian women constituted half of the workforce and received equal pay for equal jobs, but in practice, educated women were traditionally channeled into the low-income occupations of doctors, teachers, and librarians. Female collective farmers, underpaid and usually in their senior years, were at the very bottom of the social ladder. The average Ukrainian woman worked full-time, took care of the children, and did most of the shopping (read: queuing). During the 1970s, women were spending an average of twenty-seven hours per week on household duties, compared with less than twelve for men.

Alarming symptoms of social decay became apparent toward the end of the Brezhnev era. Free, but often inadequate, medical care did not make a major difference in Ukrainians' life expectancy, one of the lowest in Europe. Increased disillusionment with "developed socialism" resulted in a pandemic spread of corruption and pilfering. Rising crime, alcoholism, and drug abuse all indicated a dysfunctional society different from the one portrayed in the Soviet press and on TV. Most troublesome, disenchantment and cynicism spread among those people considered successful in Soviet society, such

as professionals and well-paid workers. A major cause of this disillusionment was to be found in a pragmatic, consumerist understanding of the
Communist ideal, which Khrushchev had introduced but was unable to
achieve. Increased access to Western goods and Western radio broadcasts
in Russian and Ukrainian meant that Soviet Ukrainians could now judge for
themselves the differences between socialism and capitalism. The citizens'
disappointment with Soviet results did not necessarily lead to their rejection
of socialism. But as an ever larger number of people realized that things were
not working as intended, their resignation resulted in a loss of optimism and
sense of direction.

One early warning bell for the Ukrainian authorities sounded in 1969,
when an American traveling exhibition "Education in the USA" arrived in
Kyiv. Although the exhibition (lasting from September 5 to October 5) was
not advertised in the local media, rumors quickly spread that its American staff was distributing free copies of *America* magazine in Russian—a
government-sponsored publication advertising the American way of life—as
well as souvenir pins and booklets. Located in a small pavilion far from the
city center, the exhibition operated at maximum capacity from opening,
accepting about 5,500 visitors a day. Embarrassed by the long lines at the pavilion, the Kyivan authorities dispatched fifty propaganda workers to blacken
the American social system. They also organized nearby distractions, such
as free circus performances, concerts, and games. On Sunday, September 14,
1969, one hour before the exhibition was to close for the day, the situation
became uncontrollable as a large crowd of those waiting to get in crushed the
police cordons and tried to storm the pavilion. Soviet officials inside stopped
the onslaught by managing to lock the door. But the rush resumed the next
day and subsided a bit only after September 23, when the Americans ran out
of free copies of the magazine after having distributed some 100,000. From
then on, average daily attendance diminished to 4,700 people, which was
still close to capacity.[43]

Skepticism about the Soviet Union's ability to ever catch up with Western
living standards became widespread throughout the country, but there were
also issues specific to the Ukrainian republic that gave ideologues cause for
concern. The largest non-Russian republic with a language closely related
to the Russian, Ukraine remained a test case of the Soviet nationality policy.
The official theory on the nationalities problem was ambiguous, holding
that, under socialism, the nationalities were both "flourishing" and "drawing
together," the latter term being deliberately vague to accommodate policy
changes but generally referring to political unity and cultural contacts among
the Soviet nationalities. Soviet ideologues held that in the future highest
stage of socialism—Communism—national distinctions would disappear,

although Marx and Lenin left no hints as to how this would come about. Especially after Khrushchev's bold announcement at the Twenty-Second Party Congress in 1961 that Soviet society would achieve Communism by 1980, the press supplemented the "drawing together" concept with that of the future "merging" of the Soviet nationalities. In preparation for "merging," the authorities of the late Khrushchev period facilitated assimilation into the Russian culture by encouraging increased population exchanges among the Soviet republics. Like many of Khrushchev's innovations, the radical concept of the "merging" of nations fell out of favor under Brezhnev, who in 1971 introduced instead the notion of the "Soviet people," a multinational community of Soviet citizens using Russian as the language of inter-republican communication. Yet, this theory also presented assimilation in a positive light.

In 1954, Ukrainian authorities dropped the Ukrainian language as a compulsory college entrance requirement. In 1958, a project for an all-Union school reform featured a proposal to make the study of a second Soviet language optional in the non-Russian republics—in the Ukrainian case, the study of Ukrainian in schools with Russian as the language of instruction and that of Russian in Ukrainian schools. The Ukrainian intelligentsia and even state officials objected to this proposal, realizing that parents would want their children to study Russian, the Soviet lingua franca, and that the casualty would be the Ukrainian language. This proposal was dropped as an all-Union measure, but the following year it became law in the Ukrainian SSR that Ukrainian was an optional subject in Russian schools in the republic while Russian remained a compulsory subject in Ukrainian schools. Present-day historians make much of this law as the best example of state-sponsored assimilation, but most of them neglect to mention that this law was never fully implemented. In practice, all permanent residents of Ukraine attending Russian schools in the republic studied Ukrainian as a second language.[44]

Instead, it was the right of parents to choose whether to send their children to a Ukrainian or Russian school that worked as the instrument of assimilation. As one of Shcherbytsky's present-day apologists writes, the first secretary "did not force" parents to choose Russian,[45] but surely he was instrumental in opening more and more Russian-language schools, as well as switching state and business correspondence to Russian. During the 1970s, the share of Ukrainian-language journals in the republic fell from 46 to 19 percent; that of books published in Ukrainian decreased from 49 to 24 percent. By the decade's end, more than half of the schoolchildren in the republic attended Russian-language schools—compared with about 30 percent in 1958. By the late 1980s, such large cities as Donetsk, Kharkiv, and Odesa did not have a single Ukrainian school, and the number of Ukrainian-language books fell to 18 percent of the total titles published.[46] Because of in-migration from the Russian Federation and increased self-identification as Russians among the offspring of mixed marriages, the proportion of ethnic Russians in the republic's population surged from 16.9 percent in 1959 to 22.1 percent in 1989.[47] By 1989, more than 4 million ethnic Ukrainians considered Russian to be their mother tongue, and an even higher number of them actually used Russian in everyday life.

However, the widely assumed "success" of assimilation in Ukraine, which the dissidents and diaspora commentators have long decried, requires reevaluation. During censuses, the percentage of ethnic Ukrainians claiming that their native language was Ukrainian decreased somewhat from 93.5 percent in 1959 to 89.1 percent in 1979 to 87.7 percent in 1989. But polls during the early 1990s presented an even gloomier picture: Only about 40 percent of the republic's adult population used Ukrainian as the language of convenience.[48] The difference between census results and polls means that millions of "assimilated" Russian-speaking Ukrainians continued in Soviet times to claim Ukrainian as their native language. Mechanisms of national self-identification are more complex than the choice of everyday language, and linguistic assimilation did not prevent these people from associating themselves with Ukraine's history and culture. Nor was the increase in the number of ethnic Russians a serious threat to the Ukrainian republic's political identity, unless interpreted from the position of exclusive, ethnic nationalism. In 1991, the majority of these Russians would support Ukrainian independence and remain in the country as loyal, if Russian-speaking, citizens of the Ukrainian state.

Overall, the cultural and nationality policy of the period from 1953 to 1985 can hardly be defined as a straightforward assimilation drive. The accomplishments of Ukrainian culture and scholarship in the 1960s and 1970s include such massive state-sponsored projects as two editions of the *Ukrainian Soviet Encyclopedia*, a twenty-six-volume history of Ukrainian regions, monumental histories of Ukrainian literature and art, an eleven-volume dictionary of the Ukrainian language, and several multivolume histories of Ukraine. All this cultural production bore the unmistakable traits of Soviet censorship and ideological control, but it furnished Soviet Ukraine with the cultural foundations of a modern nation. The state never withdrew its support of Ukrainian high culture and establishment intellectuals, and it also invested in maintaining a limited mass culture in Ukrainian.

The authorities, however, welcomed the fact that in the age of television, Ukraine became fully incorporated into the Soviet mass-cultural space, with Moscow-made films and songs as popular in the republic as they were in the Russian Federation. For all the creative innovations of the Ukrainian sixtiers, they worked for a narrow audience of intellectuals. Striking films by Serhii Paradzhanov, such as *Shadows of Forgotten Ancestors* (1965), a magical-realism glimpse of love and death in a nineteenth-century Carpathian village, had a better chance of reaching the wider public. The actor Ivan Mykolaichuk, who starred in this and other works of the "poetical school" in Ukrainian cinema, certainly enjoyed celebrity status in the republic.[49] But there was also a mass-culture aspect to Soviet Ukrainian culture. The composer and singer Volodymyr Ivasiuk became famous in the 1960s for his folk-based pop melodies, such as "Red Rue." The singer Sofiia Rotaru also rose to fame with folk-inspired songs in Ukrainian, but eventually she made a career as a Soviet pop star singing in Russian. A brilliant duo of stand-up comedians, known to millions of television viewers by the colorful names Tarapunka and Shtepsel, achieved all-Union fame with their trademark bilingual dialogues in Ukrainian and Russian.[50]

After Brezhnev's death in 1982, very little changed in Ukrainian politics, society, and culture. His successor as general secretary, Yurii Andropov, confused the causes of societal crisis with its consequences and, instead of a major economic reform, initiated a crackdown on idle workers and corrupt officials. A former KGB chief, Andropov did not entertain plans of cultural or political liberalization and hardly had time to enact them, even if he did. Andropov died in 1984 and was succeeded by Brezhnev's old crony, Konstantin Chernenko, from a family of Ukrainian peasants who emigrated to Siberia. He was too old and too ill to change anything during his year as general secretary. The Ukrainian party boss Shcherbytsky remained in office through these changes and into the age of Gorbachev's reforms, and he kept a tight lid on the republic to the best of his abilities.

❖

Although the post-Stalin period in Soviet Ukraine's history is today often characterized as a dark time of assimilation and economic stagnation, the Ukrainian SSR had impressive achievements to its credit. An urbanized society with a developed economy, the Ukrainian republic provided a national homeland for ethnic Ukrainians and was considered a desirable place to live by many national minorities. Even with the majority of state business during the last Soviet decades conducted in Russian, the institutional matrix of the Ukrainian SSR ensured the reproduction of a Ukrainian ethnic identity. Already in the early 1970s, the prominent Ukrainian émigré historian Ivan L. Rudnytsky warned against underestimating Soviet Ukraine's nominal statehood.[51] Indeed, the very existence of a Ukrainian polity within the USSR gave its citizens a potential focus of allegiance. National political institutions—the Ukrainian parliament and the Council of Ministers—for decades rubber-stamped party decisions, but if something were to happen to the Soviet center, power would revert to them almost by default. Likewise, the cultural institutions of a modern nation, from the Academy of Sciences to the national theater to historical sites, were all in place in the Ukrainian SSR.

From Chernobyl to the Soviet Collapse   **10**

Just like the revolutionary storm of 1917 through 1920, the events in Ukraine from 1985 to 1991 cannot be explained solely by the inner dynamics of Ukrainian history. By the time Mikhail Gorbachev came to power in Moscow in March 1985, the dissident movement in Ukraine was suppressed, local elites subservient, and the overwhelming majority of the population compliant with the Soviet political system. The Kremlin initiated radical reforms as a "revolution from above," and for most of this tumultuous period, Ukrainian activists followed in the steps of Russian democrats and Baltic nationalists. An independent Ukrainian state emerged in 1991 not as a result of mass nationalist mobilization or popular rebellion against Communist rule—although there were signs of these two processes as well—but as a by-product of the Soviet collapse. The path to Ukrainian independence, therefore, must be placed in a larger context. The story of how Ukraine became a sovereign state necessarily begins with Gorbachev's reforms in Moscow, continues with the creation of popular fronts in the Baltic republics, touches on the collapse of Communism in eastern Europe in 1989, and concludes with the dissolution of the Soviet Union in 1991.

This trajectory does not deny the role of internal political forces and cultural struggles. All-Union decrees created a political space, which was then filled by native movements and concerns growing from Ukraine's own past and present. Democratic activists in Moscow and the Baltics did not identify to the same degree with the disaster at the Chernobyl nuclear power plant as those close to it, the issues of language and culture never assumed in Russia the prominence they had in Ukraine, and no Union-wide process made western Ukraine a stronghold of Ukrainian national identity—the region had played this role for a century. In addition to democracy, national rights figured prominently in Ukraine's public discourse under Gorbachev. Former dissidents joined forces with establishment intellectuals to press for sovereignty, and in the moment of crisis, the republic's bureaucratic elite sided with them against the center, evoking the nation as the focus of allegiance. Finally, whereas developments in Moscow charted the course for Kyiv during most of Gorbachev's period, in December 1991 the Ukrainian people for once determined the fate of the Soviet Union when they voted overwhelmingly in favor of their republic's independence.

The Soviet legacy of nation building played a major role in the political processes of the late 1980s and early 1990s. What the state had established as "empty" forms of nationhood—republican parliaments, governments, newspapers in national languages, academies of sciences, and historical museums—could easily be turned into real vehicles of political expression.[1] The Ukrainian Soviet Socialist Republic required only a change of national symbols, such as the flag and coat of arms, to transform itself into an independent Ukrainian state. While multinational, both these polities with their identical borders owed their existence to the long twentieth-century project of creating a national homeland for their titular nationality, ethnic Ukrainians.

✢✢ Chernobyl and Glasnost

When Mikhail Gorbachev came to power in the Kremlin in March 1985 at the age of fifty-four, he was widely perceived as a "young" and energetic administrator. The new general secretary, however, had no clear plan for reforms. As Gorbachev would acknowledge later, in 1985 he saw the need for an economic restructuring but not a political transformation. Relaxing the Soviet nationalities policy was not on his agenda yet either. On a visit to Kyiv in June 1985, Gorbachev spoke primarily of Ukraine's large role in the Soviet economy and committed a serious gaffe when he referred to the Soviet Union as "Russia" during a conversation with Kyivans that was broadcast live on television.[2] Always appearing alongside Shcherbytsky, the general secretary did not hint that any political change in Ukraine was forthcoming. In fact, 1985 saw renewed repressions against Ukrainian dissidents; several were sentenced for imprisonment, and one, the prominent poet Vasyl Stus, died in a prison camp.[3]

As elsewhere in the Soviet Union, Gorbachev's ill-defined campaign for economic "acceleration" had little effect in Ukraine. Official statisticians registered a modest increase in industrial growth in the republic (less than 1 percent) and a 3 percent improvement in agricultural production, but this was achieved mainly by strengthening work discipline. Although morally laudable, the official antialcohol drive in 1985 and 1986 cost the republic's budget some 10 billion rubles. While reluctant, for ideological reasons, to embrace the free market, the Soviet leadership was looking for partial solutions and halfway measures to revitalize the economy. Late in 1986, the state began encouraging the creation of cooperatives. These grew quickly in Ukraine, totaling 24,000 organizations and 254,000 employees in 1989, but they were concentrated in trade and service industries and never created real competition for the state-run branches of the economy.[4]

Gorbachev's 1987 attempt to promote self-sufficiency for industrial enterprises did not prove a success, as managers felt more comfortable in the familiar world of guaranteed state orders. Efforts to reduce the administrative apparatus did have a visible result in the reduction of the number of Ukraine's ministries from fifty-five to forty-six by 1989, but this was too little, too late. Halfhearted reforms led only to a further decline in production. The republic's economy fully reflected the plight of the Soviet economy in general, dominated as it was by "unreformable" smokestack factories built to 1930s standards, when colossal waste, consumption of energy, and pollution seemed unimportant. Ukraine was the extreme case of this imbalance, as heavy industry was 60 percent of its economy.[5]

Within a year of coming to power, Gorbachev added to the concept of economic acceleration two equally ill-defined terms: *perestroika* (restructuring) and *glasnost* (openness). The first referred to the need for a more radical transformation in the economy and society in general, and the second implied greater freedom of the press and some degree of transparency in politics. Before the impact of these new policies could reach Ukraine, however, the republic was shaken by the worst nuclear accident in history. On April 26, 1986, a combination of the unsafe design of Soviet nuclear reactors and human error led to a steam explosion that destroyed one of the four reactors at the Chernobyl nuclear power plant, located some eighty miles north of Kyiv. Though it did not explode as a nuclear bomb, the ruined reactor discharged into the atmosphere a large cloud of radioactive dust containing ninety times the amount of radioactive products released during the bombing of Hiroshima.[6] The radioactivity was concentrated heavily in Ukraine and the neighboring Belarusian Republic, but winds carried some fallout as far away as Scandinavia.

For all their rhetoric about glasnost, the Soviet authorities did not pass the test of Chernobyl (or Chornobyl in the Ukrainian spelling). They made no official announcements for the first three days after the accident, until Swedish meteorologists protested the high level of radiation in their country. When Soviet communiqués were finally issued, they minimized the scale of the catastrophe. When Shcherbytsky called Moscow, asking if the May Day parade in Kyiv should be canceled, Gorbachev threatened him with expulsion from the party.[7] (As a result, tens of thousands of people, including this book's author, were forced on May 1, 1986, to march on the streets of the Ukrainian capital instead of fleeing the city that was receiving slight radioactive fallout.) The immediate casualties of the disaster included more than thirty firefighters and power plant personnel who were first at the scene and soon died of radiation sickness. About 135,000 people were evacuated permanently from the thirty-kilometer zone around Chernobyl, and thousands more were exposed to high levels of radiation during the extensive cleanup efforts. Soviet authorities at the time pressured Ukrainian doctors not to search for connections between exposure to radiation and diseases, but direct links were later established in the cases of 35,000 adults and 1,400 children.[8] A total of 2.4 million Ukrainians reside in regions that experienced some degree of radioactive contamination, and the full extent of damage to people and the environment may become clear only after several decades.[9]

Soviet engineers succeeded in encasing the damaged reactor in a concrete sarcophagus, but the catastrophe had major political implications for the authorities. Their initial decision to withhold information about life-threatening radioactive fallout caused resentment among the population. The Communist Party lost a great deal of legitimacy in Ukraine, and in public discourse, Chernobyl became a potent symbol of the regime's criminal negligence.

Following this public relations fiasco, the Gorbachev leadership gave new impetus to the policy of glasnost. Newly appointed editors and cultural functionaries in Moscow, including the transplanted Ukrainian writer Vitalii Korotych at the helm of the immensely popular *Ogonek* (The Spark) magazine, began to broach long-forbidden topics. At first, Ukrainians lined up at newspaper kiosks to read in the Russian press about Stalin's crimes, environmental disasters, and the misery of everyday life in the land of socialism. Soon, the Ukrainian media followed cautiously in the steps of exposé-style journalism led by the newspaper of the Writers' Union, *Literaturna Ukraina* (Literary Ukraine).

Glasnost developed slowly in Ukraine, primarily because of resistance from local bureaucrats, who were still led by the long-serving conservative First Secretary Volodymyr Shcherbytsky. Those working with him recall that Shcherbytsky "did not respect Gorbachev" and was uneasy about the reforms.[10] For reasons that remain unclear, however, Gorbachev was in no hurry to remove Shcherbytsky—perhaps he valued stability in the most populous non-Russian republic over the advancement of democracy. As a result, Ukrainian journalists were able to raise sensitive topics only by overcoming the staunch resistance of local party functionaries. The issues that galvanized Ukrainian society at the time differed somewhat from the repertoire of hot topics in the central press. In addition to Stalinist crimes, ecology, and present-day abuses of power, they included linguistic assimilation, the Famine of 1932 and 1933, and the banned Ukrainian churches—Greek Catholic and Autocephalous Orthodox.

Taking advantage of glasnost, groups of Ukrainian intellectuals also began raising these long-forbidden questions in public. During the first phase of glasnost in Ukraine, the Writers' Union and its *Literaturna Ukraina* acted as the chief pressure group. As early as June 1986, patriotic writers protested the declining use of Ukrainian in education and publishing. They subsequently spearheaded the publication of banned literary works and the rehabilitation of Ukrainian writers who had been repressed under Stalin or had died in emigration, such as Khvylovy and Vynnychenko. Beginning in 1987, public discussion of "difficult questions" went hand in hand with the creation of embryonic civic organizations.

The first "informal" organizations that lacked official sanction were usually environmentalist groups and Ukrainian culture clubs. A notable exception was the Ukrainian Helsinki Union, a successor to the Ukrainian Helsinki Group established by released political prisoners in the spring of 1988. But the union was not a typical informal organization, precisely because of continuity with its underground predecessor. Much more representative was the first organization to create a national structure with a network of local branches: the ecological association Green World (December 1987). Like most other informal bodies of the time, it was led by nondissident intelligentsia and tolerated by the authorities. Other national civic organizations were created in 1989, once Gorbachev's reforms had spread into politics, although their local branches often traced their history back to the "informals" of 1987. Inaugurated in February 1989, the Taras Shevchenko Ukrainian Language Society became the first truly mass civic organization in the republic, whose membership rose from about 10,000 at its founding to 150,000 by late 1989.[11] The "Memorial" Society, established in March 1989 as a Ukrainian branch of the all-Union "Memorial," dedicated its efforts to uncovering Stalinist crimes and commemorating their victims. But the most important civic organization of all was the Ukrainian equivalent of the Baltic "popular fronts," the Popular Movement of Ukraine for Perestroika, better known simply as Rukh ("The Movement").

Rukh originated in a series of meetings held at the headquarters of the Writers' Union in October and November 1988—right after the news arrived about the congresses of popular fronts in Estonia, Latvia, and Lithuania.[12] These gatherings of writers and democratic activists resulted in the creation of an initiative group and preparation of the movement's program. Yet, because of pressure from the authorities, no founding congress of Rukh took place in 1988. Local structures of Rukh began crystallizing in the spring of 1989, however, and by the time of its founding congress in September 1989, the organization had about 280,000 members. Rukh's name emphasized congruence with Gorbachev's reform program; indeed, it originally did not position itself as a political opposition. But in practical terms, Rukh played this very role in Ukraine, where the conservative party bureaucracy was slow in introducing democratization. Conceived as a catchall movement, Rukh sought to include Ukrainian patriots, environmentalists, minority activists, and Russian-speaking democrats from eastern and southern Ukraine. Yet the organization's early success as a mass movement contained the seeds of its eventual decline. Although for some participants the moderate slogans of democracy, humanism, and universal human rights were ends in themselves, others used them only because the authorities would not yet tolerate an open discussion of the Ukrainian national question.

The growing popularity of Rukh was just one sign of the party's crumbling control over society. In July 1989, a mass strike of miners in the Donbas undermined the party's claim to represent the interests of the working class. More than 460,000 miners participated in the strike, which began with purely economic demands but later featured calls for the resignation of local political bosses.[13] Democratic activists, however, did not manage to establish ties with the miners, and the strike committees did not turn into a Ukrainian equivalent of Poland's Solidarity.

Another challenge to Communist ideology arose from the religious revival. After decades of underground existence, the priests and faithful of the Ukrainian Greek Catholic Church in western Ukraine began coming out into the open during 1987. A series of mass rallies in support of the banned church continued until Gorbachev allowed its legalization on the eve of his historic visit to the Vatican in December 1989. The revival of the Ukrainian Autocephalous Orthodox Church also began in 1989, as a number of Russian Orthodox priests in western Ukraine defected to this church. As the leaders of both the UGCC and UAOC were preparing for their return from abroad, the Russian Orthodox Church answered their challenge by renaming its Ukrainian exarchate the Ukrainian Orthodox Church. A prolonged and acrimonious three-way struggle for parishes and buildings ensued against the background of steadily increasing church attendance for all three confessions.

The Communist Party was also gradually losing control over public discourse. Originally introduced by Gorbachev as a means of galvanizing society and overcoming bureaucratic resistance to his reforms, glasnost by 1990 had snowballed into a critique of the entire Communist project. The Kremlin could no longer contain public denigration of Lenin, which until then was a taboo topic in the press. In Ukraine, official ideologues were forced to acknowledge the Famine of 1932 and 1933, even if they continued to minimize the responsibility of Stalinist administrators. The democratic press increasingly lionized Hetman Ivan Mazepa, the historian Mykhailo Hrushevsky, leaders of the Ukrainian Revolution, and dissidents of the 1960s as the real national heroes. In the summer of 1990, mass festivals marked the 500th anniversary of the Cossack stronghold on the Dnipro, the Zaporozhian Sich. A struggle also developed between the opposition and party functionaries around the restoration of Ukraine's suppressed national symbols from the revolutionary and earlier periods: the blue-and-yellow flag, the trident, and the anthem "Ukraine Has Not Died Yet." All three were increasingly used at various public demonstrations.

Beginning in 1988, such rallies were reclaiming from the authorities public space in Ukraine's cities. Lviv led the way with the very first mass protest meeting in June 1988, when the local authorities tried to prevent a conference of the Ukrainian Language Society. Only several hundred people participated in the original protest, but 7,000 were on the streets three days later. In 1989, mass rallies in Kyiv and Lviv attracted tens and perhaps hundreds of thousands, while smaller events were becoming a common occurrence. Party archives preserve the cumulative police data about the number—probably intentionally underreported—of mass demonstrations in the republics during the first ten months of 1989: there were 927 with an estimated total number of participants of more than 500,000. Half of these events were not sanctioned by the authorities. These data must have excluded the electoral campaign during the spring of the same year for which informal organizations held some 1,200 meetings with an estimated participation of 13 million people.[14] In January 1990, Rukh commemorated the 1919 union of the two Ukrainian republics by forming a human chain of some 450,000 people between Kyiv and Lviv.[15]

✣ The Birth of Mass Politics

No matter how much the archconservative Shcherbytsky tried to suppress political expression in the republic, in March 1989 Ukrainians, along with all Soviet citizens, got their first taste of democratic politics when they went to the polls to elect the Congress of People's Deputies, Gorbachev's new parliament. These were not free and fair elections, as one third of the seats were reserved for the Communist Party and other all-Union organizations, the authorities still controlled the media, and registration committees weeded out undesirable candidates. Yet, the Kremlin announced its desire to see "democratic" elections, thus removing the threat of punishment for voting against the party line. As a result, in big cities and in western Ukraine, where vote rigging and intimidation no longer worked, the party suffered a number of humiliating losses. Four provincial party secretaries and one Ukrainian Central Committee secretary, all running unopposed, failed to obtain the required 50 percent of cast ballots. The first secretary of the Kyiv party committee and the mayor of the capital also were not elected. Of the 231 deputies elected in Ukraine, more than 40 identified with the democratic opposition. (There were as yet no legal party affiliations other than membership in the Communist Party, which stood at 88 percent among the republic's deputies.)[16]

The tempo of political change accelerated in the fall of 1989, although compared with the events rocking eastern Europe at the same time, Ukraine remained relatively quiet. Soon after the founding congress of Rukh in September, the ailing and disillusioned Shcherbytsky finally retired. (He died in February 1990.) His successor as the first secretary, Volodymyr Ivashko (1989–1990), identified more closely with Gorbachev's reforms and adopted some rhetoric about Ukrainian sovereignty, which had been hitherto the exclusive language of the opposition. Lacking charisma and independent vision, however, Ivashko could not galvanize the CPU. The party apparatus, as well as many rank-and-file Communists in Ukraine, were disoriented by the quick pace of reforms and increasingly mistrusted Gorbachev. Many ordinary citizens, especially in the western provinces, saw the collapse of Communism in neighboring Poland, Hungary, and Czechoslovakia as the writing on the wall for the CPU.

The party was thus poorly prepared for the next test at the ballot box. In March 1990, all the Soviet republics held elections to their legislatures and the local councils. In the Baltic republics, these first relatively free elections brought victory to opposition popular fronts. This did not happen in Ukraine, where "national Communists" were not yet seeking an agreement with the opposition, and rural voters, particularly in the east, could still be manipulated. Vote rigging was also widespread. Yet Rukh, the Green World, the Ukrainian Language Society, and other opposition organizations united in a single Democratic Bloc, which won a hundred seats out of 450 in the parliament, the Supreme Rada ("council"). Political lines remained permeable, though, as many Democratic Bloc deputies remained members of the Communist Party, and some Communist deputies sympathized with the opposition.

During this time of unprecedented political activism, defection from the party increased dramatically. Only 6,200 Ukrainian citizens resigned from the CPU in 1989, but some 250,951 did so during 1990.[17] The majority of the almost 3 million remaining in the party were disillusioned, nominal members who stayed by the force of inertia. Among those leaving were also disheartened supporters of the Democratic Platform in the CPU, a branch of an all-Union movement for democratic reform within the party. This group enjoyed brief popularity early in 1990 and broke away in the summer, after the mainstream party leadership rejected its proposals. Some of its deputies crossed the floor over to the Democratic Bloc.

By mid-1990, 125 deputies of the Ukrainian parliament belonged to the Democratic Bloc, 239 represented the shrunken CPU core majority, and the rest were nominally independent.[18] In sharp contrast to Soviet times, the Supreme Rada became the center of the country's political life. Its fully televised debates were often acrimonious and accompanied by protest rallies outside the building. The republic's leadership was finding it difficult to deal with the deputies. At first, local bureaucrats imitated the Moscow model, which in its original form saw Gorbachev combining the posts of party general secretary and chairman of the parliament. In Ukraine, Ivashko combined these two posts. But it soon became apparent that the busy job of parliamentary chairman or speaker left no time for running the party. To complicate matters further, in July 1990, Ivashko suddenly resigned and moved to Moscow to become deputy general secretary of the CPSU. (Ivashko was still thinking as an old Soviet careerist, valuing advancement in the party over jobs in the government and parliament. Had he remained in Kyiv, he may have been propelled to the Ukrainian presidency, whereas in Moscow he became a nonentity after the Soviet collapse and died soon thereafter.)

In selecting Ivashko's successor, the CPU leadership decided to separate the positions of first secretary and parliamentary chairman. The grim conservative bureaucrat Stanislav Hurenko became head of the party, and the parliamentary nomination went to the second-in-command and a relative newcomer among the party leadership, Second Secretary Leonid Kravchuk. Born in Volhynia when it was part of Poland, Kravchuk spoke excellent Ukrainian and made a career for himself as an ideologue specializing in the national question. As a result, he perfectly understood the logic of his former opponents, the nationalists. During the 1980s, the party leadership used him to deal with the Ukrainian intelligentsia; among other things, he tried to delay the politicization of Rukh. Eloquent and intelligent, by mid-1990 Kravchuk seemed to be the party's best choice for parliamentary chairman, although some hard-liners were already criticizing him for being too cozy with the opposition.

Following Kravchuk's nomination by the CPU, in July 1990 the Supreme Rada duly elected him as its chairman. The Democratic Bloc, now rechristened the People's Council, did not support his candidacy, and he won owing to the 239 Communist votes. Just before Kravchuk's election, on July 16 the parliament adopted the Declaration of Sovereignty. This symbolic declaration, affirming in principle the republic's sovereignty, did not mean the proclamation of independence. Rather, it was a nonbinding pronouncement about the supremacy of Ukrainian laws over those of the Soviet Union, a document imitating similar declarations recently adopted by Russia and other republics. It was significant, however, as a sign of the gradual convergence between the interests of the Communist majority and the democratic opposition, for the votes of Communist deputies made its passage possible. New "national

Communists," exemplified by Kravchuk, increasingly adopted the language of sovereignty. They realized that in the age of mass politics, the mantle of the democratic nationalists could offer the political elites a better claim for legitimacy than membership in the Politburo. Many Communist deputies attentively watched the gradual transfer of power from the party to the state and from Moscow to the republics. Some sensed that big politics and big money would soon be made in Kyiv and that their reelections would depend on their constituencies rather than their allegiance to the Communist Party. Kravchuk later recalled that in 1989 and 1990, he had heard several Communist deputies wondering aloud, "Maybe it really would be better to separate [from the Union]?"[19]

At this point, however, party stalwarts still controlled the army, the police, and the state apparatus. Angry with Kravchuk's national Communist tendencies, Hurenko told a closed party meeting in October 1990 that the parliamentary chairman "belonged only nominally to the party."[20] (Kravchuk had just resigned as the CPU's second secretary.) Signs of a conservative backlash were visible throughout the Soviet Union in the fall of 1990, particularly in the Baltic republics. In Ukraine, party conservatives pushed through measures banning demonstrations near the Supreme Rada, temporarily suspended the broadcast of its proceedings, and stripped the radical nationalist deputy Stepan Khmara of his immunity (he was arrested after a police provocation).[21] But unlike in the Baltics, the situation in Ukraine never developed into a violent clash between the military and the crowds because of a combination of popular protest and Kravchuk's skillful maneuvering.

Unexpectedly, resistance to the rollback of democracy came from Ukraine's students. In October 1990, a group of student hunger strikers put up tents on Kyiv's main plaza, then still called October Revolution Square. Before long, the strike spread to other cities, and mass demonstrations in Kyiv in support of the students involved tens of thousands.[22] The students' demands included new parliamentary elections, stationing Ukrainian conscripts to the Soviet Army within the republic, nationalization of the CPU's property, postponement of discussions about a new Union treaty, and the resignation of the government. With the party leadership disoriented and parliament divided on how to proceed, the police did not attempt a crackdown. Instead, Kravchuk invited student leaders to address the Supreme Rada, and the government promised to satisfy all their demands. In fact, the only measure taken at the time was the removal of Prime Minister Vitalii Masol. As a sort of bonus, soon after the strike the parliament voted to remove the infamous Article Six (proclaiming the Communist Party the "guiding force" in Soviet society) from the republic's constitution.

By then, multiparty politics had become a reality. The authorities delayed the formation of full-fledged political parties until after the March 1990 elections. Thereafter, parties of all ideological stripes came into existence, but almost all were small groups of activists lacking both mass support and a financial base. The first to make itself known was the nationalist Ukrainian Republican Party, the direct successor of the Ukrainian Helsinki Union, led by former political prisoners. More moderate patriotic intellectuals created the Democratic Party of Ukraine. The Green World Association transformed itself into the Green Party. While the CPU still occupied the extreme left of the political spectrum, new parties emerged there as well. The former Democratic Platform in the CPU constituted itself as the Party of Democratic Revival, and no fewer than two Social Democratic parties struggled to reconcile socialism with the defense of national rights.

One consequence of the new party politics was the changing profile of Rukh. Conceived as a catchall popular front, Rukh continued to grow numerically; by the time of its second congress in October 1990, the organization boasted a membership of 633,000. Yet, many former leaders of Rukh were now committed to their own parties, in particular the Ukrainian Republican Party, the Democratic Party, and the Party of Democratic Revival. Agreements about these groups' associate membership in Rukh were not carried through. This was connected to Rukh's own evolution from a popular front united by protest against Communist rule into a coalition with narrower political aims. The Second Congress removed the mention of perestroika from the organization's name and at the same time came out explicitly for Ukraine's independence. Rukh's leaders chose their language carefully. Programmatic documents usually demanded statehood for the inclusive "people of Ukraine" rather than the "Ukrainian people" or "Ukrainians," which could sound like a reference to the titular ethnic group. But the minorities, Russians and Jews in particular, were by and large apprehensive about breaking ties with Russia. Compared with the First Congress of Rukh, the number of ethnic Ukrainians among the delegates of the Second Congress rose from 89 percent to 95 percent—whereas their share in the general population stood at 73 percent. The proportion of delegates from eastern Ukraine also declined, as the representation of Galicia and Kyiv increased from 47 to 57 percent.[23]

Exploiting the concerns of ethnic Russians, in January 1991 party conservatives in the Crimea organized a referendum resulting in a 93 percent vote in favor of restoring the Crimean autonomous republic within the Ukrainian SSR. Ethnic Russians still constituted 67 percent of Crimea's population, although with the launch of perestroika, the Crimean Tatars began returning to their ancestral lands. The referendum aimed to forestall the reestablishment of Crimean Tatar autonomy on the peninsula and to send Kyiv a warning about the Crimea's possible separation if Ukraine broke away from the Soviet Union. Indeed, in 1991 several political groups in the Crimea began campaigning for the abolition of the 1954 decree transferring the peninsula from Russia to Ukraine. But separatists did not yet have Crimean public opinion on their side, and the Autonomous Republic of Crimea remained under the firm grip of old party functionaries.

✥ Ukraine and the End of the Soviet Union

One field in which Gorbachev never managed to make serious progress was the transition to a market economy. Several attempts were abandoned because of resistance from industrial managers and the social cost of such processes as privatization and price liberalization. In 1990, subsidies to unprofitable enterprises in Ukraine consumed about 45 percent of the state's expenditures. Yet, the economy was contracting: In 1990 and 1991, the republic's GDP declined by a whopping 27 percent.[24] As the center printed more and more money to cover the budget deficit, in August 1990, the Supreme Rada passed a law declaring the republic's economic sovereignty. But neither this declaration, nor the introduction in November of consumer coupons to protect Ukraine's shoppers from buyers from other republics, had a serious effect. Ukrainians fully felt the consequences of the all-Union price increases in April 1991 and the subsequent price liberalization. During 1991, retail prices multiplied eightfold, but citizens' savings in the state bank were not indexed.[25] Frustration and anger grew among the population, which was unsure whether to blame Moscow or Kyiv for its misery.

Although Kravchuk had no magic recipe for fixing the economy, during the winter of 1990–1991 he proved himself a skillful politician. He kept a low profile when it seemed that Moscow conservatives were taking the upper hand, but after the bloodshed in the Baltic republics compromised the stalwarts around Gorbachev, he reemerged as a proponent of Ukrainian sovereignty. Because there was no presidential post, the parliamentary chairperson acted as the de facto head of state, a position that was no longer ceremonial. In November 1990, Kravchuk hosted in Kyiv a delegation of the Russian Federation headed by Boris Yeltsin. Acting as if the Union framework was irrelevant and they were heads of independent states, the two politicians signed a broad-ranging treaty between their republics. In a final parting of ways between the national Communists and orthodox Communists in Ukraine, early in 1990 Kravchuk and Hurenko took opposite positions on all major political questions. Kravchuk and his deputy speaker, the colorful former collective farm chairman Ivan Pliushch, condemned the center's use of violence in Lithuania and expressed their disapproval of Gorbachev's plans for a new Union treaty.

Consumed with his efforts to save the federal state, in March 1991 Gorbachev managed to organize an all-Union referendum on preserving the USSR. However, because of Kravchuk's maneuvering, Communist deputies in the Supreme Rada split, allowing the addition of a second question to the ballots in Ukraine. In the end, 70.5 percent of participants sided with the Kremlin's proposal "to preserve the USSR as a renewed federation of equal sovereign republics," but at the same time 80.2 percent supported Kyiv's qualification that Ukraine should enter any future union only "on the basis of the Declaration of State Sovereignty of Ukraine." In addition, local authorities in three Galician provinces added a third question, on complete independence, which received support from 88 percent.[26] Hurenko claimed victory for the proponents of the Union, but the referendum results really meant that the majority of the population was as yet undecided about the meaning of "sovereignty." Political or economic crises could push public opinion in favor of either preservation of the Soviet Union or separation.

Gorbachev, meanwhile, continued pressing for the signing of a new Union treaty. By this time, six Soviet republics had unequivocally come out in favor of independence and were not participating in negotiations, but the remaining nine—including Ukraine—continued talks with the center. At this point, Gorbachev was prepared to relinquish much of the center's authority to the republics of the future "Union of Sovereign States," but bargaining continued throughout the summer of 1991. On August 1, President George H. W. Bush stopped in Kyiv on a trip to the Soviet Union. Ukrainian patriots were looking forward to his visit as an affirmation of Ukraine's new international standing, but Bush's cautious address to the Supreme Rada (dubbed in the Western press as the "Chicken Kiev" speech) proved a disappointment. Rather than encourage Ukrainian independence, the U.S. president endorsed Gorbachev's plan for a new union and warned Ukrainians against pursuing the "hopeless course of isolation." Americans, Bush announced, "will not aid those who promote a suicidal nationalism based upon ethnic hatred."[27]

American speechwriters were not alone in their misreading of the situation in Ukraine or the Soviet Union generally. Communist hard-liners, who since fall 1990 increasingly surrounded Gorbachev, also believed that the republics' pursuit of sovereignty could be rolled back. Gorbachev was having trouble securing signatures under any text of a new Union treaty, but party stalwarts worried that his success in this endeavor would bury the Soviet Union. On the same day that Bush poured cold water on his Ukrainian hosts, Gorbachev announced on Soviet television that the process of signing the new Union treaty would begin on August 20 with endorsements from Russia, Kazakhstan, and Uzbekistan. Others were expected to sign later; Ukraine was still negotiating with the center. This declaration spurred the conservatives to action.

On August 19, 1991, all Soviet citizens woke to the announcement that Gorbachev's ill health and the failure of his policies had led to the establishment of an eight-man emergency committee to run the country. Gorbachev, who was vacationing at his seaside residence in Crimea, was in good health, but because he had refused to play along with the plotters, they put him under house arrest and cut all communication lines. The putsch folded in three days, in large part because of the courageous stand of Russian President Boris Yeltsin against the plotters in Moscow. No dramatic standoffs took place in the republics, but the possibility of a return to old times exposed the frail nature of their sovereignty. In addition to Yeltsin, only the leaders of the Baltic republics and Moldova promptly condemned the coup. Others, including Kravchuk, adopted a wait-and-see approach.

The CPU central apparatus instructed its regional secretaries to support the Emergency Committee, and military commanders in Ukraine received analogous orders from their superiors in Moscow. But Kravchuk remained uncommitted during his meeting on August 19 with the representative of the Emergency Committee, General Valentin Varennikov. In the two TV broadcasts he gave that same day, Kravchuk called for calm and deliberation, but he did not clearly favor either side. In contrast, Rukh and other oppositional forces condemned the coup and called for a general strike. On the next day, mass protests began on Kyiv's main boulevard, the Khreshchatyk, but Kravchuk still refused to convene an emergency session of the Supreme Rada. He did so only on August 22, after the coup was over and Gorbachev had returned to Moscow.

The day before the emergency session, scheduled for August 24, Kravchuk flew to Moscow, where Gorbachev tried to persuade the republican leaders to proceed with the new Union treaty. Yet, the Soviet president lost all real power when the center self-destructed during the coup. Yeltsin humiliated Gorbachev in front of the television cameras and banned the Communist Party in the Russian Federation. Back in Kyiv on August 24, Kravchuk claimed before parliament that he had opposed the coup from the very beginning and prevented the introduction of a state of emergency in Galicia and the capital.

The deputies did not dwell for long on the question of Kravchuk's behavior during the putsch. They realized that the center had caved in and the republics, including Russia, were establishing themselves as independent states. In addition, Communist parliamentarians wanted to distance themselves from the party leadership in Moscow, which was implicated in the coup. After a short break to allow the Communist majority and the democratic opposition to meet separately, on the evening of August 24 the Supreme Rada approved a brief declaration of independence by the overwhelming margin of 346 votes in favor, 1 against, and 3 abstentions. The declaration somewhat disingenuously proclaimed the republic a fully independent state "in view of the mortal danger surrounding Ukraine in connection with the state coup in the USSR on August 19, 1991," but it also referred to the long tradition of statehood, the right of national self-determination, and the previous Declaration of Sovereignty.[28] On August 30, following in the steps of other republics, the Supreme Rada banned the CPU and nationalized its property—bank accounts, buildings, presses, and archives.

Halfhearted negotiations about the fate of the Soviet Union continued in the fall of 1991, although Kravchuk's successful trip to Canada, the United States, and France in September attracted more attention in the Ukrainian media. Political forces in Ukraine, meanwhile, concentrated on the upcoming referendum and presidential elections. According to parliament's decision, Ukraine's Declaration of Independence was to be put to a referendum on December 1, 1991. Before the coup, in July 1991, the Supreme Rada passed a law creating the office of president, in part because Russia and other republics had done so already. Now the elections were to take place on the same day.

Following the defeat of the coup, expectations of a better life after Communism ran high. In addition, the Ukrainian media converted to the cause of independence and spread the seductive myth that separating from Moscow, which had allegedly exploited Ukrainian resources, would leave the republic much better off economically. No mainstream political force agitated for a "no" vote. The only audible opposing voice came from the unpopular Gorbachev in Moscow. On December 1, 1991, an impressive 84.2 percent of Ukrainian voters turned out, with 90.3 percent in favor of independence. A majority was registered in every province, including the overwhelmingly Russian Crimea (54.1 percent). On the same day, Kravchuk, who faced no opposition from the left, took 61.5 percent of the vote in the first round of the presidential elections, easily defeating a candidate from Rukh, former dissident and political prisoner Viacheslav Chornovil, and four other candidates to become Ukraine's first president. Both of the main candidates stood unambiguously for independence, but compared with his rival, Kravchuk appeared to be a levelheaded centrist and a seasoned statesman.

Immediately after the results were announced, neighboring Poland became the first foreign country to recognize Ukraine's independence. Canada was the first G-7 country to do so. For all practical purposes, the outcome of the Ukrainian referendum buried Gorbachev's plan to save the Union. As soon as the news sank in, the leaders of the three Slavic republics—Russia (Yeltsin), Ukraine (Kravchuk), and Belarus (Stanislaŭ Shushkevich)—gathered secretly in Brezhnev's old hunting lodge in the Belarusian forests. Their first evening together was devoted to drinking, but the next day, December 8, 1991, they emerged to announce that the Soviet Union was to be dissolved and a Commonwealth of Independent States (CIS) created in its place. The majority of former Soviet republics eventually joined the CIS, but this loose organization did not evolve into a statelike structure. Gorbachev officially ended his duties as Soviet president by the year's end. The Soviet Union was no more. Ukraine had become an independent state.

⁂

With the passage of time, an event as significant as gaining independence inevitably becomes mythologized. Just as other nations embellish the foundations of their statehood, present-day Ukrainian media and history textbooks understandably prefer to emphasize the long tradition of the dissident movement and the large scale of mass demonstrations. This way, the emergence of independent Ukraine becomes the result of a popular revolution. But while the element of mass protest is undeniably present in the story of Ukraine's transformation from a Soviet republic into an independent state, the main story line is nevertheless that of the Soviet Union's disintegration—a process that was started from above by misguided Communist reformers. Independent Ukraine would not have emerged in 1991 if it were not for Gorbachev, for the example of the Baltic republics, and—most important—for the tacit understanding between the democratic opposition and national Communists. This last factor explains much about the next thirteen years in Ukrainian history. The Soviet Union and Communism were gone, but the old elites remained in charge of Ukrainian politics and economic life.

A s seen from Ukraine, the Soviet collapse in 1991 was no revolution with clear-cut victors and obvious regime change. The republic obtained independence peacefully when the Soviet Union disintegrated, and the same politicians and industrial managers who for decades had built socialism became founding fathers (and very few mothers) of an independent Ukrainian state. As happened elsewhere in the former USSR, the Communist Party was banned, but by then it was only a shadow of its former self, more dynamic functionaries having moved to the parliament and government. Lacking electoral strength to govern on its own, the Ukrainian opposition did not topple the old regime in the republic but made an implicit deal with its more flexible representatives, led by Leonid Kravchuk. Both sides wanted an independent Ukraine, the opposition for ideological reasons and the renegade elites for a fiefdom for them to rule without taking orders from the Kremlin. This pact left in power old political elites—purged of the most odious party hacks, who did not change colors well—to govern as custodians of a new state. Moreover, with the nationalist right supportive and the Communist Party banned, Kravchuk faced almost no political opposition during his first years in office.

The tremendous difficulties Ukraine has experienced after its separation from the Soviet Union, therefore, did not result from any residual Communist resistance to democratic reforms pursued by the government. Rather, they were the consequence of the former Soviet elite itself charting the course of Ukraine's post-Communist development and not starting these reforms in the first place. Both Western observers and the democratic opposition in Ukraine expected the republic to undergo a "transition" from Soviet socialism to political democracy and a market economy. Soon, however, they found themselves wondering what post-Soviet Ukraine was really being transformed into—crony capitalism coupled with political oligarchy?

In addition, general theories of post-Communist transition neglected the aspect Ukrainians saw as paramount: nation building.[1] In Ukraine, democratization and economic transformations were accompanied, and often overshadowed, by the construction of a new state and the development of a new nation. The idea of independent Ukraine as a state for ethnic Ukrainians, where their language and culture should finally become dominant, is common currency in the country's media and political discourse, but it usually reflects a protest against the persistent influence of "imperial" Russian culture rather than exclusive ethnic nationalism. Of the two models of nationhood, an ethnic one that would include only ethnic Ukrainians and a civic model inclusive of all citizens of the new Ukrainian state, Ukrainian nation builders clearly embraced the latter. Given the strong ethnic connotations of the Ukrainian word *natsiia* (nation understood as ethnocultural entity), the foundational documents of Ukrainian statehood speak instead of the "people of Ukraine" or a multinational "Ukrainian people."

Building the State: The Kravchuk Presidency

The winner of the presidential elections that were held concurrently with the independence referendum on December 1, 1991, Leonid Kravchuk (b. 1934), was sworn in as president of Ukraine later that month. In early 1992, a series of parliamentary measures established the symbolic rupture between the new state and the Ukrainian SSR by adopting the state symbols associated with the Ukrainian People's Republic (1918–1920): the blue-and-yellow flag, the trident as the state coat of arms, and the anthem "Ukraine Has Not Perished Yet." In truth, most differences were confined to ideology—to the reversal of the official position on the Communist past, the Russian big brother, and the capitalist West. The young state was being governed by institutions inherited from Soviet Ukraine. The Supreme Rada elected in 1990 served its full term until 1994. The republic's government, the Council of Ministers headed by Vitold Fokin, also continued after independence, although under the new name, the Cabinet of Ministers. Rather than scrapping the entire old administrative apparatus as true revolutionaries would do, the Ukrainian authorities adopted a new political language while preserving the old state machinery. In fact, many ministries saw their staff numbers grow, perhaps none more so than the Ministry of Foreign Affairs, which in Soviet times was a small committee responsible for receiving foreign dignitaries and maintaining a mission at the UN. Now, hundreds of people were needed to staff Ukrainian embassies abroad and to develop the new state's international policies.

Indeed, like other newly independent states, Ukraine was obsessed with obtaining international recognition of its sovereignty and borders. In practical terms, this meant establishing Ukraine's separateness from Russia. Yeltsin's Russia had played a leading role in the dissolution of the Soviet Union, but once the imperial center was gone, the Russian authorities began aggressively asserting their country's regional dominance. The Kremlin promoted a closer integration of the former Soviet republics into the Commonwealth of Independent States (CIS) and jealously guarded Russian interests in the "near abroad," which included former Soviet military bases and cultural rights of the Russian minority. In the case of Ukraine, many Russian politicians also remained ambiguous about the very existence of a separate Ukrainian nationality.[2] In the face of such attitudes, early Ukrainian foreign policy focused on affirming the republic's independence. During the initial CIS summits in 1991 and 1992, Ukraine led other dissenting republics in opposing the proposals for CIS citizenship, a joint security pact, and an interparliamentary assembly. Ukrainian resistance contributed to the fact that the CIS never developed into a supranational structure and subject of international law. But much greater tension in Russian-Ukrainian relations built up over the issues of Crimea and the Black Sea Fleet.

In 1991 and 1992, many Russian politicians questioned the legality of Ukrainian control over the Crimea, which Khrushchev had transferred in 1954 from the Russian to the Ukrainian republic as a token of the two peoples' eternal friendship.[3] Encouraged by Moscow's support, in 1992 Russian separatists took the upper hand in the Crimean parliament, which passed a declaration of independence. The declaration was soon rescinded, but at the same time the Russian parliament voted to declare the 1954 transfer unconstitutional and invalid. The Crimean problem simultaneously embodied several anxieties of post-Soviet Russia. The Crimea was a region where ethnic Russians constituted the majority, it was a base of the Soviet Black Sea Fleet, and it served as a setting for major events in Russian military history. Thus, the nation's cohesion, military might, and national pride all appeared to be threatened. Russian patriots were particularly disturbed by Ukraine's bid to take over the Black Sea Fleet and its main base of Sevastopol, the city that the tsarist army had heroically defended during the Crimean War and the Soviet Army, during World War II. Only two emergency meetings between Yeltsin and Kravchuk in the Crimea in the summer of 1992 defused tension somewhat. The two presidents agreed to establish joint Russian-Ukrainian control over the Black Sea Fleet for the next three years, with its ownership to be decided later.

But Ukraine and Russia had more military hardware to divide. After the Soviet Union's breakup, Ukraine's brand-new Ministry of Defense claimed jurisdiction over some 800,000 Soviet army personnel stationed in the republic, as well as more than 6,500 tanks, 1,500 combat aircraft, and approximately 5,000 nuclear weapons—the world's third-largest nuclear arsenal. The majority were tactical weapons, already in the process of being dismantled as part of Soviet-U.S. arms reduction agreements, and following U.S. pressure, Ukraine agreed to transfer these nuclear warheads to Russia for destruction there. However, Ukraine remained in possession of the deadliest weaponry of all, 176 intercontinental ballistic missiles with 1,240 nuclear warheads.[4] The Ukrainian authorities were reluctant to simply transfer this arsenal to Russia and preferred to make a separate deal with the West to dismantle the rockets in Ukraine. Kyiv was also seeking U.S. financial compensation and security guarantees (presumably from possible Russian aggression). Ukraine's procrastination, together with statements by some Ukrainian parliamentarians about nuclear arms as the only guarantee of independence and Western assistance, alarmed politicians around the world. After a brief stint as a "problem child" of nuclear proliferation, however, Ukraine realized it could not afford to maintain its aging Soviet arsenal. In January 1994, a trilateral agreement signed by the United States, Russia, and Ukraine resolved the standoff by compensating Ukraine with fuel from Russia for its nuclear power stations. Ukraine also received substantial U.S. aid and vague guarantees of its territorial integrity. During 1994, the Supreme Rada finally ratified the Strategic Arms Limitation Treaty and the Nuclear Non-Proliferation Treaty. The last nuclear warheads were removed from Ukrainian territory in 1996, thus making Ukraine the world's first state to give up its nuclear arsenal.

The American treatment of Ukraine during the nuclear controversy in the early 1990s was representative of initial U.S. policy in the post-Soviet space. The administration of President George H. W. Bush consistently sided with Russia as the strongest Soviet successor state that could ensure political stability in the region. Yet, Yeltsin's Russia was anything but stable. With economic reforms and democracy faltering, the Russian authorities became increasingly assertive on the international scene. Beginning in early 1994, U.S. policy makers understood the geopolitical importance of independent Ukraine as a guarantee against the restoration of the Soviet Union and the extension of Russian influence into eastern Europe. As the influential hawkish commentator Zbigniew Brzezinski put it in a *Foreign Affairs* article: "It cannot be stressed strongly enough that without Ukraine, Russia ceases to be an empire, but with Ukraine suborned and then subordinated, Russia automatically becomes an empire."[5] The improvement in U.S.-Ukrainian relations, thus, resulted from worsening American-Russian relations.

Ukraine's neighbors to the west, Poland, Hungary, Slovakia, and Romania, generally welcomed the emergence of independent Ukraine as a state shielding them from often unpredictable Russia. Notwithstanding the turbulent history of Polish-Ukrainian relations and the loss of territory to Ukraine in 1939, post-Communist Poland was the first state to recognize Ukrainian independence and consistently acted as Ukraine's advocate to the West. In contrast, minor tensions developed between Romania and Ukraine because of Romanian claims to the territories the Soviet Union had acquired in 1940: southern Bessarabia, northern Bukovyna, and the oil-rich Serpent

Island in the Black Sea. Although Romania was eventually forced to drop its territorial claims as a condition of joining NATO and the EU, relations between the two countries remained strained for much of the 1990s.[6] In general, although Ukraine's western neighbors welcomed the development of bilateral relations with Ukraine, they were reluctant to accept the new state into any regional structures (geared toward entry into the EU). The Kravchuk administration presented the "return to Europe" as a desirable alternative to Ukraine's past closeness to Russia, but until 1994 the EU did not pay much attention to Ukraine.

The lack of support from the West between 1991 and 1994 further slowed the already difficult process of Ukraine's post-Communist transition. Contrary to widespread expectations, the attainment of independence did not improve the economic situation; if anything, the breakup of economic ties among the former Soviet republics exacerbated the crisis that had begun in the 1980s. In the Soviet planned economy, most industrial production cycles involved factories located in various republics. With independence, the movement across new borders of raw materials, parts, and finished goods was impeded because of both tariffs and an undeveloped payment system. (Owing to high inflation in the early 1990s, barter was often the preferred method of exchange.) Ukraine suffered more than certain other republics because heavy industry and the military-industrial sector dominated its economy, with about 80 percent of large enterprises involved in arms production.[7] Much of Ukraine's industrial output had been intended for Russia, which was no longer interested in outdated industrial equipment or able to afford so many armaments. At the same time, the price Russia was charging Ukraine for oil and gas, on which the Ukrainian economy was heavily dependent, began increasing after 1992—although for more than a decade it would still remain well below world prices. Finally, Ukraine had been a region of early Soviet industrialization during the 1930s, and by the 1990s, many of its enterprises and mines were obsolete. Their modernization required huge investments, yet such funds were neither available in the country nor forthcoming from the West.

Preoccupied as he was with state building, President Kravchuk paid little attention to economic reform. In fact, such neglect may have been intentional, as radical "shock therapy" based on the Polish model could have led to social unrest benefiting his opponents on the left and antagonizing the Russian-speaking industrial regions in the east.[8] Instead of launching privatization, the government of Prime Minister Vitold Fokin subsidized unprofitable state factories to prevent mass unemployment, but the credits it issued were still in rubles, as Ukraine had not fully separated its financial system from that of Russia. By the fall of 1992, Russia's Central Bank realized that this Ukrainian policy fueled hyperinflation in Russia and stopped honoring ruble credits issued by the Ukrainian National Bank. In Ukraine, too, mounting public discontent over inflation—which would reach the annual rate of 2,500 percent in 1992—and the scarcity of goods forced the Supreme Rada to bring down Fokin's government in September. In November 1992, Ukraine formally withdrew from the ruble zone by introducing its own provisional currency, the *karbovanets*.[9]

But the new currency did not mean a different approach to economic reform. The new prime minister, Leonid Kuchma (b. 1938), a former director of the world's largest missile factory, Pivdenmash (in Dnipropetrovsk), attempted to introduce strict monetary controls, improve tax collection, and start privatization. But his belt-tightening measures led only to more discontent. With wage and pension arrears mounting throughout the country, the Donbas miners went on a massive strike in June 1993 that disrupted whatever remained of the functioning economy. To satisfy the miners' demands, the government had to print so much money that nominal GDP rose by 82 percent.[10] After a frustrated Kuchma resigned in September 1993, his successor, a former mine manager from the Donbas, Yukhym Zviahilsky, reversed most of his reforms and issued even more generous subsidies to failing factories and collective farms. The *karbovanets* immediately succumbed to hyperinflation, which reached 100 percent in December 1993 and 10,115 percent for the calendar year 1993.[11] As the coins became worthless, for a brief period in 1993 Ukrainians enjoyed free public phones and subway rides, until tokens and cards came into use.

Overall, however, the standard of life in Ukraine plummeted during the early 1990s. With their savings wiped out by hyperinflation, salaries not catching up with rising prices, and goods simply not being available for purchase, much of the population retreated to a subsistence economy in which a primitive barter system of goods and services, as well as cultivation of small garden plots in the countryside, ensured survival. During the early to mid-1990s, an estimated three quarters of Ukrainians lived below the poverty level.[12] With the decline of state welfare and health systems, the average life expectancy and birth rate both took a plunge, and the country's population declined rapidly from a high of 52 million in 1989, to 48.5 during the 2001 census. Another contributing factor was emigration, with Ukrainian Jews in particular leaving en masse for Israel, the United States, and Germany. Large numbers of ethnic Ukrainians were also immigrating to North America and western Europe in search of a better life. The only social group that found the situation to their liking was the new rich: a mixture of high government officials moonlighting as big-league traders and private businesspeople, who were often former Soviet industrial managers, Komsomol functionaries, or black marketeers. With the government's connivance, the new elites amassed huge fortunes by looting state assets and reselling subsidized Russian oil and gas in Europe at world prices.

The ugly face of Ukraine's early economic transformation reflected the lack of a strong democratic, reformist political force in the country. Kravchuk and his government represented the political center, which remained structurally undefined, as most ministers initially did not belong to any political party, not that there were any strong centrist parties. The new elites were essentially the old Soviet bureaucrats in Ukraine who came to power as a result of imperial collapse rather than revolution and thus felt no need to develop either democratic institutions or a market economy. The right, still represented at this stage by Rukh, was in favor of Western-style reforms, but its electoral appeal was limited by the endorsement of Ukrainian nationalism (admittedly of a democratic variety). Popular in western Ukraine as well as among the intelligentsia in big cities, the right could not break through in the Russian-speaking east. In any case, Rukh kept its part of the "Grand Bargain," which had made independence possible. It continued to support the government of the corporate center for as long as it remained committed to strengthening the Ukrainian state. Moreover, Rukh was weakened considerably after its split in 1992 into two political parties, with the larger one (led by Chornovil and claiming a membership of 50,000) retaining the name Rukh. As disillusionment with democratic nationalism set in, the Banderite wing of the OUN inserted itself into mainstream politics as the Congress of Ukrainian Nationalists (1992), although it remains a very marginal political force. Some young radicals in western Ukraine joined the far-right and fascistlike Ukrainian National Self-Defense Force (est. 1991), which is constantly in trouble with the Ukrainian authorities.

The resurfacing of the far right only added to public discontent with the state of affairs that the parties on the left would eventually benefit from. From 1991 to 1993, however, the Kravchuk administration did not face serious opposition on the left either. After the banning of the Communist Party in August 1991, the Socialist Party of Ukraine, led by Oleksandr Moroz, immediately attracted more than 60,000 members and thus became the largest political party in the country, where the majority of citizens had developed a strong revulsion against politics. If the Socialists were generally supportive of Ukrainian independence and some economic reform, this was not the case with the Communist Party, which was resurrected in 1993 at a congress in the eastern industrial city of Donetsk. Under the leadership of the hard-liner Petro Symonenko, the Communists called for the restoration of the Soviet system and opposed any economic reforms. They also advocated making Russian the second official language and, in the long run, reestablishing the

Soviet Union. Party membership momentarily swelled to 130,000, with senior citizens predominating.[13] The Communists soon positioned themselves to garner the protest vote and the nostalgia vote of those who yearned for the Soviet welfare state.

Even when the Communists were still absent from the political scene, Kravchuk was having a difficult time working with the Supreme Rada, which had been elected before the Soviet collapse. Dominated by "Red managers" and still-powerful regional bosses, the Rada successfully fought off the president's attempts to appoint presidential representatives as de facto provincial governors and establish a large advisory council to the president. Kravchuk did manage to expand presidential powers by building up the apparatus of the Presidential Administration into a mini-cabinet with an extensive bureaucracy. All in all, his state-building measures did not represent any coherent program and were an outcome of power struggles at the top and the use of old administrative methods.[14] But his most memorable and controversial contribution to state building was the top-down linguistic Ukrainization of the civil service and education.

Ukraine's post-Soviet elites emerged from the collapse of Communism with an ideology borrowed from the nationalists to justify their power. Thus, Kravchuk substantiated his rift with Russia by embracing a nationalistic concept of Ukrainian history as a long struggle against Russian oppression.[15] As part of his move away from Moscow, he took measures to strengthen Ukrainian national identity—a turn greatly appreciated by his allies on the right but highly controversial in vote-rich eastern Ukraine. The new elites understood that making the Ukrainian state more "Ukrainian" was important for state building, as national independence remained insecure as long as most bureaucratic paperwork and education were conducted in Russian. For nationalists on the right, a Ukrainization drive seemed natural, because for them the Ukrainian state represented self-fulfillment of the Ukrainian ethnic nation and, therefore, had to be thoroughly Ukrainized.

The Kravchuk administration distanced itself from a notion of forced Ukrainization, but it did promote the use of Ukrainian in government, education, and the media. Scholars have pondered whether Ukraine under Kravchuk could, like interwar Poland, be called a "nationalizing state," forcibly assimilating its minorities.[16] Yet, Kravchuk's halfhearted policies did not go beyond establishing Ukrainian as a state language in the civic and multiethnic state that is modern Ukraine. Other nation-building measures of Ukraine's first president were guided by the same logic of asserting Ukrainian sovereignty, and they caused a similar backlash. Kravchuk promoted public use of the new blue-and-yellow flag, the "trident" state emblem, and the anthem "Ukraine Has Not Yet Perished"—all of them initially rejected as nationalistic in the Russian-speaking east. He supported the Ukrainian Orthodox Church (Kyivan Patriarchate) over all other Orthodox churches in Ukraine, including the largest of them, the Russian Orthodox Church. Overall, Kravchuk's efforts brought notable improvement in the use of Ukrainian as the state language, but he paid a heavy political price for his identification with Ukrainization, which caused widespread discontent in the Russian-speaking regions of eastern and southern Ukraine. In 1994, the Russian separatist movement in the Crimea flared up again—this time without Moscow's support—with the election of Yurii Meshkov as president of the autonomous republic.[17]

Sensing trouble, official Kyiv began scaling down its Ukrainizing efforts well in advance of the parliamentary elections held in March 1994. But voters were not impressed by feverish nation building in the midst of an economic collapse and blatant corruption. Although poor voter turnout led to only 338 of 450 seats being filled, the Communist Party won 25 percent of them (35 percent together with the Socialists and the Peasant Party, which formed the left bloc with the Communists), emerging as the largest party in the Supreme Rada. Rukh elected only 6 percent of deputies, and all the parties of the right, 9 percent. The extreme right won 8 seats (2.5 percent). But independents, most of them representing the amorphous corporate center, numbered 168 (almost 50 percent).[18] With no secure majority for any bloc, the parliament proved to be dysfunctional.

Because Kravchuk had not created a political party of his own, the parliamentary elections were less of a referendum on his rule than the presidential elections that followed in the summer. Yet even before that, the new Supreme Rada sent him ominous signals by electing as its speaker the Socialist leader Oleksandr Moroz and rejecting all candidates for the head of government other than the Soviet-era prime minister Vitalii Masol. During the presidential elections in June and July 1994, Kravchuk faced six opponents of various political stripes in the first round, and his former prime minister, Leonid Kuchma, in the runoff. The incumbent had a dismal economic record and no meaningful reform plan, which forced him to campaign as a nation builder. Kravchuk was placing much hope on his recent successes in foreign policy—in early 1994, Ukraine settled the issue of its nuclear arsenal, became a major recipient of U.S. financial aid, and signed a partnership agreement with the EU. Yet disgruntled voters apparently saw these moves as being in line with his general anti-Russian policy. Kuchma skillfully exploited the themes of economic catastrophe and the divisive Ukrainization drive by connecting nationalism with mismanagement. He campaigned on a platform of economic reform, rebuilding close ties with Russia, and making Russian the second state language. In the runoff, Kuchma defeated Kravchuk by taking 52% of the vote. Overall, the elections confirmed the sharpening polarization between Ukraine's historical regions, with Kravchuk carrying the Ukrainian-speaking west and Kuchma winning substantial votes in the more populous and largely Russian-speaking east and south.

✄ Building Crony Capitalism: The Kuchma Presidency

Although he was elected on the promises of restoring ties with Russia and protecting the Russian language, President Kuchma (1994–2004) in fact continued an independent foreign policy and creeping cultural Ukrainization, for these policies provided legitimacy for the new Ukrainian ruling elites. Like Kravchuk, Kuchma preferred the status of a president of an independent state to that of a Russian pawn. He maintained close relations with the United States, with the result that Ukraine became the third-largest recipient of American financial aid (after Israel and Egypt) in the late 1990s.[19] President Bill Clinton and President Kuchma twice exchanged official visits (1995/1997 and 1999/2000), and a commission headed by Kuchma and U.S. Vice President Al Gore was established to oversee the development of bilateral relations. In fact, Kuchma went beyond Kravchuk, who had maintained Ukraine's nonbloc status, when in February 1995, Ukraine became the first CIS country to enter into a cooperation agreement with NATO, the so-called Partnership for Peace program. In 1997, NATO and Ukraine furthered their cooperation by signing the "Charter on a Distinctive Partnership." All in all, during his first term, Kuchma found it beneficial to play the West and Russia against each other. In this spirit, his government often issued pro-Western declarations, albeit without really moving too far away from its powerful northern neighbor. It was under Kuchma—and not the openly anti-Russian Kravchuk—that Ukraine officially announced its desire to join the EU.

Instead of becoming Russia's client, Kuchma used his excellent relations with the United States to normalize Ukrainian-Russian affairs. Concerned about Ukraine's overtures toward NATO, including joint NATO-Ukrainian maneuvers in the Crimea, in June 1997, President Yeltsin signed a friendship treaty with President Kuchma, recognizing Ukraine's territorial integrity and dividing the Black Sea Fleet. Ukraine ended up with 18 percent of the ships, and the Russian navy secured a long-term lease on Sevastopol's port facilities. Along the way, Kuchma also managed to extinguish the Russian separatist movement in the Crimea. Taking advantage of an internal political conflict on the peninsula, he removed Meshkov in 1995 and abolished the Crimean presidency in 1996.

Like his predecessor, however, Kuchma during his first term (1994–1999) spent much of his time and energy fighting with the Supreme Rada. A deeply divided parliament with a left plurality and an amorphous center opposed any serious reform efforts. As a result, Kuchma soon found himself following in Kravchuk's footsteps by pushing for the expansion of presidential powers, especially with the preparation of the Law on Power (1995), which caused a prolonged stalemate with the Rada. After threatening to hold a referendum that would empower him to dissolve parliament, Kuchma finally managed, during an all-night marathon session on June 28, 1996, to get a new constitution passed by the Supreme Rada. (Ukraine was the last of the former Soviet republics to promulgate a post-Communist constitution.) Although endowing the president with impressive powers, this document formally designated Ukraine as a presidential-parliamentary republic. Kuchma also built the Presidential Administration into an even larger separate bureaucracy that duplicated the functions of the Cabinet of Ministers, which he saw as a competing power center.

Kuchma's standoff with the left-leaning parliament provided him with a convenient explanation for lack of progress in the economy—a line he fed time and again to both foreign experts and the disconcerted populace—but the real reasons were more complex. In October 1994, Kuchma announced a comprehensive economic reform package envisaging privatization of state enterprises, strict fiscal discipline, and the creation of a stable currency.[20] He encountered fierce resistance from two quarters: from the Communists, ideologically opposed as they were to a free market economy, and from industrial managers, who dreaded the elimination of subsidies. Although the president publicly denounced the left, he kept quiet about the other, no less powerful, group of dissenters. In fact, Kuchma owed his electoral victory to financial support from business interests in eastern Ukraine, primarily in his home base of Dnipropetrovsk. His last job before becoming president was chairman of the Ukrainian Union of Industrialists and Business People, an organization uniting "Red directors" and new entrepreneurs. These Soviet-style "industrialists," who thrived by exploiting the system of subsidized state enterprises, staunchly resisted privatization. Only small, consumer-oriented businesses were privatized en masse from 1995 to 1997, and Kuchma watered down most other reforms as early as 1995. The new elites who had brought him to power were so accustomed to stealing from the state that they did not yet realize the benefits of becoming private operators.

During his first term, Kuchma went through four prime ministers, but it was the third one, Pavlo Lazarenko (May 1996–July 1997), who best embodied the spirit of the "crony capitalism" then under construction in Ukraine. A collective farm chairman and minor Communist Party functionary in Soviet times, after independence Lazarenko (b. 1953) grew to political prominence in his home province of Dnipropetrovsk. Through various shady business schemes, he also accumulated a considerable fortune. While he was prime minister, he moved into energy and communications businesses on a large scale (with his companies registered under other people's names) and was also accused of extortion and ordering contract killings of rival businessmen. During his short term at the helm of the government, Lazarenko allegedly stashed hundreds of millions of dollars in U.S., Swiss, and Antiguan banks. After losing in the game of big business and being removed from power, in 1998 Lazarenko was caught entering Switzerland on a Panamanian passport. When the Supreme Rada lifted Lazarenko's immunity from prosecution in 1999, he fled to the United States, where he purchased Eddie Murphy's former mansion in California. Convicted by a U.S. court of money laundering, Lazarenko was imprisoned there, with more charges against him pending in Ukraine and Switzerland.[21]

Lazarenko's saga, with all its dazzling turns, became a public spectacle only because he had had a falling-out with Kuchma's immediate circle. Hundreds of high government officials had enriched themselves in a similar way without attracting the attention of the judiciary and the media. Nor was Lazarenko the first former prime minister to flee Ukraine after being accused of corruption and illegal economic activities, as Yuhym Zviahilsky had already done a runner in the fall of 1994; he spent three years in Israel until the investigation was closed for lack of evidence. But for the Ukrainian public, Lazarenko symbolized the new class of "oligarchs," or businesspeople who had amassed fortunes by questionable means. Some oligarchs owed their business success to their own or their relatives' tenure in power, yet the majority emerged in the murky business waters of the mid-1990s and developed the right political connections during the latter half of the decade.

The heads of Ukraine's two most powerful regional economic clans under Kuchma fit this model well. Reputed to be the richest man in Ukraine, the reclusive Rinat Akhmetov (b. 1966) is an ethnic Tatar and an economist by training, who began his ascent to power by creating banks in Donetsk in the mid-1990s but soon expanded his business interests into metallurgy, machine building, and communications. He also owns the Shakhtar soccer team. Akhmetov is believed to be the head of the Donetsk economic clan, and his wealth is estimated at US$3.5 billion. He is a close ally of Viktor Yanukovych, the long-serving governor of Donetsk province and prime minister, who was also the party of power's candidate during the presidential elections in 2004. Akhmetov's competitor and sometime business partner is the head of the Dnipropetrovsk clan, the affable Viktor Pinchuk (b. 1960), a metallurgical engineer by training, who in the early 1990s established a large pipe-making enterprise. From there, he expanded into oil, gas, and metallurgy, as well as the media. Having developed close links with President Kuchma's inner circle,

Pinchuk helped finance his reelection in 1999. In 2002, he married Kuchma's daughter, Olena. By late 2004, the fortune of this art lover and philanthropist was estimated at US$2.5 billion.[22]

Given the cozy symbiosis between the oligarchs and the government, it is a miracle any economic reforms were attempted at all. In 1996, the Ukrainian authorities introduced a new and stable currency, the *hryvnia*, the only successful measure from Kuchma's original package. Yet the government continued overspending, for it had difficulties collecting taxes but needed to pay pensions and salaries on time—or risk a Communist victory at the ballot box. Ukraine's debt to Russia for deliveries of oil and gas grew at a dangerous rate. After the announcement of structural reforms in 1994, Ukraine also qualified for support from the International Monetary Fund (IMF) and soon became addicted to rolling Western credits. The IMF made further financing conditional on meeting targets in inflation control, interest rates, and tax collection. According to one scholar, "The IMF has often seemed like the only real party of reform in Ukraine, albeit one imposing its own neo-liberal agenda without much regard for Ukrainian circumstance."[23]

In any case, even when the Ukrainian ministers managed to meet the IMF's short-term targets, this did not amount to the creation of a market economy. In agriculture, inefficient Soviet-period collective farms survived under the name of "collective agricultural enterprises," while the class of individual farmers remained small, if increasingly important, in the production of meat, dairy products, and fruit. This was due in part to the fact that farmers could only rent their fields. Because the Communists and their allies were categorically opposed to the sale of land, in 2001 the Supreme Rada finally passed a land code making such transactions possible, but its implementation was postponed until 2007 or later.

Small businesses were suffocating under the burden of taxes, which sometimes reached 90 percent. Much economic activity therefore escaped into the "shadow economy," which operated underground. Even at registered enterprises, however, workers were often paid in cash to hide the business's real size and evade the employer's contribution to the state pension fund. Direct foreign investment remained so small as to be negligible. Large-scale privatization of industry began in earnest between 1996 and 1998, but the oligarchs and Red directors benefited most by buying major enterprises for next to nothing—and with privatization certificates snatched for pennies from impoverished workers. Even after they became private owners, Ukraine's new capitalists had little incentive to improve productivity, because they were getting more from government subsidies and tax privileges.[24] Yet, by the late 1990s, there were the first signs of industrial revival, especially in export-oriented metallurgy.

By the end of Kuchma's first term, popular disenchantment with his policies had become pronounced. The parliamentary elections of 1998 brought back the Communists as the largest party in the Rada with 27 percent of seats (38 percent with their allies), but overall they produced a more structured and efficient parliament. For the first time, the elections were held under a semiproportional system, with half of the 450 "people's deputies" chosen in single-member districts and another half picked proportionally from party lists of those parties that cleared the 4 percent threshold. Such a method had the effect of strengthening the party system, with the independents this time constituting only 26 percent of parliamentarians. Rukh polled only 10 percent, but the main beneficiaries were the small centrist parties, all of them misleadingly named; they were really front organizations for regional clans and business interests: the Greens, Popular Democrats, Hromada ("Community"), and Social Democrats (United). The total number of centrist deputies was 23 percent.[25] As in the previous parliament, a leftist, Oleksandr Tkachenko of the Peasant Party, became parliamentary speaker, and the left could still mount effective resistance to Kuchma's policies.

As he stood for reelection in 1999, the president focused his attentions elsewhere. In advance of presidential elections, Kuchma and his entourage lined up financial support from friendly oligarchs, tightened their control over the media, and hired experienced political strategists from Russia. The strategy that they came up with was inspired by the 1996 Russian elections, in which an unpopular Yeltsin won reelection because his opponent in the runoff was the dogmatic and uninspiring leader of the Communist Party, Gennadii Ziuganov. His Ukrainian counterpart, Petro Symonenko, was even more orthodox and less charismatic than Ziuganov. All the authorities had to do, therefore, was to prevent a liberal or moderate socialist candidate from putting up a serious challenge. The Kuchma administration freely exploited its control of the media and engaged in economic harassment of businesses associated with potential opponents. In the hope of splitting the left vote, the authorities also discreetly supported the extremist Progressive Socialist Party, which was further to the left than the Communists. In the end, the Russian-inspired strategy (reinforced by some ballot stuffing) worked perfectly. The most visible moderate leftist, Socialist leader Moroz, was a distant third in the first round, just ahead of the firebrand Natalia Vitrenko, the chief of the Progressive Socialists. In the runoff, all right and centrist forces closed ranks behind Kuchma, who easily defeated Symonenko, the "Red menace," with 56 percent of the vote to the latter's 38 percent.

During Kuchma's second term (1999–2004), however, economic recovery contrasted with dirty politics and corruption. Signs of a modest revival in the economy had been seen for some time, although the balance sheet remained negative, with the GDP decreasing every year until 1999. Based on Ukraine's rich deposits of iron ore and other minerals, metals production was the first industry to recover. During the late 1990s, new capitalists in Ukraine discovered that the export of steel and minerals was a reliable and almost completely legal way of enriching themselves—compared with their previous parasitical practice of reselling Russian oil and appropriating state loans. In other branches of the economy, many privatized enterprises also found their market niches. As they paid higher salaries, increased consumer spending, especially in the big cities, further stimulated the economy. Finally, after a painful financial default in 1998, the Russian economy began an impressive recovery, which had a positive influence on Ukraine.

Before these emerging trends could coalesce into an economic recovery, however, Ukraine needed increased fiscal discipline. In 1999, Ukraine's foreign debt had reached a historical high of US$12.4 billion, half of which was owed to the IMF, the World Bank, and Russia. The government also spent generously in advance of the presidential elections, which led to the threat of runaway inflation. With international experts warning about the possibility of a Ukrainian default and Washington urging belt tightening, in December 1999 Kuchma appointed Viktor Yushchenko (b. 1954) as prime minister. Yushchenko had a long career in banking, culminating in his recent tenure as head of the National Bank. He was known for his pro-Western liberal and reformist views—and in 1998, he married an American of Ukrainian descent, Chicago-born Kateryna Chumachenko, a former employee of the U.S. State Department. In all likelihood, Kuchma picked Yushchenko as the best candidate for conducting difficult negotiations with Western donors in the hope that, like other prime ministers, Yushchenko would last a year or so and leave after amassing a fortune for himself.

To the president's unpleasant surprise, however, Yushchenko proved to be a determined reformer and an honest civil servant. As expected, he rescheduled the debt payments. But at the same time, together with his deputy prime minister in charge of the energy sector, the energetic Yulia Tymoshenko (b. 1960), he began cracking down on the illegal resale of stolen Russian oil and gas in Europe at world prices. Tymoshenko herself was only too familiar with such schemes, as she had made her fortune in gas exports as an associate of Lazarenko. Now, however, she was shutting down the elaborate operations to siphon off Russian gas from pipelines on Ukrainian territory and hide the profits abroad. The duo also lifted tax exemptions that had been illegally granted to select oligarchs, in particular to oil exporters and electricity distributors. The incredibly generous terms on which the country's electricity system had been privatized were now revised, much to the chagrin of the previous main beneficiary, the Kyivan oligarch Hryhorii Surkis, the owner of Dynamo Kyiv soccer club and Kuchma's close ally.

While a crackdown on the worst excesses of crony capitalism was already bringing billions of dollars into the state coffers, Yushchenko also lowered income and profit taxes for Ukraine's developing middle class. Many small businesses that had been part of the shadow economy now came out in the open, because they could afford to pay lower taxes. The state treasury and national pension fund benefited by contributions from employers and employees, who in the past had come to mutual arrangements of using undeclared cash. Overall, it is estimated that during 2000 Yushchenko's reforms raised some US$4 billion, or 13 percent of the GDP.[26] As a result, his government caught up on pension and wage arrears, while managing to deliver a balanced budget. The fiscal cleanup combined with industrial revival and increased consumer spending to make 2000 the first year of economic growth since independence. After a freefall in the early 1990s and creeping decline later in the decade, in 2000 the GDP grew by an impressive 6 percent. Although the IMF temporarily suspended its loans because of electoral abuses during the 1999 presidential elections, Ukraine no longer needed them as badly as before. In the spring of 2001, another series of more transparent privatizations further boosted state revenues.

As a result of the relative success of their reforms, Yushchenko and Tymoshenko saw their popularity soar. After all, they were restoring social justice by squeezing the parasitical oligarchs and directing the money to senior citizens and workers. Their tax breaks benefited the middle class, too. But the oligarchs around Kuchma disliked the reformers intensely, and so did the president, both because of his entourage's financial losses and because Yushchenko was fast becoming the great hope of liberal democrats for the next presidential election. The president contemplated his removal as early as the spring of 2000, but in the end, it took him uncharacteristically long to get rid of his popular prime minister. The reason for the delay may be found in Kuchma's preoccupation during 2000 and 2001 with other political firestorms.

✸ Kuchma's Twilight and the Orange Dawn

As foreboding as 2000 was for Kuchma as a politician, the year actually began with what was widely seen as his important victory. In January, the authorities managed to cajole most centrist and right deputies into a pro-government majority in the Supreme Rada. Ironically, this group was originally led by the former president Leonid Kravchuk, who had returned to politics as a deputy and figurehead chairman of the Social Democratic Party (United), a puppet party of the Kyivan oligarch Surkis. Kravchuk was now doing dirty work for Kuchma, the very man who had defeated him in 1994. A parliamentary majority removed the pro-Communist speaker Tkachenko first by voting and, two weeks later, physically, as the left barricaded itself in the Rada building. For the moment, it seemed that the power struggle between the president and parliament—a hallmark of Ukrainian politics since 1991—would soon be over.

Yet, the unity imposed by bribes and arm-twisting did not last. When Kuchma went ahead with the referendum to reduce the Rada's size and power, which was planned before the parliamentary coup, the pro-government coalition quickly disintegrated. The referendum in April 2000 shocked the West with the scope of its ballot stuffing, giving Kuchma an improbable victory: All four proposals were approved by 82 percent to 90 percent of voters, with the turnout standing at 81 percent. The parliamentary reform was not implemented, however, because it had no chance of being approved by a constitutional majority (two thirds) of deputies. In general, by undermining the left and overplaying his hand with the centrists, Kuchma prepared the conditions for his regime's ultimate demise. He cleared the field for the emergence of a new, non-Communist opposition bloc, which would be best positioned to garner the protest vote.

The grand scandal that destroyed what remained of the legitimacy of Kuchma's rule began unfolding in the fall of 2000. In September, the opposition raised the alarm over the sudden disappearance of Georgii Gongadze, an Internet journalist who wrote about government abuses and oligarchs' scams. In early November, a farmer found Gongadze's headless body in the woods near Kyiv. The real scandal, however, detonated on November 28, when Moroz accused Kuchma of ordering the journalist's disappearance. During his speech in parliament, the Socialist leader revealed the existence of some 300 hours of recordings made secretly in Kuchma's office by Major Mykola Melnychenko, a security service officer responsible for sweeping it for electronic bugs. On the "Melnychenko tapes," Kuchma is heard on three separate occasions, asking his interior minister and security service chief to "take care" of Gongadze. The president even suggests a scenario for Gongadze's disappearance, with the Ukrainian security service deporting him to his native Georgia, from where he would be conveniently "kidnapped" by "Chechen guerrillas."[27]

Melnychenko, who was later granted asylum in the United States, claimed he acted alone when he made the recordings with a simple digital recorder hidden under a couch in Kuchma's office. Experts doubted these technical details, raising suspicions that the security officer was a pawn for a powerful politician or even a foreign government armed with more sophisticated equipment, but the authenticity of the voices was verified repeatedly. Some of the people heard on the tapes confirmed that these conversations had indeed taken place. Others, especially those whose recordings presented them in an unfavorable light, denied them. So did Kuchma until early 2001, when he acknowledged that the voice was his, but he claimed that the incriminating passages had been doctored. However, almost everything "Kuchma" says on the tapes presents him in a negative light. After the recordings were posted on the Internet, millions of Ukrainians discovered that Kuchma's private person was a foul-mouthed, cynical manipulator, as well as an anti-Semite and misogynist. Conversations confirmed the highest authorities' involvement in electoral fraud, manipulation of justice, fraudulent privatization, money laundering, and even illegal arms trade.

The Ukrainian public was shocked by the revelations, but with no strong opposition present, it took time for a protest movement to develop. Several demonstrations took place in Kyiv, but police took decisive action, and a harsh winter soon set in. Protest marches resumed in February 2001, with demonstrators organizing themselves into a movement known as "Ukraine without Kuchma." But the political breakthrough happened when the opposition acquired high-profile leaders. In January, the oligarchs, who were unhappy with Tymoshenko, engineered her dismissal from the government. As soon as she joined the protesters, she was arrested and imprisoned on charges of fraud and embezzlement (dating back to the mid-1990s), which were soon dismissed by the court. Back on the streets, Tymoshenko emerged as a passionate and charismatic leader with a strong populist bent. She established the National Salvation Forum and, by year's end, the Yulia Tymoshenko Bloc (BYuT), essentially a coalition of small parties and movements.

Yushchenko, meanwhile, remained prime minister until April 2001, when the front parties for oligarchs in the Supreme Rada joined together with the Communists to unseat him. A generous interpretation of the Communists' complicity is that they hated Yushchenko's capitalist reforms; the cynical explanation is that they envied his popularity and had been bribed to vote no confidence in the government. Whatever the case, Kuchma's advisors who were complicit in this affair should have realized that a disaffected Yushchenko in opposition would be much more threatening than a contented Yushchenko in the government, where he even signed a letter condemning the street protests.

Highly popular at the time of his dismissal, the moderate liberal Yushchenko emerged as an ideal candidate to unite the opposition. In preparation for the parliamentary elections scheduled for March 2002, he founded a broad center-right electoral bloc called "Our Ukraine." Although Rukh's successors and more extreme nationalists to the far right joined, Yushchenko de-emphasized the divisive issue of linguistic Ukrainization. Instead, his campaign focused on economic reform and clean government. In a pragmatic move, he signed up some disaffected oligarchs with their own small political groups and media outlets (notably, Petro Poroshenko and Yevhen Chervonenko), thereby securing the movement's financial base.

Feverish coalition building also took place in the Kuchma camp, where bribes and threats ensured the creation of the bloc "For a United Ukraine," although the Social Democrats (United) did not formally join. Incapable of establishing a popular pro-presidential party, Kuchma's command continued to rely on support from smaller parties financed by oligarchs. Such an arrangement was inherently unstable, because the oligarchs constantly competed against each other and had a weak sense of loyalty to politicians.[28] Without a united party structure, the president's team felt more comfortable ensuring the victory of its candidates who were standing for election in single-mandate districts.

On election night in March 2002, the vote for political parties and the vote for individual candidates brought very different results. Of the half of the seats filled by the proportional representation method, Our Ukraine won the largest number (70 top names from the party list), followed by the Communists (59), and For a United Ukraine (36). The BYuT, the Socialists, and the Social Democrats (United) won about 20 seats each. In single-mandate districts, though, where it was easier to apply administrative pressure and buy votes, For a United Ukraine led with 66 seats.[29] The pro-government coalition also persuaded 18 independent deputies to join its ranks. In the end, For a United Ukraine became the largest faction (119), followed by Our Ukraine (113), and the Communists (66). The opposition protested the "stolen" elections, and the West criticized the official manipulations, but the protests soon died down. The party of power secured the positions of speaker and his deputies, but the deeply divided Rada could barely function. A political impasse ensued until the 2004 presidential elections.

Meanwhile, the Kuchma regime was repositioning itself on the international scene. The disillusioned West had strongly condemned the electoral manipulations and the muzzling of the press in Ukraine, while a reinvigorated Russia under President Vladimir Putin sought to restore its influence in Kyiv. The administration of President George W. Bush was troubled by the revelation heard on the Melnychenko tapes that Kuchma had approved the illegal sale to Iraq of some US$100 million worth of weapons. The disclosure in the spring of 2003 that Ukraine had sold or agreed to sell to Saddam Hussein the high-tech Kolchuga radar systems, which can detect stealth bombers, caused fury in Washington. Of course, the West had started shunning Kuchma even earlier, ever since the Gongadze scandal. In 2002, when the pariah Ukrainian president showed up uninvited at a NATO summit in Prague, the organizers speedily changed the seating arrangement by listing country names in French rather than English, to prevent Ukraine's Kuchma from being seated next to Bush and the United Kingdom's Prime Minister Tony Blair. Kuchma could not salvage his reputation either by his official declaration in 2002 that Ukraine wanted to join NATO or by sending Ukrainian troops in 2003 to Iraq, where for some time they constituted the fourth largest contingent.

In semi-isolation from the West, the Kuchma regime found itself drawn back into the Russian sphere of influence. Led since 2000 by a dynamic and pragmatic, if authoritarian, President Vladimir Putin, Russia was increasingly using economic leverage against Ukraine. Because there was little political return on the years of delivering subsidized oil and gas to Ukraine, Russia's Gazprom began demanding payment in kind, primarily in ownership of oil refineries and other related businesses. Russian oligarchs marched in, too, and pressured the weakened Kuchma administration to approve the sale of other assets. Some nationalists on the right decried the invasion of Russian capital, but it actually helped sustain Ukraine's impressive economic growth. After the initial increase of 6 percent in 2000, the country's GDP until 2005 grew at a startling annual average of 9 percent.[30]

Economic ties to Russia, however, came with political strings attached. In 2003, Kuchma pushed through the Supreme Rada the Russian-initiated proposal to establish a "Common Economic Space" with Russia, Belarus, and Kazakhstan. Previous official pronouncements about Ukraine's Euro-Atlantic orientation gave way to the notion of the so-called multivector foreign policy, under which both Russia and the West would be seen as strategic partners. The Kuchma administration held discussions with Russia about greater economic cooperation, including in the military-industrial sector. But few projects were implemented before the country plunged into the electoral campaign leading up to the 2004 elections.

With Kuchma's second term ending late in 2004, during 2002 and 2003 his cronies had begun searching for ways to remain in power. The constitution dictated that the same person could not be president for more than two consecutive terms, but the constitution itself came into force in the middle of Kuchma's first term. In December 2003, the Constitutional Court, filled by Kuchma's appointees, ruled that he was actually completing his first term under the present constitution and, thus, could stand as a candidate in 2004. But by then, Kuchma's ratings were so low—consistently in the single digits and often less than 5 percent—that his victory could be ensured only by the most blatant fraud, which would completely antagonize the West and Ukrainian society. The authorities' further moves showed their desperation, especially several failed attempts in the spring of 2004 at an eleventh-hour constitutional reform, which would either have the president elected by parliament or would deprive the president of much of his or her powers in favor of parliament. Kuchma's camp, apparently assuming that Yushchenko would win and trying to curb his future authority, was clearly in disarray. No version of such a reform could pass the Supreme Rada, however, as they all would require a two thirds majority.

As the Kuchma administration ran out of options, it had to unite behind an official candidate. In so doing, it made an odd choice that would facilitate Yushchenko's job as a challenger—closing ranks behind Prime Minister Viktor Yanukovych (b. 1950). Yanukovych became head of the government in November 2002, when the previous cabinet of Anatolii Kinakh failed to secure consensus in the Rada on the budget. Yanukovych's candidacy was forced upon Kuchma by the increasingly powerful Donetsk clan, which Yanukovych had fronted politically since 1997 as the governor of Donetsk province. Kuchma's immediate entourage, linked closely to the rival Dnipropetrovsk and Kyiv economic clans, expressed little enthusiasm about this candidacy—and later would not hesitate before betraying Yanukovych. Buoyed by strong support from Donetsk and unlimited funds for bribing parliamentarians, Yanukovych lasted as prime minister for more than two years—longer than any other head of government under Kuchma. Yet, it was his background that made him a strange choice for an official candidate to stand against the cultured and charismatic Yushchenko.

Born and raised in the Russian-speaking Donbas, Yanukovych had a rough adolescence, including convictions for theft in 1967 and assault and battery in 1970. Both convictions were allegedly overturned in 1978, although few documents survive, and doubts persist as to whether legal procedures were followed at the time of his rehabilitation. Yanukovych soon rose through the ranks as a transportation manager, but he never received a proper higher education. He obtained his engineering degree by correspondence and, although as a prominent regional boss during the 1990s he bought himself a few degrees and titles, his writing skills remained shaky. When he registered as a candidate for presidency, he had to fill out some forms by hand, and his embarrassing mistakes created a sensation. Most infamously, he misspelled his title of professor as "proffesor." To top off his criminal convictions, lack of education, and poor literacy, Yanukovych was apparently shy in public. When he appeared on television, he stumbled in search of words, especially in Ukrainian, and generally projected a wooden public persona. All in all, his past was a treat for opposition cartoonists, who depicted him in a striped prison uniform, and his oratory was no match for that of the charming and sophisticated Yushchenko, a native speaker of Ukrainian. Yet the delicate balance of power within the ruling elites forced Kuchma to embrace Yanukovych as his chosen successor.

It was an unfortunate choice because of Yanukovych's personality and his lack of a perceptible program—some pro-Kuchma centrists would have fared better on these scores—but also because of the changes under way in Ukrainian society. The economic recovery had strengthened the Ukrainian middle class, mostly small business owners and professionals who believed in the free market and democracy and hated the oligarchs and the corrupt government. For them, Yanukovych symbolized the criminal elites who were determined to stay in power. Furthermore, unlike the previous elections, the official candidate was opposed not by a scary orthodox Communist but by a center-right reformer with a good economic record, who spoke only Ukrainian but carefully de-emphasized linguistic Ukrainization. Both the Ukrainian- and Russian-speaking middle class thus pinned their hopes on Yushchenko, as did supporters of democracy and reform among other social strata and Ukrainian speakers in western Ukraine.

Yushchenko, who had consistently led in the polls since the 2002 elections, also successfully built a broad political coalition. For a while, he kept his distance from the more radical Yulia Tymoshenko and various youth groups, but in the summer of 2004 he made a deal with Tymoshenko by promising her the position of prime minister. With BYuT on board, Yushchenko's electoral appeal broadened considerably. The well-organized radical youth movement Pora ("It's Time"), with its base in Western-supported NGOs and with veterans of the 2000 revolution in Serbia as its visiting mentors, also joined the coalition and would prove invaluable during the street protests. But above all, Yushchenko kept polishing his public image as an honest family man, a practicing Christian, and a committed reformer. Because of the influx of money both from friendly oligarchs and from the West, the opposition ran a sleek propaganda campaign with well-designed posters, extensive use of the Internet, and highly professional television ads. Yushchenko's people also came up with orange as the principal color of their banners and scarves. Although this color held no special symbolism for Ukrainians, it projected optimism, like the brand slogan "Tak!" ("Yes!"). At the time, nobody thought of Yushchenko's presumed victory as an Orange revolution. By analogy with the 2003 "Rose Revolution" in Georgia, the future victory in the Ukrainian elections was to be branded "Chestnut Revolution," for chestnut is Kyiv's trademark tree. But the final victory would come later than expected, in the winter, after the trees had shed both leaves and chestnuts.

The authorities were not thinking about naming their future victory. During the spring and summer of 2004, the Kuchma-Yanukovych camp was growing increasingly desperate. In the summer, Kuchma conducted a fire sale of some large enterprises to his supporters, including the privatization of Kryvorizhstal, the country's largest steel mill, by his son-in-law, Pinchuk, and Akhmetov for US$800 million, or about 20 percent of what it was thought to be worth. Yanukovych was trailing Yushchenko in the polls, but the government hesitated to use its last, most effective weapon—but one that was harmful for the economy—a large increase in pensions and welfare payments. Belatedly, official Kyiv again invited political strategists from Russia, who first complained about the unredeemable candidacy of Yanukovych but then suggested the old scheme. Yanukovych was to stand on the platform of close collaboration with Russia and making Russian the second official language, while Yushchenko was to be presented as a nationalist and American puppet. This, indeed, was the tenor of Yanukovych's propaganda late in the campaign, with one memorable poster combining the faces of Bush and Yushchenko into "Bushchenko." But the potentially most divisive image, that of Yushchenko as an extreme Ukrainian nationalist, did not stick, for there was little to support it.

In late September, Yanukovych played his last card by promising to allow dual citizenship with Russia, make Russian the second state language, and double state pensions. The first two promises resonated well in the east, and the third one, among the older population. As a result, the prime minister temporarily surged in the polls ahead of Yushchenko, gaining the preference of more than 40 percent of voters. Putin, whose own popularity in Ukraine then stood at an impressive 66 percent—he was perceived as a strong leader reining in the oligarchs—also visited Ukraine repeatedly, making no secret of his support for the pro-Russian Yanukovych. (Russia made a major investment in Yanukovuch's campaign, an estimated US$300 million, most of which went to bribes, vote buying, and administrative expenses for the campaign, which had few sincere volunteers.) This momentum did not last, however, as the mysterious poisoning of Yushchenko overshadowed everything and lent credibility to rumors of his opponents' criminal methods.

Late in the evening on September 5, Yushchenko and a businessman close to him drove to a villa outside Kyiv for a secret meeting with the head of Kuchma's security service and his deputy. The exact aim of the meeting remains unclear, but apparently Yushchenko was establishing contacts with the security apparatus to prevent a violent showdown during the elections. In any case, the negotiating parties ate and drank together, and on his way home, Yushchenko became violently ill. Ukrainian doctors diagnosed food poisoning, but as Yushchenko's stomach pains worsened and his internal organs swelled, an oligarch supporter had him airlifted to a private clinic in Austria. Specialists there stabilized his condition in a week and treated him again for ten days in October, but Yushchenko returned to Ukraine with his face and body scarred by lesions. He announced publicly that he had been poisoned.

The pro-government camp disgraced itself by the way they reacted to the failed assassination attempt. A fabricated fax was sent to Reuters, allegedly from the Austrian clinic, denying the possibility of poisoning. The official media in Ukraine picked up this report and suggested that Yushchenko's condition was the result of a failed Botox injection or rejuvenating inoculation of fetal stem cells (a popular procedure among the Ukrainian nouveau riche). In December, however, after the first two rounds of the presidential elections, further tests in Austria and Germany confirmed poisoning with massive amounts of dioxin, a chemical used in Agent Orange. But even before the elections, when Yushchenko appeared in the Supreme Rada, the sight of his badly pockmarked face was enough to force some political opponents to apologize for their previous suggestions that he should switch from sushi (the dish served at the fateful dinner with the security bosses) to healthy Ukrainian food. Yushchenko's poisoning became a major campaign issue in Ukraine and was featured extensively by the Western media.

✖ The Orange Revolution and After

Twenty-four candidates were on the ballot during the first round of the presidential elections on October 31, 2004, but the overwhelming majority of votes went to two of them, Yushchenko (39.9 percent) and Yanukovych (39.3 percent). At least these were the official results; it was revealed after the revolution that the Yanukovych team had access to the Central Electoral Commission's electronic database and was "correcting" the data arriving by e-mail from the electoral districts—this, in addition to the usual ballot stuffing and voter intimidation.[31] Once a serious force at the ballot box, the Communist leader Symonenko garnered only 5 percent of votes, with most of his electorate apparently moving to Yanukovych as Yushchenko's only serious opponent.

In advance of the second round of elections on November 21, middlemen for the government began approaching independent pollsters with lucrative financial offers to secure desirable exit polls. Such attempts signaled preparations for a massive fraud, on a scale much larger than during the first round. Not all pollsters agreed; in fact, some were supported by Western foundations. A major gap emerged, therefore, between reliable exit polls that gave Yushchenko a lead with 53 percent to Yanukovych's 44 percent and the first official results announced on the election night: 49.5 percent for Yanukovych against 46.9 percent for Yushchenko, with 65 percent of the votes counted.

The Yanukovych team arrived at these numbers by making changes in the Central Electoral Commission's database, a hoax that was immediately obvious, because the Yushchenko camp had the (illegally obtained) evidence: recordings of phone calls made and received by the Yanukovych team, which revealed massive fraud. In addition, foreign and Ukrainian observers filed numerous reports of manipulations in the electoral districts.

The protests began immediately. The Yushchenko side had anticipated the fraud and made preparations for a mass rally in the center of Kyiv. Several opposition rallies earlier in the year could be seen as trial runs attracting tens of thousands of protesters. Even before the polls closed, a stage was quickly built on Independence Square (known popularly by the Ukrainian word for square: Maidan), and large plasma television screens installed. On the morning of November 22, after the Kuchma-appointed Central Electoral Commission hurried to preannounce Yanukovych as the winner, more than 200,000 Kyivans gathered on the Maidan to protest. Participants from elsewhere in western and central Ukraine arrived on buses and trains, swelling the numbers even further; many of them stayed in the city, lodging free with countless local supporters or in public buildings. Yushchenko's followers also set up a city of 1,500 tents on Khreshchatyk Boulevard, which crosses Independence Square. Protest rallies, sit-ins, and strikes soon spread to other cities, especially west of Kyiv.

The Orange side was buoyed by the international response to the fraud. The United States and the EU issued strong statements and refused to recognize the official results. Putin was the first to congratulate Yanukovych on his victory, but only a few post-Soviet states followed suit. With scores of foreign journalists on the ground, orange-clad crowds on the Maidan became a familiar sight for television viewers throughout the world, while most of the Ukrainian media still toed the official line. But the continuing mass protests and Western pressure made Kuchma lose his nerve. Every night, an estimated 500,000 protesters showed up on the Maidan to listen to Tymoshenko's fiery speeches and concerts of pro-Yushchenko music stars. In the intervals between his regular appearances on the square, Yushchenko found time to take a symbolic presidential oath in a half-empty parliament and to put out feelers to Kuchma. The Pora youth organization put additional pressure on the outgoing president by starting a blockade of government buildings, forcing Kuchma to stay at his country villa. Furthermore, the Supreme Court promptly agreed to review the opposition's appeal, thus delaying the certification of Yanukovych's win.

Amid the first signs of disunity among the authorities and the media, international mediators arrived in Kyiv on November 26: President Aleksander Kwaśniewski of Poland, President Valdas Adamkus of Lithuania, EU foreign policy chief Javier Solana, and speaker of the Russian parliament Boris Gryzlov. They helped bring together Kuchma, Yanukovych, and Yushchenko for several negotiating sessions. There was no immediate result other than the commitment to wait for the Supreme Court's decision, but Kuchma showed his weakness by offering compromise solutions. His main proposal was to agree on a "package" including an election rerun, constitutional reform that would transfer much of president's power to parliament, and immunity from prosecution for him and his family. Although no deal was made at this time, the negotiations probably prevented the use of military force against the protesters (which Putin and Yanukovych had allegedly suggested) or a violent clash between the Orange side and Yanukovych's miners, who were bused in for a counterdemonstration in the capital.

Pro-Yanukovych rallies took place in many eastern cities, especially in his home base of Donetsk, but there was little popular momentum there, most of the organizational work being done by the local authorities. As Kuchma was apparently leaning toward a self-interested deal and the Supreme Rada on November 27 passed the resolution condemning the fraudulent elections, the Yanukovych camp brought out its ultimate weapon—the threat of separatism. In the last days of November, a conference of eastern Ukrainian governors demanded a referendum on the federalization of Ukraine. The Donetsk authorities, in fact, had scheduled a local referendum on the province's autonomous status for January, but it was soon called off. The Western media began discussing the possibility of civil war in Ukraine, but there was never any serious popular support for separation. In addition, Kuchma now openly abandoned Yanukovych by briefly toying with the idea of totally new elections in which neither of the two main candidates would be allowed to stand.

In any case, the Supreme Court's surprising decision on December 3 broke the political deadlock. In a display of independence atypical of Ukrainian courts, it declared the results of the runoff election invalid and decreed a repeat runoff between Yanukovych and Yushchenko to be held on December 26. This legal victory for the opposition facilitated the compromise. On December 8, 402 (out of 450) deputies to the Supreme Rada voted for the "package" agreed on by the opposing sides.[32] It included constitutional reform (to be enacted in 2006) giving more power to parliament, a new election law making the repeat rerun possible, and the dismissal of the Central Electoral Commission's head. Then, a mass defection of politicians and oligarchs from the Yanukovych camp started.

The second runoff on December 26 became one of the most monitored elections in history, with some 300,000 Ukrainian and 12,000 foreign observers present. The final results closely approximated exit polls: 51.99 percent votes for Yushchenko and 44.19 percent for Yanukovych. The regional voting patterns held in the fair election, with Yanukovych carrying the Russian-speaking east and south, and Yushchenko the Ukrainian-speaking west. What distinguished the 2004 elections from similar regional divisions in 1991, 1994, and 1998, however, was Yushchenko's triumph in central Ukraine, a Ukrainian-speaking region not connected to the nationalist stronghold of western Ukraine by religion or historical tradition. Scholars have argued that the peasants of central Ukraine, who overwhelmingly voted for Yushchenko, for the first time in history imagined themselves as members of a Ukrainian political nation. Their sense of ethnic identity was important, but it helped mobilize them in defense of an open society rather than nationalism as such.[33]

Yanukovych tried to challenge the results in both the Central Electoral Commission and the Supreme Court, but lost in both cases. On January 10, 2005, the Central Electoral Commission officially certified Yushchenko as the winner. He was sworn in as Ukraine's third president on January 23, 2005. The Orange Revolution was over, but its victors now faced the challenge of reforming their country.

During his first year in office, Yushchenko spent much of his time on foreign trips in an effort to consolidate the pro-Western turn in Ukraine's foreign policy. With so much bad blood between the Orange side and the Russian government, Yushchenko initially promised to break the tradition that had Ukrainian leaders making their maiden official foreign visit to Russia. He reversed himself at the last moment, however, and showed up in Moscow on the day after the inauguration, but this did not radically improve the tense political and economic relations between the two countries. Rather, Yushchenko's triumphant visits to the European Parliament in February and Washington in April set the tone for his presidency. As if having a pro-Western minister of foreign affairs (Borys Tarasiuk) were not enough, a new ministerial position was created with a "European integration" portfolio. Both Yushchenko and his Western supporters saw the phenomenon of the Orange Revolution as exportable. During his meeting with Bush, the Ukrainian president spoke boldly of his intention to help the United States advance freedom in neighboring Belarus and faraway Cuba. Since then, the Cedar Revolution in Lebanon and the Tulip Revolution in Kyrgyzstan (both in 2005), as well as the opposition's unsuccessful protests in Belarus in 2006, have been described as being modeled on the Orange Revolution.

The Russian opposition has continued talking about the chances of a similar upheaval in Russia. The Ukrainian authorities attempted to develop GUAM (Georgia, Ukraine, Azerbaijan, and Moldova)—a loose organization of four post-Soviet states trying to break free of Russia's influence in the region—into a closer political union. In August 2005, to Putin's great annoyance, Yushchenko and Georgian president Mikhail Saakashvili initiated the creation of the Community of Democratic Choice, an organization of democratic countries along Russia's borders.

In internal policy, Yushchenko initially deferred to Yulia Tymoshenko, who was approved by the Supreme Rada as his first prime minister. Her cabinet was a coalition of Our Ukraine, BYuT, Socialists, and other minor groups, but "Yulia" (as she is popularly known) was clearly the most dynamic force for change. With only a few (reformed) dignitaries from Kuchma's era in the higher echelons of the Orange administration, it appeared that the new authorities finally accomplished what the 1991 revolution failed to do: create a new political elite. By the summer, 18,000 middle- and lower-level civil servants were fired from their jobs and replaced by new employees. Tymoshenko's economic measures also added to the sense of a clear break with the past, although Western observers worried about their populist bent. The prime minister announced a program of "reprivatization," meaning nationalization of enterprises privatized under Kuchma and their sale to new owners. After a nervous reaction from Western investors, the authorities clarified that they had in mind only thirty or so of the most blatant cases involving the largest enterprises, but even this plan met with great resistance from business interests at home and uneasiness abroad. Reprivatization actually took place in only a few high-profile cases, in which the losers were the oligarchs associated with the old regime. Most sensational by far was the cancellation of the 2004 sale of Kryvorizhstal steel mill to Pinchuk and Akhmetov and its resale at auction in October 2005 for US$4.8 billion, or six times the original amount, to Mittal Steel, one of the world's largest steel producers. Tymoshenko also increased public sector wages and welfare payments while cutting several taxes on businesses. These measures only built up inflationary pressures, however. The prime minister also attempted to establish state control over fuel and meat prices, only to be overruled by the president.

The slowing tempo of economic growth and rising inflation were already noticeable by the spring of 2005. The new government claimed that Yanukovych's impressive numbers had been inflated by the wide proliferation of illegal tax-return schemes, in which manufacturers claimed to have produced and exported merchandise worth millions in order to collect a significant value-added tax refund on products leaving the country. Yet there were other perceptible signs of deceleration. The middle class, which had kept much of its savings in U.S. dollars, also suffered when the government upped the *hryvnia*'s exchange rate from 5.2 to 5.05 for one U.S. dollar to maintain the appearance of lower fuel prices, which were actually increasing.

Much of Tymoshenko's energy, in the meantime, was consumed by a bitter conflict with Petro Poroshenko, an oligarch close to Yushchenko and a competitor for the prime minister's position. Appointed instead as secretary of the Council of National Security and Defense, Poroshenko tried to build this body, with its vaguely defined prerogatives, into a powerful overseer of several related ministries. He also continued to have considerable personal influence over the president. Yushchenko, in turn, proved incapable of managing internal conflicts within his coalition. Indeed, his weak leadership was becoming increasingly obvious to the general public. The president was abroad too often, preferred long-winded speeches on general topics to concrete political decisions, and in general seemed aloof and distant from citizens' everyday concerns. Even more damaging, the new bureaucrats were often as cynical and corrupt as their predecessors. This was true of many low-level appointees of the new regime, but scandals were soon erupting at the highest level as well. The American-born Justice Minister Roman Zvarych voted against the law banning reexport of Russian oil to Europe. Then, it turned out that his wife was involved in just such a transit. Moreover, Zvarych's claims that he had a doctorate from Columbia University and professor's title were proven to be false. Yushchenko stepped in by defending Zvarych as a veteran of the Maidan but, in so doing, only damaged his own reputation. The minister was later quietly dismissed, but returned to the cabinet in 2006.

In the summer of 2005, Ukrainian newspapers broke the story about the luxurious lifestyle of Yushchenko's son from his first marriage. A second-year university student, the young man lived in an exorbitantly expensive apartment, drove a car valued at US$150,000 (which he parked anywhere he liked), and used a platinum-plated cell phone allegedly worth up to US$50,000.[34] The official explanation was that Yushchenko junior was given free use of all these items by his wealthy friends, but the press cried foul. The president lost his temper at a press conference and called one journalist an "ugly mug" and a "hired killer." The public concluded that corruption had spread into Yushchenko's closest circle and that the president did not have much respect for the freedom of the press.

The cultural policies of Yushchenko's administration also proved controversial. The president talked frequently about his desire to unite the competing Ukrainian churches—three Orthodox churches and the Greek Catholic Church—into a single Ukrainian patriarchate, but such statements sounded strange in the age of religious freedom and were viewed with suspicion even by church hierarchs. Non-Christians and atheists were taken aback by Yushchenko's initiative to introduce in schools a new discipline of "Christian Ethics." Although the new government did not overly promote Ukrainization of cultural life, it created a stir by harassing some artists and theaters, especially those performing in Russian, who had supported Yanukovych in 2004. In particular, the use of tax police and other administrative methods against the head of Kyiv's venerable Russian Drama Company led many to fear a sad throwback to the past. Some in the government apparently supported an aborted attempt by a friendly oligarch to wrestle the popular Dynamo Kyiv soccer club from Kuchma's old ally, Surkis. The authorities also gradually limited the availability of Russian TV channels in Ukraine (and mandated Ukrainian subtitles on Russian-language programs), although there was little they could do about mass culture. Russian pulp fiction and pop music remain the favorites of Ukrainian citizens, more than half of whom still prefer Russian for daily use.

In the fall of 2005, the simmering conflict between Tymoshenko and Poroshenko exploded into open and mutual accusations of corruption. Following the resignations of Poroshenko and some of Tymoshenko's supporters, the president fired Prime Minister Tymoshenko, which led to the automatic dismissal of the entire cabinet. Yushchenko accused Tymoshenko of engineering political conflicts and causing an economic slowdown. She retaliated by accusing him of betraying the ideals of the Orange Revolution. With the parliamentary elections scheduled for March 2006, Tymoshenko began positioning her bloc as an alternative to the party of power. The new government, headed by Prime Minister Yurii Yekhanurov, a caretaker administrator with little political capital, halted reprivatization and made overtures to oligarchs of all stripes.

Yushchenko approached the first anniversary of his inauguration with disappointing results. He squandered the year in which he still had wide-ranging powers as president before the implementation of the constitutional reform. He mismanaged his coalition and did not provide strong leadership in internal affairs. He brought his party to the elections in bad shape, while creating a powerful opposition with his acrimonious dismissal of Tymoshenko. Not to be forgotten was his split with Russia, although it was mainly the result of Putin's political choices during the Orange Revolution.

One major consequence of the rift with Russia was the gas crisis during the early months of 2006. Before the elections, the Kuchma administration had hinted that Putin's Russia would stop subsidizing energy deliveries to Ukraine if a pro-Western candidate came to power there. Russia's Gazprom, indeed, served notice in March 2005 that the price of gas for Ukraine would rise from $50 per 1,000 cubic meters to $160. In the course of difficult negotiations, Russia later upped the price to $230, which was in line with what it already charged other European countries. The Ukrainian government procrastinated, hoping for a last-minute concession. In fact, Ukraine had some aces up its sleeve, as Russia transported gas to Europe through Ukrainian territory, with Ukraine taking 15 percent of the gas passing through its pipes as transit fees. But because of its inefficient economy, Ukraine was a gas-guzzler, consuming 80 billion cubic meters per year, of which some 25 billion were Russian (bartered and purchased) and another 36 billion from Turkmenistan (but were delivered via Russia).

The two sides had not reached any agreement by the end of the year, and on January 1, 2006, Gazprom cut gas exports to Ukraine. Ukraine immediately began withholding Russian gas in transit to Europe, thus causing momentary panic in countries like Italy and Germany. The supply of gas was restored in three days, following the intervention of the United States and the EU. Ukraine agreed to pay $95 per 1,000 cubic meters, but its transit fees also increased.[35] Still, Russian political and economic circles suggested that the price of gas for Ukraine would continue to rise. The increase was bound to have a negative impact on the Ukrainian economy, especially on the chemical and steel industries. Many observers saw these moves as punishing Yushchenko for his pro-Western orientation and, perhaps, calculated to promote pro-Russian political forces in Ukraine's March 2006 parliamentary elections.

With his personal popularity sliding, Yushchenko could not do much to boost Our Ukraine, now registered as a political party, which was still the core of a larger eponymous political bloc. As president, he could not be at the top of the party list for election to the Supreme Rada, the spot occupied instead by his prime minister, Yurii Yekhanurov, a competent if colorless functionary. Yushchenko called himself an honorary chairman of Our Ukraine, but many experts considered this unconstitutional. Our Ukraine faced attacks from all sides, with Yanukovych's Party of Regions running on the traditional platform of closer ties with Russia and official status for the Russian language, the BYuT denouncing the government as corrupt traitors of the revolution, and the weakened left condemning the builders of capitalism as Western puppets.

The March 2006 parliamentary elections were the first to be held according to the full proportional representation system, without single-mandate districts. (This change was part of the compromise package passed in the heady days of the revolution.) Only five parties of the forty-five passed the required 3 percent threshold: Party of Regions (32 percent of votes, 186 seats), BYuT (22.29 percent, 129 seats), Our Ukraine Bloc (13.95 percent, 81 seats), Socialists (5.69 percent, 33 seats), and Communists (3.66 percent, 21 seats).[36] The Yushchenko administration suffered the double humiliation of garnering fewer votes than Yanukovych and fewer than Tymoshenko. But the three-way split also contained a promise of a majority coalition in the Supreme Rada. Difficult negotiations went on for months after the elections, though, with no resolution in sight. Restoring the old Orange coalition was an obvious choice, but Yushchenko and his entourage dreaded the prospect of working with Tymoshenko, whose condition for entry into an alliance was the post of prime minister for her. Our Ukraine also did not want to see the Socialist leader Oleksandr Moroz in the speaker's chair because Petro Poroshenko, an influential businessman and Yushchenko's close friend, wanted this position for himself. Meanwhile, BYuT and Our Ukraine could only achieve a majority in the Supreme Rada with the Socialists' support.

In contrast, working with Yanukovych—a mind-boggling proposal only a year earlier—was now a conceivable prospect for Yushchenko, who already had the experience of seeking and receiving Yanukovych's support for the confirmation of Yekhanurov's cabinet. Finally, in early August 2006, the Party of Regions, Socialists, and Communists formed a coalition, which Our Ukraine reluctantly and, at first, informally joined. (The president's party sent its ministers to the cabinet but claimed that the conditions of its entry into the parliamentary coalition were yet to be negotiated.) A visibly embarrassed Yushchenko introduced his old nemesis Yanukovych to the Supreme Rada as the new prime minister. Looking more confident than ever and speaking very good Ukrainian, Yanukovych even made a point of referring positively to the "ideals of Maidan," thus stripping the president of the mantle of the revolution's winner. But the coalition government, built on an uneasy rapprochement between the Party of Regions and Our Ukraine, was anything but stable, and the Bloc of Yulia Tymoshenko was likely to become a formidable opposition.

Splits within the Orange camp returned Ukrainian politics to the age of unstable coalitions and powerful business clans. This setback may be temporary, but the larger political picture—the exact distribution of power between the president and the prime minister after the constitutional reform is fully implemented—is uncertain. Regardless of the division of power between Yushchenko and Yanukovych and the shape of the governing coalition, disappointment with Orange revolutionaries has set in among Ukrainians. The population is not looking back to Kuchma's times, however, but would like to see the leaders of the Orange Revolution follow up on the promises they made to the crowds on Maidan—to build functioning democracy, corruption-free civil service, and an economy competitive in the global world of the twenty-first century.

❖❖

Ukraine gained independence as a result of the Soviet Union's collapse, rather than from a Ukrainian revolution. The new state therefore inherited the old Soviet elites and institutions, resulting in thirteen years of procrastination over reforms and the development of crony capitalism. On the international scene, Ukraine chose an independent course early on, having discovered the advantages of its strategic position between Russia and the expanding European Union. At home, however, inconsistent economic reforms and the power of oligarchs delayed economic recovery until the late 1990s. The developing civil society made possible the popular rebellion against electoral fraud in 2004. After the Orange Revolution, a more democratic Ukraine came into being, and while political and economic problems persist, Ukrainian citizens are now free to determine their country's direction.

Epilogue

Orange-clad protesters on Kyiv's Independence Square were not Ukrainian nationalists. The hundreds of thousands gathering there every evening in November and December 2004 left their homes because they could no longer stand the corruption, infringements on democracy, and grand theft in the economy. Rich and poor, Ukrainian patriots and Russian speakers, school dropouts and professors took to the streets to defend the promise of a new Ukraine. They were not demanding more rights for ethnic Ukrainians. Although the Orange side used the Ukrainian language and culture as a mobilizing tool, the ideal Ukraine they wanted was a civic and multinational state, a modern and prosperous country with a functioning democracy and transparency in economic policy.[1] This paradox of the Orange Revolution—supporters of democracy adopting the language of moderate nationalists in order to create a civic state—reflected a major trend in Ukrainian history. The present-day multinational Ukrainian state owes its existence to the nationalist project of providing ethnic Ukrainians with their national homeland, yet it was neither built by nationalists nor constructed according to their design.

Ukraine has a rich multicultural past and traces its history of state building to mighty medieval Kyivan Rus and the legendary early modern Cossack state. Yet, the modern Ukrainian state in existence between 1917 and 1920, as well as after 1991, is the direct result of imperial collapse and nationalist mobilization. The Russian, Austro-Hungarian, and Soviet empires folded because of other reasons, but their collapse made possible the creation of independent Ukraine. Both in 1917 and 1991, the founders of a Ukrainian state based their actions on the general principle of national self-determination—an ethnic nation's entitlement to its independent state—yet in both cases they were actually building a civic and multinational polity. Ethnic nationalism made brief appearances at the moments of separation from empires, but Ukrainian states born with its assistance never identified with it. Present-day Ukraine also was not built by nationalists, and it no longer has to prove its right to exist based on ethnic Ukrainians' entitlement to their state. It can therefore focus on fulfilling the promise of the Orange Revolution.

Another theme highlighted by the events of 2004, the split between the Ukrainian-speaking west and the Russian-speaking east within Ukraine, also has roots in Ukrainian history, in the difference between the nationalities policies of the Russian and Austro-Hungarian empires, as well as between the Soviet Union and interwar eastern European states. This divide highlights the role, both positive and negative, that imperial policies play in nation building. Yet, the cultural differences between eastern and western Ukraine become politically important only when the state enforces cultural uniformity, which is not likely to happen. Although political commentators like to emphasize the linguistic divide and some politicians like to exploit it, all Ukrainian citizens are slowly developing a common identity as members of a Ukrainian civic or political nation. Even if they speak different languages, they increasingly agree, for example, on rejecting hard-line Communists and accepting Ukrainian independence.[2] There is much more material to build on in the construction of a Ukrainian political nation.

But such work can be accomplished only by a government with a popular mandate and clear reform agenda. The first year after the Orange Revolution saw, instead, political infighting among the ruling coalition and slowing economic growth. It now looks possible that the great hero of the Orange Revolution, Viktor Yushchenko, will be a one-term president and will go down in history as a failed statesman. But even if this happens, his defeat at the ballot box will still be a victory for the 2004 revolution, which taught Ukrainian citizens that their votes matter.

✖✖ Notes

Introduction

1. See Geoff Eley and Ronald Grigor Suny, "Introduction: From the Moment of Social History to the Work of Cultural Representation," in Eley and Suny, eds., *Becoming National: A Reader* (New York: Oxford University Press, 1996), pp. 3–37.

2. Miroslav Hroch, *Social Preconditions of National Revival in Europe: A Comparative Analysis of the Social Composition of Patriotic Groups among the Smaller European Nations*, trans. Ben Fowkes (Cambridge: Cambridge University Press, 1985).

3. See Serhy Yekelchyk, *Probudzhennia natsii: Do kontseptsii istorii ukrainskoho natsionalnoho rukhu druhoi polovyny XIX st.* (Melbourne: Slavic Section, Monash University, 1994), pp. 36–50.

4. Roman Szporluk, "Ukraine: From an Imperial Periphery to a Sovereign State," in his *Russia, Ukraine, and the Breakup of the Soviet Union* (Stanford, Calif.: Hoover Institution Press, 2000), pp. 361–394.

5. Terry Martin, *The Affirmative Action Empire: Nations and Nationalism in the Soviet Union, 1923–1939* (Ithaca, N.Y.: Cornell University Press, 2001), p. 15.

6. For a helpful introduction, see Zenon E. Kohut, "The Development of a Ukrainian National Historiography in Imperial Russia," in Thomas Sanders, ed., *Historiography of Imperial Russia: The Profession and Writing of History in a Multinational State* (Armonk, N.Y.: M. E. Sharpe, 1999), pp. 453–477. On Hrushevsky, see the following recent works: Frank E. Sysyn, "Introduction to the *History of Ukraine-Rus'*," in Mykhailo Hrushevsky, *History of Ukraine-Rus'* (Edmonton: Canadian Institute of Ukrainian Studies Press, 1997), vol. 1, pp. xxi–xlii; and Serhii Plokhy, *Unmaking Imperial Russia: Mykhailo Hrushevsky and the Writing of Ukrainian History* (Toronto: University of Toronto Press, 2005).

7. See Stephen Velychenko, *Shaping Identity in Eastern Europe and Russia: Soviet-Russian and Polish Accounts of Ukrainian History, 1914–1991* (New York: St. Martin's, 1993); and Serhy Yekelchyk, *Stalin's Empire of Memory: Russian-Ukrainian Relations in the Soviet Historical Imagination* (Toronto: University of Toronto Press, 2004).

8. *Istoriia Ukrainskoi RSR* (Kyiv: Naukova dumka, 1977–1979), 8 vols. [in 10 books].

9. The series includes fourteen books, six of them covering the period 1800–2000: V. H. Sarbei, *Natsionalne vidrodzhennia Ukrainy* (Kyiv: Alternatyvy, 1999); O. S. Rublov and O. P. Reient, *Ukrainski vyzvolni zmahannia 1917–1921 rr.* (Kyiv: Alternatyvy, 1999); S. V. Kulchytsky, *Ukraina mizh dvoma viinamy (1921–1939 rr.)* (Kyiv: Alternatyvy, 1999); M. V. Koval, *Ukraina v Druhii Svitovii*

i Velykii Vitchyznianii viinakh (1939–1945 rr.) (Kyiv; Alternatyvy, 1999); V. K. Baran and V. M. Danylenko, *Ukraina v umovakh systemnoi kryzy (1946–1980–i rr.)* (Kyiv: Alternatyvy, 1999); and V. M. Lytvyn, *Ukraina na mezhi tysiacholit (1991–2000 rr.)* (Kyiv: Alternatyvy, 2000).

10. Yaroslav Hrytsak, *Narys istorii Ukrainy: Formuvannia modernoi ukrainskoi natsii: XIX–XX stolittia* (Kyiv: Heneza, 1996).

11. The following Ukrainian editions of their works have been particularly influential: Ivan Lysiak Rudnytsky, *Istorychni ese* (Kyiv: Osnovy, 1994), 2 vols.; and Roman Shporliuk, *Imperiia ta natsii* (Kyiv: Dukh i litera, 2001).

12. Mark von Hagen, "Does Ukraine Have a History?" *Slavic Review* 54 (Fall 1995): 658–673.

Chapter 1

1. Western readers will find a good introduction to these theories in Andrew Wilson, *The Ukrainians: Unexpected Nation* (New Haven, Conn.: Yale University Press, 2000; 2002), chapter 2, although the author does not emphasize the fact that very few professional historians in Ukraine ever embraced these speculations.

2. After Ukraine became independent in 1991, a minor boom of publications on the Trypillian culture followed, crowned by the recent appearance of a two-volume encyclopedia of Trypillian civilization: L. M. Novokhatko, ed., *Entsyklopediia Trypilskoi tsyvilizatsii* (Kyiv: Ukrpolihrafmediia, 2004), 2 vols.

3. Herodotus's visit to Scythia is being seriously questioned today. See Andrzej Poppe, "Introduction to Volume 1," in Mykhailo Hrushevsky, *History of Ukraine-Rus'* (Edmonton: Canadian Institute of Ukrainian Studies Press, 1997), vol. 1, p. liii.

4. K. P. Buniatian, V. Yu. Murzin, and O. V. Symonenko, *Na svitanku istorii* (Kyiv: Alternatyvy, 1998), pp. 117 and 163.

5. One recent example is in P. P. Tolochko, ed., *Etnichna istoriia davnoi Ukrainy* (Kyiv: Instytut arkheolohii NANU, 2000), p. 4, where Scythian plowers are called "proto-Slavs."

6. The last great discoveries of Scythian artwork were made in the late 1960s and early 1970s by the Ukrainian archaeologist Borys Mozolevsky, who analyzed his findings in his books *Tovsta mohyla* (Kyiv: Naukova dumka, 1979) and *Skifskyi step* (Kyiv: Naukova dumka, 1983). Only the treasures uncovered since World War II are kept in Ukrainian museums; most previous finds of Scythian gold were sent to the Hermitage Museum in St. Petersburg. Of several albums of Scythian art available to the Western reader, the best are *From the Land of the Scythians: Ancient Treasures from the Museums of the USSR: 3000 B.C.–100 B.C.* (New York: Metropolitan Museum of Art, 1975) and Ellen D. Reeder, ed., *Scythian Gold: Treasures from Ancient Ukraine* (New York: Harry N. Abrams, 1999).

7. The Bosporian Kingdom is featured prominently in recent Ukrainian historical works. See S. D. Kryzhytskyi, V. M. Zubar, and A. S. Rusiaieva, *Antychni*

derzhavy Pivnichnoho Prychornomoria (Kyiv: Alternatyvy, 1998), pp. 247–343; and A. S. Rusiaeva [Rusiaieva] and V. M. Zubar, *Bospor Kimmeriiskii: istoriia i kultura* (Nikolaev: Vozmozhnosti Kimmerii, 1998).

8. See Ivan Bilyk, *Mech Areia* (Kyiv: Veselka, 2003; originally published in 1972). Soviet ideologists saw this historical fantasy as a manifestation of Ukrainian nationalism and banned the novel.

9. P. P. Tolochko, *Kochevye narody stepei i Kievskaia Rus* (St. Petersburg: Aleteiia, 2003), pp. 36–43.

10. Tolochko, *Etnichna istoriia*, p. 119.

11. P. P. Tolochko, ed., *Davnia istoriia Ukrainy* (Kyiv: Instytut arkheolohii NANU, 2000), vol. 3, pp. 17 (historians), 72 (archaeological finds).

12. V. A. Smolii, ed., *Istoriia Ukrainy*, 3rd ed. (Kyiv: Alternatyvy, 2002), pp. 28–30; O. P. Tolochko and P. P. Tolochko, *Kyivska Rus* (Kyiv: Alternatyvy, 1998), pp. 51–57.

13. Aleksei Karpov, *Vladimir Sviatoi* (Moscow: Molodaia gvardiia, 1997), pp. 142–173; Petro Tolochko, *Volodymyr Sviatyi, Yaroslav Mudryi* (Kyiv: ArtEk, 1996), pp. 88–89.

14. Petro Tolochko, *Yaroslav Mudryi* (Kyiv: Alternatyvy, 2002), pp. 170–178.

15. Unlike her husband, the French king, Anna was literate. The Slavic Gospel that she brought with her from Kyiv can still be seen in the treasury of the Reims Cathedral. In the 1970s, Anna's life was the subject of a popular Soviet film; in 2005, the Ukrainian authorities donated a statue for her monument in France. President Viktor Yushchenko opened the monument to Anna in the town of Sanlis, where she died, during his state visit to France in June 2005. The Ukrainian-made inscription on the monument had to be redone after his departure, however, as it did not conform to French grammar. On Anna, see Tolochko, *Yaroslav Mudryi*, pp. 206–207. On the monument, see *Segodnia*, 11 July 2005, p. 3.

16. The Ukrainian historian Oleksii Tolochko shows that the kin of the Riurikids in general rather than any ruler in particular had been understood as the source of authority in Rus. See A. P. Tolochko, *Kniaz v Drevnei Rusi: vlast, sobstvennost, ideologiia* (Kyiv: Naukova dumka, 1992).

17. See, for example, Petro Holubenko, *Ukraina i Rosiia u svitli kulturnykh vzaiemyn* (Kyiv: Dnipro, 1993). This work was originally published in Ukrainian in New York.

18. On Turkic settlers, see Mykhailo Hrushevsky, *Istoriia Ukrainy-Rusy* (Kyiv: Naukova dumka, 1992), vol. 2, pp. 547–551.

19. The most recent Western contribution to this debate is Edward L. Keenan, *Josef Dobrovsky and the Origins of the Igor' Tale* (Cambridge, Mass.: Harvard Ukrainian Research Institute, 2003).

20. See Vasyl Nimchuk, "Pivdenni davnoruski hovory—osnova ukrainskoi movy," in S. Ya. Yermolenko and A. K. Moiseienko, eds., *Istoriia ukrainskoi movy: Khrestomatiia* (Kyiv: Lybid, 1996), pp. 257–269; and Hryhorii Pivtorak, "Koly zh vynykla ukrainska mova," in ibid., pp. 270–279. A similar disagreement exists among Western scholars.

21. See such recent works as Yaroslav Isaievych, *Halytsko-Volynska derzhava* (Lviv: Instytut ukrainoznavstva im. I. Krypiakevycha NANU, 1999), and O. S. Kucheruk, ed., *Halytsko-Volynska derzhava XII–XIV st.* (Lviv: Svit, 2002).

22. See S. C. Rowell, *Lithuania Ascending: A Pagan Empire within East-Central Europe, 1295–1345* (New York: Cambridge University Press, 1994).

23. See Jaroslaw Pelenski, "The Contest over the 'Kievan Inheritance' in Russian-Ukrainian Relations: The Origins and Early Ramifications," in Peter J. Potichnyi et al., eds., *Ukraine and Russia in Their Historical Encounter* (Edmonton: Canadian Institute of Ukrainian Studies Press, 1992), pp. 3–19.

24. N. M. Yakovenko, *Ukrainska shliakhta z kintsia XIV do seredyny XVII st. (Volyn i Tsentralna Ukraina)* (Kyiv: Naukova dumka, 1993), pp. 204–206; O. V. Rusyna, *Ukraina pid tataramy i Lytvoiu* (Kyiv: Alternatyvy, 1998), p. 202.

25. Yakovenko, *Ukrainska shliakhta*, pp. 269–270.

26. Natalia Yakovenko, *Narys istorii Ukrainy: z naidavnishykh chasiv do kintsia XVIII stolittia* (Kyiv: Heneza, 1997), p. 132.

27. See the prince's recent biography: Petro Saukh, *Kniaz Vasyl-Kostiantyn Ostrozky* (Rivne: Volynski oberehy, 2002).

28. Kyiv-Mohyla Academy existed until 1817, when it was transformed into a seminary for training clergymen and subsequently closed by the Soviet authorities in 1920. In 1992, Kyiv-Mohyla Academy reopened its doors as a secular university located in and around the old academy buildings. It is now one of the best and most prestigious universities in Ukraine.

29. On the Cossacks and the Orthodox religion, see Serhii Plokhy, *The Cossacks and Religion in Early Modern Ukraine* (New York: Oxford University Press, 2001).

30. The best source in English on the early history of the Cossacks is Mykhailo Hrushevsky's monumental history of Ukraine, which is now appearing in Canada in an excellent translation with exhaustive comments. See Mykhailo Hrushevsky, *History of Ukraine-Rus'* (Edmonton: Canadian Institute of Ukrainian Studies Press, 2000–2002), vols. 7 and 8.

31. See his recent biography: O. I. Hurzhii and V. V. Korniienko, *Hetman Petro Konashevych-Sahaidachyi* (Kyiv: Ukraina, 2004).

32. V. A. Smolii and V. S. Stepankov, *Ukrainska natsionalna revoliutsiia XVII st. (1648–1676)* (Kyiv: Alternatyvy, 1999), p. 100; Smolii and Stepankov, "Ukrainska natsionalna revoliutsiia 1648–1676 rr. kriz pryzmu stolit," *Ukrainskyi istorychnyi zhurnal*, no. 1 (1998): 17. Ukrainian historians actually take their estimates from the works of North American historians of Ukrainian background: Jaroslaw Pelenski, "The Cossack Insurrections in Ukrainian-Jewish Relations," in Peter J. Potichnyj and Howard Aster, eds., *Ukrainian-Jewish Relations in Historical Perspective* (Edmonton: Canadian Institute of Ukrainian Studies Press, 1988), p. 36.

33. See especially Valerii Smolii and Valerii Stepankov, *Bohdan Khmelnytsky* (Kyiv: Alternatyvy, 2003), pp. 12 and 399 (Bohdan the Great); L. D. Kuchma, "Dopovid na urochystykh zborakh z nahody 400–richchia vid dnia narodzhennia Bohdana Khmelnytskoho," *Ukrainskyi istorychnyi zhurnal*, no. 4 (1996): 3 (Father of the Fatherland).

34. See P. M. Sas, *Politychna kultura ukrainskoho suspilstva: kinets XVI–persha polovyna XVII st.* (Kyiv: Lybid, 1998); Frank Sysyn, "Konstruiuvannia natsionalnykh rekonstruktsii," *Krytyka* 9, no. 1–2 (2005): 28.

35. On the first point, see Frank E. Sysyn, "The Khmelnytsky Uprising and Ukrainian Nation-Building," *Journal of Ukrainian Studies* 17, nos. 1–2 (1992): 141–170; on the second, Natalia Yakovenko, "U kolorakh proletarskoi revoliutsii," *Ukrainskyi humanitarnyi ohliad*, no. 3 (2000): 58–78.

36. This point has been made in Yakovenko, *Narys istorii Ukrainy*, pp. 200–201. The best introduction in English to the discussions about the Pereiaslav Treaty remains John Basarab, *Pereiaslav 1654: A Historiographical Study* (Edmonton: Canadian Institute of Ukrainian Studies, 1982). The most representative collection of interpretations in the Ukrainian language is Pavlo Sokhan, ed., *Pereiaslavska rada 1654 roku: (Istoriohrafiia ta doslidzhennia)* (Kyiv: Smoloskyp, 2003).

37. Long branded a "traitor" in Russian and Soviet history writing, Mazepa is now lionized by Ukrainian media, and his portrait appears on the ten-hryvnia banknote. Modern-day authors often interpret his actions in the light of later political concepts of popular sovereignty and egalitarian nationalism, although this charge does not apply to a superb recent biography, which sees the hetman as a representative of the Cossack officer class disillusioned with tsarist absolutism and seeking to protect its position: Serhii Pavlenko, *Ivan Mazepa* (Kyiv: Alternatyvy, 2003).

38. See a series of excellent works by the Ukrainian historian Viktor Horobets: *Vid soiuzu do inkorporatsii: ukrainsko-rosiiski vidnosyny druhoi polovyny XVII–pershoi chverti XVIII st.* (Kyiv: Instytut istorii Ukrainy NANU, 1995); *Prysmerk Hetmanshchyny: Ukraina v roky reform Petra I* (Kyiv: Instytut istorii Ukrainy NANU, 1998); and *Politychnyi ustrii ukrainskykh zemel druhoi polovyny XVII–XVIII st.* (Kyiv: Instytut istorii Ukrainy NANU, 2000).

39. The 1785 decision came as a result of intense petitioning by Cossack officers; later, many categories of them struggled long to prove their noble status. See Zenon Kohut, *Russian Centralism and Ukrainian Autonomy: Imperial Absorption of the Hetmanate, 1760s–1830s* (Cambridge, Mass.: Harvard Ukrainian Research Institute, 1988).

40. See O. K. Fedoruk, ed., *Ukrainske barokko ta evropeiskyi kontekst* (Kyiv: Naukova dumka, 1991); and O. Myshanych, ed., *Ukrainske barokko* (Kyiv: Instytut ukrainskoi literatury im. T. H. Shevchenka NANU, 1993).

41. O. I. Hurzhii and T. V. Chukhlib, *Hetmanska Ukraina* (Kyiv: Alternatyvy, 1999), pp. 199–206 and 260–262.

42. See, most recently, Plokhy, *Unmaking Imperial Russia.*

Chapter 2

1. See Hroch, *Social Preconditions of a National Revival in Europe.*

2. My division of Russian-ruled Ukraine into just three historical regions simplifies more detailed demarcations made by scholars writing for a specialist audience. See, for instance, Ivan L. Rudnytsky, "The Role of Ukraine in Modern History,"

in his *Essays in Modern Ukrainian History* (Edmonton: Canadian Institute of Ukrainian Studies, 1987), pp. 11–36; and Roman Szporluk, "Urbanization in Ukraine since the Second World War," in Ivan L. Rudnytsky, ed., with the assistance of John-Paul Himka, *Rethinking Ukrainian History* (Edmonton: Canadian Institute of Ukrainian Studies, 1981), pp. 180–202.

3. See John Doyle Klier, *Russia Gathers Her Jews: The Origins of the "Jewish Question" in Russia, 1772–1825* (DeKalb: Northern Illinois University Press, 1986). On the numerical increase of the Jewish population in the Right Bank, see Ya. S. Khonigsman and A. Ya. Naiman, *Evrei Ukrainy: kratkii ocherk istorii* (Kyiv: Uchebno-metodicheskii kabinet Minobrazovaniia Ukrainy, 1993), vol. 1, p. 111; and Leonid Finberh and Volodymyr Liubchenko, eds., *Narysy z istorii ta kultury ievreiv Ukrainy* (Kyiv: Dukh i litera, 2005), p. 64.

4. See Patricia Herlihy, *Odessa: A History, 1794–1914* (Cambridge, Mass.: Harvard Ukrainian Research Institute, 1986).

5. See John Czaplicka, ed., *Lviv: A City in the Crosscurents of Culture* (Cambridge, Mass.: Harvard Ukrainian Research Institute, 2005).

6. Indeed, even in the 1870s, Mykhailo Drahomanov, a Ukrainian patriot from the Russian Empire, traveled to Transcarpathia by the same means. See M. P. Drahomanov, "Avstro-ruski spomyny," in his *Literaturno-publitsystychni tvory* (Kyiv: Naukova dumka, 1970), vol. 2, pp. 263–274.

7. This observation is in Wilson, *The Ukrainians*, p. 111.

8. See Hrytsak, *Narys istorii Ukrainy*, pp. 41–45.

9. See Andreas Kappeler, "Mazepintsy, Malorossy, Khokhly: Ukrainians in the Ethnic Hierarchy of the Russian Empire," in Andreas Kappeler, Zenon E. Kohut, Frank E. Sysyn, and Mark von Hagen, eds., *Culture, Nation, and Identity: The Ukrainian-Russian Encounter (1600–1945)* (Edmonton: Canadian Institute of Ukrainian Studies Press, 2003), pp. 162–181; and Kappeler, *"Great Russians" and "Little Russians": Russian-Ukrainian Relations and Perceptions in Historical Perspective*, The Donald W. Treadgold Papers, no. 39 (Seattle: Henry M. Jackson School of International Studies, University of Washington, 2003).

10. Throughout the nineteenth century, at least half of Russian government officials in the Ukrainian lands were ethnic Ukrainians, but the overwhelming majority saw themselves as Little Russians or Russians from Ukraine. See Stephen Velychenko, "Identities, Loyalties, and Service in Imperial Russia: Who Administered the Borderlands?" *Russian Review* 54, no. 2 (1995): 188–208.

11. On the role of the intelligentsia in the Ukrainian national movement during the nineteenth century, see Andreas Kappeler, *Der schwierige Weg zur Nation: Beiträge zur neueren Geschichte der Ukraine* (Cologne: Böhlau Verlag, 2003).

12. See V. V. Kravchenko, *Narysy z ukrainskoi istoriohrafii epokhy natsionalnoho vidrodzhennia (druha polovyna XVIII–seredyna XIX st.)* (Kharkiv: Osnova, 1996).

13. On Ukrainian Romantic writers' interest in nationality, see Tetiana Bovsunovska, *Fenomen ukrainskoho romantyzmu* (Kyiv: Instytut literatury im. T. H. Shevchenka NANU, 1997).

14. The other litterateur was P. P. Hulak-Artemovsky, who wrote humorous works in Ukrainian but serious belles-lettres in Russian. See Kvitka's own testimony in "Letter to P. O. Pletnov, 15 March 1839," in his *Zibrannia tvoriv u semy tomakh* (Kyiv: Naukova dumka, 1981), vol. 7, p. 215; and Oksana Yatyshchuk, *Hryhorii Fedorovych Kvitka-Osnovianenko v dukhovnii istorii Ukrainy* (Ternopil: TDPU im. V. Hnatiuka, 2003), pp. 39–40.

15. Maksymovych even signed his letters to friends as an "Old Ukrainian." See Viktor Korotkyi, "'Staryi ukrainets Mykhalio Maksymovych," in Mykhailo Maksymovych, *U poshukakh omriianoi Ukrainy* (Kyiv: Lybid, 2003), pp. 9–27.

16. Admittedly, the majority were landless nobles. Still, excluding hundreds of thousands of people from the ranks of the nobility was one of the nineteenth century's largest efforts at social engineering. See Daniel Bovua [Beauvois], *Shliakhtych, kripak i revizor: Polska shliakhta mizh tsaryzmom ta ukrainskymy masamy (1831–1863)*, trans. Zoia Borysiuk (Kyiv: Intel, 1996), pp. 195 and 383. This book is a translation of Daniel Beauvois, *Le Noble, le Serf et le Révizor. La noblesse polonaise entre le tsarisme et les masses ukrainiennes (1831–1863)* (Paris: Editions des Archives contemporaines, 1985).

17. Excellent biographies of Kostomarov are available both in Ukrainian and English: Yu. A. Pinchuk, *Mykola Ivanovych Kostomarov: 1817–1885* (Kyiv: Naukova dumka, 1992) and Thomas Prymak, *Mykola Kostomarov: A Biography* (Toronto: University of Toronto Press, 1996).

18. See Hryhorii Hrabovych [George Grabowicz], *Shevchenko, iakoho ne znaiemo* (Kyiv: Heneza, 2000) and Serhy Yekelchyk, "Creating a Sacred Place: The Ukrainophiles and Shevchenko's Tomb in Kaniv (1861–ca. 1900)," *Journal of Ukrainian Studies* 20, no. 1–2 (1996): 15–32.

19. A. M. Katrenko and Ya. A. Katrenko, *Natsionalno-kulturna i politychna diialnist Kyivskoi hromady (60–90–ti rr. XIX st.)* (Kyiv: KNU im. T. H. Shevchenka, 2003).

20. See David B. Saunders, "Russia and Ukraine under Alexander II: The Valuev Edict of 1863," *International History Review* 17 (February 1995): 23–51.

21. Viktor Dudko, "Audytoriia zhurnalu 'Osnova' (1861–1862): Kilkisnyi vymir," *Kyivska starovyna*, no. 6 (2001): 79.

22. The members of *hromadas* did not advance political demands, such as Ukrainian self-rule. But at the time, the very fact of asserting the distinctiveness of Ukrainian culture was a political statement. Scholars also stress that the *hromadas* started cultural and educational work among the masses—an important component of a national revival's cultural stage. See L. H. Ivanova and R. P. Ivanchenko, *Suspilno-politychnyi rukh 60–kh rr. XIX st. v Ukraini: do problemy stanovlennia ideolohii* (Kyiv: Mizhnarodnyi instytut linhvistyky i prava, 2004), pp. 309–310.

23. The best and most detailed study of these events remains Fedir Savchenko, *Zaborona ukrainstva 1876 r.* (Kharkiv: Derzhavne vydavnytstvo Ukrainy, 1930).

24. The most sophisticated analysis of Drahomanov's political views is in Anatolii Kruhlashov, *Drama intelektuala: politychni idei Mykhaila Drahomanova*

(Chernivtsi: Prut, 2001). On his political activities, an older book remains unsurpassed: R. P. Ivanova, *Mykhailo Drahomanov u suspilno-politychnomu rusi Rosii ta Ukrainy* (Kyiv: Vydavnytstvo Kyivskoho universytetu, 1971).

25. Of the two main organizers of the 1881 assassination, Andrii Zheliabov was a student from Odesa who had been previously involved in the local Ukrainian *hromada*, and Sofiia Perovskaia was descended from the Rozumovskys, the family of Ukraine's last hetman. On the revolutionary populists in Ukraine, see V. A. Smolii, ed., *Politychnyi teror i teroryzm v Ukraini XIX–XX st.: istorychni narysy* (Kyiv: Naukova dumka, 2002), pp. 39–61.

26. Serhy Yekelchyk, "The Nation's Clothes: Constructing a Ukrainian High Culture in the Russian Empire, 1860–1900," *Jahrbücher für Geschichte Osteuropas* 49, no. 2 (2001): 230–239.

27. Ernest Gellner has contributed an influential argument that modern nationalism's cultural work consists of creating from the elements of the folk tradition a new high culture appropriate to the industrial age. See Ernest Gellner, *Nations and Nationalism* (Oxford: Blackwell, 1983), p. 57.

28. Hrytsak, *Narys istorii Ukrainy*, pp. 51–52.

29. Sarbei, *Natsionalne vidrodzhennia Ukrainy*, pp. 122–125.

30. See Hrytsak, *Narys istorii Ukrainy*, pp. 73–74. By the late 1860s, however, Gołuchowski's policy of undermining the conservative Ruthenian clergy and pro-Russian intellectuals in Galicia cleared the field for a younger generation of Ukrainian patriots. See Stanislav Piiai [Stanisław Pijai], "Polityka Agenora Golukhovskoho shchodo halytskykh ukraintsiv u 1866–1868 rokakh ta ii naslidky," *Visnyk Lvivskoho universytetu. Seriia istorychna* 37, no. 1 (2002): 246–267.

31. See Sarbei, *Natsionalne vidrodzhennia Ukrainy*, pp. 200–201. On the various ways in which Galician intellectuals imagined the Ruthenians' place among modern nationalities and why certain options were not as viable as others, see John-Paul Himka, "The Construction of Nationality in Galician Rus': Icarian Flights in Almost All Directions," in Ronald Grigor Suny and Michael D. Kennedy, eds., *Intellectuals and the Articulation of the Nation* (Ann Arbor: University of Michigan Press, 1999), pp. 109–166.

32. Vasyl Hutkovsky, Ivan Krupsky, and Oksana Oleksyn, *Ukrainska zhurnalistyka na zakhidnoukrainskykh zemliakh: derzhavotvorcha funktsiia, tematychni aspekty (1848–1919 rr.)* (Lviv: Vilna Ukraina, 2001), pp. 27–33; Yu. H. Shapoval, *"Dilo" (1880–1939 rr.): Postup ukrainskoi suspilnoi dumky* (Lviv: NDTs periodyky LNB im. V. Stefanyka, 1999).

33. V. Herman, ed., *"Prosvita": istoriia ta suchasnist (1868–1998)* (Kyiv: Prosvita, 1998), p. 73.

34. See John-Paul Himka, *Religion and Nationality in Western Ukraine: The Greek Catholic Church and the Ruthenian National Movement in Galicia, 1867–1900* (Montreal: McGill-Queen's University Press, 1999), and idem, "The Construction of Nationality."

35. Other fruits of this short-lived compromise included the introduction of modern Ukrainian as the language of school instruction in Ukrainian schools (1893),

the creation of the large Ukrainian insurance company "Dnister," and a government subsidy to the Shevchenko Scientific Society. See I. P. Chornovil, *Polsko-ukrainska uhoda 1890–1894 rr.: Geneza, perebih podii, naslidky. Avtoreferat* (Lviv: Instytut ukrainoznavstva im. I. P. Krypiakevycha NANU, 1995).

36. See Plokhy, *Unmaking Imperial Russia*.

37. His only up-to-date political biography in any language is in a short book by Yaroslav Hrytsak, *"Dukh, shcho tilo rve do boiu": Sproba politychnoho portreta Ivana Franka* (Lviv: Kameniar, 1990). Professor Hrytsak is preparing a longer study of Franko's life and legacy.

Chapter 3

1. Andreas Kappeler, "The Ukrainians of the Russian Empire, 1860–1914," in Andreas Kappeler, ed., with the participation of Fikret Adanir and Alan O'Day, *The Formation of National Elites: Comparative Studies on Governments and Non-Dominant Ethnic Groups in Europe, 1850–1940* (New York: New York University Press, 1992), vol. 6: 106; Andreas Kappeler, "A 'Small People' of Twenty-Five Million: The Ukrainians circa 1900," *Journal of Ukrainian Studies* 18, nos. 1–2 (1993): 85–92.

2. See Paul R. Magocsi, "The Ukrainian National Revival: A New Analytical Framework," *Canadian Review of Studies in Nationalism* 16, nos. 1–2 (1989): 45–62.

3. Sarbei, *Natsionalne vidrodzhennia Ukrainy*, p. 176.

4. V. H. Sarbei, "Stanovlennia ukrainskoi natsii," in Sarbei, ed., *Ukrainske pytannia v Rosiiskii imperii (kinets XIX–pochatok XX st.)* (Kyiv: Instytut istorii Ukrainy NANU, 1999), vol. 1: 40.

5. I. K. Rybalka and F. H. Turchenko, "Sotsialno-klasova struktura naselennia Ukrainy naperedodni Zhovtnevoi revoliutsii," *Ukrainskyi istorychnyi zhurnal*, no. 11 (1981): 29 and 32.

6. See Eugene Weber, *Peasants into Frenchmen: The Modernization of Rural France, 1880–1914* (Stanford, Calif.: Stanford University Press, 1976).

7. T. I. Lazanska, "Narodonaselennia Ukrainy," in Sarbei, *"Ukrainske pytannia" v Rosiiskii imperii*, vol. 1: 94.

8. Bohdan Krawchenko, *Social Change and National Consciousness in Twentieth-Century Ukraine* (Edmonton: Canadian Institute of Ukrainian Studies, 1985), pp. 16–17 and 42–43.

9. Kappeler, "The Ukrainians," p. 108.

10. Lazanska, "Narodonaselennia Ukrainy," p. 96. Ethnic Russians constituted 50.2 percent and Jews, 23 percent.

11. See A. I. Miller, *"Ukrainskii vopros" v politike vlastei i russkom obshchestvennom mnenii (vtoraia polovina XIX v.)* (St. Petersburg: Aleteiia, 2000) and Roman Szporluk, "Ukraine: From an Imperial Periphery to a Sovereign State," *Daedalus* 126 (Summer 1997): 85–120.

12. Yu. P. Lavrov, "Vynyknennia i diialnist ukrainskykh politychnykh partii," in Sarbei, *"Ukrainske pytannia" v Rosiiskii imperii*, vol. 2: 252–258 and 280–283.

13. Volodymyr Holovchenko, "Politychnyi portret Mariana Melenevskoho," *Kyivska starovyna*, no. 4 (2000): 100; M. S. Karmazina, "Revoliutsiia 1905–1907 rr. v Ukraini: paradoksy strimkoi polityzatsii," in I. F. Kuras, ed., *Politychna istoriia Ukrainy: XX st.* (Kyiv: Heneza, 2002), vol. 1: 161–165 and 180–185.

14. Nina Doroshchuk, "Kulturnytska diialnist ukrainstva mizh dvoma revoliutsiiamy (1907–1917 rr.)," *Kyivska starovyna*, no. 2 (2000): 162; O. V. Lysenko, "Ukrainska vydavnycha sprava," in Sarbei, *"Ukrainske pytannia v Rosiiskii imperii*, vol. 2: 82–85.

15. See V. M. Volkovynsky, "Hromadski orhanizatsii velykoruskykh shovinistiv," in Sarbei, *"Ukrainske pytannia" v Rosiiskii imperii*, vol. 2: 160–203.

16. S. A. Makarchuk, *Ukrainskyi etnos (Vynyknennia i istorychnyi rozvytok)* (Kyiv: Navchalno-metodychnyi kabinet Ministerstva osvity, 1992), p. 80.

17. See Himka, "The Construction of Nationality" and idem, "Young Radicals and Independent Statehood: The Idea of a Ukrainian Nation-State, 1890–1895," *Slavic Review* 41, no. 2 (1982): 219–235.

18. A. I. Pavko, "Posylennia vplyvu politychnykh partii Skhidnoi Halychyny na hromadske zhyttia kraiu u 1900–1907 rr.," *Ukrainskyi istorychnyi zhurnal*, no. 5 (2002): 75.

19. On Hrushevsky's conceptual revolution, see Sysyn, "Introduction to the *History*" and Plokhy, *Unmaking Imperial Russia*.

20. Yaroslav Hrytsak, "Yakykh-to kniaziv buly stolytsi v Kyievi? Do konstruiuvan-nia istorychnoi pamiati halytskykh ukraintsiv u 1830–1930–ti roky," *Ukraina moderna*, no. 6 (2001): 77–98.

21. Sarbei, *Natsionalne vidrodzhennia Ukrainy*, pp. 296–297.

22. See a new Russian study of the tsarist policies in occupied eastern Galicia: A. I. Bakhturina, *Politika Rossiiskoi Imperii v Vostochnoi Galitsii v gody Pervoi mirovoi voiny* (Moscow: AIRO-XX, 2000).

23. See Mark von Hagen, "Derzhava, natsiia ta natsionalna svidomist: rosiisko-ukrainski vidnosyny v pershii polovyni XX st.," *Ukrainskyi istorychnyi zhurnal*, no. 1 (1998): 128; and Eric Lohr, *Nationalizing the Russian Empire: The Campaign against Enemy Aliens during World War I* (Cambridge, Mass.: Harvard University Press, 2003).

24. For an up-to-date treatment of the Union, see Yu. P. Lavrov, "Pochatok diialnosti Soiuzu vyzvolennia Ukrainy," *Ukrainskyi istorychnyi zhurnal*, no. 4 (1998): 3–32; no. 5 (1998): 3–15.

Chapter 4

1. Recent works that go beyond the traditional historiographical models and chart out a new research agenda include Mark von Hagen, "The Dilemmas of Ukrainian Independence and Statehood, 1917–1921," *The Harriman Institute Forum* 7 (January 1994): 7–11; John-Paul Himka, "The National and the Social in the Ukrainian Revolution of 1917–20," *Archiv für Sozialgeschichte* 34 (1994): 95–110; Yaroslav Hrytsak, "Ukrainska Revoliutsiia, 1914–1923: novi interpretat-sii," *Ukraina moderna*, nos. 2–3 (1999): 254–269; Roman Szporluk, "Ukraine: From an Imperial Periphery to a Sovereign State," *Daedalus* 126 (Summer

1997): 85–119; and a special issue of the *Journal of Ukrainian Studies* 24 (Summer 1999), edited by John-Paul Himka.

2. See V. F. Shevchenko, ed., *Ukrainski politychni partii kintsia XIX–pochatku XX stolittia: prohramovi i dovidkovi materialy* (Kyiv: Feniks, 1993) and S. O. Teleshun, *Natsionalne pytannia v prohramakh ukrainskykh politychnykh partii v kintsi XIX–na pochatku XX st.* (Kyiv: n.p., 1996).

3. For decades, these two numbers—the 100,000 manifestation participants and the 300,000 "Ukrainized" soldiers—passed from one book to another as proof of the popular support for the Central Rada. It is refreshing to see a present-day Ukrainian historian interpreting these numbers as a reflection of wider social and national upheavals of 1917 that was *construed* by contemporaries as a sign of mass support for the Central Rada. See V. F. Soldatenko, *Ukrainska revoliutsiia: istorychnyi narys* (Kyiv: Lybid, 1999), pp. 139, 292.

4. The English translation of the Universals is found in Taras Hunczak, ed., with the assistance of John T. von der Heide, *The Ukraine, 1917–1921: A Study in Revolution* (Cambridge, Mass.: Harvard Ukrainian Research Institute, 1977), pp. 382–395.

5. Vladyslav Verstiuk, *Ukrainska Tsentralna Rada* (Kyiv: Zapovit, 1997), pp. 90, 99.

6. V. M. Boiko, "Uchast ukrainskykh partii u munitsypalnii kampanii 1917 r.," *Ukrainskyi istorychnyi zhurnal*, no. 5 (1997): 37.

7. Steven L. Guthier, "The Popular Base of Ukrainian Nationalism in 1917," *Slavic Review* 38 (March 1979): 30–47.

8. Ivan Khmil and Ihor Kutashev, "Narostannia selianskoho ekstremizmu v Ukraini (berezen-zhovten 1917 r.)," in V. F. Verstiuk, ed., *Problemy vyvchennia istorii Ukrainskoi revoliutsii 1917–1921 rr.* (Kyiv: Instytut istorii Ukrainy NANU, 2002), pp. 53–76; Mark R. Baker, "Peasants, Power and Revolution in the Village: A Social History of Kharkiv Province, 1914–1921," Ph.D. thesis (Harvard University, 2001).

9. The correct translation of this polity's name, *Ukrainska Narodnia Respublika*, is the Ukrainian People's Republic, and indeed, this was the English version of its name used by the republic's diplomats. After World War II, the term "People's Republic" became associated with Soviet satellite states, causing Ukrainian émigré historians in the West to prefer the wording "the Ukrainian National Republic." See a perceptive comment in Hunczak, *The Ukraine*, p. 388, note 3.

10. I. L. Hoshuliak, "Pro prychyny porazky Tsentralnoi Rady," *Ukrainskyi istorychnyi zhurnal*, no. 1 (1994): 36.

11. A. P. Hrytsenko, *Ukrainski robitnyky na shliakhu tvorennia natsionalnoi derzhavy* (Kyiv: Instytut istorii Ukrainy NANU, 1992), pp. 4–6, 13–18; O. M. Movchan and O. P. Reient, "Mizhpartiina politychna borotba u profspilkovomu rusi Ukrainy (1917–1922)," *Ukrainskyi istorychnyi zhurnal*, no. 5 (1995): 8–27; O. P. Reient, *Ukrainska revoliutsiia i robitnytstvo* (Kyiv: Instytut istorii Ukrainy NANU, 1996), pp. 5–7.

12. Before tabling the Fourth Universal at the Small Rada, Hrushevsky noted that its aims were "to allow our government to complete the peace process and to defend our country from various incursions" (V. F. Verstiuk, ed., *Ukrainska*

Tsentralna Rada: Dokumenty i materialy [Kyiv: Naukova dumka, 1997], 2: 101). See also V. Vynnychenko, *Vidrodzhennia natsii* (Kyiv: Vydavnytstvo politychnoi literatury Ukrainy, 1990), 2: 243, 283.

13. Smolii, *Istoriia Ukrainy*, p. 230.

14. V. S. Lozovyi, "Ahrarna polityka Dyrektorii UNR," *Ukrainskyi istorychnyi zhurnal*, no. 2 (1997): 70–71.

15. P. P. Prytuliak, "Ekonomichnyi dohovir UNR z Nimechchynoiu ta Avstro-Uhorshchynoiu 1918 r.," *Ukrainskyi istorychnyi zhurnal*, no. 1 (1997): 62–72; O. S. Rublov and O. P. Reient, *Ukrainski vyzvolni zmahannia 1917–1921 rr.* (Kyiv: Alternatyvy, 1999), p. 81.

16. Hrytsak, *Narys istorii Ukrainy*, p. 129.

17. O. V. Pavliuk, "Dyplomatiia nezalezhnykh ukrainskykh uriadiv (1917–1920)," in V. A. Smolii, ed., *Narysy z istorii dyplomatii Ukrainy* (Kyiv: Alternatyvy, 2001), pp. 327–335.

18. See Oleksandr Reient, *Pavlo Skoropadskyi* (Kyiv: Alternatyvy, 2003), pp. 218–227.

19. Oleh Pavlyshyn, "Orhanizatsiia tsyvilnoi vlady ZUNR u povitakh Halychyny (lystopad-hruden 1917 roku)," *Ukraina moderna*, nos. 2–3 (1997–1998): 132–193, here 143–144.

20. See M. R. Lytvyn and K. Ye. Naumenko, *Istoriia halytskoho striletstva*, 2nd ed. (Lviv: Kameniar, 1991), p. 97 (60,000 by February 1919).

21. M. R. Lytvyn and K. Ye. Naumenko, *Istoriia ZUNR* (Lviv: Instytut ukrainoznavstva NANU, 1995), pp. 119–120.

22. See V. S. Lozovy, "Poshuk Dyrektoriieiu ideino-politychnykh zasad vidnovlennia diialnosti UNR," *Ukrainskyi istorychnyi zhurnal*, no. 5 (2000): 32–37.

23. Vynnychenko, *Vidrodzhennia natsii*, 3: 322–323.

24. In addition to existing literature in various languages, new Ukrainian and Russian books on Makhno and Hryhoriiv include Volodymyr Horak, *Povstantsi otamana Hryhoriiva* (Fastiv: Polifast, 1998); S. P. Mosiiash, *Odisseia batki Makhno* (Moscow: Veche, 2002), V. F. Verstiuk, *Makhnovshchyna: selianskyi povstanskyi rukh na Ukraini (1918–1921)* (Kyiv: Naukova dumka, 1991); and Valerii Volkovynsky, *Nestor Makhno: lehendy i realnist* (Kyiv: Perlit, 1994). On the three Marusias, see *Holos Ukrainy*, March 26, 1994, p. 7.

25. Henry Abramson, "Jewish Representation in the Independent Ukrainian Governments of 1917–1920," *Slavic Review* 50 (Fall 1991): 548.

26. See Serhy Yekelchyk, "Trahichna storinka Ukrainskoi revoliutsii. Symon Petliura ta ievreiski pohromy v Ukraini (1917–1920)," in Vasyl Mykhalchuk, ed., *Symon Petliura ta Ukrainska natsionalna revoliutsiia* (Kyiv: Rada, 1995), pp. 165–217; and V. I. Serhiichuk, ed., *Pohromy v Ukraini: 1914–1920* (Kyiv: Vydavnytstvo im. Oleny Telihy, 1998). The most recent and reliable work in English is Henry Abramson, *A Prayer for the Government: Ukrainians and Jews in Revolutionary Times, 1917–1920* (Cambridge, Mass.: Harvard Ukrainian Research Institute and Harvard Center for Jewish Studies, 1999). See also Taras Hunczak, "A Reappraisal of Simon Petliura and Jewish-Ukrainian Relations 1917–1921," *Jewish Social Studies* 31, no. 3 (1969): 163–183.

27. Lytvyn and Naumenko, *Istoriia halytskoho striletstva*, pp. 147–148.

28. Isak Mazepa, *Ukraina v ohni i buri revoliutsii: 1917–1922* (Kyiv: Tempora, 2003), pp. 317–324.

29. Rublov and Reient, *Ukrainski vyzvolni zmahannia 1917–1921 rr.*, p. 228.

30. See Andrea Graziosi, *The Great Soviet Peasant War: Bolsheviks and Peasants, 1917–1933* (Cambridge, Mass.: Harvard Ukrainian Research Institute, 1996), pp. 28–37.

Chapter 5

1. Western scholars made this point well before the USSR showed any signs of crumbling. See Ivan L. Rudnytsky, "Soviet Ukraine in Historical Perspective," in his *Essays in Modern Ukrainian History* (Edmonton: Canadian Institute of Ukrainian Studies Press, 1987), pp. 463–475 (originally presented as the Shevchenko Memorial Lecture at the University of Alberta in 1970).

2. See Martin, *The Affirmative Action Empire.*

3. Quoted in S. V. Kulchytsky, *Komunizm v Ukraini: pershe desiatyrichchia (1919–1928)* (Kyiv: Osnovy, 1996), p. 114.

4. S. V. Kulchytsky, *Ukraina mizh dvoma viinamy (1921–1939 rr.)* (Kyiv: Alternatyvy, 1999), pp. 11–12; O. M. Movchan, "Robitnychyi straikovyi rukh v Ukraini (20–ti rr.)," *Ukrainskyi istorychnyi zhurnal*, no. 6 (1998): 12–21.

5. Kulchytsky, *Komunizm v Ukraini*, p. 175.

6. S. V. Kulchytsky and O. M. Movchan, *Nevidomi storinky holodu 1921–1923 rr. v Ukraini* (Kyiv: Instytut istorii Ukrainy NANU, 1993), pp. 60–61.

7. Smolii, *Istoriia Ukrainy*, p. 298; M. M. Oliinyk, "Polityka derzhavnykh ta partiinykh orhaniv Ukrainy shchodo pryvatnykh pidpryiemtsiv u period NEPu," *Ukrainskyi istorychnyi zhurnal*, no. 1 (2001): 22.

8. O. O. Sushko, *Nepmany: sotsialno-istorychnyi typ pryvatnykh pidpryiemtsiv v USRR (1921–1929)* (Kyiv: Natsionalnyi pedahohichnyi universytet im. M. P. Drahomanova, 2003), p. 36.

9. See Kulchytsky, *Komunizm v Ukraini*, pp. 274–291.

10. These statistical data are found in Krawchenko, *Social Change*, pp. 99–100.

11. V. A. Hrechenko and Yu. I. Shapoval, "KP(b)U u mizhvoiennyi period," in Kuras, *Politychna istoriia Ukrainy*, 3: 87, 93.

12. L. P. Salyha, "Borotba Kh. H. Rakovskoho za rozshyrennia prav Ukrainy pid chas konstytutsiinoho oformlennia SRSR (traven-lypen 1923 r.)," *Ukrainskyi istorychnyi zhurnal*, no. 1 (1992): 122–123.

13. These two cities are currently known as Dnipropetrovsk and Donetsk, respectively.

14. Lebid stated his views in a 1923 article in the party newspaper *Kommunist*. See George Y. Shevelov, *The Ukrainian Language in the First Half of the Twentieth Century (1900–1941): Its State and Status* (Cambridge, Mass.: Harvard Ukrainian Research Institute, 1989), p. 114.

15. See Martin, *The Affirmative Action Empire.*

16. Lazar Kaganovich, *Pamiatnye zapiski* (Moscow: Vagrius, 1997), p. 377. Note that the Communist Party of Ukraine was the only regional party organization in

the USSR that had its own Politburo. The Central Committee of the All-Union Communist Party also elected a Politburo from among its members, but this structure was not imitated in any other republic.

17. V. A. Smolii, ed., *"Ukrainizatsiia" 1920–30-kh rokiv: peredumovy, zdobutky, uroky* (Kyiv: Instytut istorii Ukrainy NANU, 2003), pp. 64, 81.

18. V. S. Lozytsky, "Polityka ukrainizatsii v 20–30-kh rokakh: istoriia, problemy, uroky," *Ukrainskyi istorychnyi zhurnal*, no. 3 (1989): 50–51.

19. Smolii, *"Ukrainizatsiia" 1920–30-kh rokiv*, pp. 137–145; V. L. Borysov, "Ukrainizatsiia ta rozvytok zahalnoosvitnoi shkoly v 1921–1932 rr.," *Ukrainskyi istorychnyi zhurnal*, no. 2 (1999): 76–80.

20. Smolii, *"Ukrainizatsiia" 1920–30-kh rokiv*, p. 8; and Martin, *The Affirmative Action Empire*, pp. 122–123. Note also an earlier suggestion by George O. Liber that "in the end, the Ukrainian language and culture did not become hegemonic in the cities" (*Soviet Nationality Policy, Urban Growth, and Identity Change in the Ukrainian SSR, 1923–1934* [New York: Cambridge University Press, 1992], p. 178).

21. James E. Mace, *Communism and the Dilemmas of National Liberation: National Communism in Soviet Ukraine, 1918–1922* (Cambridge, Mass.: Harvard Ukrainian Research Institute, 1983), p. 99.

22. Ibid., p. 100.

23. Ibid., pp. 161–190; and Liber, *Soviet Nationality Policy*, pp. 126–131.

24. On Khvylovy, see Mykola Khvylovy, *The Cultural Renaissance in Ukraine: Polemical Pamphlets, 1925–1926*. Ed., trans., and with an Introduction by Myroslav Shkandrij (Edmonton: Canadian Institute of Ukrainian Studies Press, 1986); Mace, *Communism and the Dilemmas*, pp. 120–160; Myroslav Shkandrij, *Modernists, Marxists and the Nation: The Ukrainian Literary Discussion of the 1920s* (Edmonton: Canadian Institute of Ukrainian Studies Press, 1992); O. V. Kresin, "Natsionalna kontseptsiia Mykoly Khvylovoho," *Ukrainskyi istorychnyi zhurnal*, no. 6 (1997): 58–62.

25. In addition to Mace's book, see the following Ukrainian works on Yavorsky: H. V. Kasianov, "Akademik M. I. Yavorsky: dolia vchenoho," *Ukrainskyi istorychnyi zhurnal*, no. 8 (1990): 75–80; and A. V. Santsevych, "M. I. Yavorsky—vydatnyi ukrainskyi istoryk," in V. A. Smolii and Yu. A. Pinchuk, eds., *Istorychna spadshchyna u svitli suchasnykh doslidzhen* (Kyiv: Instytut istorii Ukrainy NANU, 1995), pp. 108–122.

26. See especially Dzheims Meis [James Mace] and Mai Panchuk, *Ukrainskyi natsionalnyi komunizm: trahichni iliuzii* (Kyiv: Instytut natsionalnykh vidnosyn i politolohii NANU, 1997), pp. 63–69; but also V. F. Soldatenko, *Nezlamnyi: Zhyttia i smert Mykoly Skrypnyka* (Kyiv: Knyha pamiati Ukrainy, 2002), p. 143.

27. Martin, *The Affirmative Action Empire*, p. 123.

28. Hrechenko and Shapoval, "KP(b)U u mizhvoiennyi period," p. 121.

29. B. V. Chirko, *Natsionalni menshyny v Ukraini (20–30 roky XX stolittia)* (Kyiv: Asotsiiatsiia Ukraina, 1995), p. 47.

30. Vasyl Sokil, *Zdaleka do blyzkoho* (Edmonton: Canadian Institute of Ukrainian Studies Press, 1987), p. 65.
31. See Liber, *Soviet Nationality Policy*, p. 77.
32. Since the late 1980s, a flood of publications has appeared in Ukraine about cultural life in the 1920s. Perhaps the best summary is found in Myroslav Popovych, *Narys istorii kultury Ukrainy*, 2nd ed. (Kyiv: Art Ek, 2001), pp. 587–612. Only a few aspects of this cultural flowering received monographic treatment in English. See Oleh S. Ilnytzkyj, *Ukrainian Futurism, 1914–1930: A Historical and Critical Study* (Cambridge, Mass.: Harvard Ukrainian Research Institute, 1997); Irena R. Makaryk, *Shakespeare in the Undiscovered Bourn: Les Kurbas, Ukrainian Modernism, and Early Soviet Cultural Politics* (Toronto: University of Toronto Press, 2004); Shkandrij, *Modernists, Marxists and the Nation*; Maxim Tarnawsky, *Between Reason and Irrationality: The Prose of Valerijan Pidmohyl'nyj* (Toronto: University of Toronto Press, 1995).
33. See the new biography of Dovzhenko: George O. Liber, *Alexander Dovzhenko: A Life in Soviet Film* (London: BFI Publishing, 2002). The most convenient introduction in English to his cinema remains Vance Kepley Jr., *In the Service of the State: The Cinema of Alexander Dovzhenko* (Madison: University of Wisconsin Press, 1986).
34. See Shkandrij, *Modernists, Marxists and the Nation*.

Chapter 6

1. Kulchytsky, *Ukraina mizh dvoma viinamy*, p. 135.
2. After the collapse of Communism, researchers allowed to work in Russia's Presidential Archive dug up Stalin's baptismal certificate, showing that the future dictator was really born in December 1878. Beginning in the early 1920s, however, and for reasons that remain unclear, Stalin began listing 1879 as the year of his birth. Thus, his fiftieth birthday was celebrated in 1929 rather than 1928. See Edvard Radzinsky, *Stalin* (New York: Doubleday, 1996), pp. 11–14.
3. V. M. Danylenko, H. V Kasianov, and S. V. Kulchytsky, *Stalinizm na Ukraini: 20–30-ti roky* (Kyiv: Lybid, 1991), pp. 80–81; Smolii, *Istoriia Ukrainy*, p. 306.
4. V. A. Smolii, ed., *Istoriia Ukrainy: nove bachennia* (Kyiv: Naukova dumka, 1994), vol. 2: 220.
5. Kulchytsky, *Ukraina mizh dvoma viinamy*, p. 222.
6. Krawchenko, *Social Change*, p. 117.
7. Liber, *Soviet Nationality Policy*, p. 171.
8. Krawchenko, *Social Change*, p. 118.
9. Ibid., pp. 118–119.
10. See Serhy Yekelchyk, "The Making of a 'Proletarian Capital': Patterns of Stalinist Social Policy in Kiev in the mid-1930s," *Europe-Asia Studies* 50, no. 7 (1998): 1229–1244.
11. Kulchytsky, *Ukraina mizh dvoma viinamy*, p. 152.
12. V. M. Danylenko, H. V. Kasianov, and S. V. Kulchytsky, *Stalinizm na Ukraini: 20—30-ti roky* (Kyiv: Lybid, 1991), p. 103.

13. Valerii Vasilev and Lynne Viola, eds., *Kollektivizatsiia i krestianskoe soprotivlenie na Ukraine (noiabr 1929–mart 1930 gg.)* (Vinnytsia: Logos, 1997), pp. 251–253. On women's riots, see Lynne Viola, "Bab'i Bunty and Peasant Women's Protest during Collectivization," *Russian Review* 45, no. 1 (1986): 23–47.

14. Smolii, *Istoriia Ukrainy*, p. 312.

15. Krawchenko, *Social Change*, pp. 125–126.

16. James E. Mace and Leonid Herets, eds., *Oral History Project of the Commission on the Ukrainian Famine* (Washington, D.C.: U.S. Government Printing Office, 1990), 3 vols.; Lidiia Kovalenko and Volodymyr Maniak, eds., *33–ii: Holod. Narodna knyha-memorial* (Kyiv: Radianskyi pysmennyk, 1991).

17. Martin, *The Affirmative Action Empire*, pp. 302–307. The decree in question has been published in Valerii Vasyliev and Yurii Shapoval, eds., *Komandyry velykoho holodu* (Kyiv: Heneza, 2001), pp. 310–313.

18. See Marco Carynnyk, "Making the News Fit to Print: Walter Duranty, the *New York Times* and the Ukrainian Famine of 1933," in Roman Serbyn and Bohdan Krawchenko, eds., *Famine in Ukraine, 1932–1933* (Edmonton: Canadian Institute of Ukrainian Studies Press, 1986), pp. 67–96; and Lubomyr Luciuk, ed., *Not Worthy: Walter Duranty's Pulitzer Prize and The New York Times* (Kingston, Ont.: Kashtan Press, 2004).

19. S. Kulchytsky, "Teror holodom iak instrument kolektyvizatsii," in *Holodomor 1932–1933 rr. v Ukraini: prychyny i naslidky* (Kyiv: Instytut istorii Ukrainy NANU, 1995), p. 34.

20. Although it is now the Ukrainian state's official view that the Famine was a manmade Soviet "genocide" against ethnic Ukrainians, Western scholars continue to be divided on this issue. For examples of the "genocide" interpretation, see Robert Conquest, *The Harvest of Sorrow: Soviet Collectivization and the Terror-Famine* (New York: Oxford University Press, 1986), and Miron Dolot, *Execution by Hunger: The Hidden Holocaust* (New York: Norton, 1985). For examples of works arguing that the famine was not limited to Ukraine and was not fundamentally or exclusively man-made, see R. W. Davies and Stephen G. Wheatcroft, *The Years of Hunger: Soviet Agriculture, 1931–1933* (New York: Palgrave, 2004) and Mark Tauger, "The 1932 Harvest and the Famine of 1933," *Slavic Review* 50 (Spring 1991): 80–89.

21. On Hrushevsky and the Soviet authorities, see Vsevolod Prystaiko and Yurii Shapoval, *Mykhailo Hrushevskyi i HPU-NKVD: Trahichne desiatylittia, 1924–1934* (Kyiv: Ukraina, 1996) and idem, *Mykhailo Hrushevskyi: sprava "UNTs" i ostnanni roky, 1931–1934* (Kyiv: Heneza, 1999). On Yavorsky, see Yu. I. Shapoval, "Stalinizm i Ukraina," *Ukrainskyi istorychnyi zhurnal*, no. 7 (1991): 29–30.

22. First published in R. Ya. Pyrih, ed., *Holod 1932–1933 rokiv na Ukraini: ochyma istorykiv, movoiu dokumentiv* (Kyiv: Politvydav Ukrainy, 1990), pp. 292–294.

23. V. A. Hrechenko and Yu. I. Shapoval, "KP(b)U u mizhvoiennyi period," in Kuras, *Politychna istoriia Ukrainy*, 3: 132.

24. See a new, archival-based biography of Skrypnyk: V. F. Soldatenko, *Nezlamnyi: zhyttia i smert Mykoly Skrypnyka* (Kyiv: Knyha pamiati Ukrainy, 2002).

25. On the Poles, see a recent book by Kate Brown, *A Biography of No Place: From Ethnic Borderland to Soviet Heartland* (Cambridge, Mass.: Harvard University Press, 2004).

26. Yu. I. Shapoval, *Ukraina 20–50-kh rokiv: storinky nenapysanoi istorii* (Kyiv: Naukova dumka, 1993), pp. 255–256.

27. Ivan Bilas, *Represyvno-karalna systema v Ukraini, 1917–1953: suspilno-politychnyi ta istoryko-pravovyi analiz* (Kyiv: Lybid-Viisko Ukrainy, 1994), vol. 1: 379.

28. Smolii, *Istoriia Ukrainy: nove bachennia*, 2: 252.

29. Hiroaki Kuromiya, *Freedom and Terror in the Donbas: A Ukrainian-Russian Borderland, 1870s–1990s* (New York: Cambridge University Press, 2003), pp. 246–247.

30. V. M. Nikolsky, "Natsionalni aspekty politychnykh represii 1937 r. v Ukraini," *Ukrainskyi istorychnyi zhurnal*, no. 2 (2001): 78–79.

31. Tsentralnyi derzhavnyi arkhiv hromadskykh obiednan Ukrainy (Ukrainian Central State Archive of Civic Organizations, hereafter TsDAHO), Fond 1, List 1, Case 446, Fol. 3–5.

32. See a new, archival-based book on Soviet cultural policies in Ukraine during the 1930s: Hennadii Yefymenko, *Natsionalna-kulturna polityka VKP(b) shchodo Radianskoi Ukrainy (1932–1938)* (Kyiv: Instytut istorii Ukrainy, 2001).

33. All statistics in this paragraph come from Krawchenko, *Social Change*, pp. 134–141.

34. Smolii, *Ukrainizatsiia 1920–30-kh rokiv*, p. 342.

35. For a new work on the "Great Retreat" in general, see David L. Hoffmann, *Stalinist Values: The Cultural Norms of Soviet Modernity, 1917–1941* (Ithaca, N.Y.: Cornell University Press, 2003). Specifically on the restoration of Russian nationalism and parallel processes in Ukraine, see David Brandenberger, *National Bolshevism: Stalinist Mass Culture and the Formation of Modern Russian National Identity, 1931–1956* (Cambridge, Mass.: Harvard University Press, 2002), and Yekelchyk, *Stalin's Empire of Memory*.

36. William Taubman, *Khrushchev: The Man and His Era* (New York: Norton, 2003), pp. 116 and 120.

37. S. V. Kulchytsky, "Forma i sut ukrainskoi radianskoi derzhavnosti," in Kuras, *Politychna istoriia Ukrainy*, 3: 216–217.

38. Kulchytsky, *Ukraina mizh dvoma viinamy*, p. 254.

39. See Liber, *Alexander Dovzhenko*.

Chapter 7

1. John-Paul Himka, "Western Ukraine between the Wars," *Canadian Slavonic Papers* 34 (December 1992): 391–393.

2. See Rogers Brubaker, *Nationalism Reframed: Nationhood and the National Question in the New Europe* (New York: Cambridge University Press, 1996), pp. 83–93.

3. Jerzy Tomaszewski, *Rzeczpospolita wielu narodów* (Warsaw: Czytelnik, 1985), pp. 30–32. It is possible that some peasants feigned ignorance because open identification with the Ukrainian nationality could be disadvantageous. See Hrytsak, *Narys istorii Ukrainy*, p. 189.

4. According to the calculations of present-day Ukrainian historians, in the late 1930s the total number of Polish colonist households in the region stood at 47,000. See Kulchytsky, *Ukraina mizh dvoma viinamy*, pp. 189–190.

5. Ivan Forhel, "Rozvytok kooperatyvnoho rukhu v Zakhidnii Ukraini u 1918–1939 rr.," in K. K. Kondratiuk, ed., *1939 rik v istorychnii doli Ukrainy i ukraintsiv* (Lviv: LNU im. Ivana Franka, 2001), pp. 62–65.

6. V. L. Komar, "'Ukrainske pytannia' v politytsi uriadiv Polshchi (1926–1939 rr.)," *Ukrainskyi istorychnyi zhurnal*, no. 5 (2001): 124–127.

7. On Józewski, see Timothy Snyder, *Sketches from a Secret War: A Polish Artist's Mission to Liberate Soviet Ukraine* (New Haven, Conn.: Yale University Press, 2005).

8. See Oleksandr Zaitsev, "Ukrainska narodna trudova partiia (1919–1925)," *Ukraina moderna*, no. 7 (2002): 69–90; and Mykola Kuhutiak, *Istoriia ukrainskoi natsional-demokratii* (1918–1929) (Kyiv and Ivano-Frankivsk: Plai, 2002), vol. 1.

9. Volodymyr Kucher and Valerii Pavlenko, "Zakhidna Ukraina: borotba za sobornist ukrainskykh zemel (1923–1939 rr.)," *Kyivska starovyna*, no. 1 (1999): 82.

10. O. S. Rublov and Yu. A. Cherchenko, *Stalinshchyna i dolia zakhidnoukrainskoi intelihentsii: 20–50-ti roky XX st.* (Kyiv: Naukova dumka, 1994), pp. 72–73; Kulchytsky, *Ukraina mizh dvoma viinamy*, p. 277.

11. Kulchytsky, *Ukraina mizh dvoma viinamy*, p. 302.

12. The most recent Ukrainian work on Dontsov is Serhii Kvit, *Dmytro Dontsov: Ideolohichnyi portret* (Kyiv: Vydavnychyi tsentr "Kyivskyi universytet," 2000).

13. Yu. Z. Yurchuk, *Orhanizatsiia ukrainskykh natsionalistiv u borotbi za rozviazannia ukrainskoho pytannia v 1929–1935 rr. Avtoreferat* (Lviv: Natsionalnyi universytet "Lvivska politekhnika," 2004), pp. 12–13.

14. Most of historical Bessarabia is currently a part of Moldova, but southern Bessarabia was incorporated into Soviet Ukraine in 1940 and remains a part of Ukraine.

15. I. A. Piddubny, "Politychne zhyttia ukraintsiv Pivnichnoi Bukovyny u pershe mizhvoienne desiatylittia (1928–1928 rr.)," *Ukrainskyi istorychnyi zhurnal*, no. 5 (2001): 133–139.

16. Ivan Lysiak-Rudnytsky, "Karpatska Ukraina: narod u poshukakh svoiei identychnosti," in his *Istorychni ese* (Kyiv: Osnovy, 1994), vol. 1: 466–468.

17. A. V. Kentii, *Narysy istorii Orhanizatsii ukrainskykh natsionalistiv (1929–1941 rr.)* (Kyiv: Instytut istorii Ukrainy NANU, 1998), pp. 92–93.

18. Paul Robert Magocsi, *The Shaping of a National Identity: Subcarpathian Rus', 1848–1948* (Cambridge, Mass.: Harvard University Press, 1978), p. 242; and Mykhailo Shvahuliak, "Ukrainske pytannia v mizhnarodnykh politychnykh kryzakh peredodnia Druhoi svitovoi viiny (1938–1939)," *Visnyk Lvivskoho universytetu. Seriia istorychna*, nos. 35–36 (2000): 303–304.

19. Kulchytsky, *Ukraina mizh dvoma viinamy*, p. 317.

20. The classic study of the Soviet invasion and initial policies in the region is Jan T. Gross, *Revolution from Abroad: The Soviet Conquest of Poland's Western Ukraine and Western Belorussia* (Princeton, N.J.: Princeton University Press, 1988).

21. Yekelchyk, *Stalin's Empire of Memory*, p. 24.

22. Konstiantyn Kondratiuk, "Politychni, sotsialno-ekonomichni i dukhovni aspekty 'radianyzatsii' zakhidnykh oblastei Ukrainy u 1939–1941 rr.," in Kondratiuk, *1939 rik v istorychnii doli Ukrainy i ukraintsiv*, p. 26.

23. TsDAHO, Fond 1, List 6, Case 564, Fol. 134; Fond 1, List 9, Case 70, Fol. 27.

24. Smolii, *Istoriia Ukrainy*, p. 337; Iurii Slyvka, ed., *Deportatsii: Zakhidni zemli Ukrainy kintsia 30-kh—pochatku 50-kh rr.* (Lviv: Instytut ukrainoznavstva NANU, 1999), vol. 1: 8, 11.

25. See Kubijovyč's own memoir: Volodymyr Kubiiovych, *Ukraintsi v Heneralnii Hubernii, 1939–1941: Istoriia Ukrainskoho Tsentralnoho Komitetu* (Chicago: Vydavnytstvo Mykoly Denysiuka, 1975).

Chapter 8

1. *Komunist*, November 15, 1939, p. 1.

2. These ideological transformations in Ukraine are discussed in Yekelchyk, *Stalin's Empire of Memory*, and, in the Soviet Union in general, in Brandenberger, *National Bolshevism*.

3. M. V. Koval, *Ukraina v Druhii svitovii i Velykii Vitchyznianii viinakh (1939–1945 rr.)* (Kyiv: Alternatyvy, 1999), p. 39.

4. G. F. Krivosheev, ed., *Grif sekretnosti sniat: poteri Vooruzhennykh Sil SSSR v voinakh, boevykh deistviiakh i voennykh konfliktakh* (Moscow: Voenizdat, 1993), pp. 166–167; and Alexander Dallin, *German Rule in Russia, 1941–1945: A Study of Occupation Policies* (New York: St. Martin's, 1957), p. 69, note 1.

5. The exact number was 3,184,726. In 1944 and 1945, another 4.5 million Ukrainian citizens joined the Red Army. See Ivan Drobot, Volodymyr Kucher, Anatolii Sliusarenko, and Petro Cherneha, *Ukrainskyi narod u Druhii svitovii viini* (Kyiv: Shkoliar, 1998), pp. 219–220.

6. Bilas, *Represyvno-karalna systema*, 2: 267–271.

7. Karel C. Berkhoff, *Harvest of Despair: Life and Death in Ukraine under Nazi Rule* (Cambridge, Mass.: Belknap Press of Harvard University Press, 2004), pp. 22–23 and 30–32.

8. See, most recently, Rudolf A. Mark, "The Ukrainians as Seen by Hitler, Rosenberg and Koch," in Taras Hunczak and Dmytro Shtohryn, eds., *Ukraine: The Challenges of World War II* (Lanham, Md.: University Press of America, 2003), pp. 23–36.

9. Dallin, *German Rule in Russia*, pp. 56–57.

10. See Mark Kupovetsky, "Osoblyvosti etnodemohrafichnoho rozvytku ievreiskoho naselennia Ukrainy v druhii polovyni XX stolittia," *Filosofska i sotsiolohichna dumka*, nos. 5–6 (1994): 166; Feliks Levitas, *Yevrei Ukrainy v roky Druhoi Svitovoi viiny* (Kyiv: Vyrii, 1997), pp. 266–267; and Leonid Finberg and Volodymyr Liubchenko, eds., *Narysy z istorii ta kultury ievreiv Ukrainy* (Kyiv: Dukh i litera, 2005), p. 182.

11. *Kievskie vedomosti*, September 25, 2004, p. 2.

12. See Aharon Weiss, "Jewish-Ukrainian Relations in Western Ukraine during the Holocaust," in Peter J. Potichnyj and Howard Aster, eds., *Ukrainian-Jewish*

Relations in Historical Perspective (Edmonton: Canadian Institute of Ukrainian Studies Press, 1988), p. 417. Sheptytsky died in 1944. The primary reasons for his not having been honored as "Righteous Gentile" are the welcome he extended to the German army in 1941 and his endorsement of the recruitment drive for the SS Galicia Division in 1943.

13. B. M. Petrov, "Shcho robyly Hitler i Mussolini v Umani u serpni 1941 r.?" *Ukrainskyi istorychnyi zhurnal*, no. 1 (1994): 82–87.

14. Berkhoff, *Harvest of Despair*, p. 133. See also Mykola Slobodianiuk, "Seliany Ukrainy pid natsystskym okupatsiinym rezhymom, 1941–1944," *Kyivska starovyna*, no. 2 (2000): 44–57.

15. This number sums up deportations to Germany from the entire present-day territory of Ukraine. A 1945 archival source, which refers to Ukraine in its prewar borders, gives the number of 2,145,500. See TsDAHO, Fond 1, List 23, Case 1479, Fol. 2.

16. See two new Ukrainian studies of Nazi policies in Galicia and Bukovyna: Andrii Bolianovsky, "Sotsialnyi aspekt hitlerivskoho 'novoho poriadku' v Halychyni u 1941–1944 rokakh," *Visnyk Lvivskoho universytetu: Seriia istorychna*, no. 33 (1998): 186–194; and Arsen Zinchenko, "Rumunskyi okupatsiinyi rezhym u Podnistrovi v roky Druhoi svitovoi viiny," *Kyivska starovyna*, no. 2 (2000): 116–134.

17. New Ukrainian publications on this episode and in general on the relations between the OUN and the German administration include Stanislav Kulchytsky, "Lviv, 30 chervnia 1941 roku," *Kyivska starovyna*, no. 2 (2000): 32–44; and Andrii Bolianovsky, "Nimetska okupatsiina administratsiia i natsionalnyi rukh oporu Ukrainy u 1941–1944 rokakh," *Zapysky NTSh* 238 (1999): 348–381.

18. See Amir Weiner, *Making Sense of War: The Second World War and the Fate of the Bolshevik Revolution* (Princeton, N.J.: Princeton University Press, 2001), chapter 5; and Brown, *A Biography of No Place*, chapter 8.

19. Volodymyr Kubiiovych, *Meni 70* (Paris: Vydavnytstvo NTSh, 1970), p. 57.

20. Oleh Shablii, *Volodymyr Kubiiovych: Entsyklopediia zhyttia i tvorennia* (Lviv: Feniks, 1996), pp. 112 and 115.

21. Myroslav Yurkevich, "Galician Ukrainians in German Military Formations and in the German Administration," in Yuri Boshyk, ed., *Ukraine during World War II: History and Its Aftermath* (Edmonton: Canadian Institute of Ukrainian Studies Press, 1986), p. 76.

22. The most recent, archival-based Ukrainian work on the Galicia Division and other Ukrainian military formations in the German army is Andrii Bolianovsky, *Ukrainski viiskovi formuvannia v zbroinykh sylakh Nimechchyny, 1939–1945* (Lviv: LNU im. I. Franka, 2003).

23. See I. I. Iliushyn, *Volynska trahediia 1943–1944 rr.* (Kyiv: Instytut istorii Ukrainy NANU and Kyivskyi slavistychnyi universytet, 2003), pp. 167, 191–194, and 221–222.

24. Koval, *Ukraina v Druhii svitovii i Velykii Vitchyznianii viinakh*, pp. 270–271. In 1948, the still-incomplete name count stood at 136,668 partisans and 21,342 "underground fighters" (*Holos Ukrainy*, 23 May 1995, 13).

25. See *Radianska Ukraina*, October 15, 1944, pp. 1–2.

26. See V. A. Hrynevych, "Utvorennia Narkomatu oborony URSR u 1944 r.: z istorii odniiei politychnoi hry," *Ukrainskyi istorychnyi zhurnal*, no. 5 (1991): 29–37; and V. A. Hrynevych, "Utvorennia Narodnoho komisariatu zakordonnykh sprav Ukrainskoi RSR: proekty i realii (1944–1945 rr.)," *Ukrainskyi istorychnyi zhurnal*, no. 3 (1995): 35–46.

27. See O. Ye. Lysenko, *Tserkovne zhyttia v Ukraini, 1943–1946* (Kyiv: Instytut istorii Ukrainy NANU, 1998).

28. Bilas, *Represyvno-karalna systema*, 2: 314 and 549–570.

29. Ibid., pp. 604 and 608.

30. Marta Dyczok, *The Grand Alliance and Ukrainian Refugees* (New York: St. Martin's, 2000), p. 136.

31. O. V. Butsko, *Ukraina-Polsha: migratsionnye protsessy 40–kh godov* (Kyiv: Institut istorii Ukrainy NANU, 1997), pp. 61 and 69.

32. Ihor Vynnychenko, *Ukraina 1920–1980–kh: deportatsii, zaslannia, vyslannia* (Kyiv: Rada, 1994), p. 82.

33. See Jeffrey Burds, *The Early Cold War in Soviet West Ukraine, 1944–1948*, The Carl Beck Papers in Russian & East European Studies, no. 1505 (Pittsburgh: Center for Russian and East European Studies, University of Pittsburgh, 2001).

34. See a new Polish study: Roman Drozd, *Polityka władz wobec ludności ukraińskiej w Polsce w latach 1944–1989* (Warsaw: TYRSA, 2001).

35. See Bohdan R. Bociurkiw, *The Ukrainian Greek Catholic Church and the Soviet State (1939–1950)* (Edmonton: Canadian Institute of Ukrainian Studies Press, 1996).

36. Scholars attribute the delay with collectivization to Soviet concern with security in the countryside. See David R. Marples, *Stalinism in Ukraine in the 1940s* (Edmonton: University of Alberta Press, 1992), pp. 88–90.

37. Roman Szporluk, "The Soviet West—or Far Eastern Europe?" in his *Russia, Ukraine, and the Breakup of the Soviet Union* (Stanford, Calif.: Hoover Institution Press, 2000), p. 267.

38. N. S. Khrushchev, *The "Secret" Speech* (Nottingham: Bertrand Russell Peace Foundation, 1976), p. 58.

39. See V. A. Smolii, ed., *Holod v Ukraini 1946–1947: dokumenty i materialy* (Kyiv: Vydavnytstvo M. P. Kots, 1996), p. 13.

40. Serhy Yekelchyk, "Celebrating the Soviet Present: The *Zhdanovshchina* Campaign in Ukrainian Literature and the Arts," in Donald J. Raleigh, ed., *Provincial Landscapes: Local Dimensions of Soviet Power, 1917–1953* (Pittsburgh: University of Pittsburgh Press, 2001), pp. 255–275.

41. Amir Weiner, "The Making of a Dominant Myth: The Second World War and the Construction of Political Identities within the Soviet Polity," *Russian Review* 55, no. 4 (1996): 638–660.

42. Krawchenko, *Social Change*, p. 243.

43. One recent Ukrainian study speaks of 5.5 million civilians and 2.5 million soldiers (Drobot et al., *Ukrainskyi narod u Druhii svitovii viini*, 227). A 2002 TV

report referred to new research indicating an estimate of 8.5 million: 5 million civilian victims and 3.5 million soldiers (ICTV Fakty news program, Ukrainian television, May 9, 2002). In the summer of 2003, scholars working on two multivolume projects, *Ukraine's Book of Remembrance* and *Ukraine's Book of Sorrow*, announced that these book series will contain the names of 4.5 million civilians and 6 million soldiers who perished during World War II (*Segodnia*, June 21, 2003, p. 2).

Chapter 9

1. On Kyrychenko, see D. V. Tabachnyk and Yu. I. Shapoval, *O. I. Kyrychenko: Shtrykhy do politychnoho portretu pershoho sekretaria TsK Kompartii Ukrainy v 1953–1957 rr.* (Kyiv: Instytut istorii AN URSR, 1990). The previous ethnic Ukrainian party leader in Ukraine was Dmytro Manuilsky, but in the early 1920s, this position was relatively unimportant.
2. On the history of this ideological document, see Yekelchyk, *Stalin's Empire of Memory*, pp. 154–156.
3. V. K. Baran and V. M. Danylenko, *Ukraina v umovakh systemnoi kryzy (1946–1980-ti rr.)* (Kyiv: Alternatyvy, 1999), p. 82.
4. On Pidhorny, see V. L. Saveliev, "Storinky politychnoi biohrafii M. V. Pidhornoho," *Ukrainskyi istorychnyi zhurnal*, no. 1 (1991): 78–86.
5. The Canadian sociologist Bohdan Krawchenko originally advanced this thesis in his *Social Change and National Consciousness in Twentieth-Century Ukraine* (London: Macmillan, 1985), chapter 5, but it has since migrated to Ukrainian scholarship. See, for instance, V. K. Baran, "Ukraina v dobu Khrushchova," in Kuras, *Politychna istoriia Ukrainy*, 6: 105.
6. V. Prystaiko, "Yak pochynalas reabilitatsiia," in S. V. Kulchytsky, ed., *Pochatok destalinizatsii v Ukraini (do 40-richchia zakrytoi dopovidi M. Khrushchova na XX zizdi KPRS)* (Kyiv: Instytut istorii Ukrainy NANU, 1997), pp. 67 and 72.
7. Baran, "Ukraina v dobu Khrushchova," pp. 133–136; Amir Weiner, "The Empires Pay a Visit: Gulag Returnees, East European Rebellions, and the Soviet Frontier Politics," *Journal of Modern History* 78 (2006): 333–376.
8. Baran and Danylenko, *Ukraina v umovakh*, p. 85.
9. Volodymyr Baran, *Ukraina 1950–1960-kh rr.: evoliutsiia totalitarnoi systemy* (Lviv: Instytut ukrainoznavstva in I. Krypiakevycha, NANU, 1996), pp. 196–197.
10. Baran, "Ukraina v dobu Khrushchova," p. 151.
11. Derzhavnyi arkhiv Kyivskoi oblasti (State Archive of Kyiv Province, hereafter DAKO), Fond P-5, List 6, Case 248.
12. Baran, *Ukraina 1950–1960-kh rr.*, pp. 182–183.
13. Shelest's interviews of 1989 and 1990 are conveniently reprinted in Yurii Shapoval, ed., *Petro Shelest: "Spravzhnii sud istorii shche poperedu": spohady, shchodennyky, dokumenty, materialy* (Kyiv: Heneza, 2004), pp. 635–703. See also Shelest's memoirs (in Russian!): P. E. Shelest, *"Da ne sudimy budete": Dnevnikovye zapisi, vospominaniia chlena Politbiuro TsK KPSS* (Moscow: Original, 1995).

14. Contemporary Western works on Shelest include Yaroslav Bilinsky, "Mykola Skrypnyk and Petro Shelest: An Essay on the Persistence and Limits of Ukrainian National Communism," in Jeremy R. Azrael, ed., *Soviet Nationality Policies and Practices* (New York: Praeger, 1978), pp. 105–143; Jaroslaw Pelenski, "Shelest and His Period in Soviet Ukraine (1963–1972): A Revival of Controlled Ukrainian Autonomism," in Peter J. Potichnyj, ed., *Ukraine in the 1970s* (Oakville, Ont.: Mosaic Press, 1975), pp. 283–305; and Lowell Tillett, "Ukrainian Nationalism and the Fall of Shelest," *Slavic Review* 34, no. 4 (1975): 752–768. More recent treatments are found in Taras Kuzio and Andrew Wilson, *Ukraine: Perestroika to Independence* (Edmonton: Canadian Institute of Ukrainian Studies Press, 1994), pp. 44–47; Bohdan Nahailo, *The Ukrainian Resurgence* (Toronto: University of Toronto Press, 1999), pp. 26–38; and Andrew Wilson, *Ukrainian Nationalism in the 1990s: A Minority Faith* (Cambridge: Cambridge University Press, 1997), pp. 98–99.

15. A representative selection of archival documents related to Shelest's policies is in Shapoval, *Petro Shelest: "Spravzhnii sud istorii shche poperedu,"* pp. 427–626. Also, this collection features an insightful introduction by Yurii Shapoval, "Petro Shelest u konteksti politychnoi istorii Ukrainy XX stolittia," pp. 5–20.

16. Krawchenko, *Social Change*, pp. 246–248.

17. Viktor Haman, *Korydory TsK: Deshcho iz zapysnykiv 1968–1972 rokiv ta piznishykh dopovnen* (Kyiv: Ukrainskyi pysmennyk and Vyr, 1997), pp. 4 and 345.

18. *Naspravdi bulo tak: Interviu Yuriia Zaitseva z Ivanom Dziuboiu* (Lviv: Instytut ukrainoznavstva im. I. Krypiakevycha, 2001), p. 68.

19. *Kievskie vedomosti*, September 27, 2004, p. 21.

20. See especially Tillett, "Ukrainian Nationalism and the Fall of Shelest."

21. See S. V. Kulchytsky, "Novitnia istoriia Ukrainy," *Ukrainskyi istorychnyi zhurnal*, no. 10 (1991): 4; and *Den*, June 7, 2003, p. 7.

22. A good biography of Shcherbytsky remains to be written. Dmytro Tabachnyk has published a helpful short biographical essay, which, however, does not use any archival sources: "'Apostol zastoiu': Eskiz do politychnoho portreta Volodymyra Shcherbytskoho," *Vitchyzna*, no. 9 (1992): 159–163; no. 10 (1992): 107–113; no. 11 (1992): 119–123.

23. Baran and Danylenko, *Ukraina v umovakh*, p. 75.

24. Petro Tronko, "V. V. Shcherbytsky (1918–1990)," in V. F. Vozianov, ed., *Zirky i terny doli: Volodymyr Shcherbytsky: Spohady suchasnykiv* (Kyiv: In Iure, 2003), p. 22. Balanced evaluations of Shcherbytsky are very rare in present-day Ukrainian history surveys. One exception is V. O. Kotyhorenko, V. P. Andrushchenko, V. H. Kremen, O. V. Lisnychuk, and V. M. Nahirny, "'Rozvynutyi sotsializm' v Ukraini," in Kuras, *Politychna istoriia*, 6: 225–227.

25. See P. T. Tronko, O. H. Bazhan, and Yu. Z. Danyliuk, eds., *Ternystym shliakhom do khramu: Oles Honchar v suspilno-politychnomu zhytti Ukrainy: 60–80-ti rr. XX st.* (Kyiv: Ridnyi krai, 1999), p. 84. There also exists a helpful journalistic account of the *Cathedral* affair: Vitalii Koval, *"Sobor" i navkolo soboru* (Kyiv: Molod, 1989).

26. Heorhii Kasianov, *Nezhodni: Ukrainska intelihentsiia v rusi oporu 1960–80-kh rokiv* (Kyiv: Lybid, 1995), pp. 88–90.

27. This book is available in an English translation: Ivan Dziuba, *Internationalism or Russification? A Study in the Soviet Nationalities Problem* (New York: Monad Press, 1974).

28. See Levko Lukianenko, *Ne dam zahynut Ukraini!* (Kyiv: Sofiia, 1994), pp. 8–35; Anatolii Rusnachenko, *Natsionalno-vyzvolnyi rukh v Ukraini: Seredyna 1950-kh-pochatok 1990-kh rokiv* (Kyiv: Vydavnytstvo im. Oleny Telihy, 1998), pp. 92–97. Given its membership, this organization was known more appropriately in the West as the "Jurists' Group."

29. A. M. Rusnachenko, "Ukrainskyi natsionalnyi front–pidpilna hrupa 1960-kh rr.," *Ukrainskyi istorychnyi zhurnal*, no. 4 (1997): 81–94.

30. Kasianov, *Nezhodni*, pp. 70–72 (events of 1967); Baran, *Ukraina 1950–1960-kh rr.*, pp. 408–409 (Kyivan Spring 1973).

31. See Yu. O. Kurnosov, *Inakomyslennia v Ukraini (60-ti-persha polovyna 80-kh rr. XX st.)* (Kyiv: Instytut istorii Ukrainy NANU, 1994), pp. 186–215.

32. Vasyl Ovsiienko, ""Pravozakhysnyi rukh v Ukraini (seredyna 1950-kh–1980-i roky," in Ye. Yu. Zakharov, ed., *Ukrainska Hromadska Hrupa spryiannia vykonanniu Helsinkskykh uhod* (Kharkiv: Folio, 2001), vol. 1: 31.

33. I. P. Merkatun, "Antyrelihiina kampaniia 50–60-kh rokiv na Ukraini," *Ukrainskyi istorychnyi zhurnal*, no. 10 (1991): 75; Nataliia Shlikhta, "Tserkva za umov khrushchovskoi antyrelihiinoi kampanii," *Ukraina moderna*, nos. 4–5 (1999–2000): 255.

34. Kuzio and Wilson, *Ukraine: Perestroika to Independence*, pp. 61–62.

35. Krawchenko, *Social Change*, pp. 250–251.

36. See V. I. Dmytruk, *Reaktsiia ukrainskoho suspilstva na podii 1968 r. v Chekhoslovachchyni: Avtoreferat* (Kharkiv: Kharkivskyi natsionalnyi universytet im. V. N. Karazina, 2000); Amir Weiner, "Déjà vu All Over Again: Prague Spring, Romanian Summer, and Soviet Autumn on Russia's Western Frontier," *Contemporary European History* 15 (May 2006): 159–194.

37. See Volodymyr Baran, *Ukraina: novitnia istoriia (1945–1991 rr.)* (Lviv: Instytut ukrainoznavstva in. I. Krypiakevycha NANU, 2003), pp. 237–254.

38. Ibid., p. 318.

39. P. P. Panchenko, "Deformatsii v rozvytku ukrainskoho sela u 80-kh–na pochatku 90-kh rokiv," *Ukrainskyi istorychnyi zhurnal*, no. 1 (1992): 23.

40. Data from the late 1960s show that 31 percent of meat, 29 percent of milk, 50 percent of eggs and potatoes, 35 percent of fruits, and 24 percent of vegetables produced in the republic came from peasants' individual plots. See Baran, *Ukraina 1950–1960-kh rr.*, p. 165.

41. Baran and Danylenko, *Ukraina v umovakh*, p. 92.

42. L. V. Kovpak, *Sotsialno-pobutovi umovy zhyttia naselennia Ukrainy v druhii polovyni XX st. (1945–2000 rr.)* (Kyiv: Instytut istorii Ukrainy NANU, 2003), pp. 59 (household appliances) and 61 (housing wait-list).

43. DAKO, Fond P-1, List 22, Case 452, Fol. 82–86.

44. Simplistic interpretations of the 1959 law have now passed from Western works into Ukrainian textbooks, which is even more astonishing because surely at least some of their authors attended Russian schools and studied the Ukrainian lan-

guage and literature. The only children exempted from taking Ukrainian were those moving into the republic after starting school elsewhere in the USSR. For an excellent, if largely neglected by textbook writers, Western account of this law and its implications, see Krawchenko, *Social Change*, pp. 231–236.

45. V. Vrublevsky, *Vladimir Shcherbitsky: pravda i vymysly. Zapiski pomoshchnika* (Kyiv: Dovira, 1993), p. 130.

46. Rusnachenko, *Natsionalno-vyzvolnyi rukh*, pp. 46–53.

47. V. O. Kotyhorenko, V. P. Andrushchenko, V. H. Kremen, O. V. Lisnychuk, and V. M. Nahirnyi, "'Rozvynutyi sotsializm' v Ukraini," in Kuras, *Politychna istoriia Ukrainy*, 6: 310 and 313.

48. Wilson, *Ukrainian Nationalism*, p. 22, with reference to research by the Ukrainian sociologist Valerii Khmelko.

49. Recently, there has been renewed scholarly interest in Ukraine in the "poetical school" and Mykolaichuk's career. See L. I. Briukhovetska, *Ivan Mykolaichuk* (Kyiv: Kino-Teatr and KM Akademiia, 2004) and L. I. Briukhovetska, ed., *Poetychne kino: zaboronena shkola* (Kyiv: Kino-Teatr, 2001).

50. Soviet Ukrainian mass culture remains an understudied subject. There is a helpful, but uneven, collection of articles in Ukrainian: Oleksandr Hrytsenko, ed., *Narysy ukrainskoi populiarnoi kultury* (Kyiv: Ukrainskyi tsentr kulturnykh doslidzhen, 1998).

51. "The nominal statehood of the Ukrainian SSR is, in terms of contemporary political reality, a sheer myth manipulated to the advantage of the rulers. But a myth which has entered the consciousness of the people becomes a latent force. The clever manipulators may well find themselves someday in the position of the sorcerer's apprentice, unable to master the genie whom they have conjured" (Rudnytsky, "Soviet Ukraine in Historical Perspective," p. 467. This essay was originally published in 1972.)

Chapter 10

1. On the Soviet efforts to control the nationalities issue by granting the republics "empty" forms of nationhood, and the ultimate failure of this project, see Ronald Grigor Suny, *The Revenge of the Past: Nationalism, Revolution, and the Collapse of the Soviet Union* (Stanford, Calif.: Stanford University Press, 1993).

2. Bohdan Nahailo, *The Ukrainian Resurgence* (Toronto: University of Toronto Press, 1999), p. 53.

3. The last prison sentence for "anti-Soviet agitation" was handed down in Ukraine as late as December 1986. See Yurii Danyliuk and Oleh Bazhan, *Opozytsiia v Ukraini (druha polovyna 50-kh–80-ti rr. XX st.)* (Kyiv: Ridnyi krai, 2000), pp. 213–214.

4. See Oleksandr Boiko, *Ukraina u 1985–1991 rr.: Osnovni tendentsii suspilno-politychnoho rozvytku* (Kyiv: Instytut politolohiii i etnonatsionalnykh doslidzhen NANU, 2002), pp. 23–24.

5. Smolii, *Istoriia Ukrainy*, p. 387. Stephen Kotkin has made an argument about the unreformability of Soviet heavy industry in his *Armageddon Averted: The Soviet Collapse, 1970–2000* (Oxford: Oxford University Press, 2001).

6. Baran and Danylenko, *Ukraina v umovakh.*

7. Vrublevsky, *Vladimir Shcherbitsky*, pp. 210–211.

8. M. I. Omelianets, S. S. Kartashova, and V. F. Torbin, "Medyko-demohrafichni naslidky," in V. H. Bariakhtar, ed., *Chornobylska katastrofa* (Kyiv: Naukova dumka, 1996), p. 436.

9. For the best introduction in English to the Chernobyl catastrophe and its immediate consequences, see David R. Marples, *Chernobyl and the Nuclear Power in the USSR* (London: Macmillan, 1986) and idem, *The Social Impact of the Chernobyl Disaster* (New York: St. Martin's, 1988).

10. Leonid Kravchuk, "Shcherbytskyi buv liudynoiu volovoiu, z sylnym, zahartovanym kharakterom," in Vozianov, *Zirky i terny doli*, pp. 70–71.

11. O. V. Haran, *Ubyty drakona: Z istorii Rukhu ta novykh partii Ukrainy* (Kyiv: Lybid, 1993), p. 27.

12. Boiko, *Ukraina u 1985–1991 rr.*, pp. 69–71.

13. See David R. Marples, *Ukraine under Perestroika: Ecology, Economics and the Workers' Revolt* (New York: St. Martin's, 1991), and Anatolii Rusnachenko, *Probudzhennia: robitnychyi rukh na Ukraini v 1989–1993 rr.* (Kyiv: Vydavnychyi dim "KM Academia," 1995).

14. O. D. Boiko and V. M. Lytvyn, "Nove myslennia," in Kuras, *Politychna istoriia Ukrainy*, 6: 377 and 395.

15. This number is a police estimate. Some Rukh activists cited a much higher number, up to 5 million participants. See Haran, *Ubyty drakona*, p. 81. The distance between Kyiv and Lviv is about 300 miles.

16. Volodymyr Lytvyn, *Politychna arena Ukrainy: diiovi osoby ta vykonavtsi* (Kyiv: Abrys, 1994), pp. 139–141.

17. Lytvyn, *Politychna arena Ukrainy*, p. 223.

18. Boiko, *Ukraina u 1985–1991 rr.*, p. 147.

19. Leonid Kravchuk, *Maiemo te, shcho maiemo: Spohady i rozdumy* (Kyiv: Stolittia, 2002), p. 56.

20. Wilson, *Ukrainian Nationalism*, p. 107.

21. See Kuzio and Wilson, *Ukraine: Perestroika to Independence*, pp. 152–156.

22. Boiko, *Ukraina u 1985–1991 rr.*, p. 217.

23. Wilson, *Ukrainian Nationalism*, p. 67.

24. M. R. Pliushch, "Zminy v materialnykh osnovakh suspilstva," in P. P. Panchenko, ed., *Ukraina: druha polovyna XX st.: Narysy istorii* (Kyiv: Lybid, 1997), p. 286.

25. Smolii, *Istoriia Ukrainy*, p. 393.

26. Wilson, *Ukrainian Nationalism*, pp. 125–126.

27. Nahailo, *The Ukrainian Resurgence*, p. 369.

28. Ibid., p. 391.

Chapter 11

1. On this omission in much of "transitological" literature, see Valerie Bunce, "Should Transitologists Be Grounded?" *Slavic Review* 54 (Spring 1995): 117–127 and Taras Kuzio, "Ukraine: A Four-Pronged Transition," in Kuzio, ed., *Contem-*

porary Ukraine: Dynamics of Post-Soviet Transformation (Armonk, N.Y.: M. E. Sharpe, 1998), pp. 165–180.

2. See Szporluk, *Russia, Ukraine, and the Breakup of the Soviet Union*, esp. pp. 319–342.

3. S. V. Kulchytsky, "Utverdzhennia nezalezhnoi Ukrainy: pershe desiatylittia," *Ukrainskyi istorychnyi zhurnal*, no. 3 (2001): 51–52.

4. "Nuclear Weapons," in Zenon E. Kohut, Bohdan Y. Nebesio, and Myroslav Yurkevich, *Historical Dictionary of Ukraine* (Lanham, Md.: Scarecrow Press, 2005), pp. 385–386.

5. Zbigniew Brzezinski, "The Premature Partnership," *Foreign Affairs* 73, no. 2 (1994): 80.

6. F. M. Rudych, "Heopolitychnyi vymir Ukrainy," in Kuras, *Politychna istoriia Ukrainy*, 6: 650.

7. O. D. Boiko, *Istoriia Ukrainy*, 2nd ed. (Kyiv: Akademvydav, 2004), p. 569.

8. Wilson, *Ukrainian Nationalism*, pp. 112–113.

9. See Ilya Prizel, "Ukraine's Hollow Decade," in Yitzhak Brudny, Jonathan Frankel, and Stefani Hoffman, eds., *Restructuring Post-Communist Russia* (New York: Cambridge University Press, 2004), pp. 102–105; Paul D'Anieri, Robert Kravchuk, and Taras Kuzio, *Politics and Society in Ukraine* (Boulder, Colo.: Westview Press, 1999), pp. 188–192.

10. Wilson, *The Ukrainians*, p. 257.

11. Anders Åslund, "Why Has Ukraine Failed?" in Anders Åslund and Georges De Menil, eds., *Economic Reform in Ukraine: The Unfinished Agenda* (Armonk, N.Y.: M. E. Sharpe, 2000), p. 265.

12. O. P. Derhachov, "Formuvannia hromadianskoho suspilstva," in Kuras, *Politychna istoriia Ukrainy*, 6: 542; O. Kyselova, "Bidnist v Ukraini," *Politychna dumka*, no. 3 (1990): 5.

13. Nahailo, *The Ukrainian Resurgence*, p. 455.

14. Bohdan Harasymiw, *Post-Communist Ukraine* (Edmonton: Canadian Institute of Ukrainian Studies Press, 2002), p. 164.

15. Wilson, *Ukrainian Nationalism*, pp. 110–111.

16. For arguments for and against seeing Kravchuk's Ukraine as a "nationalizing state," see Dominique Arel, "Ukraine: The Temptations of the Nationalizing State," in Vladimir Tismaneanu, ed., *Political Culture and Civil Society in the Former Soviet Union* (Armonk, N.Y.: M. E. Sharpe, 1995), pp. 157–188; and Taras Kuzio, "Nation Building or Nationalizing State? A Survey of the Theoretical Literature and Empirical Evidence," *Nations and Nationalism* 7 (April 2001): 135–154.

17. Another factor fanning the flames of separatism was the mass return of the Crimean Tatars, some 250,000 by the end of 1993, to their ancestral homeland and the resulting tensions over land possession. See O. M. Maiboroda, "Natsiotvorennia," in Kuras, *Politychna istoriia* 6: 578–579.

18. Sarah Birch, *Elections and Democratization in Ukraine* (New York: St. Martin's, 2000), p. 84.

19. Smolii, *Istoriia Ukrainy*, p. 419.
20. See Taras Kuzio, *Ukraine under Kuchma: Political Reform, Economic Transformation and Security Policy in Independent Ukraine* (New York: St. Martin's, 1997), pp. 138–142.
21. "Lazarenko, Pavlo," in Zenon E. Kohut, Bohdan Y. Nebesio, and Myroslav Yurkevich, *Historical Dictionary of Ukraine* (Lanham, Md.: Scarecrow Press, 2005), pp. 305–307; Andrew Wilson, *Ukraine's Orange Revolution* (New Haven, Conn.: Yale University Press, 2005), pp. 39–40.
22. *KP v Ukraine*, September 29, 2004, p. 2.
23. Wilson, *The Ukrainians*, p. 262.
24. Robert S. Kravchuk, "Kuchma as Economic Reformer," *Problems of Post-Communism* 52, no. 5 (2005): 51.
25. Birch, *Elections*, p. 106. On the proliferation in Ukraine of "fake" parties that were created to give oligarchs seats in the Rada, and thus immunity from prosecution, see Andrew Wilson, *Virtual Politics: Faking Democracy in the Post-Soviet World* (New Haven, Conn.: Yale University Press, 2005).
26. Anders Åslund, "Ukraine's Return to Economic Growth," *Post-Soviet Geography and Economics* 42, no. 5 (2001): 320.
27. Wilson, *Ukraine's Orange Revolution*, p. 53.
28. Lucan A. Way, "Kuchma's Failed Authoritarianism," *Journal of Democracy* 16 (April 2005): 137.
29. Bohdan Harasymiw, "Elections in Post-Communist Ukraine, 1994–2004: An Overview," *Canadian Slavonic Papers* 47 (September–December 2005): 202 and 230–231.
30. Anders Åslund, "The Economic Policy of Ukraine after the Orange Revolution," *Eurasian Geography and Economics* 46, no. 5 (2005): 328.
31. Wilson, *Ukraine's Orange Revolution*, p. 106.
32. Danylo Yanevsky, *Khronika "Pomaranchovoi" revoliutsii* (Kharkiv: Folio, 2005), pp. 212–213.
33. Dominik Arel [Dominique Arel], "Paradoksy Pomaranchevoi revoliutsii," *Krytyka* 9 (April 2005): 2–4.
34. The story first broke in a popular Internet news outlet, *Ukrainska Pravda*. See Serhii Leshchenko, "Andriy Yushchenko—A Son of the God?" *Ukrainska Pravda*, July 25, 2005 (available in English at http://www.pravda.com.ua/en/news/2005/7/25/686.htm).
35. Mara D. Bellaby, "Ukraine Signs Off on Gas Supply Deal" (Associated Press, February 2, 2005).
36. See the official Web site of the Central Electoral Commission (http://www.cvk.gov.ua/vnd2006/w6p001e.html).

Epilogue

1. Arel, "Paradoksy Pomaranchevoi revoliutsii," pp. 2–4.
2. Here I develop Yaroslav Hrytsak's suggestion made in his *Strasti za natsionalizmom: istorychni esei* (Kyiv: Krytyka, 2004), p. 225.

❖ Recommended Reading

General Works

Concise Encyclopaedia of Ukraine. 2 vols. Toronto: University of Toronto Press, 1963–1971.

Čyževs'kyj, Dmytro. *A History of Ukrainian Literature (From the 11th to the End of the 19th Century)*, trans. Dolly Ferguson, Doreen Gorlsine, and Ulana Petyk; ed. George S. N. Luckyj, 2nd ed. With an overview of the twentieth century by George S. N. Luckyj. New York: Ukrainian Academic Press, 1997.

Encyclopedia of Ukraine. 5 vols. Toronto: University of Toronto Press, 1984–2001.

Grabowicz, George G. *Toward a History of Ukrainian Literature*. Cambridge, Mass.: Harvard Ukrainian Research Institute, 1981.

Hann, Christopher, and Paul Robert Magocsi, eds. *Galicia: A Multicultured Land*. Toronto: University of Toronto Press, 2005.

Kappeler, Andreas, Zenon E. Kohut, Frank E. Sysyn, and Mark von Hagen, eds. *Culture, Nation, and Identity: The Ukrainian-Russian Encounter*. Edmonton: Canadian Institute of Ukrainian Studies Press, 2003.

Kohut, Zenon E., Bohdan Y. Nebesio, and Myroslav Yurkevich. *Historical Dictionary of Ukraine*. Lanham, Md.: Scarecrow Press, 2005.

Lindheim, Ralph, and George S. N. Luckyj, eds. *Towards an Intellectual History of Ukraine: An Anthology of Ukrainian Thought from 1710 to 1995*. Toronto: University of Toronto Press, 1996.

Magocsi, Paul R. *A History of Ukraine*. Toronto: University of Toronto Press, 1996.

———. *Ukraine: A Historical Atlas*, cartography by Geoffrey J. Matthews, rev. ed. Toronto: University of Toronto Press, 1985.

Potichnyj, Peter J., ed. *Poland and Ukraine, Past and Present*. Edmonton: Canadian Institute of Ukrainian Studies, 1980.

Potichnyj, Peter J., and Howard Aster, eds. *Ukrainian-Jewish Relations in Historical Perspective*, 2nd ed. Edmonton: Canadian Institute of Ukrainian Studies Press, 1990.

Potichnyj, Peter J., Mark Raeff, Jaroslaw Pelenski, and Gleb N. Žekulin, eds. *Ukraine and Russia in Their Historical Encounter*. Edmonton: Canadian Institute of Ukrainian Studies Press, 1992.

Reid, Anna. *Borderland: A Journey through the History of Ukraine*. London: Wiedenfeld & Nicolson, 1997.

Rudnytsky, Ivan L. *Essays in Modern Ukrainian History*. Edmonton: Canadian Institute of Ukrainian Studies Press, 1987.

Rudnytsky, Ivan L., ed. with the assistance of John-Paul Himka. *Rethinking Ukrainian History*. Edmonton: Canadian Institute of Ukrainian Studies Press, 1981.

Snyder, Timothy. *The Reconstruction of Nations: Poland, Ukraine, Lithuania, Belarus, 1569–1999*. New Haven, Conn.: Yale University Press, 2003.

Subtelny, Orest. *Ukraine: A History*, 3rd ed. Toronto: University of Toronto Press, 2000.

Szporluk, Roman. *Russia, Ukraine and the Breakup of the Soviet Union*. Stanford, Calif.: Hoover Institution Press, 2000.

———. *Ukraine, a Brief History*, 2nd expanded ed. Detroit, Mich.: Ukrainian Festival Committee, 1982.

Torke, Hans-Joachim, and John-Paul Himka, eds. *German-Ukrainian Relations in Historical Perspective*. Edmonton: Canadian Institute of Ukrainian Studies Press, 1994.

Wilson, Andrew. *The Ukrainians: Unexpected Nation*, 2nd ed. New Haven, Conn.: Yale University Press, 2002.

Wynar, Bohdan S., ed. *Independent Ukraine: A Bibliographic Guide to English-Language Publications, 1989–1999*. Englewood, Colo.: Ukrainian Academic Press, 2000.

———. *Ukraine: A Bibliographic Guide to English-Language Publications*. Englewood, Colo.: Ukrainian Academic Press, 1990.

Ukraine before 1800

Baron, Samuel H., and Nancy Shields Kollman, eds. *Religion and Culture in Early Modern Russia and Ukraine*. DeKalb: Northern Illinois University Press, 1997.

Basarab, John. *Pereiaslav 1654: A Historical Study*. Edmonton: Canadian Institute of Ukrainian Studies Press, 1982.

Fisher, Alan W. *The Russian Annexation of the Crimea, 1772–1783*. New York: Cambridge University Press, 1970.

Franklin, Simon, and Jonathan Shepard. *The Emergence of Rus, 750–1200*. London: Longman, 1996.

Frick, David. *Meletij Smotryc'kyj*. Cambridge, Mass.: Harvard Ukrainian Research Institute, 1995.

Gordon, Linda. *Cossack Rebellions: Social Turmoil in the Sixteenth-Century Ukraine*. Albany: State University of New York Press, 1983.

Gudziak, Borys A. *Crisis and Reform: The Kyivan Metropolitanate, the Patriarchate of Constantinople, and the Genesis of the Union of Brest*. Cambridge, Mass.: Harvard Ukrainian Research Institute, 1999.

Hrushevsky, Mykhailo. *History of Ukraine-Rus'*. Vols. 1, 7, 8, and 9. Edmonton: Canadian Institute of Ukrainian Studies Press, 1997–2005.

Kohut, Zenon E. *Russian Centralism and Ukrainian Autonomy: Imperial Absorption of the Hetmanate, 1760–1830s*. Cambridge, Mass.: Harvard University Press, 1988.

Pelenski, Jaroslaw. *The Contest for the Legacy of Kievan Rus'*. Boulder, Colo.: East European Monographs, 1998.

Plokhy, Serhii. *The Cossacks and Religion in Early Modern Ukraine*. New York: Oxford University Press, 2001.

———. *Tsars and Cossacks: A Study in Iconography*. Cambridge, Mass.: Harvard Ukrainian Research Institute, 2002.

Pritsak, Omeljan. *The Origin of Rus'*. Cambridge, Mass.: Harvard University Press, 1981.

Saunders, David. *The Ukrainian Impact on Russian Culture: 1750–1850*. Edmonton: Canadian Institute of Ukrainian Studies Press, 1985.

Senyk, Sophia. *History of the Church in Ukraine*. Vol. 1. Rome: Pontifical Oriental Institute, 1993.

Ševčenko, Ihor. *Ukraine between East and West: Essays on Cultural History to the Early Eighteenth Century*. Edmonton: Canadian Institute of Ukrainian Studies Press, 1996.

Subtelny, Orest. *The Mazepists: Ukrainian Separatism in the Early Eighteenth Century*. Boulder, Colo.: East European Monographs, 1981.

Sydorenko, Alexander. *The Kievan Academy in the Seventeenth Century*. Ottawa: University of Ottawa Press, 1977.

Sysyn, Frank E. *Between Poland and the Ukraine: The Dilemma of Adam Kysil, 1600–1653*. Cambridge, Mass.: Harvard Ukrainian Research Institute, 1985.

Velychenko, Stephen. *National History as Cultural Process: A Survey of the Interpretations of Ukraine's Past in Polish, Russian, and Ukrainian Historical Writing from the Earliest Times to 1914*. Edmonton: Canadian Institute of Ukrainian Studies Press, 1992.

Nineteenth-Century Ukraine

Friedgut, Theodore H. *Iuzovka and Revolution: Life and Work in Russia's Donbass, 1869–1924*. Princeton, N.J.: Princeton University Press, 1989.

Grabowicz, George G. *The Poet as Mythmaker: A Study of Symbolic Meaning in Taras Ševčenko*. Cambridge, Mass.: Harvard University Research Institute, 1982.

Hamm, Michael F. *Kiev: A Portrait, 1800–1917*. Princeton, N.J.: Princeton University Press, 1993.

Herlihy, Patricia. *Odessa: A History, 1794–1914*. Cambridge, Mass.: Harvard Ukrainian Research Institute, 1986.

Himka, John-Paul. *Galician Villagers and the Ukrainian National Movement in the Nineteenth Century*. Edmonton: Canadian Institute of Ukrainian Studies Press, 1988.

———. *Religion and Nationality in Western Ukraine: The Greek Catholic Church and the Ruthenian National Movement in Galicia, 1867–1900*. Montreal: McGill-Queen's University Press. 1999.

———. *Socialism in Galicia: The Emergence of Polish Social Democracy and Ukrainian Radicalism, 1860–1890*. Cambridge, Mass.: Harvard Ukrainian Research Institute, 1983.

Kozik, Jan. *The Ukrainian National Movement in Galicia, 1815–1849*. Edmonton: Canadian Institute of Ukrainian Studies Press, 1986.

Luckyj, George S. N. *Panteleimon Kulish: A Sketch of His Life and Times*. Boulder, Colo.: East European Monographs, 1983.

———. *Young Ukraine: The Brotherhood of Saints Cyril and Methodius in Kiev, 1845–1847*. Ottawa: University of Ottawa Press, 1991.

———. *Between Gogol and Ševčenko: Polarity in the Literary Ukraine: 1798–1847*. Munich: W. Fink, 1971.

Luckyj, George S. N. et al. *Shevchenko and the Critics, 1861–1980*. Toronto: University of Toronto Press, 1980.

Magocsi, Paul R. *The Shaping of a National Identity: Subcarpathian Rus', 1848–1948*. Cambridge, Mass.: Harvard University Press, 1978.

Markovits, Andrei S., and Frank E. Sysyn. *Nationbuilding and the Politics of Nationalism: Essays on Austrian Galicia*. Cambridge, Mass.: Harvard Ukrainian Research Institute, 1982.

Miller, Alexei. *The Ukrainian Question: Russian Nationalism in the 19th Century*. Budapest: Central European University Press, 2003.

Prymak, Thomas M. *Mykola Kostomarov: A Biography*. Toronto: University of Toronto Press, 1996.

Wexler, Paul. *Purism and Language: A Study in Modern Ukrainian and Belorussian Nationalism (1840–1967)*. Bloomington: Indiana University Press, 1974.

Wynn, Charters. *Workers, Strikes, and Pogroms: The Donbass-Dnepr Bend in Late Imperial Russia, 1870–1905*. Princeton, N.J.: Princeton University Press, 1992.

Zaitsev, Pavlo. *Taras Shevchenko: A Life*, trans. and ed. by George S. N. Luckyj. Toronto: University of Toronto Press, 1988.

Zipperstein, Steve Jeffrey. *The Jews of Odessa: A Cultural History, 1794–1871*. Stanford, Calif.: Stanford University Press, 1986.

Ukraine from 1900 to 1939

Abramson, Henry. *A Prayer for the Government: Jews and Ukrainians in Revolutionary times, 1917–1920*. Cambridge, Mass.: Harvard Ukrainian Research Institute, 1999.

Adams, Arthur E. *Bolsheviks in the Ukraine: the Second Campaign, 1918–1919*. New Haven, Conn.: Yale University Press, 1963.

Armstrong, John Alexander. *Ukrainian Nationalism*, 3rd ed. Englewood, Colo.: Ukrainian Academic Press, 1990.

Bohachevsky-Chomiak, Martha. *Feminists Despite Themselves: Women in Ukrainian Community Life, 1884–1939*. Edmonton: Canadian Institute of Ukrainian Studies, 1988.

Borys, Iurij. *The Sovietization of Ukraine, 1917–1923: The Communist Doctrine and Practice of National Self-Determination*. Edmonton: Canadian Institute of Ukrainian Studies Press, 1980.

Brown, Kate. *A Biography of No Place: From Ethnic Borderland to Soviet Heartland*. Cambridge, Mass.: Harvard University Press, 2004.

Commission on the Ukraine Famine. *Investigation of the Ukrainian Famine, 1932–1933. Report to Congress*, ed. James E. Mace and Leonid Heretz. Washington, D.C.: U.S. Government Printing Office, 1988.

Conquest, Robert. *The Harvest of Sorrow: Soviet Collectivization and the Terror-Famine*. New York: Oxford University Press, 1986.

Fedyshyn, Oleh S. *Germany's Drive to the East and the Ukrainian Revolution, 1917–1918*. New Brunswick, N.J.: Rutgers University Press, 1971.

Gross, Jan Tomasz. *Revolution from Abroad: The Soviet Conquest of Poland's Western Ukraine and Western Belorussia*, 2nd ed. Princeton, N.J.: Princeton University Press, 2002.

Hunczak, Taras, ed. *The Ukraine, 1917–1921: A Study in Revolution.* Cambridge, Mass.: Harvard Ukrainian Research Institute, 1977.

Kepley, Vance. *In the Service of the State: The Cinema of Alexander Dovzhenko.* Madison: University of Wisconsin Press, 1986.

Khvylovy, Mykola. *The Cultural Renaissance in Ukraine: Polemical Pamphlets, 1925–1926,* ed. by Myroslav Shkandrij. Edmonton: Canadian Institute of Ukrainian Studies Press, 1986.

Kostiuk, Hryhory. *Stalinist Rule in the Ukraine: A Study of the Decade of Mass Terror, 1929–39.* New York: Praeger, 1961.

Krawchenko, Bohdan. *Social Change and National Consciousness in Twentieth-Century Ukraine.* New York: St. Martin's, 1985.

Kuromiya, Hiroaki. *Freedom and Terror in the Donbas: A Ukrainian-Russian Borderland, 1870s–1990s.* Cambridge: Cambridge University Press, 1998.

Liber, George. *Soviet Nationality Policy, Urban Growth, and Identity Change in the Ukrainian SSR, 1923–1934.* Cambridge: Cambridge University Press, 1992.

Livezeanu, Irina. *Cultural Politics in Greater Romania: Regionalism, Nation Building & Ethnic Struggle, 1918–1930.* Ithaca, N.Y.: Cornell University Press, 1995.

Lohr, Eric. *Nationalizing the Russian Empire: The Campaign against Enemy Aliens during World War I.* Cambridge, Mass.: Harvard University Press, 2003.

Luckyj, George S. N. *Literary Politics in the Soviet Ukraine, 1917–1934,* 2nd ed. Durham, N.C.: Duke University Press, 1990.

Mace, James E. *Communism and the Dilemmas of National Liberation: National Communism in Soviet Ukraine, 1918–1933.* Cambridge, Mass.: Harvard Ukrainian Research Institute, 1983.

Mace, James E., and Leonid Heretz, eds. *Oral History Project of the Commission on the Ukraine Famine.* 3 vols. Washington, D.C: U.S. Government Printing Office, 1990.

Malet, Michael. *Nestor Makhno in the Russian Civil War.* London: Macmillan, 1982.

Martin, Terry. *The Affirmative Action Empire: Nations and Nationalism in the Soviet Union, 1923–1939.* Ithaca, N.Y.: Cornell University Press, 2001.

Motyl, Alexander J. *The Turn to the Right: The Ideological Origins and Development of Ukrainian Nationalism, 1919–1929.* Boulder, Colo.: East European Quarterly, 1980.

Palij, Michael. *The Anarchism of Nestor Makhno, 1918–1921: An Aspect of the Ukrainian Revolution.* Seattle: University of Washington Press, 1976.

Plokhy, Serhii. *Unmaking Imperial Russia: Mykhailo Hrushevsky and the Writing of Ukrainian History.* Toronto: University of Toronto Press, 2005.

Procyk, Anna. *Russian Nationalism and Ukraine: The Nationality Policy of the Volunteer Army during the Civil War.* Edmonton: Canadian Institute of Ukrainian Studies Press, 1995.

Prymak, Thomas M. *Mykhailo Hrushevsky: The Politics of National Culture.* Toronto: University of Toronto Press, 1987.

Radziejowski, Janusz. *The Communist Party of Western Ukraine, 1919–1929.* Edmonton: Canadian Institute of Ukrainian Studies Press, 1983.

Reshetar, John S. *The Ukrainian Revolution, 1917–1920: A Study in Nationalism.* Princeton, N.J.: Princeton University Press, 1952.

Serbyn, Roman, and Bohdan Krawchenko, eds. *Famine in Ukraine, 1932–1933.* Edmonton: Canadian Institute of Ukrainian Studies Press, 1986.

Shevelov, Yurii. *The Ukrainian Language in the First Half of the Twentieth Century (1900–1941): Its State and Status.* Cambridge, Mass.: Harvard Ukrainian Research Institute, 1989.

Shkandrij, Myroslav. *Modernists, Marxists and the Nation: The Ukrainian Literary Discussion of the 1920s.* Edmonton: Canadian Institute of Ukrainian Studies Press, 1992.

Snyder, Timothy. *Sketches from a Secret War: A Polish Artist's Mission to Liberate Soviet Ukraine.* New Haven, Conn.: Yale University Press, 2005.

Ukraine from 1939 to 1991

Berkhoff, Karel C. *Harvest of Despair: Life and Death in Ukraine under Nazi Rule.* Cambridge, Mass.: Harvard University Press, 2004.

Bilinsky, Yaroslav. *The Second Soviet Republic: The Ukraine after World War II.* New Brunswick, N.J.: Rutgers University Press, 1964.

Bilocerkowycz, Jaroslaw. *Soviet Ukrainian Dissent: A Study of Political Alienation.* Boulder, Colo.: Westview Press, 1988.

Bociurkiw, Bohdan R. *The Ukrainian Greek Catholic Church and the Soviet State, 1939–1950.* Edmonton: Canadian Institute of Ukrainian Studies Press, 1996.

Boshyk, Yuri, ed. *Ukraine during World War II: History and Its Aftermath: A Symposium.* Edmonton: Canadian Institute of Ukrainian Studies Press, 1986.

Chornovil, Viacheslav. *The Chornovil Papers.* New York: McGraw-Hill, 1968.

Dallin, Alexander. *German Rule in Russia, 1941–1945: A Study of Occupation Policies,* 2nd rev. ed. Boulder, Colo.: Westview Press, 1981.

Dougan, Andy. *Dynamo: Triumph and Tragedy in Nazi-Occupied Kiev.* Guilford, Conn.: Lyons Press, 2002.

Dyczok, Marta. *The Grand Alliance and Ukrainian Refugees.* New York: St. Martin's, 2000.

Dziuba, Ivan. *Internationalism or Russification? A Study in the Soviet Nationalities Problem,* 3rd ed. New York: Monad Press, 1974.

Farmer, Kenneth. *Ukrainian Nationalism in the Post-Stalin Era: Myth, Symbols, and Ideology in Soviet Nationalities Policy.* Hingham, Mass.: Martinus Nijhoff, 1980.

Kamenetsky, Ihor. *Hitler's Occupation of Ukraine, 1941–1944: A Study of Totalitarian Imperialism.* Milwaukee: Marquette University Press, 1956.

Koropeckyj, I. S. *Development in the Shadow: Studies in Ukrainian Economics.* Edmonton: Canadian Institute of Ukrainian Studies Press, 1990.

———. *The Ukrainian Economy: Achievements, Problems, Challenges.* Cambridge, Mass.: Harvard Ukrainian Research Institute, 1992.

Kosyk, Volodymyr. *The Third Reich and Ukraine.* New York: P. Lang, 1993.

Krawchenko, Bohdan, ed. *Ukraine after Shelest*. Edmonton: Canadian Institute of Ukrainian Studies Press, 1983.

Levytsky, Borys. *Politics and Society in Soviet Ukraine, 1953–1980*. Edmonton: Canadian Institute of Ukrainian Studies Press, 1984.

Lower, Wendy. *Nazi Empire-Building and the Holocaust in Ukraine*. Chapel Hill: University of North Carolina Press, 2005.

Marples, David R. *Chernobyl and Nuclear Power in the USSR*. Edmonton: Canadian Institute of Ukrainian Studies Press, 1986.

———. *Stalinism in Ukraine in the 1940s*. New York: St. Martin's, 1992.

———. *Ukraine under Perestroika: Ecology, Economics, and the Workers' Revolt*. New York: St. Martin's, 1991.

Redlich, Shimon. *Together and Apart in Brzezany: Poles, Jews, and Ukrainians, 1919–1945*. Bloomington: Indiana University Press, 2002.

Shumuk, Danylo. *Life Sentence: Memoirs of a Ukrainian Political Prisoner*. Edmonton: Canadian Institute of Ukrainian Studies Press, 1984.

Siegelbaum, Lewis H., and Daniel J. Walkowitz, eds. *Workers of the Donbass Speak: Survival and Identity in the New Ukraine, 1989–1992*. Albany: State University of New York Press, 1995.

Solchanyk, Roman, ed. *Ukraine from Chernobyl' to Sovereignty: A Collection of Interviews*. New York: St. Martin's, 1992.

Velychenko, Stephen. *Shaping Identity in Eastern Europe and Russia: Soviet and Polish Accounts of Ukrainian History, 1914–1991*. New York: St. Martin's, 1993.

Weiner, Amir. *Making Sense of War: The Second World War and the Fate of the Bolshevik Revolution*. Princeton, N.J.: Princeton University Press, 2001.

Yekelchyk, Serhy. *Stalin's Empire of Memory: Russian-Ukrainian Relations in the Soviet Historical Imagination*. Toronto: University of Toronto Press, 2004.

Ukraine since 1991

Åslund, Anders, and George De Menil. *Economic Reform in Ukraine: The Unfinished Agenda*. Armonk, N.Y.: M. E. Sharpe, 2000.

Banaian, King. *The Ukrainian Economy since Independence*. Northampton, Mass.: Edward Elgar, 1999.

Birch, Sarah. *Elections and Democratization in Ukraine*. New York: Macmillan Press, 2000.

D'Anieri, Paul J. *Economic Interdependence in Ukrainian-Russian Relations*. Albany: State University of New York Press, 1999.

D'Anieri, Paul J., Robert S. Kravchuk, and Taras Kuzio. *Politics and Society in Ukraine*. Boulder: Westview Press, 1999.

Dawson, Jane I. *Eco-Nationalism: Anti-Nuclear Activism and National Identity in Russia, Lithuania, and Ukraine*. Durham, N.C.: Duke University Press, 1996.

Garnett, Sherman W. *Keystone in the Arch: Ukraine in the Emerging Security Environment of Central and Eastern Europe*. Washington, D.C.: Carnegie Endowment for International Peace, 1997.

Isajiw, Wsevolod W., ed. *Society in Transition: Social Change in Ukraine in Western Perspectives*. Toronto: Canadian Scholars' Press, 2003.

Kravchuk, Robert S. *Ukrainian Political Economy: The First Ten Years*. New York: Palgrave Macmillan, 2002.

Kubicek, Paul. *Unbroken Ties: The State, Interest Associations, and Corporatism in Post-Soviet Ukraine*. Ann Arbor: University of Michigan Press, 2000.

Kuzio, Taras. *Ukraine: State and Nation Building*. New York: Routledge, 1998.

———. *Ukraine under Kuchma: Political Reform, Economic Transformation and Security Policy in Independent Ukraine*. New York: St. Martin's, 1997.

Kuzio, Taras, ed. *Contemporary Ukraine: Dynamics of Post-Soviet Transformation*. Armonk, N.Y.: M. E. Sharpe, 1998.

Kuzio, Taras, Robert S. Kravchuk, and Paul J. D'Anieri. *State and Institution-Building in Ukraine*. New York: St. Martin's, 1999.

Kuzio, Taras, and Andrew Wilson. *Ukraine: Perestroika to Independence*. New York: St. Martin's, 1994.

Molchanov, Mikhail A. *Political Culture and National Identity in Russian-Ukrainian Relations*. College Station: Texas A&M University Press, 2002.

Moroney, Jennifer D. P., Taras Kuzio, and M. Molchanov. *Ukrainian Foreign and Security Policy: Theoretical and Comparative Perspectives*. Westport, Conn.: Praeger, 2002.

Motyl, Alexander J. *Dilemmas of Independence: Ukraine after Totalitarianism*. New York: Council on Foreign Relations Press, 1993.

Nahaylo, Bohdan. *The Ukrainian Resurgence*. Toronto: University of Toronto Press, 1999.

Prizel, Ilya. *National Identity and Foreign Policy: Nationalism and Leadership in Poland, Russia and Ukraine*. Cambridge: Cambridge University Press, 1998.

Solchanyk, Roman. *Ukraine and Russia: The Post-Soviet Transition*. Lanham, Md.: Rowman & Littlefield, 2001.

Wanner, Catherine. *Burden of Dreams: History and Identity in Post-Soviet Ukraine*. University Park: Pennsylvania State University Press, 1998.

Wilson, Andrew. *Ukraine's Orange Revolution*. New Haven, Conn.: Yale University Press, 2005.

———. *Ukrainian Nationalism in the 1990s: A Minority Faith*. Cambridge: Cambridge University Press, 1996.

Wolchik, Sharon L., and Vladimir A. Zviglianich. *Ukraine: The Search for a National Identity*. Lanham, Md.: Rowman & Littlefield, 2000.

Wolchuk, Roman. *Ukraine's Foreign and Security Policy, 1991–2000*. New York: Routledge Curzon, 2003.

❖ Glossary

BYuT	Bloc of Yulia Tymoshenko
Cheka	Extraordinary Commission (first Soviet security police)
CP(B)U	Communist Party (Bolshevik) of Ukraine (before 1952)
CPSU	Communist Party of the Soviet Union
CPU	Communist Party of Ukraine (after 1952)
DP	displaced person
Einsatsgruppen	SS extermination units during World War II
EU	European Union
Gestapo	Nazi secret police, part of the SS
Hetman	Cossack military commander or head of the Cossack state
hryvnia	Ukrainian currency (since 1996)
IMF	International Monetary Fund
KGB	Committee on State Security (Soviet security police)
Komsomol	Young Communist League
KPZU	Communist Party of Western Ukraine
MTS	machine and tractor station
NATO	North Atlantic Treaty Organization
Natsiia	Ethnic nation
NEP	New Economic Policy
NGO	nongovernmental organization
NKVD	People's Commissariat of Internal Affairs (Soviet police)
Otaman(sha)	Cossack chieftain or guerilla band leader
OUN	Organization of Ukrainian Nationalists
OUN-B	Organization of Ukrainian Nationalists (Bandera faction)
OUN-M	Organization of Ukrainian Nationalists (Melnyk faction)
Politburo	Political Bureau, the elected ruling core of the Communist Party's Central Committee
POW	prisoner of war
Rada	council or legislative assembly
Rukh	"The Movement," a Ukrainian popular front
RUP	Revolutionary Ukrainian Party
samvydav	"self-publishing," underground dissident literature in Soviet Ukraine
Sejm	Polish parliament
SS	SS: *Schutzstaffel*, elite security and military corps in Nazi Germany
SSR	Soviet Socialist Republic

UAOC	Ukrainian Autocephalous Orthodox Church
UCC	Ukrainian Central Committee
UGCC	Ukrainian Greek Catholic Church
UHG	Ukrainian Helsinki Group
UNDO	Ukrainian National Democratic Union
UPA	Ukrainian Insurgent Army (*Ukrainska povstanska armiia*)
URDP	Ukrainian Radical Democratic Party
USSR	Union of Soviet Socialist Republics, formal name of the Soviet Union
ZUNR	Western Ukrainian People's Republic

✣ Index

Italicized figure references refer to photo gallery images.